TRIBES

How Race, Religion, and Identity

Determine Success in the

New Global Economy

JOEL KOTKIN

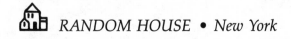

RANDOM HOUSE • *New York*

Grateful acknowledgment is made to
Paul Craft Music for permission to
reprint an excerpt from "Working for
the Japanese" by Ron Delacy.
Copyright © 1991 by Paul Craft Music, administered by Copyright
Management, Inc. All rights reserved.
International copyright secured. Used by permission.

Library of Congress Cataloging-in-Publication Data
Kotkin, Joel.
Tribes: how race, religion and identity determine success in the
new global economy / Joel Kotkin.
p.   cm.
Includes bibliographical references and index.
ISBN 0-679-75299-4
1. Success in business.   2. Ethnic groups.   I. Title.
HF5386.K776   1992
650.1—dc20   92-53638

Manufactured in the United States of America on acid-free recycled
paper

9 8 7

Book design by Carla Weise/Levavi & Levavi

For my father

Seest thou a man diligent in his business? he shall stand before kings

PROVERBS 22:29

ACKNOWLEDGMENTS

FOR THE BETTER PART of three years this book dominated my life. The extraordinary research and travel requirements of the project demanded constant intellectual, financial and, most important, moral support. In this respect, I have been most fortunate to have had so many willing and able to assist me.

In any such list it is usually difficult to cite one person in particular, but in this case there is no such problem. No person contributed more to the making of *Tribes* than my researcher and friend Hal Plotkin. The huge research involved in making this book rested primarily on Hal's extensive knowledge of and skillful use of the resources of the Stanford University libraries. At Stanford, Hal was ably assisted by two students, Julie Chien and Wei Shun Mao, whose insights and energy also benefited this undertaking. He also conducted numerous interviews, both here and abroad, while offering cogent analyses critical to the construction of the book.

In putting this research into words, and hopefully some sort of coherent construct, I was fortunate to have the assistance of two excellent editors. From the very early drafts onward Mark Benham provided the dogged editing and intellectual curiosity that perhaps more than anything else resulted in whatever literary quality this manuscript now has. At the same time I received constant encouragement and direction from Ann Godoff, executive editor at Random House, whose faith in this project never wavered throughout the duration.

I would also like to thank here the steady assistance provided by my assistant, Mari Arizumi. Besides preventing my files from catching fire or suffocating me, Mari also provided invaluable assistance in the translation of documents and dialogue during several trips to Japan. Her advice, particularly about younger people in her native country, was consistently helpful throughout the research.

The project would also not have been possible without the steadfast support of two major institutions whose financial and moral assistance played a particularly critical role. The Center for the New West, a think tank based in Denver, and the Pepperdine University School of Business and Management both supported me throughout the research and writing of *Tribes*; without them, this book would not exist. I am particularly grateful to Dr. Phil Burgess and Kent Briggs, both at the Center, for their constant intellectual contributions and moral support, as well as that offered by my colleagues at Pepperdine, most notably Dr. James Wilburn, Dr. John Nicks and Keith McFarland.

Several other institutions also deserve mention for their help. In Taiwan, I received assistance from the Pacific Cultural Foundation for research in that often underappreciated but increasingly critical country. I also would like to thank the DeTocqueville Institution, located at the Hoover Institute at Stanford University, for their financial and logistical support of my work on immigration policy and its effects. Finally, I would like to thank several editors, notably Greg Critser, formerly with *California Magazine* and now with *Buzz*; Nathan Gardels, editor of *New Perspectives*; Jodie Allen of *The Washington Post*; George Gendron at *Inc.*; Gary Spiecker and Allison Silver of the *Los*

Angeles Times; and Steve Solomon of *Family Business,* all of whom supported this project with assignments critical to the research.

Given the nature of this book, it was crucial to gain the insights of people with particular knowledge of each ethnic group. For the Jewish chapters, I am particularly indebted to Katriel Schory, Nomi Ben-Nathan and their staff at Belbo Films in Tel Aviv and for the excellent research assistance of Rachel Perisco. In France, I was helped greatly by the insights of Leon Masliah of the *Consistoire de Paris* and his many contacts. Closer to home, Rabbi Mel Gottlieb of Congregation Kehillat Ma'Arav in Santa Monica, California, also kindly read the Jewish chapter with an eye for correcting any mistakes within my own highly secularly oriented analysis.

The British chapters were greatly enhanced by the help of Jeremy Davies of Price Waterhouse and the worldwide network of that estimable organization. I also owe a debt of gratitude to Doug Beckett, formerly of Los Angeles and Hong Kong and now back in Standard Chartered's London main offices, for his assistance. I also received warm support from the British consulate in Los Angeles, most particularly Angus Mackay. Through their good offices, I had the pleasure of working with their staff in both London and Edinburgh, each of whom helped arrange numerous appointments and provided invaluable practical assistance. I also benefited from the sharp analysis, particularly on Protestant religious matters, from Virginia Postrel, editor of *Reason* magazine, and on Anglo-American business culture from Robert Kelley, president of the Southern California Technology Executives Network.

Within Europe I was fortunate to have the aid of many kind and knowledgeable people. My work in France benefited greatly from the assistance of the Los Angeles consulate, including Consul General Gerard Coste and press attaché Marie Twining. In Paris, Madame France Raguin provided invaluable logistical aid and many useful insights. The Adenauer Foundation in Germany also provided a ten-day visit to their remarkable country, which proved useful to me in understanding many of the dynamics now shaping Europe. I also wish to thank the insightful research work done by Dirk Grosse-Leege, particularly on the topics of immigration and demographics.

The former Soviet Union also played an important role in the research. Here I have to thank most two remarkable young Russians, entrepreneur Vladimir Sidorov and Lev Yellin, a correspondent with *New Times*, who worked as translators and provided an essential road map during my trip to Moscow and its environs. Without their assistance, I would never have received the exceptional warmth and understanding of the country from which my grandparents emigrated.

For years Japan has been critical to developing my analysis of the changing role of ethnicity in economics. As usual I have relied throughout on the guidance of my two longtime *sensei*, Jiro Tokuyama and Aki Tsurukame. I am also grateful for the assistance of Shisuku Hirano and Masatoshi Hayase of the Japan External Trade Organization, Professor Hideo Ohtsubo of the Technical University in Fukuoka, Akira Hase of the Dentsu Institute of Human Studies and Professor Tadao Kiyonari of Hosei University.

I would also like to thank Kenji Wada of Sony Corporation and Kazuo Wada of Yaohan Corporation, who assisted us in setting up numerous interviews with their colleagues not only in Japan, but also around the world. I also appreciate the thorough and insightful reading of this manuscript by Dr. David Friedman, a respected friend and Los Angeles–based Japan research fellow at the Massachusetts Institute of Technology. Finally, the support and assistance of my agents in Japan, Tom Mori and Miyoko Kai, and my publishers at Fusosha, particularly Yoichi Matsui, helped me immeasurably with my research there.

In the Chinese-related chapters I would most like to cite the contribution of my friend Vincent Diau, a Los Angeles–based reporter for the *Chinese Daily News*, and his associates at the *World Journal* in Taipei. I also received notable assistance there from Luk Kwanten and Lily Chen of the Tuttle Mori Big Apple Agency. In Hong Kong, I would like to thank the staff of the Hong Kong Government Information Service, who, at the prodding of Peter Johnson and Melinda Parsons of their San Francisco office, helped me immeasurably in my many weeks of research in that most dynamic center of cosmopolitan Chinese capitalism.

When I started this book, of all the major tribes, my knowledge of Asian Indians was perhaps the scantest. But this situation was greatly relieved by my many Indian friends here in the United States who offered their worldwide networks to me. I would particularly like to thank Mira Advani of Los Angeles, who arranged many interviews in Britain and Southeast Asia as well as here in the United States. Her assistance on my trip to India was also invaluable and the friendship shown by her family and friends remains one of the enduring pleasant memories of this experience. I also would like to extend thanks to financier Nitin Mehta of San Francisco and Prakash Chandra, president of the Silicon Valley Indian Professionals Association, for their insights and assistance in making contacts with Indians around the world.

I would also like to thank several other people for their help in the project, including Victor and Paul Ajlouny, for their assistance with the Palestinian community; Paul Akian of Los Angeles, for offering his global network among the Armenians; and Keith Atkinson and Donald Lefevre of the Church of Jesus Christ of Latter-day Saints.

Yet even so exhaustive a list barely touches the surface of the many people who helped with this project. But at the end of this long process, I have perhaps the most gratitude for those who have worked with me longest, through other projects as well, most notably my agent, Melanie Jackson, and my publicist, Jacqueline Green. In this regard I would also like to thank Mark Kotkin for his insightful readings of this manuscript, my wife, Julie Kotkin, and my mother, Loretta Kotkin, for putting up with me through this often arduous process. Without my family, I would probably have given myself up for lost at one of numerous turns at which this book seemed like a road without signposts, leading nowhere.

Los Angeles, California

CONTENTS

PROLOGUE: GLOBAL TRIBES

BORN AMIDST OPTIMISM for the triumph of a rational and universal world order, the twentieth century is ending with an increased interest in the power of race, ethnicity and religion rather than the long-predicted universal age or the end of history. The quest for the memory and spirit of the specific ethnic past has once again been renewed; the results will shape the coming century. In the words of sociologist Harold Isaacs: "Science advanced, knowledge grew, nature was mastered, but Reason did not conquer and tribalism did not go away."[1]

For many in enlightened society this trend represents a throwback to the basest kind of clannishness. Usually identified with the excesses of Islamic fundamentalism, irredentist chaos within the former Soviet bloc, or racial strife in American cities such as Los Angeles, increased emphasis on religion and ethnic culture often suggests the prospect of a humanity breaking itself into narrow, exclusive and often hostile groups.

Yet beyond such visions lies the emergence of another kind of tribalism, one forged by globally dispersed ethnic groups. These global tribes are today's quintessential cosmopolitans, in sharp contrast to narrow provincials. As the conventional barriers of nation-states and regions become less meaningful under the weight of global economic forces, it is likely such dispersed peoples—and their worldwide business and cultural networks—will increasingly shape the economic destiny of mankind.

Global tribes combine a strong sense of a common origin[2] and shared values, quintessential tribal characteristics, with two critical factors for success in the modern world: geographic dispersion and a belief in scientific progress. Such cosmopolitan groups—from the Jews and British of the past to today's ascendant Asian global tribes—do not surrender their sense of a peculiar ethnic identity at the altar of technology or science but utilize their historically conditioned values and beliefs to cope successfully with change.

The collapse of communism and the end of the Cold War further boost the prospects for global tribes. As ideologies such as "scientific socialism" have collapsed, the world has experienced a renaissance of interest in the symbols of the tribal past. Like desert flowers after a rain, churches, mosques, synagogues, Buddhist temples and family shrines across the former communist empire have come back to life. Other icons of national sentiment, such as the Russian tricolor, have been unfurled as symbols of a rebirth of renewed popular identity.

This remarkable historical reversal leads to our critical point: ethnicity as a defining factor in the evolution of the global economy. In the post–Cold War era, where ideology has faded and peoples seek definition from the collective past, dispersed groups such as global tribes seem particularly well adapted to succeed within today's progressively more integrated worldwide economic system.

In defining global tribalism, I have set out to examine five principal groups—the Jews, British, Japanese, Chinese and Indians—all of whom powerfully illustrate this phenomenon. Although each of these five tribes possesses a vastly different history, they all share the following three critical characteristics:

1. A strong ethnic identity and sense of mutual dependence that helps the group adjust to changes in the global eco-

nomic and political order without losing its essential unity.

2. A global network based on mutual trust that allows the tribe to function collectively beyond the confines of national or regional borders.

3. A passion for technical and other knowledge from all possible sources, combined with an essential open-mindedness that fosters rapid cultural and scientific development critical for success in the late-twentieth-century world economy.

Of course, these five groups are not alone in displaying some or all of the above traits. Dispersed ethnic groups, in one form or another, have existed since the beginnings of history. Often originating as small, highly distinct tribes, some ultimately extended their influence over wide swaths of territory. Their unmistakable imprint on distant lands at times lingered for centuries following their departure or even their own society's ultimate collapse. In Western antiquity, Babylonians, Egyptians, Phoenicians, Greeks and Romans, for example, played such critical formative roles. Similarly the ancient Native Americans—the Incas, Mayans and Aztecs of meso-America—and the great Chinese and Islamic empires left profound marks upon the language, religion, custom, architecture, agriculture and science of cultures well beyond their formal borders.

Later, other groups, armed with a strong sense of self-identity and a passion for knowledge, established themselves in the byways of global economy. During the centuries after the Middle Ages, Italians, Dutch, Portuguese, Spanish and Germans extended their cultural and technological influence over various portions of the world. More recently, other peoples, including the Armenians, Palestinians, modern Greeks, Ibos, Cubans and Koreans, among others, have also spread across national lines, often with potent economic and cultural effects.

All these, and no doubt many others as well, can be defined as sharing some of the characteristics of global tribes. But for the purposes of this book, I have chosen to concentrate on the five major ethnic groups that today most powerfully demonstrate the effectiveness of global tribalism. Among the European-derived groups, for example, I concentrate on the Anglo-Americans because their worldwide sway—expressed in global investments, multinational corporations and cultural and political influence—remains far greater than that of the Germans, Italians or French, who, for all their economic or cultural prowess, are now concentrated in a European-centered sphere of influence. Similarly I have chosen the Japanese, Chinese and Indians among the Asians due not only to their growing influence on the contemporary world but also their potential to impact massively the course of history in the next century.

It is not my intention to argue for, nor do I believe in, the essential moral or racial superiority of any of these groups. In each case, the global tribe has grown as much through intimate contact with other civilizations as through any intrinsic cultural superiority, much less any supposed racial purity. In fact, global tribes such as the British or Japanese have variously been known as imitators par excellence. Similarly, the Jews, British and Indians, far from being pure examples of a particular genetic stock, are among the most racially diverse of peoples.

Certainly fate, often the prime genetrix of history, has played a critical part in assigning these groups their role as global tribes—and then compelled them to play it. This is clearly evident in the case of the Jews, my own people, who in many ways represent the archetype of global tribalism. From the time of Abraham—or so goes the mythology—the Jews have been defined by their own historic sense of uniqueness, based largely on their identification with God. Their stubborn adherence to this belief both led to their millennia of dispersion and sustained their particularly strong sense of identity.

Isolated in their own communities among strangers who were frequently hostile, the Jews were forced to develop both a powerful tradition of self-help and a particular skill at adjusting to changing economic and social conditions. Empires rose and fell, economies collapsed, great religious waves swept across continents, yet the Jews—their social institutions, their laws and family traditions—survived.

As a dispersed people with a widespread network of communities, the Jews benefited greatly from the early emergence of an increasingly globalized economy. From the last days of Rome until the end of the Middle Ages, Jews endured not only by trading goods but also through the acquisition of knowledge in areas such as medicine or mathematics from regions as diverse as India and Spain. Later, when the European ascendancy created a far more advanced international economy, the Jews, as a people stretched beyond national boundaries, were ideally suited to take advantage.

If the Jews represent the archetypical global tribe, easily the most consequential one to this point in history has been the British and their progeny. Originating on a small and relatively infertile island in antiquity's northwest fringe, the British and their empire molded the pattern of modern technologic development and commerce far more than any of their European rivals.

As writers such as Max Weber and R. H. Tawney have observed, this British ascendancy was propelled largely by the powerful moral and cultural influence of Calvinism. Much like the Jews, the British Calvinists—and other dissenting, but theologically distinct groups such as Quakers—were animated by a sense of specialness through the discipline of their faith. Calvinism, as both Tawney and Weber pointed out, also fostered attitudes conducive both to trade and to an interest in the acquisition of technical knowledge.

The dissenting culture, first in Britain and later in their American diaspora, helped create many of the forms of capitalist organization that still prevail throughout the world economy. Even where American or British power has all but evaporated, Anglo-American standards of business behavior and cultural forms, as well as the English language, remain preeminent.

The gradual erosion of the Anglo-American hegemony over the past few decades stems largely from the erosion of many of the core values that previously drove its ascendance. Like the late Soviet empire, the Anglo-Americans, and European capitalism in general, now suffer from the growth of corrupt and lethargic elites, a loss of competitive will, rising criminality, decay in basic values such as thrift, and the importance of hard work.[3]

Many of these vital ethical principles and attitudes are today more evident among the emerging global tribes from Asia. These ascendant ethnic groups—notably the Japanese, Chinese and Indians—have successfully exploited the commercial pathways created by the Anglo-Americans with often devastating success.

The Japanese—the most prominent of these new Asian tribes —are, like the British, an island people animated by a peculiar ethos, reflected in the extraordinary organization and industriousness that have been critical to their success in the modern world-system. Yet unlike the British or the Jews, whose dispersions were carried out essentially through permanent settlement, the Japanese diaspora, as I will argue, has been largely by design, characterized by the dispatch of temporary corporate sojourners to the various corners of the globe. Aided by new technologies of communications and transportation, the Japanese tribe has employed this unique system to challenge the centuries-old economic hegemony of the Anglo-Americans.

Yet even as the world, particularly the West, trembles at Japan's advance, the quickening pace of internationalization and technology has spawned the emergence of other, potentially even more potent tribal groups. The Chinese, the world's most populous race and possessors of one of the most venerable ethnic traditions, have in recent decades reemerged as a power on the world stage after centuries of decline.

Like the Jews or the British, the Chinese have developed a powerful global diaspora, with strong communities stretched from the Southeast Asian tropics to the great cities of North America. Today this diaspora—centered in Taipei, Hong Kong and Singapore—constitutes one of the world's wealthiest, most technically sophisticated and highly entrepreneurial groups. The Chinese already have carved out an economic empire along the edges of the Pacific Basin, the world's most vibrant region; more important, they also now increasingly direct the monumental task of building China's own enormous industrial potential.

As communism fades and linkages among the Chinese become ever closer, the diaspora's influence will likely grow more critical. Able to combine their cosmopolitan resources in North

America and Southeast Asia with a revived mainland, the Chinese seem the best positioned of any group to challenge the insular Japanese for preeminence in the increasingly Pacific-dominated world economy. By the early twenty-first century, the Chinese global tribe likely will rank with the British-Americans and the Japanese as a driving force in transnational commerce.

Further in the future lies the possible emergence of yet another great Asian tribe, the Indians. The Indians—meaning here not only Hindus but Muslims, Parsis and Sikhs as well—also boast a long historical memory and a well-developed cultural sense of uniqueness. Though currently burdened by deep fratricidal divisions and the desperate poverty of hundreds of millions, they have in recent decades developed their own increasingly potent global diaspora, from North America and the United Kingdom to Africa and Southeast Asia.

The Indians boast one of the world's deepest reservoirs of scientific and technical talent. If their homeland can be liberalized and reformed, they have the potential to develop into the next powerful global economic force. Viewed in the light of today's often destitute and corrupt reality, such an assertion might yet seem a product of fancy. Yet only a century ago similar doubts were cast about the potential of the Japanese and the Chinese.

The end of the Cold War opened a new era of opportunity for the cosmopolitanism embodied by these global tribes. The consequent fading of military force as the prime element in determining economic position naturally reduces the traditional power of nation-state structure that long has served as the essential counterweight to globalism. Similarly, the collapse of the socialist model makes moot much of the traditional ideological debate over rival economic systems, focusing attention instead on those cultures and attitudes most effective within the global economic system.

In this respect, the history and development of global tribes is particularly enlightening. Clearly identifiable values—such as a strong ethnic identity, a belief in self-help, hard work, thrift, education and the family—have proved universally successful in all these different groups; stripped of the burdens of Cold War ideology and racism, the relationship between such values and group success is simply too self-evident to ignore.

This perspective already has produced, among other things, a critical debate among groups such as African-Americans. In contrast to the legalistic, civil rights–oriented traditions of the black establishment, African-American leaders as different in temperament and approach as Booker T. Washington, Marcus Garvey, Malcolm X, Louis Farrakhan and Tony Brown have emphasized the importance of developing a more self-affirming, economically and intellectually self-sufficient social culture as the primary means of overcoming racial oppression. Similarly, as the appeal of Marxism wanes in Africa, Latin America and other parts of the developing world, the focus on the development of such values has also shifted—as peoples look for clues to the success of the Japanese or the overseas Chinese rather than mimic the old Soviet model.

Yet tribalism, to be successful in the modern context, must also be leavened with a willingness to learn from and accept others or it will prove ultimately self-destructive. Each of the global tribes featured in this book retains, along with its cosmopolitan characteristics, aspects of a more hostile and primitive clannishness as well. As Japanese social theorist Hidetoshi Kato has observed: "A culture is an aggregate of divergent and contradictory pictures, and each picture is true."[4]

Among Jews, for example, a dogged desire to repel outside influences has at times fostered narrow and exclusive perspectives within the tribe. Such attitudes, according to Max Weber, nurtured among Jews a kind of "pariah capitalism," motivated largely by resentment of others, with one set of rules for members of the tribe, another for the Gentiles.[5] This, Weber believed, made the "traditionalistic" Jewish businessman prone to some forms of double-dealing and "speculatively oriented capitalism."[6]

Such negative images of Jews—for example, as penny-pinching slumlords, con men and financial manipulators—have within them a certain element of historical truth, up to and including the involvement of a number of Jews in both traditional organized crime[7] and some of the more monumental securities scandals of the late 1980s.[8] Yet similar claims have been made about many other immigrant groups and some global tribes—from the Scots in early New England to the Indian owners of dilapidated apartment complexes in contemporary San Francisco—and Korean shopkeepers in numerous American cities who also developed reputations for making profits in ways that are often seen as less than "respectable."

More disturbing, with the recovery of the historic homeland in Palestine, some Jews have reverted to a racially tinged kind of tribalism. At times, the advocates of such measures as the "removal" of Arabs from the West Bank, or even pre-1967 Israel, reintroduce the most brutish aspects of the biblical conquest of Palestine under Joshua. Religious fundamentalism, hostility to outsiders and racism within contemporary Israel represent the dark obverse of the cosmopolitanism characteristic of the diaspora; unchecked, they could lead not only to the continued cycle of endless war, but will impair the Jewish experience as a cosmopolitan global tribe.

The British-American tribe also faces its own moral crisis, one that may determine its long-term future. In many English-speaking countries the increased presence of outside groups—as immigrants, competitors and investors—has tapped a deep reservoir of resentment and racial loathing. The descendants of the Anglo-America heritage—particularly in such ethnically hybrid cities as New York, Los Angeles, Toronto, Sydney and London—must still overcome a deeply held assumption of racial superiority that, shaped over centuries of worldwide hegemony, simply does not fit with contemporary realities.

Such a shift in attitudes may prove critical in determining whether the British tribe and indeed the entire European-descended peoples can thrive in a world where other ethnic groups play increasingly important, even leading, roles. By learning from the experience of the Japanese as well as by drawing upon the energies of their recent immigrants, Europeans and Americans can hope to resuscitate their own lagging industrial and commercial skills. The alternative—to cower behind the confines of a white "fortress Europe" or "fortress

America"—would simply repeat the tragic mistakes that, in the past, fostered the decline of these same Asiatic societies and their subsequent domination by Europeans.

For the Japanese, as well, the challenge of balancing a highly effective ethnic ethos with an understanding for other cultures represents a particularly daunting task. Arguably the most insular of the global tribes, the Japanese may be the least prepared one for an increasingly multiracial economic reality. In their rapid expansion over the past four decades, they have been notable in their failure to adequately accommodate others within their organizations, supply networks and industrial development strategies.

In this book, I have devoted a great deal of time to discussing this particular issue. This is not to suggest that Japanese racism is any worse inherently than that of the Jews, the British or any other ethnic group. If I were writing this book in 1950, for example, the racial attitudes of Anglo-Americans, then the world's clearly predominant force, would have commanded similar attention. A successor volume—written, say, in 2030—might concentrate instead on the racial exclusivity of the Chinese, or even the Indians, who might then appear as the most expansionist of global tribes.

Despite such inherent problems, these cosmopolitan groups —dispersed, armed with a strong belief in themselves and the power of knowledge—will almost inevitably flourish within an increasingly denationalized and demilitarized world economy. This increased power, in most cases, will not be expressed through the traditional medium of the nation-state, but through more cosmopolitan mechanisms such as the multinational corporation or financial conglomerate; it is as globalized ethnic group that Japan, Inc., or its Anglo-American, Jewish, Chinese or Indian analogues, will find their fullest future expression.

As the global economy evolves, we soon may approach a situation in the advanced countries where, as one Tokyo executive once put it, "there will be no Japan, only Japanese." In this new cosmopolitan society, the primacy of global tribes will likely only increase, each tribe adding its own peculiar influence in each of the world's primary cities. Already—in such emerging global centers as Singapore, Toronto, Los Angeles, New York and London—one can discern the outlines of a new pattern of human coexistence that reflects not an enforced sameness but the entire enormous richness and range of the human experience.

CHAPTER ONE

THE MAKING OF GLOBAL TRIBES

THERE IS NO HINT of grandeur, no shining corporate logo, no edifice of modern art outside the imposing nineteenth-century mansion on Faubourg Saint Honoré. The stuffy, carpeted interior, with antique clocks and pictures, exudes more the hushed, reverently preserved atmosphere of a museum than the manic bustle of a worldwide financial empire.

Alone, in an office lined with books and photos, Edmond Rothschild sits nervously, pondering his far-flung concerns. Today the baron, whose title is a holdover from an epoch when his family dominated the finances of the aristocracies of Europe, seems in ill humor, agitated by the political turmoil in Yugoslavia, Argentina's chronic debt and rising religious fanaticism in the Middle East, among other global problems.

A man born to wealth, Rothschild could well have lived without confronting such problems, not to mention the preoccupations of his chairmanship of over a dozen financial firms spanning from the West Indies to Tel Aviv, including the family's sprawling Paris-based Compagnie Financière.[1] Yet like generations before him, he believes that being a Rothschild means choosing not to live comfortably from the accumulations of the past.

This, perhaps more than anything else, sets the Rothschilds apart from other wealthy families of the nineteenth and early twentieth centuries who long ago faded into relative obscurity. Though they possessed all the accoutrements of the landed gentry, the Rothschilds rarely opted to lose themselves in the good life. They chose instead to accumulate capital and invest:

> We are different for a simple reason. Many families disappear in one generation because they don't realize that whatever they had, you must have discipline and that you have to work whether you like it or not. Otherwise why not become a drug addict or a drunk.
>
> It's very simple. Discipline. I received it from my mother and my father and hopefully my son is going to give it to his children. It's the discipline of tradition.[2]

For the Rothschilds, however, the "discipline of tradition" meant something quite different from merely the noblesse oblige that has been the creed of the best wealthy Europeans since the ascendancy of capitalism. They did not suffer the hangover of Medieval ideals about the piety of poverty—or the supposed wickedness of profit seeking.[3] Indeed, when Nathan Rothschild, the founder of the British house, was asked in the 1830s whether he wished his children to be as capitalistic as himself, he responded: "I wish them to give mind, and soul, and body, and everything to business; that is the way to be happy."[4]

Within less than a century, this ethos primed an ascendancy so great that Baron James Rothschild, the Paris-based son of Frankfurt coin dealer Mayer Amschel, stood, in popular accounts of the time, as "the absolute monarch of the financial world," with the power to determine the fiscal fate of nations. By the 1840s the family, in the estimation of Austria's Prince Metternich, possessed more influence over the affairs of France than any foreign government, save that of its arch-rival, Great Britain.[5]

But the Rothschilds did not live purely by a capitalist ethos, what German Chancellor Otto von Bismarck disparagingly referred to as their "absurd desire to leave to each of their children as much as they themselves inherited."[6] No single-minded worship of money in itself, Edmond Rothschild insists, would have maintained a family tradition against the temptation to fully assimilate over the generations. Along with love of business, the Rothschilds remain united by another, larger vocation, one extending beyond business, family and even nation—the vocation of being Jews. As his cousin David Rothschild, who heads up a family merchant bank not far from the squat estate on Faubourg Saint Antoine, puts it: "Judaism creates the cement —the Jewish family has the tradition of solidarity."[7]

THE WORLD AS STAGE

At a time when global economics is often perceived in the abstract, defined by cold statistics and computer-driven models, it might seem odd, even anachronistic, to speak of "the discipline of tradition" and ethnic "solidarity" as critical elements in understanding the ways of commerce. Yet the history of modern capitalism has been shaped largely by the progress of such global tribes, dispersed groups held together by a common culture.

The power of global tribes derives from their successful coalescing of two principles that, in classic liberal thought, have been separated: an intrinsic "tribal" sense of a unique historical and ethnic identity and the ability to adapt to a cosmopolitan global economy. In this respect, the Jews present the archetypical, but hardly the only, example of a global tribe. Over the past four centuries the dynamics of various global diasporas (from the Greek, meaning a scattering) have shaped the world economy, from the great ascendancy of the British and their descendants in the seventeenth century to the recent growth in influence of the Asiatic global tribes, principally the Chinese, Japanese and Indians. Other smaller but influential groupings— such as Armenians, Cubans and Palestinians—also represent what Wesleyan University's Khachig Toloyan calls "transnational groups," often combining homelands with colonies dispersed around the world.[8]

These dispersed ethnic groups have exercised a disproportionate influence on the growth patterns of nations, cities and regions. On this level, the continuous interaction of capitalism with dispersed ethnic groups—not just the staid history of financial flows or the heroic stories of nation builders—constitutes one of the critical elements in the evolution of the global economy. As the economist Joseph Schumpeter observed:

> . . . a process [such as] railroadization, or the electrification of the world transcends the boundaries of individual countries in such a way as to be more truly described as one world-wide process than as the sum of distinct national ones. Capitalism itself is, both in the economic and the sociological sense, essentially one process, with the whole earth as its stage.[9]

In this process, global tribes represent a critical dynamic element—the historical protagonist—on the world economic stage. Where they appear, new combinations of technology, industry and culture flourish. When they leave, by choice or through compulsion, the commercial lifeblood, more often than not, runs dry; to the countries that subsequently receive them come the blessings of new ideas, technologies and intelligence. "Every advance of culture," noted economist Carl Bucher, "commences with a new period of wandering."[10]

At the onset of transnational commerce, even before the emergence of the Jews as traders, the Phoenicians, arguably the world's first global tribe, served as key transmitters of culture, technology and products across the ancient world. These "bedouins of the sea" not only sold products from remote places such as Britain, with its tin deposits, or silver-rich Spain, they also brought the art of mining to the Greeks.[11] As advisers to rulers in Babylon, Ashur, Persepolis and Thebes,[12] they helped marry technology and resources from India and interior Africa with those of classical antiquity.[13]

In the ensuing centuries, other largely commercial empires, perhaps most prominently the Portuguese[14] and the Dutch, also played important economic roles, developing trade and political spheres of influence from Europe to the furthest reaches of Africa, Asia and the Americas. Yet no global tribe in history has endured longer than the Jews. Forerunner of all other global tribes, from the British to the modern Asian diasporas, the Jews developed a unique set of attitudes toward themselves and the world. In a pattern seen today most noticeably with the Japanese or the Chinese, the Jews maintained a ferocious loyalty to their own identity even as their power reached its fullest expression through dispersion. Mormon historian Spencer Palmer has observed:

> A sense of *insularity* that the Japanese and the Jews nurtured was *combined with openness to the outside world.* This has made the Jews and the Japanese very conservative, but at the same time very innovative.[15]

Serving as middlemen, traders and arbitrageurs of information and products on a global basis, much like today's Japanese, they appeared in most of the major cities of the known world, representing, in Oswald Spengler's somewhat derogatory phrase, "a new kind of nomad cohering unstably in fluid masses, the parasitical city-dweller . . ."[16] Yet for their host countries these "nomads" became indispensable not only as traders but as transmitters and translators of knowledge among at least three major cultures—Christian, Arabic and Indian.[17] Indeed, according to at least one medieval account, it was a Jewish scholar, sent to India by an Arabic ruler, who brought back the Indian numerical inscriptions thereafter widely known as "arabic" letters.[18]

In Spain, first under the Moors and later under the Christian kings, Jews rose to intellectual heights perhaps unequaled in modern times. But with the expulsion of 1492, as Spanish social critic Angel Gavinet has observed, Spain emptied itself of much of its scientifically curious population. The Ottoman sultan, who received much of this gifted population, with its cadre of cartographers, swordsmiths and metallurgists, was astounded by his good fortune. "And you call this man, the King of Spain, a politically wise King, he who impoverishes his kingdom to enrich ours?" asked Bejazet II, whose descendants would use Jewish physicians extensively over the next several centuries.[19] "I receive the Jews with open arms."[20]

Later these same Jews from Spain and Portugal would play critical roles in the emergence of new world cities, such as Amsterdam, London and, eventually, New York. Meanwhile the Hispanic peninsula, after a century of rapid conquests, fell into a long period of decline.

When the Jews left their ghettos and entered European society, even sympathetic observers supposed that the Jews would lose their separate identity. In the early 1830s, for instance, the poet Heinrich Heine, a German-Jewish apostate, foresaw the inevitable assimilation of Jews in France as the "witty acid" of rationalism demolished all traces of ethnic identification.[21] Similar views were held by Karl Marx, son of a Jewish convert to Christianity, who believed that in the struggle for a socialist rational universe all such ethnic distinctions would fade away, replaced by the overarching imperatives of class.[22]

Others, particularly among the Anglo-American elite, saw the Jews as a hopelessly backward people, largely incapable of adjusting to the new demands of advanced capitalist societies. One prominent academic, H. H. Godard, director of research at a school for mentally impaired children in New Jersey, in 1913 found over four out of every five Jewish immigrants to be "feebleminded." Godard and others of his time wondered if the best use for the Jews would be to employ them at tasks requiring an "immense amount of drudgery" that would be unacceptable to more advanced and intelligent races.[23]

Yet rather than causing the Jews to be overwhelmed by modernity or to lose their sense of identity, the encounter with the new conditions of advanced societies generally stimulated the Jews' progress. To some extent, notes Jewish religious scholar Jacob Neusner, the tribe's tradition of "systematic skepticism"

—particularly in Talmudic reasoning—proved fortuitous in aiding its adjustment to the emerging technological order.[24] Once animated by the Western liberal and scientific spirit, no ethnic group anywhere in the world likely has produced so many gifted intellectuals per capita, whether in the sciences, the arts or technology. As early as 1934 Jews, most of them Europeans, constituted the third largest group of recipients of Nobel Prizes, behind only the *countries* of Germany and France.[25] Later the Jewish intelligentsia shifted largely to North America, where by 1983 fully one quarter of America's Nobel Prize winners were Jews.[26]

Even the depredations of Nazism failed to blunt their growth. Since the Holocaust, in fact, Jewish influence has reached levels unprecedented in their history; in virtually every society where they are represented in any significant number—from the Americas to South Africa and Europe[27]—their levels of educational achievement and occupational and economic status remain far above the national averages.[28] By the 1990s in virtually every country of their dispersion they have achieved significant global influence in critical fields as varied as entertainment, fashion, communications and finance.

THE BRITISH TRIBE: SHAPERS OF MODERNITY

Yet if the Jews remain the prototype of the global tribe, the most important and enduring diaspora has been that originating in the British Isles. Although in the Middle Ages they remained, in Lewis Mumford's phrase, "one of the backward countries of Europe,"[29] by the seventeenth and eighteenth centuries the British increasingly emerged as the primary force in the emerging global economy.

As with the Jews, much of the British genius stemmed from adapting to changing conditions and from an openness to acquiring skills from other cultures. And like the Japanese earlier in this century, they borrowed shamelessly the best techniques from France, Germany or Asia for everything from shipbuilding to the construction of waterworks and spinning mills and land-clearance schemes.[30] As Defoe remarked, perhaps a bit unfairly, the British improved everything and invented nothing.[31]

In America, these innovative and inquiring traits became even further developed, primarily in New England. There, amidst the virgin forest, the migration of well-educated Puritans, as Max Weber later pointed out, brought an unprecedented explosion of "mass intellectualism" as well as "the rational spirit, the rationalization of the conduct of life in general and the rationalist economic ethos."[32] Later on, American industrialists—like their British forebears—spared little expense to garner technical and scientific knowledge from any source, most notably Great Britain itself.

Weber suggested that such acquisitive attitudes found their roots in the Calvinistic faith of the British and their progeny. Today, the epitome of this mentality can perhaps be found among the Mormons, a spin-off of radical British Protestantism, who in their institutions and faith have made even more explicit the connection between religion on one hand and education, science and technology on the other. "The Glory of God," explains the Mormon *Doctrine and Convenant,* "is intelligence."[33]

Driven by such attitudes, the British tribe ultimately developed most of what has come to be the basis of modern industrial, scientific and technological process. Between 1750 and 1950, the two primary English-speaking nations, the United Kingdom and the United States, according to one detailed survey, accounted for nearly three out of every five major inventions, discoveries and innovations in the world.[34]

As the world's first fully industrialized nation, Britain in particular carved out a unique hegemonic role in the developing world economy. Flush with the profits from its precocious technological leap, British financiers and industrialists—including the descendants of emigrants such as the Rothschilds—dominated the flow of capital throughout the world, financing, among other things, the emergence of eventual rivals for global dominance, including Japan, Germany and Russia.[35]

But the most important edge for the expansion of the British tribe, and its culture, lay in the mass migration of English-speaking people. No other major competing European nation sent nearly as many of its native sons abroad; by 1700, for instance, over 400,000 British had left for North America, compared to only 27,000 Frenchmen. By that date, Britons and their descendants totaled twice the number of expatriates represented by the peninsular Spaniards and Creoles, although their migration to the "new world" had begun a century earlier.[36]

Indeed, between 1832 and 1932 the British Isles accounted for over one third of all European emigration, twice as much as any other country, the vast majority going to the United States and Britain's vast colonial possessions.[37] As no group before them, the British extended their diaspora—which includes the culturally distinct but English-speaking Irish—through the entire breadth of the known world, from North America and India to Africa and Oceania, everywhere carrying their technology and ways of doing business. By the mid-nineteenth century British firms were constructing irrigation canals and railroads from India to Patagonia. In Asia, they established many of the great commercial centers such as Hong Kong, Bombay, Singapore and Calcutta.[38]

Linked together by language, culture and traditions of political economy, the descendants of Britain forged the largest cultural and economic diaspora in world history. Even as other Europeans—notably Germans and Italians—started to emigrate in large numbers to the new lands of settlement, nearly four in five found themselves forced to adjust to a country either under direct British control or, like the United States, an English-speaking former colony.[39]

Only the Great British tribe combined mass immigration with political and cultural dominance over the lands of settlement, in the process creating a mass global business and political culture never before seen in history. As early as the mid-nineteenth century, enthusiasts, including some espousing various theories of an inherent Anglo-Saxon racial supremacy, envisioned these various offshoots of Britain as part of a single global entity destined to rule the world. Charles Wentworth Dilke, a prominent purveyor of this idea, wrote in his 1868 polemic *Greater Britain*:

There are men who say that Britain in her age will claim the Great England across the seas. They fail to see that she has done more than found plantations of her own—that she has imposed her institutions upon the offshoots of Germany, of Scandinavia, of Spain. Through America, England is speaking to the world.[40]

The power of this unique connection between the various offshoots of home islands helped sustain the cultural, financial and political influence of Great Britain long after its decline from the pinnacle of global power. Through its diaspora, and most particularly the United States, the British tribe has created most of the critical standards—in everything from the world language to political economy, science and basic business practice—for the contemporary global economy.

Over the past half century, numerous attempts have been made to overcome these standards. European fascism, Arab petrodollars, communism and, most recently, Islamic fundamentalism attempted to erect alternative systems of value, but none have come close to eclipsing those established by the progeny of Britain.

FROM NATIVES TO GLOBAL TRIBES

Yet the triumph of the Anglo-American system does not guarantee the continuing preeminence of its racial progenitors. In contrast to other groups who sought to create their own separate standards, the emerging Asian global tribes—the Japanese, the Chinese and the Indians—chose instead to exploit the technologies and use the pathways established by the British diaspora. Now, with the center of economic dynamism shifting from Europe to Asia, these emerging global tribes are powerfully positioned for future expansion.

This reflects a major shift in the history of world capitalism. Until the mid-twentieth century, most Asians, with the possible exception of the Japanese, were relegated to the periphery of the world economy, serving largely as petty brokers or middlemen, with the central commanding heights belonging almost exclusively to Europeans. As Jean Paul Sartre noted in 1966:

Not so very long ago earth numbered two thousand million inhabitants: five hundred million men and one thousand five hundred million natives.[41]

The transition of the Indians, Chinese and Japanese from the status of "natives" to that of global tribes stems largely from the fact that, like the Jews and Anglo-Saxons of earlier times, they have developed a strong, ethnically based, morally anchored form of capitalism. Today, the rationalistic capitalism developed by the Anglo-American diaspora has lost its grip on its ethical moorings, in particular, its intrinsic belief in family and self-help and the need for continuous self-improvement. Instead those virtues seem more evident today among the Asiatic global tribes. Indeed, in one critical measurement of capitalist vitality—investment as percentage of GDP—East Asia by 1990 led all regions of the world, investing in domestic industry at a rate 25 percent higher than America or Europe.[42]

The rise of globalized Asian tribes has had two crucial outstanding preconditions: the emergence of a comprehensively transnational economy and huge leaps in communication and transportation technology. The development of a world economy under British and later Anglo-American hegemony provided the critical infrastructure and, ultimately, the scientific and technological knowledge underpinning the expansion of Indians and Chinese into other regions of the world. Indeed, even as colonial rule devastated the patterns of life in India and elsewhere in Asia, European science and technology also slowly reawakened the slumbering technical, scientific and industrial potential of the primary Asian ethnic groups. In the face of the obvious exploitation that took place in China and India, historian Tony Smith notes that:

These admittedly negative factors must . . . nevertheless be weighed against the transfer of technology and capital that association with the world market brought these lands and that there is no reason to think they would have developed on their own. In fact, one of the persistent myths propagated by southern nationalists and Marxists is that European and North American economic expansion inevitably occurred in a fashion detrimental to the economic well-being of the peoples on the periphery.[43]

It was under the British flag, first and foremost, that Indians —ranging from "semi-slaves" on tropical farms to government clerks and merchants—first gained a permanent foothold in Africa and the China coast.[44] Those in closest contact with the Europeans, such as the Parsis in the region around Bombay, quickly adopted the new technology and developed their own global trading network under British protection.[45] Ultimately British attempts to encourage science and technology[46] led to the founding of new schools and colleges, creating in the process a large cadre of technically competent Indians.

Similarly, the Chinese followed the British flag from Hong Kong to Malaysia and Singapore. They came initially as coolies, as petty merchants and skilled artisans, first establishing themselves at the root of newly developing economies, then subsequently moving on to California and Hawaii. It was these Chinese, operating in areas fully integrated into the world economy, who were most directly exposed to the full force of European and American business; quickly they grasped the value of acquiring their technology, science and organizational principles.[47]

Later on, Japanese traders, moving along trade routes developed largely by the Anglo-Americans, branched aggressively into diverse markets from the Americas to Southeast Asia. Writing in the late nineteenth century, Marx described Japan as a backward feudal society, much like Britain before its rise, offering "a truer picture of the European Middle Ages than all our history books."[48] Yet faced with the sudden realization of their enormous technological backwardness, the Japanese after the Meiji Restoration of 1868 launched a modernization drive on a scale unprecedented in the non-European world. Students were dispatched to all the leading centers of Western technology, while at the same time new institutions of learning at home accelerated the creation of a local technical elite. Within five years of its founding in 1872, Tokyo's engineering college—today the Tokyo Institute of Technology—had become the largest technological university in the world.[49]

Yet despite these efforts, until the latter part of the twentieth century Anglo-Americans and other Europeans dominated the financial, transportation and communication infrastructure. But as international business expanded—by the 1980s growing more than twice the rate of global GNP[50]—the gap between Asia and the American-European world began to dissipate, creating a more equal relationship between the two largest economic regions.

Sparked initially by American aid, investment and technology, Southeast Asia by the 1970s clearly emerged as the world's fastest growing economic region, growing at an average of two to three times the older industrial economies. Equally important, Asia's population between 1950 and 1990 jumped to roughly half the world's total, while the share of Europe and North America combined slipped by nearly one third, to under 15 percent of humanity.[51] This development played to the basic strengths of the Asian tribes, who long had focused more of their efforts on the area, as opposed to the Europeans and Americans, who have primarily been interested in each other's regions. By the late 1980s both Japanese-owned and Chinese-owned firms were investing twice as much as firms from the United States in rapidly growing nations such as Thailand, Indonesia and Malaysia.[52]

At the same time, the rapid improvements in communication and transportation technology accelerated the development of the key Asian tribes. In the past, dispersed peoples like the Jews were forced to operate on the basis of only infrequent, and often unreliable, contact. A sunk ship, or a road closed by bandits, could interrupt the critical flow of information among the various tribal centers. Today instantaneous communications link dispersed groups with an ease unimaginable to the scattered traders of the past. Between 1980 and 1989, for example, the volume of phone traffic across international lines increased more than 400 percent in the United States[53] while the cost of transcontinental calls has been dropping roughly fivefold per decade.[54]

Moreover, since the end of the Second World War, Asian tribal links have been further enhanced by the creation of a comprehensive global air transport system. Because the real cost of air travel has dropped—by roughly 50 percent—since 1950,[55] the opportunities for regular contact among dispersed groups have exploded. Between 1978 and 1988, the number of passengers transported by plane more than doubled, and by the year 2000 is expected to more than double once again, with the highest rates of growth expected in the Pacific region.[56]

These developments have helped create a world where dispersed Asians, rather than being culturally isolated, can now find in most major world cities easy access to everything from Asian-language broadcasts and newspapers to shops selling videotapes in Japanese, Mandarin or Hindi. The "little Tokyos," "little Punjabs" or Chinatowns of the late twentieth century are more than merely quaint reproductions of ethnic villages; increasingly, they are transplanted portions of transnational world cities, complete with modern telecommunications linkages to other key tribal outposts. The trip from Taipei to Monterey Park, California, therefore now resembles little more than a commute across different parts of the same Chinese world city.

These new technologies also have facilitated the successful globalization of traditional, highly consensual Asian business forms, from the Japanese *keiretsu* to the Indian joint-family companies to Chinese family networks. Certainly Asian entrepreneurs felt themselves compelled to study Western science, learn the basics of Anglo-Saxon business practices, gain fluency in English or French, don the coat and tie. As the old south Indian proverb puts it: "If you put on the garb of a dog, you must bark like one."[57] Yet, through the use of fax machines, telephones and direct computer linkups, Asian firms have managed to maintain, in a way never before possible, their traditional forms without dissipating their competitive advantage.

The new technology has been particularly critical in allowing for the outward expansion of Asian family-owned businesses. At the family-owned Chung Cheong Group, faxes and frequent air connections allow for the monitoring of literally dozens of businesses scattered from Los Angeles to Thailand without the need for a central control system or a formal board of directors. Using the new technology, decisions can be made between Hong Kong and Zurich more reliably than in the 1920s, for example, when the group's patriarch relied on the often unreliable telegraph service from Canton to Hong Kong. Members of the clan even keep up on family gossip through a regular newsletter called "The Chungs' Times," faxed regularly from Los Angeles to family members dispersed globally.[58]

The emergence of the new Asian global tribes, with their philosophies and ways of doing business, marks a new epoch in the history of capitalism. Peoples who were once remotely distant to each other suddenly find themselves face-to-face in the marketplace, the stock exchange, the labor market. Indeed, a nineteenth-century English or American entrepreneur, transported to our times, would be struck by nothing so much as the leading role played in the affairs of London or New York by Japanese, Chinese, Indians and Arabs. Where once the only strangers were the Jews, today there are other Rothschilds of differing complexions operating along networks far vaster than just a few nations in western and central Europe.

THE VOCATION OF UNIQUENESS

Yet it is their enduring sense of group identification and global linkages, far more than their dispersion, or the extensiveness of their business empires, that most clearly distinguishes global tribes from other migrating populations. In other migrating groups—such as Italians or Germans—the acquisition of skills and intelligence has meant a quick assimilation into the cultures, and even the elites, of their adopted countries. For global tribes, this process of assimilation tends to be slower, less sure, and attenuated by the continued tug of old affinities and memories.

For many global tribes, depredations visited upon them by

others have created particularly acute attachments among scattered members of the group, something most clearly seen in ties among diaspora Jews and Israel due to the Holocaust.[59] Similarly, the cohesion of Armenians worldwide developed through their centuries-long struggle against Muslim invaders who conquered and persecuted them, culminating in the infamous Turkish genocide after World War I. Memory of this genocide is so intense that even everyday articles left over from that era— dishes, photographs, clothing—are treated with reverence. A priest at a recent Armenian service, reports author Jenny Phillips, compared the handling of one such relic, a torn pair of child's trousers, to "touching the robe of the Lord."[60]

Like the Jews, Armenians worldwide consider themselves essentially one people, albeit living in numerous different countries. It was natural, then, that when the former Soviet Republic of Armenia declared its independence it received immediate support from its large diaspora community, even recruiting as its foreign minister a thirty-two-year-old native of Los Angeles whose father, a professor at UCLA, had insisted on speaking Armenian at home and instructing his son in his people's traditions.[61]

Khachig Toloyan, editor of *Diaspora: A Journal of Transnational Studies*, himself an Armenian-American brought up in Syria, Lebanon and Egypt, suggests that diaspora groups such as his, or the Jews, are fundamentally different from other emigrant peoples in that:

> [They] have kept alive in their consciousness [themselves] as something in their host country; and that [they] either hope to go back to the homeland or care enough about it to try to interact with it in some way. For example, Italian-Americans are *only* an ethnic community, not a diaspora; they don't particularly worry about the cultural and political life in Italy, or about Argentineans of Italian descent. Armenian-Americans are an ethnic community but we're more than that. . . .[62]

For global tribes, such transnational group loyalties constitute a critical distinguishing characteristic, what Jewish philosopher

Martin Buber once called a "vocation of uniqueness."[63] In many cases, this "uniqueness" is built around an elaborate mythology of origin, which serves to provide a common link between all members of the group. Armenians such as Toloyan, for instance, trace their lineage to a common mythological ancestor, Haig, and later to a series of kingdoms that were among the first to espouse Christianity and even experience an apparition of Christ.[64]

Like the Armenians, other global tribes possess a similarly shared sense of tribal lineage and mythology.[65] For Indians, their origination myths derive from the ancient stories of the Vedas, "the first Bible of the Hindus"[66]; the legends associated with the rise of the first "Yellow Emperor" serve as the mythological basis for the unique sense of venerable and noble beginnings of the Chinese[67]; the Japanese concept of the "divine" origin of their land and the Yamato race underlies a particularly well developed sense of their tribal uniqueness.[68]

Origin myths can even include those borrowed from others. In the case of the British, much of the mythology of uniqueness —including the myth of King Arthur and the Holy Grail— draws on themes derived from the Jewish Holy Land.[69] Perhaps more important, Old Testament stories dominated the ideology and imagination of the Puritans, who, historian Barbara Tuchman observes, "were the self-chosen inheritors of Abraham's covenant with God, the re-embodied saints of Israel, the 'battle axe of the lord.' "[70] Later on, at the height of empire, this messianic urge was expressed in poet Rudyard Kipling's concept of "the White Man's Burden," with the British divinely chosen to bring religion and civilization to the nonwhite masses.

This same sense of mission developed early as well in Britain's North American colonies. The Puritans, notably, envisioned themselves as builders of "the new Jerusalem." Today Anglo-American messianism is reflected by Mormonism, North America's fastest growing major religion. Although initially consisting overwhelmingly of English and other North European immigrants, the Mormons trace their origins from Hebrews who allegedly migrated to North America. Not coincidentally, when they escaped their persecutors to their haven near the Great Salt Lake, they named their theological center Zion, after the Jewish homeland.

For the archetypical global tribe, the Jews, the descent myth—beginning with the story of the patriarch Abraham and his progeny—has had peculiar significance. For the Jews, the Old Testament, as the German philosopher Friedrich Nietzsche noted, was more than a religious text; it was a national epic.[71] Nietzsche, who despite his later usurpation by the Nazis despised anti-Semitism, saw the Jews' adherence to their biblical legacy not as religious piety but as a demonstration of "the toughest life-will that has ever existed in any people on earth."[72]

The force of this "life-will" became noticeable early in the history of the dispersion. In the period after the conquests of Alexander, as the cultures of other peoples faded before the brilliance of Hellenistic civilization, the Jews, even those speaking the language and enjoying the culture of the Greeks, remained, in the phrase of classical historian Michael Grant, "not only unassimilated, but unassimilable."[73]

Even then, the links between scattered Jewish communities remained remarkably strong. The Israel restored by the Maccabees—much like the modern state founded in 1947—depended heavily upon aid from more affluent Jews from the diaspora, then largely concentrated in Alexandria and Babylon.[74] The ties forged by this "vocation of uniqueness" may help to explain why the Jews, virtually alone amongst the peoples conquered by Rome, continued to struggle against their imperial masters for over two centuries after the initial conquest,[75] including some Jews living in the diaspora communities.[76]

And even after the loss of their homeland to the Romans, the scattered Jewish communities retained their unique identity, to the wonderment and frequently the annoyance of other peoples. Mass conversions, often at the threat of death,[77] reduced their numbers to a pitiable fraction of their former population, yet the surviving remnants kept their covenant with their ancient religious traditions[78] as well as their sense of obligation to other Jews.

With the homeland lost, preservation of "the vocation of

uniqueness" quickly became a struggle, particularly in the increasingly intolerant environment of early Christian Europe. To preserve the economic self-sufficiency of Jewish families, the holding of slaves was denounced as onerous.[79] The preference, wherever possible, was for hiring other members of the tribe as free laborers. "He who increases the number of his slaves increases sin and iniquity in the world," wrote the Spanish sage Maimonides, "whereas the man who employs poor Jews in his household increases merits and religious deeds."[80]

This sensibility of self-help helped the medieval and early modern European Jewish communities survive such natural disasters as the Black Death; a combination of ritual sanitary injunctions and the practice of providing professional medical care to the impoverished sick, known as *Bikur Holim* ("visiting the sick"), helped quarantine the tiny communities across Europe from devastation.

But perhaps the most remarkable feature of this self-help was that it extended beyond local communities. In 1627, when Dutch Jews learned through the Venice ghetto about the depredations on the small community in Jerusalem, they arranged payment to the local Turkish despot to mitigate "the great calamity and misery" of their distant brethren. Similar efforts were made by Italian and Dutch Jews on behalf of Jewish captives in the central European cities of Prague, Budapest and Belgrade.[81]

When Jews began to achieve a greater measure of economic power, they were not loath to use it for the protection of even the most distant branches of the tribe.[82] In 1904 and 1905, on the eve of the Russo-Japanese War, the New York investment bank of Kuhn, Loeb,[83] led by its German-born president, Jacob H. Schiff, extended a critical series of loans to Japan as a means of taking revenge for the anti-Semitic outrages of the Tsarist regime.[84]

As Jews began their first mass migrations from Russia, the tradition of self-help brought critical assistance to newcomers from the already established communities, particularly in Britain, France, Germany and the United States. In 1914, there were over 514 different Jewish benevolent societies in the United

States alone, providing everything from insurance and burial plots to summer camps for children.[85]

And when Alain de Rothschild, descendant of the great French Baron James de Rothschild, died in 1982, the shopkeepers of the poorest Jewish district in Paris—largely immigrants from North Africa who had benefited from his philanthropy—closed their doors for an hour in mourning.[86] Leon Masliah, director of the Consistoire General of the French Jewish communities, who himself emigrated from Tunisia in 1961, recalls:

> When we came, we had help with money, with housing, with the synagogue. We had a whole administration dedicated to our people. When a Jew comes to France, he knows where to go, where to worship. I am a North African—I know what *fraternité* really means. It means people waiting for you at the airport.[87]

Perhaps more important, newly arriving Jews, whether in France or America, developed their communities by building their own, largely self-contained economy. Following Maimonides's advice, Jews tended to hire as well as buy from their own community. In early-twentieth-century New York, notes author Irving Howe, Jews went to their own doctors, butchers, dry goods dealers, shoe stores, coalmen and grocers; both their apartments and their places of employment were owned largely by fellow Jews.[88]

But perhaps nothing reflects the remarkable bonding of the Jewish tribe more than the establishment and successful maintenance of the state of Israel. The revived Jewish state was conceived, financed and led from the diaspora. Virtually all the great names of Jewish business—Rothschild, Kadoorie and Warburg, among others—contributed to the building of the state.[89]

During crises, the diaspora's support for Israel has often taken dramatic forms. In the initial struggle for the establishment of the state, French Jews, with the tacit support of their government, helped provide training facilities for thousands of young Jewish military recruits streaming in from Europe, Canada and the United States.[90] In 1967, at the onset of the Six-Day

War, over ten thousand American Jews volunteered for service in Israel.[91]

By 1990 contributions of Jews abroad, particularly from the United States—as well as American government support, secured largely through their political influence—accounted for as much as 12 percent of Israel's total GDP.[92] Similarly, diaspora Jews have applied much of the political pressure and financial wherewithal behind the massive exodus of their landsmen from the collapsing former Soviet Union, most of whom had little previous knowledge of their heritage.

This ethos of self-help, with all of its occasional flaws and excesses, characterizes virtually all the ascendant global tribes, from the Chinese and Japanese to the Indians, Armenians and Palestinians—some of whom at times express a desire to model their organizational and communal ethos around a Jewish template. "What we need is something like the United Jewish Appeal for Palestinians," explains Paul Ajlouny, the New York–based publisher of the Jerusalem Palestinian newspaper *El Fajr*. "Be together like the Jews. That should be our goal."[93]

As Ajlouny suggests, group survival, particularly in dispersion, relies on a combination of factors: group self-help, a strong ethnic sense of identity and a powerful ethos of self-preservation. The conscious cultivation of ties based on enduring feelings of family, ethics and ethnic solidarity has been a consistent element in the education of young Palestinians, in Detroit or San Francisco as well as in Middle Eastern centers such as Amman, Tunis or Nablus.

Similarly, each of the major dispersed Asiatic groups has established elaborate systems of educational institutions, religious centers and social clubs. Japanese *salarimen* abroad support a worldwide network of schools, Buddhist temples and associations designed to maintain their identity in far-off countries. Members of the overseas Chinese communities, even after generations in diaspora, maintain membership in clan and regional groups whose origins lie on the mainland.[94] Indians abroad have established cultural and religious institutions so they can keep their *man* (heart) in India even as they place their *dhan* (wealth) in Britain and their *tan* (body) in a third country such as one in Asia or Africa.[95]

Like the Asian tribes, the Jews also have retained their own communal educational and cultural institutions. An estimated 50 percent or more of American Jews send their children to an ethnic school, and over three quarters of young men undergo the traditional bar mitzvah ceremony.[96] In contrast, counterpart systems promoting specifically Italian or German language, culture and history largely have disappeared in most major countries of their immigration. Even among intermarried couples— roughly half of all Jews now marry outside the tribe—a large majority claimed that most of their friends were Jews and two thirds observed at least some family religious rituals.[97]

Even as the world economy becomes ever more intertwined, Jews and other global tribes may find these ancient linkages still a powerful asset, as they have been for generations. Nothing on the disorderly horizon that suggests the struggle for economic survival will become any less brutal or difficult in the years ahead, with family groups, multinational corporations and state enterprises battling for dominance across the global economic landscape. In such an environment, the medieval Arab historian Ibn Khaldun once noted, a powerful sense of belonging constitutes perhaps the most essential element for survival. "Only tribes held together by group feeling," he noted, "can live in a desert."[98]

CHAPTER TWO

THE SECRET
OF THE JEWS

BEHIND A LOCKED DOOR on the top floor of a modern high rise overlooking Singapore's Orchard Road, faxes whine with the business of the Afghan Malaya trading company. Orders and communications come in from the *misproche* (relations) in New York and Tel Aviv as the Khafi family conducts instantaneously across the continents its commerce in diamonds, cultured pearls and jewelry.

The technology might be new, but the basic business—the trading of goods across national lines—has been the means of existence for the Khafi family for generations. Originally from Herat in Afghanistan, the Khafis have traded across the Asian continent, sometimes out of Russia, other times from their home base in Afghanistan. The company's president today, Savi Khafi, first came to Singapore in 1954 seeking new markets in the emergent economies of Asia for gemstones and other Afghan products.

He stayed, largely because Afghanistan, in the aftermath of

the establishment of Israel, had turned against its Jewish community after generations of trading. Many other surrounding countries—Indonesia, Malaysia, Brunei—also were Muslim and anti-Jewish, so Singapore, with its predominantly Chinese regime and strong business infrastructure, became home.

"I stayed here because I could not accept why I should be discriminated against," said Khafi, a heavyset fifty-seven-year-old nattily dressed in a newly pressed cotton shirt, the height of formality in the tropical business capital. "I did a lot of business with Afghanistan. I exported everything the country had and imported everything they wanted. Then they wanted Muslim names—I gave them two Muslim names!"[1]

Like other Asian trading capitals, such as Bombay, Calcutta, and Hong Kong, Singapore has long played its part in the history of the Jewish experience in East Asia. Jewish traders first entered the region from the Middle East and India in pre-Christian times, and a small community of Chinese Jews, most likely from the Arab Middle East, developed as early as 1100.[2] For several centuries they flourished, serving as traders, mandarins and artisans centered in the city of Kaifeng, capital of the Sung Empire and a city many times the size of any contemporary European capital.[3]

To a large extent, in contrast to their counterparts in the West, the Chinese Jews were generally tolerated by the surrounding population, with whom they gradually intermarried. Eventually, cut off from contact with other Jews by the Chinese Empire's conscious policy of isolation,[4] the isolated Jewish communities on the mainland died out by the end of the nineteenth century—despite last-minute efforts by Jews in Shanghai and New Orleans to revive the community.[5]

But even as the last traces of Chinese Judaism faded, Iraqi Jews began establishing colonies in Asia. They came both to escape persecution under Daud Pasha and to involve themselves in the rapid growth of trade brought on by the expansion of British capitalism. By the 1840s Iraqi Jewish colonies had been established from Calcutta[6] to Hong Kong[7] and Shanghai,[8] where leading Jewish trading families such as the Kadoories and Sassoons established strongholds.

The Jews first came to Singapore shortly after its founding by Stamford Raffles in 1819. From inception the city developed as a multiethnic trading community, serving as the key Southeast Asian outpost of the burgeoning British empire.[9] By 1846, Jews owned six of the eighteen merchant houses in the thriving young commercial city.[10]

Fed by immigrants from India, the Middle East and Europe, Singapore's Jewish community by 1930 reached nearly one thousand strong.[11] The Japanese occupation, the turmoil experienced before the establishment of the Singaporean state in 1960, fear of local Communists, as well as the hostility of Muslim neighbors threatened to extinguish this Jewish outpost; as a result, its population fell by more than half. In Shanghai, where the Communists actually took power, the community virtually disappeared, leaving en masse for either the United States or Israel.[12]

Today, however, despite all the depredations, the Jewish presence continues in both Hong Kong and Singapore. The Hong Kong community, albeit still tiny, is still several times larger than it was in the 1930s. At the same time, Singapore's community has retained a respected position in local politics. The son of an Iraqi Jewish trader, David Marshall, played a pivotal role in the city-state's independence struggle and later served as the city's chief minister[13] and ambassador to France.[14]

Nor does it seem likely that this community will disappear in the coming years. In addition to the local synagogue, the elite Tanglin Club, which boasts over sixty Jewish family members, remains a busy, informal social center, a place where conversations over the large Olympic-size swimming pool quickly turn to family relations and business deals in process as far away as Istanbul, San Francisco or Johannesburg.

As in other parts of the world, Israelis, too, have become part of the Singapore diaspora business world. Israeli merchants using Malaysian or Indonesian manufacturing facilities, due to political sensitivities in those Muslim countries, maintain their bases within more congenial Singapore. Particularly sensitive, notes Savi Khafi, are Israeli arms traders and elite military training teams who, for the purposes of mollifying Muslim public opinion both inside Singapore and in neighboring countries, pass themselves off as "Mexicans" to the local citizenry.

Other newcomers include the more traditional Jewish traders, men like Sandy Schwartz, a native New Yorker who dabbles in everything from garments and food dyes to Chinese and Indonesian herbs. His is the traditional trader's art, transferring raw materials from one Asian country to another and selling Asian products in the United States. "The Jews used to own Orchard Road but they all thought [Prime Minister Lee Kwan] Yew was a Communist so they fled," the peripatetic entrepreneur, who considers Singapore his home base, recalls. "But they are coming back. Why? Because there is money to be made here."[15]

As for himself, the forty-five-year-old trader exclaims excitedly about being on the verge of a new "blockbuster deal" involving a supposed surefire Indonesian herbal concoction that spurs weight loss regardless of dietary habits. "A secret combination of herbs and roots that, I swear, will cause you to lose weight no matter what you eat. I'm testing it now," the corpulent trader explains, feasting on Peking duck and Chinese beer at a small restaurant two blocks from the Maghain Aboth Synagogue.

"I don't even like beer but I've been drinking it for the last three weeks and stuffing my face with cakes and pastries. I've lost twenty-five pounds," he adds, reaching quickly for a picture of an even more expansive self. "The only problem is you fart a whole lot."

WANDERERS, INC.

Sandy Schwartz and Savi Khafi draw their lessons from a long heritage as wandering skilled workers, traders and arbitrageurs, members of a tribe whose economic history has been, in large part, shaped by the conditions of its global extension. More than any other major ethnic group through history, the Jews from their origins have been a dispersed people, with more of their historical experience outside their homeland than within. The Jews, notes Israeli historian Raphael Patai, were born of a "historical fission" between promised Palestine and the two earliest centers of Western civilization, Mesopotamia and Egypt.[16]

Barely four centuries after establishing their first kingdoms in Palestine, the Jews were scattered, a large portion of the population carried off toward Mesopotamia, where many stayed even after the restoration of the Israelite kingdom. As early as 500 B.C. Jewish colonies had spread to Persia and North Africa. By the second century before Christ the basic patterns of the diaspora —its huge spread, its uniqueness, its prohibitions on intermarriage[17] with other peoples—became evident. As the Greek Sibylline Oracles proclaimed: "Every sea and every land is full of you, and everyone hates you, because of your ways . . ."[18]

At the time of the birth of Christ, Palestine, although always the spiritual center of the Jews, already had lost its primacy as the economic and, arguably, the intellectual center of the tribe. Aided by rapid conversions, Jews constituted as much as one in every eleven people within the Roman Empire,[19] with as many as two thirds living outside the confines of Palestine.[20][21] One million alone lived in Egypt, concentrated in the thriving cultural and trading center of Alexandria.[22]

Even before the destruction of the Jerusalem temple by the Romans in A.D. 70 these "global" ties made the Jews, in the words of the early-twentieth-century sociologist Ferdinand Toennies, "predestined for their role as intermediaries."[23] Often fluent in many languages, they served as traders and financiers,[24] first under the Romans and later under the Byzantines and Arabs. By the height of the Muslim empire around the end of the first millennium, Jewish trading communities were operating from Spain to China,[25] with members of the tribe reaching new heights as wine merchants,[26] bankers and physicians.

Within increasingly isolated Western Europe, Jewish entrepreneurs known as Radanites traded on behalf of the eighth-century Franks, with a knowledge of languages that sometimes included Persian, Latin, Arabic, early versions of French and Spanish, as well as various Slavic dialects.[27] Among these dispersed traders, a common culture based on mutual trust provided a special asset, a common set of values and rules facilitating deal making "on a handshake."[28]

With the advent of capitalism in northern Europe, these international links—connected largely to professions such as coin dealing and money lending—became virtually the only safe means of support for the scattered and often persecuted Jewish communities. The Jew became, as sociologist George Simmel later noted, "the stranger," profoundly different from the native, the "owner of the soil." Jews paid taxes not as citizens but as "Jews"; they were excluded from land ownership and membership in various guilds.[29] As a twelfth-century German rabbi, Eliezer ben Nathan, complained: "Nowadays we are living on commerce only."[30] Although some Jews became wealthy in the period of the great European ghettos, the limitations of trade clearly could not be enough to sustain an entire people, one third of whom were forced to depend on charity.[31]

For a long-dispersed people—working largely as money brokers, artisans and traders—the growth of capitalism was a boon of enormous proportions, playing directly to their skills in finance, cross-border commerce and arbitrage. The essential rationalism of the new order broke down the feudalistic strictures relegating Jews to ghettos and, equally important, unleashed their intellectual gifts on other than religious concerns. The Jews, although not the architects or even the greatest practitioners of the new system, proved among the best positioned to benefit from its development. As the American Jewish historian Ellis Rivkin has noted:

> . . . the fate of the Jew and of Judaism came to hinge on the triumph of the capitalist revolution and on its success in shaping a form of society which reliably augmented wealth, profitably liquidated poverty, and by the demands of its very nature educated the individual for freedom.[32]

One example of the new opportunities can be seen in the career of the Franco clan—an eighteenth-century family of Iberian *marranos*, or secret Jews—who operated with two brothers in Italy, two in London, a fifth in Amsterdam, with cousins in France and nephews in Turkey. The Francos' far-flung "intelligence service," in the words of historian Leon Poliakov, allowed them to be among the few groups capable of conducting complex commercial transactions from St. Petersburg to Algiers.[33]

The critical Jewish role in the early growth of the New World capitalism has led some people, such as the German writer Werner Sombart, to identify the Jews as prime architects and initiators.[34] Perhaps more reasonably, the Jews' dispersion and relative lack of national roots helped them to identify and exploit more quickly the most lucrative emerging markets.

Jewish merchants were operating in Venice, destined to become the first great epicenter of Europe's economic revival, long before it emerged into prominence in the thirteenth century.[35] They played critical roles in the expansion of Spain and Portugal, where Hispanic Jews, known as *sephardim*, numbered roughly 200,000.[36] Even after the Inquisition, Jews as both *marranos* and as sincere new Christians emerged as prominent investors and participants in the opening of what Europe saw as "the New World." Some participated directly as sailors while others drew maps for the earliest voyages of exploration.[37]

Later, as repression in Spain grew and economic power shifted to the north, Jewish merchants and financiers drifted first toward Amsterdam, later to London and finally toward New York. As the great French historian Fernand Braudel explained:

> The Jews, being experienced businessmen, naturally gravitated towards prosperous economies. Their arrival in a country generally meant that business was good there or improving. If they withdrew, it did not always mean business was bad, but it was probably not so good.[38]

Jewish advantages were particularly telling where they could exploit the frontiers of trade—whether on the Brazilian frontier[39] or in Muslim nations off-limits to most Christian traders. The "secret" of the Jews was not simply greater mobility but an essential opportunism born of the cosmopolitan spirit. Faced with frequent threats to their trades by the majority populations, Jews, as Poliakov points out, "took refuge in the dynamic security of acquiescence in change."[40]

Jews often found themselves excluded or overwhelmed by the stronger resources of the Gentiles. Unable to compete in the higher circles of industrial capitalism, they fixed their attention on many of the emerging niches of the developing world economy, for which they are now best known, such as diamonds, communications, fashion, retailing, entertainment and the professions.

These occupational choices also conformed to a cultural preference for self-employment. As the old rabbinic watchword had it: "Skin a carcass on the streets, rather than be dependent on other people."[41] Simply put, Jews usually could not look toward the state, or the wider society, for a "security blanket." Jobs on the land, in the government bureaucracy, or in state-sponsored institutions were frequently off-limits.

For them, the path of self-help and the private sector became the only reasonable alternatives. Throughout late-nineteenth-century and early-twentieth-century Europe, Jews emerged as prominent entrepreneurs and innovators. In the German empire in 1913, for example, they represented roughly one quarter of all directors of public companies, while constituting barely 1 percent of the total population.[42] Perhaps even more remarkable was the overall rate of self-employment among German Jews, which by the early 1930s stood at a remarkable 46 percent, more than three times the national average.[43] Jews were particularly active in the Berlin Stock Exchange, where they accounted for as many as four fifths of leading members.[44]

A similar situation existed in other European countries. By the late 1930s Hungarian Jews, roughly 5 percent of the population, owned over 36 percent of the retail stores, warehouses and offices.[45] Without the Jewish presence, complained Hungary's Fascist and thoroughly anti-Semitic regent, Admiral Miklos Horthy, the country's banks, communication infrastructure and commercial establishment would become "bankrupt" virtually overnight.[46]

Jews also used their legendary savvy and cosmopolitan connections in less respectable ways. From Arnold Rothstein and Meyer Lansky to their modern-day successors in the Americas,

Israel or the former Soviet Union, Jewish criminals have succeeded in everything from murder-for-hire to smuggling and the founding of Las Vegas. Yet, even in crime, both emphasis and cultural preference lay with the successful use of *sechel* (smarts) rather than mere brute force.[47]

Even in the aftermath of the Holocaust, this tradition of Jewish entrepreneurism—what Sombart called "the curious mixture of stubbornness and elasticity"[48]—has more than overcome prejudice. Russian and other Eastern European Jews maintain the highest rates of self-employment of any major ethnic group in America, more than two times above the national average,[49] a pattern repeated in both Great Britain and the Continent.[50]

Yet behind these remarkable successes lies the legacy of the tragic European experience. Even in Britain, arguably the most consistently tolerant society in Europe over the past century, "a sense of outsiderness," observes Christopher Longley, a columnist with the *Times* of London, "still permeates the British Jewish community."[51]

To understand Jewish progress, believes British entrepreneur Harry Solomon, one has to look at the often bitter reality of ghetto life, with patterns of behavior learned by generations of itinerant traders—people without a land, always wandering, searching for sustenance. As the penultimate outsiders, notes Solomon, chairman of Hillsdown Holdings, a retailing firm with almost two hundred subsidiaries in North America and Europe as well as the United Kingdom,[52] Jews felt comfortable with—and often compelled to—experimentation.

Sitting in his modest offices on a suburban commercial street in Hampstead, Solomon, the grandson of an impoverished Polish Jewish immigrant, whose 1989 net worth was estimated at near $50 million,[53] recalled:

> The reason we were different in this society was because we had no preconceived idea, no sense of the tradition of the business. It was easier when you come up with a revolutionary idea to just go with it.
>
> For us it was important first to make money—it's the insecurity of the immigrant in somebody else's country. You're always

trying to prove something. We [Jews] are all the victims of our backgrounds.[54]

A DIASPORA OF SKILLS

Like Harry Solomon's grandfather, Phil Weisel grew up in the *shtetl* world of Eastern Europe. In the small town of Steinslaw in Galicia, on the eastern edge of the Austro-Hungarian Empire, his middle-class family of small landowners and tobacco traders was among the fortunate of Eastern European Jewry, living under the relatively benign rule of the last Hapsburg emperor, Franz Josef.

After a decade in New York, the Weisels did something unusual for Jews—they returned to their home, now part of the newly reconstituted nation of Poland. In the new Polish state, however, conditions proved more precarious than under the old emperor. On a warm summer night in a large home in suburban Woodmere, New York, Weisel remembers:

Poland started getting hard. They were very anti-Semitic, the Poles. We tried to have as little as possible to do with them. They were so hostile, we had to run, not walk. At Christmas and Easter, you had to stay in the house all the time.[55]

Within a year, the Weisels had hurried back to New York. Phil's mother, Celia, an educated woman who spoke German, Polish, Yiddish and Russian, now had to take work in a garment factory. Like many Jews, the Weisels lost much—their social status, their property, their traditional way of life—in the collapse of their old world. Yet what they retained in terms of values stressing the importance of learning, family and thrift proved of inestimable value.

Another thing that helped Jews such as Weisel was the close-knit nature of their family units. For those who were too young to have gained skills, there was often a relative to show the way. A cousin gave Phil's mother her first job as a finisher; young Phil also joined the business, starting first as a sweeper, then a packer, and eventually learned the skill of cutting fabrics, as did his brother Herman.

Ultimately for Jews such as Phil Weisel, the garment business provided an exceptionally lucrative living. By the mid-1970s, when Weisel retired, Jody Juniors, which he had launched for $12,500, owned six factories, employed 250 people and had revenues of over $3.5 million.

But as Weisel himself makes plain, the success of the Jews in the garment business was not purely made in America. Much of it grew from roots planted in the Eastern European experience, which, although it ended in unspeakable tragedy, also provided many skills and attitudes beneficial to Jews as they migrated to more promising parts of the world.

Reading from their own experience with nineteenth-century Tsarist persecutions and the horrors of the Holocaust, Zionist theoreticians have tended to write off the entire diaspora experience. The *galut*, or exile, wrote the words of Zionist theoretician Jacob Klatzkin, was "not worth keeping alive" since exile constituted "nothing more than a life of deterioration and degeneration, a disgrace to the nation and a disgrace to the individual, a life of pointless struggle and futile suffering, of ambivalence, confusion and eternal impotence."[56]

Yet in reality, even the diaspora experience in Eastern Europe provided its blessings. In the sixteenth century, when their counterparts in Western Europe were still small in numbers and penned into ghetto existences, the Jews of the East enjoyed new opportunities in lands largely underdeveloped and in desperate need of their abilities, allowing them a far broader field of endeavor.[57] At the same time, their essential culture, in contrast to that of the Roman Catholics or Russian Orthodox surrounding them, did not recognize any essential virtue in being poor. As the Talmud put it: "Poverty in the home is more painful than fifty lashes."[58]

In many parts of the Polish kingdom, such attitudes, at least initially, paid off financially. The Jewish willingness to seek profits led them not only to become petty traders or usurers but to occupy much of the middle ground left between the agricultural masses and the upper nobility.[59]

As Eastern Europe began to industrialize in the late nineteenth century, the opportunities for the expanding Jewish middle class exploded.[60] Just before the turn of the century Russian Jews were twice as likely as other Tsarist subjects to be artisans or industrial workers and fifteen times more likely to be merchants. Around the same time in Galicia, Jews accounted for no more than a tenth of the population, but represented well over half the merchants and one fifth of the total industrial work force.[61]

In the newly independent Poland after the First World War, this pattern toward skilled labor, the professions and entrepreneurial development continued. Around 10 percent of the population, Jews represented 40 percent of the shoemakers and 80 percent of the tailors.[62] In Cracow they accounted for fully 60 percent of the doctors and lawyers.[63] And by 1931 they were in the majority among Poland's independent manufacturers.[64]

Local Fascists, the Nazis and Joseph Stalin would deprive the Jews of the opportunity to capitalize on these achievements. But the skills developed there benefited enormously the roughly 2.5 million Eastern European Jews who immigrated to the United States around the turn of the century[65] as well as the additional 200,000 who went to Great Britain.[66] In the United States, the Jews arrived with skills more ideally suited for a rapidly industrializing economy than did other immigrants; around the turn of the century, 75 percent of newcomers from Poland and southern Italy were either farmers or manual laborers while two thirds of the Jews came as skilled workers.[67]

These skills transferred from "the old country" keyed the rapid ascendancy of Jews in the garment trade. Wherever Jews migrated in large numbers, they flocked to the "rag trade." As early as 1860, a Jewish tailoring firm called E. Moses and Sons claimed to have set up "the first house in London . . . in the World, that established the system of *New Clothing Ready Made*" (italics original).[68]

By the late 1880s, Jews, most of them Polish and Russian immigrants, had established themselves as the masters of the emerging ready-to-wear business from London to Glasgow.[69] Conditions, even for the artisan or small entrepreneur, were often degrading, but their ability to use their skills for forward advancement was also remarkable. Beatrice Potter, writing about the late-nineteenth-century heavily Jewish "sweaters" of London's East End, comments:

> His earnings are scanty . . . But the chances of trade were open to him with indefatigable energy and with a certain measure of organizing power he may press forward into the ranks of the large employers. . . .[70]

By the 1950s the descendants of these "sweaters" had established themselves as the leading manufacturers in both men's and ladies' garments. Their ability to mass-manufacture and merchandise clothing, notes author Stephen Aris, became the Jewish British immigrant's "most characteristic and spectacular achievement."[71] Other Eastern European refugees played similarly important roles in other diaspora countries, most notably in France.

As Jewish survivors migrated to Israel, so too did the garment industry, working closely with both European and American Jews. Garments emerged in the 1960s as one of Israel's first competitive mass-production industries, with an estimated 50,000 to 60,000 workers and $600 million in sales, today second only to electronics. One of the leading Israeli garment manufacturers, Dov Lautman, son of Polish immigrants, studied production science at MIT and worked as a manager before teaming up with a French Jewish investor in 1967. By 1975 Lautman's firm, Gibor, was among the largest panty hose manufacturers in the world. Today Lautman has launched yet another venture, Delta Ltd., an underwear manufacturer that exports 85 percent of its production, mostly to Europe.

But it was in North America—and most particularly New York City—where the Jews of Eastern Europe found their ultimate opportunity. From its beginnings New York has been the center of the modern garment industry—and Jews ran the city's garment business. As early as 1885, for instance, Jews, mostly from Germany, owned 97 percent of all the garment factories.[72] By early in the twentieth century Jewish domination of the "rag trade" was virtually complete, with Jews accounting for between 50 and 80 percent of all hatmakers, furriers, seamstresses and tailors in the country.[73]

Although other cities—such as Philadelphia, Boston and Chicago—had thriving industries, New York by the 1870s had outstripped the production of its four largest competitors.[74] It may also not be coincidental that New York, which by the 1930s was home to two million Jews, roughly half the national total, would become the trade's preeminent center.[75] Despite the "resistance" of some intellectuals and politicians to acknowledge the impact of ethnic culture, tradition and skills on economic development, the connection seems obvious. Observes sociologist Thomas Sowell:

> One academic writer, for example, said that the nineteenth-century Jewish immigrants to the United States were fortunate to arrive just as the garment industry in New York began to develop. I could not help thinking that Hank Aaron was similarly fortunate—that he often came to bat when a home run was due to be hit.[76]

By the mid-1930s, Jews accounted for not only a majority of the key skill positions in the rag trade but also had gained a powerful hold on virtually all aspects of garment merchandising, design and final production. "We knew how to do everything—I made my own cuts and patterns. Jewish people did the packing, shipping and the selling," recalls Phil Weisel. "Everybody you sold to—at J. C. Penney's, Macy's, Gimbels, the whole ready-to-wear business was Jewish."

Already a billion-dollar business by the 1920s, the rag trade produced an entire generation of well-to-do Jews[77] while accounting for as much as 40 percent of female and 20 percent of male employment in the New York Jewish community.[78] Rather than being a "modern" industry with a small number of dominant firms, the garment trade was—and remains—a largely decentralized agglomeration of smaller, often quite specialized firms. Instead of huge capital resources, usually unavailable to newcomers, quick instincts, family networks and a sense of changing market trends are often the most critical elements of success, much as had been the case with the Radanite and other Jewish traders of early modern Europe.

"The primary reason people did it was every refugee wanted his own business and this was a business you could go into for very little cash," recalls Bernie Brown, whose Russian immigrant family in 1938 founded Koret of California, still one of the leading manufacturers of women's sportswear in Los Angeles. "You have contractors, shippers who can do the business. You don't need big machines or a load of money and a big office. As long as you have fabric and you have something worthwhile to sell, you can do it."[79]

But, like many of his generation, Bernie Brown wonders how long the Jewish hold on the industry will remain as the younger generation goes on to other, less demanding and less risky fields. Already, for instance, most of the cutting and other skills are most well developed elsewhere, particularly in Asian centers such as Hong Kong or Singapore. In fact, many Jewish entrepreneurs, such as Iraqi-born Jack Shamash and Hong Kong–based Ira Dan Kaye, played critical roles in shifting production outside North America and are considered pioneers in the development of the Asian-based garment industry.[80]

Increasingly, notes Doreen Gorman, a twenty-year industry veteran, Jews are concentrated at the "fashion end" or retailing side of the business, further and further away from control of the means of production. "The [Ashkenazic] Jews don't have the balls—they're not gutsy and they don't want to put up the bucks," believes Gorman, a Manhattan designer and now a top executive with Pinky Originals, a fast-growing Indian-owned firm. "The parents want their kids to be professionals. The Asians have the stick-to-it-iveness to fight in this manufacturing business. That's why down the line it will be all Indians, Orientals and maybe a few Sephardis."[81]

But, as Gorman suggests, the Jews have not exactly disappeared from the business. Her son, Jay, twenty-five, has already launched his own first fashion private label. Equally important, the gradual exodus of the Eastern Europeans has been offset in part by newcomers, such as Israelis or, in both France and North America, by North African Jews. Arguably the most successful blue jeans label of the 1980s, Guess?, was founded by four Algerian Jews who grew up in Marseilles but settled in Los Angeles.[82]

Syrian Jews, who have clustered in Brooklyn, New York, have also emerged as a major force in the sportswear industry, particularly blue jeans lines such as Jordache and Gitano. In many ways, these newcomers constitute, if anything, a throwback to an even earlier tradition of transnational Jewish businessmen. Products of a community under constant siege, they travel the world like bedouins on jets, with few loyalties beyond their immediate family operations. "There are no borders anymore," explains Charles Dayan of Bonjour, yet another of the new Syrian garment makers. "China, El Paso, or Nashville—the only difference is that sometimes you have to carry a passport."[83]

THE ROAD TO RAMAT GAN

The steel towers along Jabotinsky Road rise starkly across the flat Mediterranean coastal plain, a profile indistinguishable from Miami, Los Angeles or Singapore. Inside, within the steel-encased inner entry of the Israel Diamond Exchange, even the guards are cosmopolitan—greeting entrants in Spanish, English, French or Hebrew with seemingly equal aplomb as they pass through metal detectors, searches and identity checks.

At the Diamond Center—like New York's garment district—the legacy of the European diaspora is alive, well and making money. Past the gates, heading toward the trading floor, the sense of being in the Holy Land dissolves into the more mundane hustle of deal making on a global scale. Rather than being a celebration of Zionist austerity, the Diamond Center bustles with scores of elegantly dressed, heavily bejeweled men and women, absorbed in the age-old traditions of haggling, hustling and trading.

From his office at the pinnacle of the tower, Moshe Schnitzer, a graying man in an open white shirt, looks down over the hazy sprawl of suburban Ramat Gan with a regal bearing one might have expected from Nathan Rothschild at the London Stock Exchange in the early nineteenth century or a movie mogul in the early days of the film industry in California. Like those Jewish entrepreneurs in their venues, Schnitzer and his fellow *diamantaires* have turned Israel into the world's most important trading and diamond-cutting center, the source of roughly one third of the country's export earnings.

Like the garment manufacturers of New York, the Israeli diamond industrialists have succeeded by building upon skills and attitudes developed in the diaspora. The industry's recent roots lay in the migration to Palestine by Jewish *diamantaires* from Holland and Belgium on the eve of the Second World War. Arriving in Tel Aviv, they possessed little but their skill at cutting and trading diamonds. Yet, in diamonds, like garments, skill and *sechel* are more important than finance or even fancy connections.

"The success in this business is in the cutting," recalls Schnitzer, who started out as a diamond cutter himself in 1944. "It's a question of knowledge; whether you end up with 45 percent or 60 percent waste is a critical issue. This is a big knowledge business—like being a surgeon or a designer."

The men from whom Schnitzer learned his trade were successors to a commercial tradition developed over hundreds of years. Jews, who long have been dealers of precious stones, began dealing diamonds to the Fatimid caliphs as early as the eleventh century. When larger quantities of stones from India became available in the sixteenth century, Jewish traders seized the opportunity and, using their already existing trade links with the subcontinent, became the critical European source of distribution, marketing and repair.[84]

In Europe, the intricate web of Jewish communication and trading—already in place for the trading of other precious stones and jewelry[85]—provided an unsurpassed medium for the exchange of diamonds. By the late seventeenth century, the remarkable *Memoirs of Gluckel of Hameln* details a highly dispersed network of Jewish stone dealers buying "pearls and precious stones" that had been established from Russia to Holland. The cleverer traders, such as Gluckel, a German-Jewish widow, used their knowledge of such specialized markets to carve out a decent livelihood in even the harshest of economic climates.[86]

But the key players were the Sephardic Jews, who, escaping from Portugal and Spain, shifted the focus of Jewish commerce to Amsterdam, Antwerp and London.[87] Despite repeated attempts by powerful competitors such as the British East India Company, the Jewish traders maintained their control of both supply and marketing.[88] By 1770, some twenty-eight Jewish houses accounted for nearly four fifths of all the diamonds imported out of India.[89]

Jewish leadership—in marketing, sales, even in the mines— further strengthened with the discovery of diamonds in South Africa. Bernie Barnato, a prospector originally from London's working-class East End, emerged as the prime competitor and later partner of the great imperialist Cecil Rhodes, an alliance that resulted in the DeBeers syndicate.[90] And over the years Jews have taken leading positions at DeBeers, which today controls roughly four fifths of the world's output of unpolished diamonds.[91]

But for the onset of the Second World War the industry would have likely remained happily in the diaspora. For ambitious young men like Moshe Schnitzer, the movement of the *diamantaires* to Palestine represented a unique opportunity. Already, the elder Schnitzer could see this migration of diamond cutters transforming Palestine into the new center for polishing and marketing, creating an industry that would mushroom almost overnight from 200 to over 4,000 workers.[92]

With the war's end, however, the industry seemed to evaporate. Many of the Belgian merchants—who traditionally used predominantly non-Jewish cutters—began to pull up stakes,[93] by 1948 reducing employment to less than a third of its 1945 level.[94] Following its old customers, DeBeers drastically redirected its supply of rough stones back to Belgium and away from the Palestine-based upstarts.

It was then that Moshe Schnitzer, who by then had become a competent cutter, saw his opportunity. With $300—"I was a big capitalist for those days," he recalls with a laugh—the relative newcomer hired three cutters and started the seemingly unprofitable business of competing against the long-established South African and European connection.

Like diaspora Jews down the ages, the Israeli diamond cutters like Schnitzer found ways around their supply problems. Some simply redirected the stones via third countries. The more adventurous secured new supplies from Ghana, Sierra Leone, the Central African Republic, Zaire and Guinea.[95] Later on, when competition arose from lower-cost centers such as India and Thailand, the Israelis responded with rising investment in innovative machinery and processes. Their efforts made Israel's industry, which now cuts and polishes roughly half of the global supply of gem-quality rough diamonds, the world's leader.[96]

The intensely cosmopolitan Israeli diamond traders also forged close links with dealers and suppliers around the world. Despite the problems posed by renewed European competition in the 1950s, they carefully reestablished their ties to DeBeers and many, largely Jewish, partners in key diamond-processing centers such as New York and Belgium. Even more remarkable, they also worked closely with the diamond traders and processors in countries, such as India, that do not recognize the Jewish state and with those nations that long have participated in the Arab boycott, such as Japan,[97] where they now find their second largest market.[98]

In an Israel that still often disparages the dispersion, the diamond industry—with over 25,000 employees—has shown that business acumen does not necessarily disappear when Jews reach their promised land. "No one comes here out of sentiment —Jews don't come here to do business because they're Jews but because we do it better and cheaper," Schnitzer observes, pausing to take a puff on a cigarette. "There's no room for sentiment in business, even among Jews."[99]

JEWS IN PARADISE

As he breakfasts in the Victorian-style dining room of the City Club, Mort Fleishacker seems to fit in, almost like the old furniture, serenely comfortable in this most establishmentarian of settings. "You have to remember," explains Fleishacker, whose family first arrived in San Francisco in the middle of the nineteenth century, "that Jews were here at least as soon as anyone else, except for perhaps the Indians and the Spaniards. . . . The Jewish community, we were in on the founding of San Francisco. We're not hyphenated anythings. We're San Franciscans. We never experienced the feeling that we didn't belong here."[100]

Fleishacker's casual acceptance of his rightful place in San Francisco characterizes a unique departure in the history of the Jews. For the first time since the destruction of the Temple, the Jews in America established themselves on a mass scale, not as a specialized caste of traders, *schmatte* (rags) manufacturers or diamond cutters but in a vast array of activities, from industrial pioneers to leaders in the sciences, arts and political life.

There remains, of course, the residue of prejudice—as late as the early 1980s more than 75 percent of surveyed business executives told the Harvard Business School that being Jewish represented a "handicap" to achieving upper-level positions in the corporate hierarchy.[101] But Jews in America have managed to achieve a level of economic success, on the basis of average household income, higher than that of any religious group, including such traditional elite congregations as Unitarians and Episcopalians.[102] By 1990 Jews also constituted as many as one fifth of the sixty-four identifiable individual billionaires in the United States, more than the combined total for Britain and France combined, a number of whose own billionaires are themselves Jewish.[103]

From the beginning, the Jewish experience in America retained a character far different from that experienced anywhere else. Under colonial regimes, both Dutch and British, they faced some of the same restrictions as back in Europe. Yet the open field provided by the young colonies, particularly after independence, gave some earlier settlers ample opportunities to use their global connections profitably to tie then remote North America with the rest of the developing world economy.[104]

In America, for the first time in many centuries, Jews found themselves full citizens of a nation where for the most part they were allowed, to an extent rare in the European context, to participate in the overall development of the country.[105] As one German immigrant to New York wrote in 1835:

> When I look at America in general I can in truth maintain despite its shortcomings it is nevertheless much better than Europe because not only is there no difference in the civic relations between Christians and Jews and everybody can do what he wishes, but what is more everybody who is ready to exert himself only a little can easily find work and his efforts in every trade are rewarded.[106]

Yet perhaps the most remarkable examples of this new freedom, found in its purest form, lay not so much on the already crowded eastern shores but farther west, toward the developing frontier. Here Jews found themselves in rough societies with weak and, in some cases, nonexistent elites. By the 1830s, in the newly developing economic environment of the Mississippi, members of the New Orleans Jewish community, many of them from French-speaking backgrounds, had managed to secure positions on the ground floor of the city's expansion—not only as merchants but as owners of major plantations.[107] One prominent New Orleans Jew, Judah P. Benjamin, became the first to enter a national cabinet, albeit in the service of the ill-fated Confederacy.

Farther west, the transformation from the old European diaspora patterns diverged even more dramatically. The frontier provided the stage for Jews who, in their time, were as much pioneers as the Zionist settlers of the early twentieth century. These Jews entered a society with few preconceptions. Like other settlers of the West, they had a wide latitude to indulge their idiosyncrasies and ambitions.

In this vast new world, Jewish traders could move into fields virtually unplowed. In city after city, from Dallas and Phoenix to Salt Lake City, they were able to establish themselves in the leading mercantile businesses.[108] But nowhere were the opportunities greater than in California. "Especially influential are the

Jews in the West," wrote Werner Sombart, with typical over-statement. "California is for the most part their creation."[109]

Yet the German writer was not too distant from the reality. Jews were in San Francisco before the gold rush, and by 1852, as noted historian Hubert Howe Bancroft has observed, among the "medley of races and nationalities" in the bustling boom town stood prominently "the ubiquitous Hebrews."[110] They were prominent in the provisioning of the mines, they helped finance the railroads and they dominated retailing up and down the coast. Some of the emerging prominent Jewish merchant banking families—such as the Seligmans and the Lazards—achieved prominence as local merchants and financial intermediaries between European capitals, the East Coast and the California gold rush.[111]

Even blue denim jeans, the "uniform" of the gold rush—and, indeed, the American West—owe their origination and popular name to Levi Strauss, a gold rush–era immigrant to San Francisco.[112] Although the age-old prejudice remained, the passion for profits on the frontier simply overwhelmed all other considerations. Here was a free field of play for all the bottled-up ambitions of a global tribe. As one contemporary observer noted:

> Never since the great Egyptian exodus have the Hebrews found a soil and society better suited to their character and taste, better adapted to their prosperity and propagation than California. All nations have come hither; shades of color, of belief, peculiarities of physique, of temper and habit were less distinctly marked. Gold was here, and in common with the Gentiles, the Jews loved gold. For the rest, all he asked was to be let alone, and here that blessing was granted him more fully than in any country he had ever seen. Gold, and golden opportunities, moneymaking and freedom of thought, speech and action, they were here, and these were the Jews' earthly paradise.[113]

In this "Jews' paradise," the tribe felt themselves, and were largely regarded, as first-class members of the local establishment. In the rough-and-ready Los Angeles of the 1860s, members of the Jewish Newmark clan served variously as city attorney, city councilman and county supervisor.[114] Another Jew helped found the city's first chamber of commerce.[115] Similarly, in San Francisco several Jews, including a prosperous merchant named Samuel Fleishacker,[116] sat on the famous 1851 Committee of Vigilance. By the 1870s, the San Francisco Jews— by then roughly 10 percent of the city's population[117]—were among the wealthiest and best positioned in the nation, in the estimates of contemporary Jewish observers.[118]

With this social liberation, Jews felt free to enter into businesses, such as commercial banking, that, even in places like New York, remained largely off-limits until later in the twentieth century. The Hellman family of Los Angeles, for example, virtually invented banking in Los Angeles during the 1860s,[119] by the 1920s controlling both the Farmer's and Merchants Bank in Los Angeles and San Francisco–based Wells Fargo.[120] In 1902, Achille Levy founded the Ventura County, California, bank that still bears his name—the Bank of A. Levy[121]—while another *landsman*, Kaspare Cohn, founded the Union Bank, which for decades stood as Los Angeles's premier middle-market bank.[122]

Perhaps most significantly of all, the Jews of Paradise felt free to seize the leadership of an entirely new industry—motion pictures—which, hitherto, barely existed. Ironically, these were not largely the same Jews who had, in previous decades, emerged as the West's leading bankers and merchants. Instead, the creators of the motion picture industry, much like the *schmatte* manufacturers, were largely drawn from more recent immigrants from the Eastern European diaspora.

Indeed, in sharp contrast to the more mainstream tastes of their assimilated California-bred brethren, the Jewish entrepreneurs in movies and their predecessor, the popular stage, were inspired largely by the explosion in the Yiddish theater that had begun first in Eastern Europe, in rapidly modernizing cities like Bucharest and Odessa. There, and afterward in America, the theater captured the struggles of a people caught between their medieval past and an uncertain present.

Based sometimes on old traditional Purim plays and adaptations of age-old stories, the Yiddish theater in America became an early form of mass media, by the turn of the century offering over 1,100 performances annually for an estimated two million patrons.[123] As a media it played a critical role in acculturating the new urban Jewish masses. As historian Moses Rischin observed:

> The "greenhorn" mélanges, bursting with absurdities of immigrant bewilderment, the incongruities of mispronunciation, the heartbreak of parting, the tears of reunion with loved ones, were constant favorites. These performances, momentarily dissolving the loneliness outside, schooled folk in the rough surfaces of city living, and knowingly familiarized them with the tenement wilderness.[124]

Although attempts were made to transform Yiddish theater into a serious art form, the predominant trend, Rischin notes, was toward mass entertainment—vaudeville routines, musicals and comedies—and ultimately the primitive nickelodeon became ever more predominant.[125] Like garments, it was an ideal sort of immigrant business—low cost of entry, low overhead, and not already dominated by some other group.

Jewish experience in retailing and catering to the mass consumer also proved useful. Years of experience as itinerant peddlers, shopowners and garment manufacturers established close contact with the "public" and a unique understanding of its ever-changing fancies. And when the Jewish entrepreneurs moved into production and out to Hollywood, like the Radanites trading Oriental goods to illiterate Frankish nobles or the merchants in the rough world of the gold rush mine fields, they retained the feel for mass tastes that already had turned furriers Marcus Lowe and Adolph Zukor into successful owners of vaudeville theaters.

In the ghetto streets and on the ramshackle stages of the Bowery and Brooklyn, they nurtured talent soon to become world famous, from George Burns and Al Jolson to Eddie Cantor and Milton Berle.[126] Slightly later on, while others pondered over questions of art, pioneer filmmakers like Carl Laemmle, author

Neil Gabler observed, took instead to "marketing movies like clothing," something rather natural for a man who came from the *schmatte* business in the first place.[127]

By the 1930s Jewish domination of the movie business was palpable. They controlled six of the eight largest studios[128] and, according to a 1936 study, accounted for almost two thirds of all the major producers.[129] Jews also accounted for a large portion of the agents and, often working under Anglicized names, many of the actors as well.[130]

Initially, the Hollywood Jews were, if anything, less than enthusiastic about identifying themselves with their ethnic heritage. Even at the height of their power, they rarely spoke openly about their Jewish identity; "an abyss," noted one history of the region, existed between the Hollywood Jews and the already well established Jewish community of Los Angeles.[131] When writer Ben Hecht asked David Selznick to contribute for guns for Jewish soldiers in Palestine, Selznick replied rather typically: "I'm an American. Why should I be interested in Jewish guerrillas?"[132]

Threatened first by the rising threat of anti-Semitism at home, then by the onset of the Second World War, the mostly Jewish moguls actually accelerated their conscious assimilation, beginning what one film historian calls the "de-Semitization" of the movies. Jewish themes, jokes, accents began to disappear from the screen. Only after the war did Jewish themes and characters begin to seep back into the mainstream industry.[133]

Yet the power of the Jews in Hollywood, and their ability to fashion fantasies not only for America but the world, flowed from their ethnic consciousness and experience. Like many of their fellow Jews in America, they shared the wonder of the relative tolerance and open vistas America had suddenly opened for them. Author Irving Howe observed:

> It was something of a miracle and something of a joke. They had come from the Ukraine and Poland and Austria-Hungary; they still spoke with Yiddish accents; but it was they, more than anyone else, who reached the fantasies of America, indeed of the entire world—a universalism of taste which shaped the century

and which they could shrewdly exploit because they innocently shared it.[134]

Today, with Jewish direct control of the studios greatly reduced, the ethnic imprint has weakened. Yet the Jewish community in both Greater Los Angeles and California, which more than doubled during the 1970s and 1980s,[135] continues to grow in power and size, attracting Jews from other parts of the United States,[136] as well as Iranian, Israeli and Russian immigrants. By 1990 the Jewish population in Los Angeles—which in 1920 had fewer Jewish residents than Buffalo, New York[137]— had expanded by over 150,000 to some 600,000,[138] making it the second largest center for the diaspora after New York.[139]

In this environment, Jewish performers, producers and other artists are part of a larger community, whose professional base extends well beyond Hollywood.[140] In the context of this wider Jewish life, few consider the existence of a Synagogue of the Performing Arts or the involvement of Jewish stars in issues concerning the Holocaust remembrance and the Middle East as anything out of the ordinary.[141]

While movies are no longer, strictly speaking, a "Jewish" industry, the role of Jews within Hollywood and the related entertainment field remains pervasive. Although virtually all the studios have been bought out by public corporations, foreign investors and individual financiers, most of them non-Jewish, complaints about strong Jewish influence in the industry still crop up, from as diverse sources as Italian film mogul Giancarlo Parretti to black film director Spike Lee and elements of the National Association for the Advancement of Colored People.

Although not in control of the media and the arts, as some anti-Semites suggest, Jews clearly possess a disproportionate influence in movies, publishing, advertising and theater. In the media, according to one survey in the 1970s, one quarter of the leading figures were Jewish, more than ten times their percentage in the general population.[142] "The Jewish role in the American elite is only partly a function of money," notes historian David Biale. "It is perhaps more a function of knowledge."[143]

In Hollywood today the difference is not so much one of

degree as one of method. Jewish power in Hollywood no longer centers on those whom own the studios but on the assorted agents, independent producers and writers who increasingly dominate the industry, including promoters such as Arnon Milchan,[144] Michael Ovitz and David Geffen, a former agent and record producer whom *Forbes* in 1990 identified as "the richest man in Hollywood."[145] Traditional Jewish skills in selling , marketing, assembling the various "elements" needed for mounting a production remain critical.

But gone forever are the big Jewish names like Thalberg, the Mayers or the Harry Cohns, who dominated the film industry's golden era. Yet even now much of the real power in Hollywood —deciding what gets made and what does not—remains with those who have the ability to judge talent, make a quick decision, spot an opportunity, make a deal. Sitting in her San Fernando Valley office, Margo Bernay, a craft union business agent whose family first started commuting to Hollywood from the old Jewish neighborhoods of East Los Angeles in the 1930s, observes:

> If you look at the real deal power in this town it's the agents, the producers; it's not with the studios. In the old days the studios owned the talent; now the talent owns the studios. So that's where the Jews are, where the creativity is, the talent, the glamour, the power. It's the *sechel* side of the business, the mentality. It's the part of the business that doesn't have boundaries that you get in big corporations—it gives you the space Jews have been brought up to push for.[146]

THE LIMITS OF ZION

Even four decades after the reestablishment of the Jewish state in Palestine, the Jews—including those in Israel—retain much of their essentially transnational character and their peculiar attachment to commerce. Jewry overall, which lost one third of its total population during World War II, has grown from a low of eleven million to at least thirteen million.[147] Some smaller and weaker diaspora communities have disappeared, while others, such as those in France, Australia and the United States, have grown in size and prosperity.[148] "The reality of Jewry life remains complex and protean," observes Israeli historian David Vital. "Jewry has no formal boundaries; its informal boundaries are subject to constant movement, change and debate."[149]

Perhaps most revealing, the diaspora has continued to prove attractive to those who feel compelled, due to persecution or economic circumstance, to migrate abroad. Only one third of the French-speaking Jews from North Africa chose to make the *aliyah* to Israel,[150] a far larger number opting instead to immigrate to their "mother country," France.[151] Indeed, despite the losses suffered in the Holocaust, since the 1930s the French Jewish community, one of the most ancient in the world, has *doubled* in size and now stands as the world's fourth largest.[152]

More important, despite repeated predictions of its demographic demise,[153] the American Jewish community has continued to expand; between 1970 and 1990—in the face of rising rates of intermarriage and a low birthrate—the number of self-defined Jews in America grew by 300,000.[154] This small population growth has come about in part due to large-scale immigration from diaspora communities in Iran and South Africa. Most important, however, has been emigration from the Soviet Union, totaling over 250,000[155]; as of 1991, an additional 100,000 with visas await their turn to leave.[156]

Reasons behind this preference for the hated *galut*, or exile, vary. For some, presence of relatives in the United States, with by far the largest community of Russian Jews' descendants, made all the difference. Another factor is frankly economic; America, where Jews are the wealthiest of all major ethnic groups,[157] generally offers a far better field of opportunity for the largely well-educated Soviet Jews than does tiny Israel. Certainly those who have come, despite the usual problems of adjustment, have done reasonably well. Within a few years, according to one recent nationwide survey, the average Soviet Jewish family earns more annually than the average American one.[158]

Given their success in America, few American Jews have migrated outside the confines of the United States. Yet, the Jewish bedouin tradition lives on in other members of the tribe, most notably and ironically the Israelis. Rather than becoming the "sons of the land" celebrated by the earlier Zionists, as many as 800,000 Israelis—products of a small, relatively poor and war-torn country—have sought better opportunities elsewhere.[159] In some years, particularly before the mass migration from Russia, the number of outbound Israelis has actually exceeded the number of immigrants.[160]

Although present in countries as distinct as Finland and Singapore, their favored place to settle has been the United States, with as many as a half million concentrated in major colonies in New York and Los Angeles.[161] In comparison, total American Jewish immigration to Israel during the four decades after 1948 has numbered no higher than 60,000, less than half the number of Israelis who legally applied for full American immigrant status between 1970 and 1987.[162]

Like other Jewish sojourners, the Israelis come to the United States mainly for economic opportunity, often for a chance to participate more fully in those activities—from filmmaking and finance to garment manufacturing—that have been mainstays of the Jewish economy for generations. Yet, in contrast to the Russians, most will likely not settle permanently in America. By 1990, only one third of the estimated Israeli residents have applied for immigrant status. "For most *kibbutzniks*—though not a few decide to stay on—Los Angeles is like a gas station," comments one, Danny Ziskind, a thirty-year-old Israeli immigrant. "We come here, en route to extended visits to the Far East, to fill up."[163]

This movement parallels the increasing mobility of the global tribes generally, most particularly those with high levels of education, skill in highly globalized industries or capital resources. Like thousands of their Irish, British, Indian, Chinese, Palestinian or other counterparts, the "wandering Israelis" of today, for example, have achieved positions within the more elite ranks of technical and other professional workers. Engineers alone account for nearly 20 percent of the total,[164] with an estimated 13,000 laboring as scientists, engineers and other professionals in California's high-technology industries alone,[165] a population roughly one third the size of Israel's native-born technical work force.[166]

These new Jewish wanderers also include a disproportionate number of former government officials, garment manufacturers and film production artists,[167] as well as several thousand similarly skilled and highly educated recent Russian émigrés to Israel.[168] Itzhak Kol, a recent immigrant to Los Angeles and as former president of three of Israel's leading studios a two-time Academy Award nominee, explains:

> The secret truth is you meet Israelis wherever you go—in New York, Thailand, Europe. You sometimes wonder how many of the old guys are left in Israel.
>
> When my mother made a cake, you need the right amount of yeast. If it's the right amount, the cake is good. But in Israel there's too much yeast. When Jews are a minority they are great —producers, directors, writers, successful people. When there are too many in a small place, it's ruined, a little bit like Israel.[169]

The continuing appeal of the diaspora, most notably to Israelis themselves, reveals the bankruptcy of some of the most fundamental portions of traditional Zionist dogma. Once the state was formed, many Zionists assumed that Jews in the diaspora would sooner or later either migrate to Israel or accept absorption into their adoptive countries. To Golda Meir, the children of dispersion constituted objects of "pity," not equal beings to the vital young Israelis "growing up in the desert."[170] Along similar lines, French sociologist Georges Friedmann predicted in his 1962 book *End of the Jewish People?* that the very existence of Israel had destroyed the essential "Jewish personality," which he defined as the product of anti-Semitism and faith built around the Law.[171] "The 'Jewish people,' " he predicted, "is disappearing and giving way to the Israeli nation."[172]

Yet, the continuing out-migration of Israelis as well as the enormous costs created by absorbing recently arrived Russian and Ethiopian refugees suggests that Israel will unlikely be able to reduce its longstanding dependence on the diaspora. This reflects, to some extent, the fears of the early Jewish pioneers in Palestine, including those left-wing Zionists who as early as the 1930s feared their embryonic Jewish state would become little more than a "colony" of "the rich Jews of America and Europe."[173] Fearful of such a result, many Zionist pioneers sought to create, in the words of A. D. Gordon, one of their leading ideologists, "a new re-created Jewish people, not a mass colony of *diaspora* Jewry, not the continuation of diaspora Jewish life in a new form."[174]

In the process the "old Jew"—with the diaspora legacy of trading, whether in rags, pounds sterling, diamonds or fantasies—would disappear. The new "re-created Jews" would gravitate instead toward "natural" work, most notably farming.[175] To many mainstream Zionists this also meant that instead of embracing capitalism, which first had liberated Jews from their medieval bondage, Israel should devote itself to the ideals of *mamlachtiut*, or statism, an approach that even today leaves two fifths of the industrial economy controlled by either the state or the national labor co-operative, Histadrut.[176] In the place of entrepreneurs, the economy became dominated by an overarching bureaucratic state that Israeli sociologist Baruch Kimmerling has described as "a paternalistic body deciding what was good for the citizens and the collectivity as a whole."[177]

Ironically, the pursuit of socialism—and later the Likud's ultranationalistic and ultraorthodox religious policies—created an Israel ever more economically dependent on the diaspora and its power abroad. By 1991 Israel had emerged as the single largest recipient of charity, grants and assistance per capita in the world, the bulk of it from America.[178]

In fact, with the exception of a few industries derived from the diaspora, most notably diamonds, Israel has failed miserably to create an independent economic existence, setting on its head any preconception that Jews, operating in their own land and free from the stimulative effects of diaspora life, are genetically better suited than others for business success. In 1989, four decades after independence, Israel's trade deficit, for example, stood at 10 percent of GNP,[179] more than five times higher on a percentage basis than America's and among the highest in the world.[180] Foreign investment, which dropped 50 percent during the 1980s,[181] has fallen to a level one fifth that enjoyed by an even smaller state such as Singapore.[182] Even the great symbols of the Zionist past—the orange industry,[183] the *kibbutz* movement, even the vaunted military industries, particularly in an era of global military cutbacks—have fallen on hard times.[184]

For some in the Jewish state, these realities—compounded by the mass migration of Russian Jews—suggest the necessity of a radical reorientation in Israel and its attitude toward the diaspora. Aharon Dovrath, who spent a quarter century as president and chief executive officer of Clal, one of Israel's largest industrial conglomerates, believes the Jewish state can win back its independence only by rediscovering traditional diaspora values of enterprise and self-help. Rather than creating a "new" Jew or playing on the guilt of wealthy Jews outside, Israel must become an economy worthy of investment, the diaspora ethos of economic opportunism replacing the traditional Zionist ethic of sacrifice or the messianic ultranationalism of the Israeli Right.

> The Jews in Israel have succeeded where they failed in diaspora —agriculture, building, military, but they failed in the areas where we are everywhere else dominant. To get efficiency was a violation of Zionism. That's why we've done a lousy job.[185]

This transition, Dovrath points out, represents an expansion quite at odds with the sort of Jewish Lebensraum, "a big and powerful state," espoused during the Likud era.[186] He suggests that an Israel at peace with its neighbors—and particularly with the Palestinians—would enjoy the economic dividends of peace and join their successful diaspora cousins in the flourishing postnational economic order.

"We would like the diaspora to give us the flexibility to adjust to reality," Dovrath, himself an immigrant from Argentina, explains. "If we had this quality, we would give back the land to the Arabs. We should act like Jews, not like Prussians."

In a sense, as Israeli economist Daniel Doron has observed, there are models for such intelligent global tribalism, most notably the Chinese in Hong Kong and Taiwan. Over the past few decades, the Chinese—whose sense of superiority and identity is quite possibly as ingrained as that of the Jews—have used their pooled investment capital and entrepreneurial and technical gifts to absorb even larger numbers of more destitute members of their tribe. And they have done so with far less charity, without the conquest of an inch of additional territory and with the achievement of higher average incomes.[187]

Having created the archetype of the global tribe, the Jews, particularly in Palestine, might look closely at the success of others who, although newer to the diaspora experience, have learned far better the lesson that economic success remains the key to long-term survival. In adapting to the new realities of an increasingly internationalized economy, the Jews can once again display the enormous resourcefulness that has carried them through the millennia as the oldest and most persistent of the global tribes.

CHAPTER THREE

LEGACY OF EMPIRE

AS MINISTER OF JUSTICE, adviser to Charles de Gaulle, and an author, Alain Peyrefitte has long pondered the British diaspora's remarkable expansion and continuing global influence. It is a question that has confounded generations of Frenchmen—as well as other Europeans—who have watched the island race and its offspring snatch the largest share of the world's riches, power and influence.

Certainly, Peyrefitte explains, there was no external logic dictating that Britain, rather than France, would play so dominant a role. France certainly had been blessed with a far richer endowment, a kinder climate, a longer history of civilization. Even as late as the 1780s France surpassed Britain in overseas colonial trade,[1] its population was more than four times larger, its industry at least as well developed.[2] The French culture and language stood second to none throughout Europe.

Yet today it is the diaspora of the British, not the French, Germans or Italians that constitutes the core of modern world society. A century has passed since the apogee of the British empire, but the nations it spawned—the United States, Canada, Australia and New Zealand—still account for thirteen of the world's fifteen largest companies,[3] over half the GDP of the world's seven leading industrialized countries,[4] and by far the largest portion of overseas foreign investment stock, more than Japan and Germany combined.[5] Similarly, the English-speaking countries also account for by far the vast preponderance of all inbound direct investment and the majority capitalization of the world's stock markets.[6]

At the same time, the English-speaking world has remained at the center in noneconomic spheres as well, from culture and politics to science and technology. Its political legacy—from the British and American constitutions to the Marshall Plan[7] and the American-directed recovery of Japan—survived the Cold War as the essential building blocks of the modern world. Its cultural hegemony, from fast food to Hollywood, continues to gain ground on the more narrowly based national pop cultures in both Japan and Europe.[8] Today, the United States' export of pop culture stands as the country's second largest export, behind only aerospace.[9]

Even in technology, where Asian power is increasingly evident, the United States, according to a 1991 Japanese government study, leads in over forty-three critical areas—including new materials, environmental science and pharmaceuticals—to thirty-three for Japan, with Europe generally far behind.[10] In basic science, where Japan still barely figures, the Anglo-American preeminence is even more palpable, since 1950 compiling six times as many Nobel Prizes as the combined totals for all of continental Europe.[11]

To Peyrefitte, the source of this enormous Anglo-American triumph lies not in any inherent technological or managerial genius, or even in the existence of superior political institutions. Instead Peyrefitte turns to the underlying motivations and attitudes that drove the British on their global quest. Unlike his own people and other Europeans, the British, he notes, even at the height of empire, had chosen to place profits ahead of grandeur, commercial gain over strengthening the state. Standing in his office in Paris, in front of a photograph of de Gaulle, the thin, gray-haired former civil servant observed:

> The British and Americans invented a society that was at heart essentially mercantile, that saw trade as its object. The French were basically rural. France made a choice of their earth and England chose the seas and trade. We stayed back and even abroad looked to re-create home.[12]

THE COMMERCIAL CONQUERORS

Like many great peoples over history, including the Spanish, the French, Peyrefitte points out, saw colonial expansion, first and foremost, as a way to expand their nation and its greatness. The concept of *la mission civilitrice* suffused the entire process of French colonialism, with its insistence on the standard use of French language and the absorption of "natives" into the metropolitan culture of Paris.[13] Their inclusion in the French body politic, including representation in the National Assembly, boasted one French politician in 1923, transformed a nation of forty million into a global entity with over one hundred million members.[14]

The British diaspora's priorities were less grandiose and notably more commercially oriented, revolving around the search for markets, resources and, where possible, prospective lands for new economically viable colonies. Yet even within its colonies of settlement there remained a distinction between motherland and periphery. The very idea of delegates from Canada or Australia, much less Ghana or Nigeria, serving in Westminster would have seemed almost absurd to most British politicians.

Rather than seeking to export a civilization, the British, and later the Americans, focused primarily on business expansion. In some sense, their enthusiasm for commerce was their raison d'être, their "vocation of uniqueness." To men such as Richard Cobden, the great early-nineteenth-century apostle of free trade, the creative expansion of modern business and technology itself would ultimately serve mankind's needs most effectively.

Commerce is the grand panacea which, like a beneficent medical discovery, will serve to inoculate with the healthy and saving taste for civilization all the nations of the world. Not a bale of merchandise leaves our shores but it bears the seeds of intelligence and fruitful thought to the members of some less enlightened community . . .[15]

Money, not glory, then, drove the British first into the Americas and India, and later to the borders of China, Africa and the deserts of Oceania. Even the great imperialist Cecil Rhodes himself, as Hannah Arendt would later write, was not an adventurer in the medieval or pure nationalist mold but "an ambitious businessman with a marked tendency toward megalomania."[16] To Rhodes, the national flag was not a holy cloth but "a commercial asset."[17]

By the late nineteenth century, the virulence of this expansionism reached a fever pitch, with the British in possession of the largest empire in history, extending over a territory three times larger than that colonized by its arch-rival, France,[18] and ruling over one fourth of the globe's population.[19] As Rhodes himself proclaimed: "Expansion is everything . . . I would annex the planets if I could."[20]

Often this expansionism led to the most brutal forms of commercial exploitation. Along the China coast, British traders—including Scots such as the Jardines and Mathesons, who had fled their ghetto in rocky, infertile Scotland[21]—grew rich primarily through a massive trade in opium,[22] in the process helping to turn nearly one of every eight Chinese nationals into a drug addict.[23] Not surprisingly, the beneficiaries of this bounty sought to harvest it quickly and return home to assume a more respectable standing. As one British China trader of the 1840s put it:

In two or three years at furthest, I hope to realize a fortune and get away. . . . You must not expect men in my position to condemn themselves to prolonged exile in an unhealthy climate for the benefit of posterity. We are money-making, practical men. Our business is to make money, as much and as fast as we can—

and for this end all modes or means are good which the law permits.[24]

Yet, over time, the opium traders and their financiers formed powerful trading houses and became the bedrock of the local establishment. Across the breadth of Asia—in an archipelago extending from Aden and Bombay to Calcutta, Singapore and Hong Kong—islands of Britain arose, dominated by small elites from the home islands and administered according to British law and customs.

Although protected by the might of British arms, and particularly that of the British navy, this was not an empire primarily based on the sword, the state and religion. Its greater power— extending far beyond the imperial boundaries—grew from the power of money and commerce.[25] As historian Karl Polanyi observed: "The Pax Britannica held its sway sometimes by the ominous poise of a heavy ship's cannon, but more frequently by the timely pull of a thread in the international monetary network."[26]

In the process the British indeed created not just an empire but a whole world, a global network through which fortunes and careers could be made in accordance with predominately British standards and methods. Even long after the empire had receded, men such as Ron Carstairs, like generations of Scotsmen before him, could find in Britain's commercial network unique opportunities for upward mobility.

The grandson of a farm laborer from outside Edinburgh, Carstairs had worked his way up from Saint Andrews College through the bureaucracy of the Chartered Bank, whose origins lay with another Scotsman, James Wilson, the scion of a successful Quaker family of woolen manufacturers and also one of the founders of that bible of British capitalism, *The Economist*. The Chartered Bank was established in 1852 as the Chartered Bank of India, Australia and China, to capitalize on the growing market for financing trade between those far-flung regions of the world and Great Britain.[27] By 1990 more than four out of every five of the bank's nearly 30,000 employees[28] and nearly three fifths of its total assets remained outside the United Kingdom.[29]

For Carstairs, this global presence provided a career path likely unavailable if he had simply remained in Britain. After a brief stint in the bank's London operation, he served almost three decades in the cities founded or shaped by British and Anglo-American expansionism—Kuala Lumpur, Singapore, Los Angeles, Manila and, ultimately, Hong Kong, where he concluded his career as general manager.

With his well-tailored suit, narrow frame and neatly combed straight white hair—almost a caricature of the British man of empire—the fifty-three-year-old banker still reveres the legacy of the great commercial conquerors like Rhodes and Wilson. Even in Hong Kong, the citadel of Asiatic capitalism, he notes, Britishers have remained at the core of the business leadership, with United Kingdom–based portfolio investment still accounting for roughly 30 to 40 percent of all Hong Kong's listed companies.[30] For these firms, stubborn remnants of empire, Hong Kong—despite the impending takeover by China scheduled for 1997—endures as the preferred place for living and for the making of money.

In fact, in 1991, Carstairs, who was unwilling to transfer back to Britain, announced his resignation from Standard Chartered and instead accepted the presidency of a local Chinese-owned bank. Explaining his decision to remain behind, Carstairs peered down over the harbor from his high-rise office and observed:

> We British were a people born of "Go east, go out, young man." . . . Even now, when we look at the Asia-Pacific area, where the wealth is being created—they are driving to a standard, and that standard is ours. Not everything from the past is broken. The British migration to Asia happened. We can't change that. There's a lot left on the table.

THE TRIUMPH OF ENGLISH

In some ways, however, the ultimate expression of the preeminence of British and, later, American influence lay not in its financial or technological power, but through its cultural and linguistic legacy. Again, perhaps the most useful contrast lies with the cultural and linguistic heritage of the French, whose language as recently as the eighteenth century had more speakers than English, but today is spoken by less than a third as many.[31]

As in their whole approach to global expansion, notes Peyrefitte, the French were largely unwilling to accept the "particularist genius" and diversity that characterized the commercially driven English. To them, "the universality" of French language and culture implied one shared set of norms, which, of course, could be regulated—and preserved from adulteration —by the Academie Française in Paris.[32] Although roughly half Europe's business deals were conducted in English even into the 1990s,[33] the French Ministry of Education opposed attempts to embrace plans for the education of multilingual Europeans in France, claiming such students would not meet their standards.[34]

The approach of the British, and later the Americans, could not have been more different. To a large extent, the English admixture reflected the ethnic development of the British, who, according to at least one prominent ethnologist, are "among the most composite of Europeans," a mixture formed by waves of invading Celts, Germanic Saxons, Danes, Flemish and Normans, among others.[35] As Defoe wrote in his caricature *The True-Born Englishman*:

> All these the Barb'rous Off-spring left behind,
> The Dregs of Armies, they of all Mankind;
> Blended with Britons who before were here,
> Of Whom, the Welch ha' blest the Character.
> From this Amphibious Ill-born Mob began
> That vain Ill-natured thing, An Englishman.[36]

Yet despite its mongrel origin, English, a language spoken in the eleventh century by only 1.5 million people on a remote island, today ranks second only to Chinese in the number of speakers, with as many as 700 million users.[37] Most important, it is spoken commonly in more countries, and on more continents, than any other language.[38] By 1980, nearly 100 million non-English speakers—three out of five of them Asian—were studying some variant of the Queen's English.[39]

Equally important, English, due largely to Anglo-American technological and commercial hegemony, also emerged uncontested as the global language of science. By the early 1970s, nearly three in four scientific journals and more than four in every five engineering journals were published in English.[40] Three quarters of the world's mail and 80 percent of the information stored in electronic retrieval systems is written in English.[41] By the 1980s even French scholars, their language's share of science publications dropping below 5 percent of the world total, were being forced to publish in the British tongue.[42]

The ability of English to develop a mutually recognizable standard contradicted the prophecies of many experts, such as one nineteenth-century Oxford linguist who saw in the language's dispersion the creation of several "mutually unintelligible" offspring. Others, like author Henry James, listened to the rich vernacular of "fluent Eastside New Yorkese" and wondered if "inward assimilation" eventually would destroy both the language and culture of his forefathers.[43]

Yet English, although spoken with a multitude of accents and inflections, has remained essentially one language. The accents of an Indian, Singaporean, American or British speaker of English may be difficult at times for outsiders, but the common communication media—from the CNN and BBC television networks, to the *Straits Times* of Singapore, to the *Times* of India, London, New York or Japan—still utilize a fundamentally standard idiom.[44] Although deeply affected by the immigrant experience, most particularly through the impact of Irish migration, English has persisted, if not as the purest of tongues, as easily the most universal.[45]

Perhaps nowhere is this peculiar "genius" more evident than in the developing world. In East Asia, the focal point of world economic and technological growth, English has become the primary means of international communication. In Hong Kong,

90 percent of students attend Anglo-Chinese bilingual schools and attempts to bifurcate the system by language group have met stiff opposition from parents concerned that students learning only Mandarin would be disadvantaged for future success.[46] Arch-rival Singapore uses English not only for business but as the primary language of communication and government.

In India and some other former colonies, English—once derided as an instrument of colonial rule—has emerged as one of the basic elements helping to create a common culture among peoples long separated by linguistic differences. "It was in the English classroom," notes one Indian scholar, "that the Indian literary renaissance was born." In African countries, such as Nigeria, noted one African writer, English provided "a language with which they could talk to one another. If it failed to give them song, it at least gave them a tongue for singing."[47]

Similarly, in Japan, where German once held a strong appeal, English emerged completely dominant after the American occupation. By the late 1970s nearly eight million Japanese were studying English—as many as in all of Western Europe[48]—and Japanese corporations, in their brochures and manuals, used it as the primary means of international communication.[49] So pervasive has the English culture become that throughout the Far East, Chinese, Korean and Japanese products use the language as what one author calls "a status marker, a talisman of modernity." Sometimes, however, this results in such nonsensical English slogans as "The Good Feeling of Fine"[50] or "I Feel Coke and Sound Special."[51]

The contrast with the linguistic and cultural legacy of other European peoples is startling. Upon independence, the Indonesians quickly scrapped Dutch, their colonial language, replacing it immediately with English, which was seen as an estimably more important and effective language. By the 1980s the local Indonesian vernacular had been transformed into something that one French linguist referred to as "Indonglish."[52]

The predominance of English is particularly maddening for many Europeans, who have long regarded the British, and even more so the Americans, as relatively unsophisticated and uncultured. Yet Europeans, whose fashions and art once enraptured the wealthy parvenus of Manchester, London and New York, now look increasingly to English speakers for the latest cultural, scientific and political trends. Although many Europeans, particularly within the French elite, deny the importance of American culture,[53] it remains easily the preeminent influence across national boundaries. As French television commentator Christine Ockrent put it: "The only true pan-European culture is the American culture."[54]

The triumph of the English language is particularly obvious in the popular culture. Between 1980 and 1991 European film production fell nearly 30 percent while English-language movies, primarily from Hollywood, expanded rapidly, capturing the lion's share of revenues. Indeed, only 15 percent of European films from a heavily subsidized local industry ever reach outside their nation or, at best, European borders; French movies garner barely 4 percent of the market share in other Francophone countries, much less in the rest of the world.[55]

Attempts to halt this tide, particularly in Europe, have, at times, bordered on the ludicrous, with millions of dollars spent in Paris or Brussels to fight off the British-American cultural thrust.[56] In 1990 French Culture Minister Jack Lang—fed up with the successful invasion by Hollywood's "industrialized international music"—set aside $8 million to support the development of French rock and roll. Yet the dreams of Bruno Lion, the unofficial but well-paid "Minister of Rock and Roll," seem to have had little effect; a year later, back home in France, Anglophone rock videos outsold their Francophone competitors four to one.[57]

Other elites outside the British diaspora have also worked to overcome this primacy. Japanese media, most notably the government-owned NHK network, have labored mightily to create alternative systems opposing the Anglo-American dominion, only to find themselves—even in their own Asian backyard—a distant second, particularly among the young.[58] Governments in some developing countries, such as India, have felt compelled to invest their scarce resources to fend off a growing wave of "alien" satellite transmissions, which bring with them the world as seen from London, Atlanta or Washington.[59]

Throughout the 1980s and early 1990s the influence of English-language, largely American news and information expanded rapidly, not only in Western Europe and Asia but also in new markets in the Soviet Union, Eastern Europe and throughout the developing world.[60] Like rock and roll and Hollywood movies, these views of current events carry within them the seeds of the British-American tribe, its viewpoints and its legacy.

Even an emerging trans-European economy will likely do little to reduce English's leadership. Already both German and French firms employ English as their lingua franca for international business.[61] Similarly, German, the language of Europe's premier economic power, has not even expanded beyond the less than 100 million speakers it possessed in 1925.[62] Even bordering countries, such as Denmark and the Netherlands, have shifted away from German, which, as one Danish linguist described it, can barely compete against the "unstoppable deluge of English."[63]

To some Germans, the emergence of a united Europe, and more particularly the liberation of Eastern Europe, could possibly provide a last-ditch opportunity to regain some of this lost ground.[64] Yet by 1991, in Hungary—where it is no longer mandatory to study Russian, and all other major European languages are now offered—roughly four out of every five students opted for English.[65]

Much the same tendency holds within the former Soviet Union itself. In the Russian Republic, the majority of students, and nearly two in three in the Ukraine, opt for English over other foreign languages.[66] As Dr. Manfred Heid, who supervises East European programs for the Goethe Foundation, a German-financed cultural institute devoted to spreading his nation's language and culture, explained:

In Eastern Europe, the popular culture from the Russians didn't exist—by the time we got there, English was already the language of young people. The origins of high-tech and worldly spread of technologies lies in the United States. Of course, there will be attempts by everyone to promote their local language but the language of science, technology is English. Even the Pasteur Institute in France publishes in English. Nothing can reverse this trend.[67]

THE CALVINISTIC DIASPORA

The worldwide hegemony established by the British tribe sprang from ideological and religious tendencies existent even before Britain's emergence as an unrivaled world empire. Although Britain, like France or Spain, had its swashbucklers and chivalric dreamers, the wellspring of its unique expansion came not from the aristocracy but from more practical, less well-born men of the middle or even working classes.[68] Many came from dissenting Protestant faiths—like the Presbyterians, Methodists and Quakers—whose counterparts had been subject to severe persecution on the Continent.

This Protestant business class possessed attitudes ideal for commercial endeavors. As the British author R. H. Tawney observed, they rejected the very idea, implicit in Catholicism and even within the Anglican Church, of society as "an organism with different grades," a series of hierarchies held together by rules and obligations imposed by a central Church. In the traditional system, economic expediency and individual improvement were held subordinate to the moral authority of the Church.[69]

Protestants—whether strict Calvinists or members of other dissenting groups such as Methodists or Quakers—largely rejected this feudal inheritance, throwing in their lot with the emerging capitalist order. To Calvin, the profits of the artisan, merchant or speculator were no less worthy than the rents harvested by the old land-owning aristocracy. "What reason is there," he asked, "why the income from business should not be larger than that from landowning? Whence do the merchant's profits come, except from his own diligence and industry?"[70]

The Roman Church, dominated by its own ecclesiastic hierarchy and tied to the old aristocratic order, was slow to accept such an approach.[71] But in the Protestant congregation, the financier was no longer a pariah but was regarded as an essential part of society[72]; successful enterprise was regarded as an expression of godliness. As Tawney noted:

> Baptized in the icy waters of Calvinist theology, the business of life, once regarded as perilous to the soul, acquired a new sanctity. Labour is not merely an economic means; it is a spiritual end.[73]

Like the Jews, in whose ancient origins they found so much of their inspiration, the Calvinists were supremely prepared for their commercial roles. As dissenters they had been largely excluded from the mainstream of a still mainly rural British aristocracy, and so heavily favored careers in commerce and industry. Stern and judgmental, rejecting the magical, they were also utter pragmatists. Questioning the notion of the innate goodness of men and the sanctity of the existing social order, they embraced instead a gospel of discipline and constant self-improvement.

With the revolution under Oliver Cromwell largely financed and led by the Nonconformists, the once overweening power of the competing feudalistic order collapsed. Even after Cromwell's regime itself fell, the ensuing set of compromises that came to be known as the Glorious Revolution helped shape a new kind of political order, one that gave unprecedented rein to the powers of individuals and private capital. From this soil soon sprang the economic gospel of the individual capitalist, the laissez-faire political economy of Adam Smith.[74]

In Britain, and later America, the individualist businessman, backed up by the force of law, became the prime source for explosive economic growth. As Alexis de Tocqueville observed in the mid-nineteenth century:

> Looking at the turn given to the human spirit in England by political life, seeing the Englishman, certain of the support of his laws, relying on himself and unaware of any obstacle except the

limits of his powers, acting without constraint . . . I am in no hurry to inquire whether nature has scooped out ports for him, and given him coal and iron. The reason for his commercial prosperity is not there at all: it is in himself.[75]

The massive immigration of such people to new and relatively underdeveloped lands unleashed enormous energies. Eager for profit, willing to adjust to new conditions, Puritans and other members of what Weber later called "the Calvinistic diaspora"[76] had a commercial impact greater than their numbers. As early as the seventeenth century, networks of Puritan business owners, bound by extended kinship and friendship, had developed extensive connections throughout New England and into the port cities of the other colonies.[77]

But the New World witnessed more than the simple re-creation of nonconforming England. In many ways, away from the old bastions of aristocracy and the established Church, the Puritans could express their ideology even more fully. In economic thought, they achieved their apotheosis in the writings of Benjamin Franklin, who epitomized the capitalist ethos of thrift and careful accumulation.

Remember, that *time* is money. He that can earn ten shillings a day by his labour, and goes abroad, or sits idle, one half of that day, though he spends but sixpence during his diversion or idleness, ought not to reckon *that* the only expense; he has rather spent, or rather thrown away, five shillings besides.[78]

As the nineteenth century unfolded, the transfer of these attitudes—and their further development under new conditions—accelerated and the British imprint on the New World deepened. Between 1846 and 1932, British immigration was four times that from Spain,[79] while Britain's main rival, France, despite its huge empire, sent only a handful abroad, less than two or three for every hundred Britishers,[80] and by the 1880s actually became more a country of immigration than a supplier of emigrants.[81]

And when other Europeans—notably Germans and Italians—

started to emigrate in large numbers to the new lands of settlement, nearly four in five found themselves forced to adjust to a country either under direct British control or, like the United States, an English-speaking former colony.[82] Only the great British tribe combined mass immigration with essential political and cultural dominance in the lands of settlement. This distinctive pattern, perhaps more than any other factor, lent to British imperialism a global force never exceeded again by any other ethnic group.

Equally important, British immigration brought with it a transfer of skills from the most advanced industrial nation on earth to countries of seemingly inexhaustible natural resources. Shifting European control to underdeveloped regions, such as those in South America, notes historian Claudio Veliz, was not enough; without the *attitudes* of the industrial revolution, white men in other peoples' lands—most notably in Peru, Mexico and even Argentina—did not guarantee a rush toward progress and development.[83]

Like today's Indian technician or Israeli filmmaker, the British immigrant of the nineteenth century was, more often than not, an economic migrant, seeking to use his skills in a more opportune environment. In the years following American independence, these immigrants increasingly came from the industrialized parts of Britain, and many brought with them considerable skills.[84] By the late eighteenth century as many as half were skilled artisans, mechanics and craftsmen.[85] A century later, nearly half the British workers in the textile industries had been in similar jobs back home.[86]

The old schoolbook picture of British immigrants showed them as sturdy yeoman farmers seeking freedom, but for many British immigrants by the latter part of the nineteenth century the passage across the Atlantic instead largely constituted a move from one part of the developing transnational industrial economy to another. With the rigors of travel eased by the shift from sail to steam-powered ships, as many as two out of every five British immigrants ultimately returned home, evidence of their largely mercantile orientation.[87] "When they spoke of liberty in the United States," notes historian Charlotte Erickson from the study of their diaries, "they usually referred to its low taxes and want of tithes."[88]

THE ATLANTIC ECONOMY

Yet, whether as sojourners or full-fledged immigrants, the British left in their wake the imprint of the particular form of industrial capitalism nurtured on the home islands. As the Rothschilds and other European Jews brought their trading skills from the Continent to London, the British immigrants of the early nineteenth century carried with them technical skills and entrepreneurial attitudes necessary for rapid industrialization, providing the sinews for the development of what historian Brinley Thomas has called the Atlantic Economy. Throughout the nineteenth century, the two giants of the English-speaking world dominated the industrial revolution, accounting for roughly half the world's major inventions, discoveries and innovations.[89]

Samuel Slater, a pioneer of New England's textile industry, for instance, was a native of Belper, England, and learned the trade from Jedidiah Strutt, one of Britain's most progressive industrialists. Strutt's factories were classic studies of early British industrial efficiency, with the hours of their operatives adjusted to the factory schedule, in turn determined by the speed and regularity of machinery. Self-control, Bible study, punctuality, discipline and the other Protestant virtues were drummed into the workers on Sundays, with attendance mandatory.[90]

By the time Slater emigrated to the United States in 1789, he had learned "the mystery" of the textile business: blending grades of cotton, repairing machinery, training disciplined hands and maintaining factory routines. Even more valuable was his knowledge of the mechanical spinning machinery itself, for both export of the machinery and emigration by knowledgeable mechanics were punishable by fine and imprisonment in England.

Slater used his skill as a commodity to gain a part ownership of the first mill in Pawtucket,[91] whose initial success spawned a "cotton mill fever" all over the northeastern United States in the early years of the nineteenth century.[92] His extensive Quaker family links gave him access to a continuing source of capital and a network of skilled machine makers and mill managers.[93] By the time of his death in 1835, Slater controlled or held interest in at least ten separate mills, employing over 1,000 people throughout New England.[94]

Like their British cousins, the American industrialists were committed to continuous improvements and refinements. Under supervision from immigrant craftsmen, they soon were making their own machines, by the 1830s achieving rough technological parity with the mother country. Relatively high labor prices and a burgeoning domestic market stimulated the development of new, more-mass-production-oriented techniques. Increasingly, the new models of factory organization were also American. By the 1840s British visitors, such as Charles Dickens, were visiting the plants established by Boston merchant Francis Cabot Lowell, now at the cutting edge of both technology and modern corporate organization.[95]

In addition to immigrants and technology, Britain also supplied America with vital supplies of capital, the last critical ingredient in developing Thomas's Atlantic Economy.[96] From 1870 to 1914 London provided between 55 and 60 percent of all the foreign investment in the rapidly developing nation, accounting for roughly 5 to 7 percent of the *total* American capital formation,[97] a larger percentage than the total for all foreigners put together in 1990.[98]

These relations increasingly tied all the settlements of the British diaspora closer together. By the eve of the First World War, the English-speaking countries accounted for three fifths of Britain's huge long-term international investment,[99] with the United States the largest single recipient. In contrast, France's colonial empire attracted less than one fifth of its external investment, the largest portion of which was expended and, ultimately, lost in Russia.[100]

Over time, these capital relations became increasingly two-way, with American bankers winding their way to London. In

1854 Junius Morgan arrived from Boston,[101] which led to possibly the most important of the cross-Atlantic linkages between Anglo-Saxon financial interests. Perhaps more than any single force, it was the Morgans who melded the worlds of New York and London ever closer together, placing British investors in the lead for financing American railroads, while the Jewish houses kept closer ties to continental European sources.[102] Through these and other connections, notes historian Mira Wilkins, the British investors gained access to "information channels" that improved their returns compared to those of less well-connected Europeans, such as the French.[103]

By the turn of the century, the nature of the relationship between New York and London began to change dramatically. Bolstered by the country's enormous economy, American equity markets now surpassed those of the City, and U.S. banking resources were twice as large.[104] The child was clearly outgrowing the parent, although Britain still lent out roughly six times as much money overseas as late as 1914, largely neglecting a home economy that no longer seemed to promise commensurate returns.[105]

Like their British cousins, American investors in the early twentieth century looked naturally toward other English-speaking countries. By 1914, the United States was already the fourth largest investor in the world,[106] and rapidly expanding its dominion both in the British possessions, most notably in Canada, and in Great Britain itself.

But it was in the realm of industrial power that America surged most impressively. In 1870, Great Britain accounted for roughly one third of world industrial output, but by 1914 it was the Americans who dominated to an equivalent extent.[107] Roughly equal to the British in 1880, American steel production was nearly five times larger by 1913.[108]

The trade linkages in particular underscored the new relationship between the English-speaking countries. By the early twentieth century the Americans, who had long furnished raw materials and food to Britain in exchange for manufactured items, had turned the mother country into their largest single customer for the latest industrial products of its burgeoning factories.[109] Overall, the United States sold the British empire three dollars' worth of goods for every one it took in.[110] Even culture and fashion, long the domain of the London metropolis, seemed to be falling to "the American invaders." As turn-of-the-century British writer Fred McKenzie lamented:

> Our very jokes are machine-made in the offices of New York publishers, for almost every English "comic" paper of the cheaper sort gets its humor, so-called, week by week from journals on the other side. Our babies are fed on American foods, and our dead buried in American coffins . . . In fact the time seems coming when we shall find our chief export across the Atlantic will be scions of our nobility, whom America can not produce on account of the limits imposed by her constitution.[111]

America's enormous power troubled many in Britain, yet the fundamental similarities in culture and ways of thinking tied the two societies ever closer together. British immigrants in America, for instance, intermarried with native-born Americans at a far higher rate than any other group of newcomers. Unlike the Poles, Germans, Jews or even the Irish, English and Scottish immigrants founded virtually no "districts" of concentrated settlement in the great cities of Canada or the United States.[112] As British philosopher J. S. Mill noted in 1840: "The American people as a whole in their good qualities and in their bad resemble anything so much as an exaggeration of our own middle class."[113]

Even in the last few decades, there remains a remarkable affinity among these English-speaking nations. Until the immigration reforms of the mid-1960s, Canada and the United Kingdom represented the two largest sources of new immigrants to the United States following the Second World War. In the ensuing decades these two countries still sent an estimated one million immigrants,[114] including a large proportion of scientists, engineers,[115] artists, corporate executives and other professionals.[116]

At the same time Britain also sent out another wave of technical, professional and managerial talent—totaling as many as

200,000 during the 1950s and early 1960s—to Canada.[117] Even into the late 1980s, British and Irish immigrants together, as in the nineteenth century, constituted by far the largest group of Western Europeans immigrating not only to the United States but also to Canada,[118] Australia and New Zealand.[119]

But beyond simple migration patterns, the nations of the British diaspora—despite the United Kingdom's entry into the European Economic Community—also retain exceedingly close economic links. The French empire might today be little more than a memory, but even into the early 1990s, Britain and America constituted the leading mutual overseas telephone connection[120] and tourist destinations.[121] Despite its relatively small economy, Britain remains America's largest European market, while the United States accounts for the second largest single market for Britain's exports.[122]

Similarly, Canada, by far the leading trading partner of the United States, accounts for over one fifth of America's trading volume,[123] while the combined nations of British descent remain the destination of nearly one third of American exports.[124] At the same time, the United States provides the largest non-Asian market for both Australia and New Zealand, as well as accounting for two thirds of all exports from Canada.[125]

Investment flows also illustrate the persistence of these diaspora ties. As the 1990s opened, Britain accounted for two fifths of all American investment in the European community.[126] In 1988 Britain attracted over thirty-eight U.S. manufacturing projects, the most in Europe and more than twice the number for West Germany or France.[127] American firms also accounted for four fifths of the manufacturing revenues in Scotland's high-tech "Silicon Glen."[128]

Despite enthusiasm for the prospects of business in Europe, British financial interests likewise remain firmly entrenched in their former imperial possessions. Throughout the 1980s, British firms solidified their position as the preeminent investors in North America, with an overall value of direct investment two thirds larger than Japan's[129] and 50 percent greater than Britain's entire investment in the European community.[130] American holdings also accounted for roughly 30 percent of all the

1992 earnings of companies listed on the London stock exchange.[131]

SETTING THE STANDARDS

But the British tribe's greatest legacy extends far beyond its physical assets and investments. In their conquest of the world in the nineteenth and early twentieth centuries, the Anglo-Americans established the essential standards by which the world economy now functions. Even as the Atlantic Economy fades in importance, the technologies, ideas and methods by which it was developed will likely shape the world that is to come.

Unlike other empires, whose legacies follow racial bloodlines, bureaucratic systems or great religious concepts, the practical and commercial character of the British diaspora brought in its wake something more subtle, yet arguably more essential to the operations of modern society. In a host of critical fields—from accounting and advertising to culture, science and, finally, the operations of government—the Anglo-Saxons created standards not just for their own race, or for their colonies, but also for the entire modern world. Even the very word *international* sprang from the writings of British eighteenth-century philosopher Jeremy Bentham.[132]

The unsurpassed industrial power of Britain and the vastness of the empire made London—as early as 1700 the largest city in the world[133]—the natural center for the development of a global finance and commercial empire far larger, and arguably more powerful, than the one run from Whitehall. As Nathan Rothschild observed in 1832:

> The whole world . . . all transactions in India, in China, in Germany, in Russia, and in the whole world, are all guided here and settled through this country.[134]

Until the last quarter of the nineteenth century, Britain's industrial machine dominated on a global basis, accounting for one third of all the world's commerce.[135] Control over access to new technology—most particularly steamships, trains and telegraphs—gave the British almost insurmountable advantages over competitors, most notably in Asia. And therefore the British, and later the Americans, forged the rules by which men traveled, communicated, financed and managed their enterprises across the globe.[136]

When Britain did not itself manufacture or export, it frequently served as intermediary, insurer and financier. By the eve of the First World War, Britain held two fifths of the world's international debt,[137] owned roughly half the world's cargo tonnage[138] and controlled more than 60 percent of all the trade passing through the Suez Canal.[139] As British economist Lilian Knowles noted in 1921: ". . . the United Kingdom was organized for world trade when other countries were only developing national unity."[140]

As the unchallenged financial hegemons, the British naturally set the standards of the world monetary regime, with a solid sterling, backed by the Bank of England. The "Old Lady of Threadneedle Street" not only set the rules for London but for much of the world.[141] After the First World War, this role was shared in tandem with the Federal Reserve system, particularly its New York–based bank.[142] At the end of the Second World War, the Americans asserted the decisive world leadership[143] until the emergence of the more collaborative "G-7" mechanism in the 1980s.

Other advanced nations that experienced rapid industrial and technological development, notably Japan and Germany, did not face the necessity of constructing global standards and systems. Like the Japanese later, the Germans of the late nineteenth century, as Thorstein Veblen later noted, were able to "take up the technological heritage of the English without having paid for it in the habits of thought, the use and wont, induced in the English community by the experience of achieving it."[144]

Britain's commercial leadership, and its role as pioneer of industrial modernity, naturally led other countries, not only colonies or former colonies, to mimic British ways of thinking. In the late nineteenth century popular author and lecturer Samuel

Smiles—like other formulators of the new ethic—constantly received letters and requests for advice from various nations around the world. On the walls of the khedive's palace in Cairo, written in Arabic, were inscriptions not from the Koran but from Smiles's seminal work, *Self-help.*[145]

Perhaps nowhere is the legacy of this experience more compelling than in such business fields as accounting. It was in Britain, and later America, where virtually all the rules and regulations of modern accounting were first formulated and developed. Among the sixteen original founders of the world's leading accounting houses, ten were either English or Scottish.[146]

The British, of course, did not invent the practice of accounting. Other commercial diaspora, such as the Phoenicians and Italians, all had learned the fundamentals of arithmetic and basic double-entry bookkeeping[147] to keep track of their far-flung activities. Similarly, Japan[148] and China also boasted a strong tradition of accounting. The name of Mount Hui-chin, in the present-day Shao-hsing district of China, for instance, means "the mountain of accounting," and the mountain is indeed where the founder of the first Chinese dynasty collected, and counted, his tributes.[149]

Yet in none of these settings were conditions ripe for the development of modern accounting principles. For one thing, enterprises in classical China, Tokugawa Japan or Renaissance Italy tended to be family-owned affairs, with no need or compulsion to provide extensive bookkeeping for outside investors. At the same time, none of these cultures imbued profit and loss with the sort of quasi-religious importance characteristic of nineteenth-century Britain. Indeed, Italian Catholic, Tokugawa, and Confucian value systems remained ambivalent at best toward profit, much less its effective measurement. As one Confucian aphorism puts it: "The mind of the superior man is conversant with righteousness; the mind of mean man is conversant with gain."[150]

To founders of today's modern accounting firms, such as Edwin Waterhouse, profit and morality were not diametrically opposed principles. Like many of the early British entrepreneurs,

Waterhouse had his roots in the Nonconformist tradition, being himself the grandson of a Quaker cotton merchant from Manchester[151] who eschewed music, light literature, anything that smacked of frivolity, much less scandal. "His bringing up had not endowed him with much softness of character," Edwin would write later, "and the narrowness of Friends' views did not bring him into sympathy with others."[152]

Edwin's own father, Alfred, although no longer in the Society of Friends, remaining true to the stony essence of nonconformity, was harsh, judgmental, relentlessly hardworking and honest. In the Waterhouse home, music and light literature were actively discouraged.[153] In 1861, after his education at University College in London, the young Edwin took a job, arranged through his father, in an accountant's firm not far from Price Waterhouse's current London headquarters overlooking the Thames. Four years later, at age twenty-four, he joined as partners with William H. Hollyland and Samuel L. Price, who had first established his own firm in 1849.[154]

Bright and ambitious, Waterhouse would dominate the new partnership. Relentlessly driven, he sought out new ways to improve the efficiency and accuracy of the accounts he audited. His meticulous nature, and his sense of organization, impressed many clients from all over England.[155] Although he eventually joined the Church of England, his Quaker sense of mores, including an almost single-minded dedication to work and detestation of even minor vices such as smoking, remained central to his character.[156]

But it was not only the virtues of Protestant Britain that explained the emergence of both his new partnership and the other, largely British-based, giants of accounting. The rapid growth of the British economy itself had forced changes in the very technology of financial record keeping. Money seemed to be generated at rates unimagined even in the recent past. "Anybody who devotes himself to making money, body and soul, can scarcely fail to make himself rich," proclaimed Samuel Smiles. "Very little brains will do."[157]

Such massive and explosive growth had no true precedent in the history of capitalism and produced the usual complications.

Speculation in railway stocks, for example, seemed to promise almost instantaneous riches and thus quickly fell subject to massive frauds. Demand for careful scrutiny of such businesses played a critical role in the early growth of British accounting firms, including Price Waterhouse, Deloitte, and the predecessor firm of Peat, Marwick.[158]

The demand for accurate accounting also increasingly gained the power of law. Starting with the 1844 Joint Companies Act, a new series of laws established basic regulations for modern corporations, mandating, among other things, impartial accounting of corporate performance. With its principle of limited liability and public accountability, the new form of corporate organization became favored by investors, with the number of firms growing from 1,000 in 1858 to over 18,000 in 1894.[159] The need for accurate accounting transformed a more or less unregulated trade into a profession, with ever more carefully crafted standards for entrance.[160]

By the end of the nineteenth century, Britain had established itself as the undisputed world leader in accountancy, and firms soon started moving into other regions of the diaspora. As early as 1874, Price Waterhouse was established in Sydney, followed by New York in 1890 and Toronto seventeen years later. Within a few decades British accountants were plying their trade in locales as diverse as India, Australia, South Africa, Brazil, Argentina, Japan and New Zealand.[161] In 1895 another of these Scotsmen, James Marwick, opened up his offices in New York.[162]

As other countries began to industrialize, they too adopted the standards set by the Anglo-Americans. With the modernizing drive of the Meiji emperor came almost immediately a demand for the latest in accounting texts, with British and American accountants playing a central role in teaching the new skills to their eager Japanese pupils. The first commercial school for this purpose was set up in Tokyo in 1875—an institution that later became Hitotsubashi University. By the end of the nineteenth century works on accounting had been published by no less than ninety Japanese authors.[163]

The Chinese, who had invented accountancy before Britain

acquired a written language, similarly turned to the Anglo-Americans for modern accounting after their revolution in 1911.[164] Indeed, throughout the world today, the Anglo-American standard of accounting is largely the only recognized form for the assessment and auditing of corporations. Firms such as Price Waterhouse and Ernst and Young have expanded well beyond their racial roots, extending themselves well beyond their traditional bastions in New York and London to Asia, continental Europe and throughout the developing world.[165]

As a collection of national partnerships connected only loosely to the Anglo-Saxon core, firms such as Price Waterhouse have shifted from being expressions of tribal expansion to instruments of global business society. Even as occasional scandals such as BCCI and questions of insufficient regulation are raised inside Britain or America,[166] there remains no possible challenger to the reigning giants of the field. Hans Steskal, a German refugee from Czechoslovakia who joined Price Waterhouse in the 1960s, served in São Paulo for three years, working for such German clients as Mannesman, Henkel and Volkswagen. Today the senior partner in the firm's Munich office, Steskal remarks:

> Twenty years ago it seemed that the world had to adjust to the Anglo-Saxon norms, to be part of the world. Now those norms are like *esperanto*, everyone buys it. I am no longer part of an Anglo-Saxon institution, but part of international society, which is what Price Waterhouse really is.[167]

Even today, when mastery in many of the industrial arts has passed to Asia, British- and American-descended firms continue to establish the basic standards in *how* business is conducted and managed worldwide. To an ambitious Indian such as Pravin Ghatalia, his partnership in Price Waterhouse reflects his own separation from the less admirable traits of Indian society, where family ties and political connections often overrule business logic.

But within a worldwide network consisting of 43,000 employees working out of 107 countries,[168] Ghatalia and other Indian partners at Price Waterhouse see themselves as able to offer their clients, many of them multinational corporations, the assurance that, in accounting at least, their business in India will follow the standards expected in London or New York. Amidst the corruption, confusion and poverty around him, Ghatalia takes pride in Price as an island of stability where the ideals of meritocracy, accuracy and diligence take priority. Taking a break from his Bombay practice, which now employs over 100 persons, he reflected:

> I am more committed to Price Waterhouse than to my wife and family. It's in my blood. I think it's a great organization. Here if I am good, I rise. If I'm poor, I fail. I don't need a godfather. And if my son joins, he gets to be partner only if he performs to standards. That's not the way things usually work in India.[169]

Indeed, since the industrial revolution began to spread outside the confines of Europe, such essentially Anglo-Saxon standards have extended beyond accounting to most of the key criteria for economic development. Vitually every developing nation of the late nineteenth and early twentieth centuries looked primarily to Britain and the United States for models of industrial organization. If Germany produced more brilliant science, France greater art, Italy finer music, the British and Americans excelled in the management of the routine of everyday business.

This pattern became even more marked following the Anglo-American triumph in the Second World War. In postwar Japan, for example, American business theorists such as Peter Drucker, James Burnham and W. Edwards Deming shaped the consciousness of the rising new business class. Many of the essential ingredients of Japan's modern success—quality control, automation, strategic planning—came first from American sources.[170]

Much the same process took place in Europe after the Second World War. First under the occupation authorities, and then with the great wave of American private investment, new technologies and management styles were introduced into the continental system. As markets grew, technology spread, and old class lines began to blur, what business historian Alfred Chandler called "all the paraphernalia of modern management"—associations, journals, training schools, consultants—suddenly surfaced prominently on the Continent.[171]

More recently, as the clear industrial supremacy of the British tribe has faded, this leadership in the setting of basic business standards has remained largely intact. In 1990, in fact, British diaspora countries alone billed roughly one third of the total worldwide export of business services, covering such activities as accounting, travel, communications, public relations and advertising.[172]

At the same time, American-based firms—McKinsey, Anderson Consulting, Bain, Booz Allen—dominate the lucrative world of consulting, even in such difficult markets as Japan.[173] Similarly, of the world's ten leading advertising agencies in 1990 seven were either American or British.[174] In addition, the two leading Japanese agencies on the list depended almost totally on domestic billings, compared to the one third or more of revenues represented by international business among their leading Anglo-Saxon competitors.[175]

In the process, New York and, most particularly, London have managed to retain their status as the global centers for business and financial services. Nearly every leading global accounting, law, banking, consulting and advertising operation has its world headquarters, or a significant regional office, in one of these two cities.

London's continued importance is particularly revealing given the relatively marginal status of Britain as a world economic power. The City's roughly 900,000 accountants, lawyers, financiers and other business service workers make their living predominately selling their expertise to the world.[176] Despite having an equity market far smaller than New York's or Tokyo's, London's turnover of foreign stocks today exceeds *all* its global competitors combined[177] and also leads all other centers in foreign exchange turnover and share of international banking assets.[178]

To a remarkable extent, this confluence of power is a direct result of the spread and cohesiveness of the British diaspora. At its nadir in the 1950s, London recovered its position as a world financial center largely through the movement of American moneymen who offset the limited resources of Britain with fortunes made elsewhere but invested in and through the City.[179] Even in 1991 one out of every three of the estimated 50,000 work permits issued in Britain were to Americans and their dependents, a large portion centered in the network of Anglo-American interests in the City of London.[180]

Similarly, those regions within the historic "sphere of influence" of Britain, such as countries in the Middle East, also established their key financial links in London, with over eighty-five Arab banks registered in Britain today.[181] Tied by language, race and commerce to London, institutions such as the Commonwealth Bank of Australia, the Imperial Bank of India, the National Bank of South Africa, Bank of South Africa, the Hong Kong and Shanghai Bank, as well as scores of others, use London as their primary source of funding and the locus for their international activities.

Even those who never experienced direct British rule find in London, and to some extent New York, the ideal place to conduct business and devise global marketing, financial and public relations stratagems. By 1989, British institutions accounted for less than one fifth of all international lending out of London, less than half the share of the Japanese, whose four large securities firms dominate the City's Eurobond market.[182] As a result, rather than being merely Europe's financial center, London remains first and foremost the financial capital of the global tribes. Taken together, Japanese, Chinese, other English-speaking countries, and the former dependencies in the Middle East represent an absolute majority of the City's international business.[183]

Over tea and cookies in his crowded office, a top Bank of England official credits London's continuing appeal to the accumulation of unsurpassed experience working with an ever-changing cast of global businessmen. Even as they are criticized for their reluctance to embrace the grand designs for a politically united Europe, the official points out that for the Japanese financier, Indian parvenu, Arab sheik, Jewish refugee[184] or American company man, all roads still lead to London, the standard setter of modern capitalism. Dropping two sugars into his whitened tea, he noted:

> The rest of the country has lagged behind, but we have a willingness, a desire to operate on a global basis. Narrow national concern, European concerns are not nearly so important. We are interdependent with the rest of the world; they are our customers. Of course, we have to operate on a European level, but what makes London special is the overseas linkages. It is our heart and soul.[185]

CHAPTER FOUR

THE NEW CALVINISTS

NORTHEASTERN OHIO is classic America, a land of rolling green hills, well-tended Amish farms and old red-brick industrial towns whose best times seem largely past. Yet where many have seen only the fading of a great industrial tradition, Vinny Gupta looked out upon a vista of opportunity and renewal.

"The fundamental thing is that by and large people in America have forgotten what the next world can be. They think luxury is a birthright," the Indian-born entrepreneur said in his spartan office in the old Ohio industrial town of Canton. "The only way it's going to go ahead is changing the way business is done. You have to bring back the ethics that there used to be."

For Vinny Gupta, these "ethics" are not the stuff of parental scolding but the foundation of business principles that have helped him turn around three failing Midwestern foundries. In the past, one might think of the values proposed by Gupta as typical of Max Weber's "Calvinistic diaspora"—epitomized by thrift, the willingness to defer gratification and single-minded devotion to building an enterprise. Today, however, one is more likely to hear such archetypical attitudes from resourceful Hindus, or refugees from Southeast Asia, than from "natives" who inherited their wealth.

Vinny Gupta first arrived at Michigan Tech during the early 1970s, intent on learning the latest about industrial technologies. After graduation, he planned to return to India, hoping to lend his newfound expertise to his family's small steel business. But Nita, his wife, who had waited patiently in Bombay for him to return, also wanted to experience life in America.

At first, the reality probably didn't seem so promising. Arriving back in 1975, Gupta's promised fellowship at Case Western Reserve in Cleveland was delayed, leaving him with no means of support. The young couple survived largely on handouts from Indian friends; schoolmates loaned them cars and even arranged for credit cards. Nita added to the family's finances by cleaning houses in upscale Shaker Heights, something she kept secret from her husband for over six months. Since she wouldn't spend money on boots, she often trudged through the Midwestern snow in slippers.

These experiences, and the hostility, even outright racism, Gupta encountered in the corporate world strengthened his resolve. In one case, when he was working for Gould Corporation, helping to turn around several of its troubled foundries, he was suddenly ordered to help smooth a sale to a subsidiary of the McGraw Edison company. Years later, Gupta recalls:

> They came in with a show to tell us how good they were, how big they were. So I asked them, "You say how good you are. So I want to know are you making money?"
>
> They hated me for that. The president of the division later came up to me and said, "How are you doing, elephant boy?" Now, no one calls me elephant boy, not even my father.[1]

Yet behind the racist bravado, Gupta noted as well an erosion of the old industrial values the British and Americans had once so confidently employed to dominate the world. As a metallurgist at plants in Wisconsin and Saint Louis, he saw an industry dominated by conglomerates who, to a large extent, were either feverishly getting out of the business or milking their foundries dry. Whether at Gould or later, at Condec, another conglomerate, Gupta saw "the hotshots in their corporate jets" as fundamentally disinterested in the basic operation of their businesses.

Condec, based in Connecticut, controlled the Orrville, Ohio, foundry where he worked as general manager. The old plant was just one of several businesses that included more highly prized operations in robotics, power-control devices and military electronics. "The managers in Connecticut didn't know anything about the business," Gupta, a short forty-year-old with thinning black-gray hair, recalls. "You'd go to these meetings in Connecticut and you'd go into the dining room—everyone had one of those beepers—and I'd get to spend ten minutes talking business and they'd spend two and half hours eating lunch. They were talking about scuba diving and what they'd do on their vacations."

By the early 1980s, Condec was under financial attack by Bill Farley's Northwest Industries and was scrambling for cash. Orrville, which was losing a quarter of a million dollars annually, seemed ripe for closing. Gupta saw an opportunity to make his mark and employ his approach on a mill no one wanted. Using his own savings, a long-term note from Condec and cash from Cincinnati investor Jerry Pollack and some Indian businessmen, he took a majority interest in the plant.

Finally in control, Gupta proceeded to do all the things that previously he could not push through Condec management. He cleaned up the plant, often taking up the broom himself. Rather than "milk" the operation, he invested when necessary in new machinery and, wherever possible, found economical ways to purchase raw materials and processing equipment.

From the time he bought the facility in 1984 until 1991, sales at Gupta's new company, renamed Technocast, soared from under $2 million to near $10 million. Productivity among the plant's 125 employees improved fourfold and quality improved to the point where the company has gained a lengthy list of new, top-drawer customers for its castings.

Subsequently, Gupta bought two other plants, one in Michigan and another in Ohio, where he is attempting to duplicate his previous success. "The way I see it, foundries are dirty work," remarked the casually dressed Gupta, walking through his recently purchased century-old Ohio foundry. "The rationale I see is that having an education in a dirty business is a unique skill. A lot of educated people don't want to work in a dirty business."

RETURN OF THE NATIVES

The movement of newcomers such as Vinny Gupta to the United States reflects the growing influence of commercially and technically gifted people from Asia on the Anglo-American metropolis. Not since the mass movement of Europeans into North America, South Africa and Oceania—what historian Brinley Thomas has called "the great re-shuffle"[2]—has there been such a movement of global tribes from one region of the world to another.

Like the British and the Jews in their time, these new immigrants bring along with them a common ethos of discipline, work ethic and frugality—a sort of Asiatic form of Calvinism. Among Indians, the roots lie within a strong family system and a predisposition to maintain traditional values and linkages.[3] Among East Asians—the Japanese, Chinese, Koreans—Confucianist value systems provide some of the basic attitudinal elements that so characterized the Calvinists of the early Anglo-American industrial revolution. "There is a value congruence," notes Korean sociologist Illsoo Kim, "between Confucianism and the Protestant ethic in the sense that both are directed toward self-control and self-abnegation."[4]

Like the Jews, Scots and dissenters, as sociologist Thomas Sowell has pointed out, such migrating Asians have been forced by their "precarious" existence as outsiders and immigrants to practice thrift.[5] In the classic Calvinist mold of Benjamin Franklin, they often willingly eschew immediate pleasure in order to own property or found a business, often raising their capital among kinsmen and connections from home. As one Pakistani real estate agent in northern England explained: "Why pay rent for property that can never be yours? Better to save money and buy a house, so you can also live in it and also make more money."[6]

Many of these Asians have used their entrepreneurial and professional skills to rise up through the supposedly impassable barriers of the British class system. Indian and Pakistani males in Britain have a 60 percent higher rate of self-employment than their white counterparts and a 300 percent higher rate than other nonwhite immigrants. They also account for a disproportionate share of managers and professionals among the British working population.[7] David Cooksey, a close adviser to the Conservative party and chairman of Advent International, Britain's leading venture capital firm, notes:

> The British have reached the point where they want social status first but if you look at the immigrants, they've had to fight for their place. The need to succeed was burned out of the Brits. The immigrants still keep the fires burning.[8]

To a remarkable extent, these efforts have had the desired results. During the 1970s Indians and Pakistanis raised their class status three times more often than either whites or other immigrants.[9] Their commitment to enterprise often would not compare unfavorably with that of the English Rothschilds, or a Victorian businessman attending a Samuel Smiles lecture in mid-nineteenth-century Leeds. "You have to understand," says Sudhir Mulji, of the Great Eastern Shipping Company, "how much Indian businessmen love business. It isn't just their work, it's a way of life, it's their passion."[10]

As happened with the Jews in Europe and America, difficulties associated with being an immigrant—and an ethnic outsider—help shape such entrepreneurial attitudes. Almost by definition, the immigrant faces an uncertain and unfamiliar world, often playing by unfamiliar codes of behavior and organization. And within most societies in the West, their welcome has often been less than enthusiastic. In the 1970s and 1980s

British hostility to new Asian immigrants intensified,[11] and nonwhite immigrants turned, as two British experts put it, from "the object of public acclaim" to "public enemies."[12] A 1990 survey found Asians fifty times more likely to be victims of violent attacks than whites.[13]

A similar process has taken place in the nations of the British diaspora. By the late 1980s, Australian liberal leader John Howard made public his concern over a possible loss of "social cohesion" from an influx of too many Asians.[14] According to a 1991 poll, nearly two out of three Australians favored curtailing or stopping all immigration.[15]

On the West Coast of North America, where the Asian population more than tripled in the two decades between 1970 and 1990, fears of rising immigration incited outright hostility. In Vancouver, where the massive influx of Hong Kong Chinese has led some locals to rename their city Hong-Couver, the newcomers have been blamed for everything from rising real estate values to the denuding of old-growth forests.[16]

The intensity of opposition to immigration is, if anything, even greater farther south, in California, the region most deeply affected by Asian trade, capital and immigration flows. By January of 1989 57 percent of all Southern Californians felt there were "too many" immigrants in the region, where within twenty years the majority of the population will be Asian or Latino. Fears over economic competition, gangs and environmental impacts from immigration have led to mounting tensions between the region's bewildering assortment of ethnic groups.[17]

Such prejudices influence the behavior of even well-educated Asians, who often feel their careers are limited by a "glass ceiling" that restricts their mobility beyond strictly technical jobs. Indeed, according to one 1985 study, Asians accounted for *three times* as many professionals and technicians as managers.[18] Indian-born professionals, according to a study by Alka Saberwal, of the State University of New York at Stony Brook, earn some 17 percent less than their similarly qualified American-born counterparts. British-born professionals, she points out, earn only 4 percent less.[19]

As a result, rather than seek acceptance within the established

order, many such immigrants create a controllable space outside, drawing upon family and culture as resources in the new
environment. In the immigrant generation particularly, many of
these ethnic businesspeople develop what UCLA researcher
Ivan Light has called "entrepreneurial collectivism." Rotating
credit associations among Japanese and Chinese, *kye* among
Koreans and the *susus* of West Indians all help overcome discrimination or lack of familiarity with local conditions.[20] These
ethnic businesses often operate in networks, with shops and
other businesses passing from one member of the group to another, keeping the enterprise, so to speak, "in the family."
Nearly 30 percent of Koreans in Los Angeles in the 1980s, for
instance, found jobs in firms run by other Koreans, although the
group accounted for barely 1 percent of the enterprises in the
region.[21]

THE URBAN PIONEERS

Koreans, much like the Jewish or British skilled tradesmen of
the nineteenth and early twentieth centuries, come well versed
in the ways of sophisticated urban economies. As many as 70
percent of the Korean shopkeepers in Los Angeles are college
graduates,[22] and half come from the capital city, Seoul.[23] Although they are often unable to find professional jobs in the
United States, their transition to urban America does not also
involve—as it does for many other Third World migrants—the
difficult shift from rural life to urban reality. "Korean migration
to the United States," notes Illsoo Kim, "resembles an internal
migration from city to city."[24]

Many of the same characteristics can be found in other Asian
newcomers. Nearly four in five Indian workers immigrating to
the United States between 1965 and 1979 hailed from professional, technical or managerial backgrounds. Less than 10 percent of total Indian immigration in the English-speaking
countries was made up of laborers or service workers.[25]

The nature of this migration stems largely from the massive
and rapid changes enveloping Asia. Many newcomers come

from places—such as Hong Kong, Taiwan, Korea and Singapore —that recently have undergone a rapid shift from labor-and-resource-intensive industries to more human-capital and technology-intensive industries.[26] In all these cultures, education, particularly for technical and commercial purposes, has been widespread and highly encouraged.

Others come from minorities inside Third World countries whose prior success in adjusting to European language, culture, technology and business methods has placed them in conflict with anticapitalist and nativist postcolonial regimes. As a result, groups such as Chinese in Vietnam, Indians in East Africa and Sindhis in Pakistan over the past few decades faced mass confiscations of property, expulsions and even full-fledged pogroms. And even *within* countries such as India, pervasive corruption, socialist policies and, increasingly, special preferences for lower castes have propelled educated commercial elites to seek refuge in the stable capitalist democracies of the European-descended countries. Even for those who felt no such pressure, the move to the old imperial core also offered an opportunity—much like that taken by the European migrants of the nineteenth century—to shift from areas of limited opportunity to those more economically fertile.

In Britain the most dramatic movement involved an estimated half million or more Indians and Pakistanis, who migrated there under their Commonwealth passports between 1945 and the 1970s.[27] For many Indians of his generation, recalls J. S. Gill, now a London-based real estate mogul, Great Britain offered a reality far more pleasant than that of home. Gill's father, a Sikh soldier wounded in the First World War, came back to India with tales of his convalescence in Brighton. "We were astounded," Gill recalled over tea in his basement office in the Bayswater section of London, "that it was so honest. No one stole."[28]

Sikhs had a special status in Britain, having served first as soldiers in their wars and, like other Indians, later proving themselves indispensable in the far-flung administrative apparatus of the empire, most particularly in the police and the army.[29] When the Second World War broke out, Gill was serving as a sergeant and clerk for the royal forces in Hong Kong. Taken prisoner by the Japanese, he survived the war in the camp by learning Japanese and making whiskey in a home-made still, something that helped placate his often irascible captors.

When the war—and soon afterward, the empire—ended, Gill returned to his native Punjab. But the only source of wealth there was land, which was becoming scarcer as overcrowding, compounded by the arrival of refugees from Pakistan, increased. So in 1951 Gill immigrated to England with six pounds in his pocket, joining thousands of other Punjabis who soon accounted for three out of every five Indians there.[30]

Yet even with the presence of friends, a network of Sikh temples and a rudimentary immigrant economy, life was difficult. Anti-Indian discrimination was rife in the factory, in housing, in the pubs, yet still the essential fairness of the British impressed him. "It was difficult for a man in a turban," he recalled. "I had no qualifications. People called you names, but sometimes you'd run into old soldiers who remember the Sikhs as people who didn't fear death. They'd speak to you in Punjabi and buy you drinks."[31]

Finding a job in a glass factory, he took every opportunity to work overtime. On weekends, he sold shirts in the London flea markets. In a little over a year he had saved enough to buy his first London property. Within three years he had quit the glass factory and opened a wholesale shop in the East End, where he still maintains a wholesale knitwear outlet.

But like many Indians, real estate became his main obsession. By 1965 he had accumulated over 85,000 pounds' worth of property, mostly around London. Today Gill, still ramrod straight despite his seventy years, controls property valued at over 10 million pounds, including over 105 London flats and a 600-acre private airport near Houston, Texas. As he walked briskly down blocks of white pastel London row houses, many of which he owns, Gill reflected:

For the Indians who came this was the logical place. It seemed that no matter what happened, there was no security in India.

Here if you worked, you could save and we liked to work, including overtime. If the British didn't want to work, well, we would do it. Here we could take our good qualities and make a good account of it.

The expulsion of 74,000 Indians—most of whom fled to Britain—from Uganda in 1972 by then President-for-life Idi Amin further increased the Indian impact on Britain. But even as the desperate refugees arrived, the doors for any further Asian influx were beginning to close in front of them, as the British imposed ever more severe limitations on new immigration.

Today Britain, with well over 1.5 million Indians and Pakistanis, no longer serves as the principal destination for emigrants from the subcontinent.[32] But by the 1970s, new avenues of immigration had opened in the traditionally far more highly restrictive nations of the British diaspora.[33] Even Australia, once renowned for its "all-white" immigration policies, by the late 1980s received 57 percent of its recent immigrants from Asia.[34] A majority of the "business immigrants"—investors and entrepreneurs admitted to jump-start the nation's languid economy during the 1980s—came from Asia, including many from the countries of the Chinese diaspora.[35]

More significant, however, has been the emergence of Canada as a major center of Asian immigration. By the late 1980s Asians were arriving at nearly twice the numbers of all European emigrants, accounting for nearly two in every five new arrivals.[36] And, according to some studies, nearly 40 percent of the males came with university educations, nearly two times the average for Canadian-born men.[37] Those Asian immigrants who have stayed in Canada for more than twenty years are almost twice as likely to be employers as immigrants from the United Kingdom or native-born Canadians.[38]

But the United States, more than any other country, has emerged as the most important, and favored, nation of immigration. A nation with no real Asian imperial legacy outside of Hawaii and the Philippines, America after the end of the Second World War forged extraordinarily close ties with a host of Asian countries, including Japan, South Korea, the ill-fated Republic of Vietnam, Thailand and, after the loss of power on the mainland, the rump remains of the Nationalist regime on Taiwan.

For many in these countries, particularly the young, the United States emerged as a sort of surrogate mother country, a role model for East Asians living outside the Communist sphere. As these countries first began to acquire consumer products like televisions, the cultural "software" filling their screens came largely from American shows, accounting for as much as 50 percent of all imported programming in the Philippines and 90 percent in Korea.[39]

Equally important, as many of these young Asians grew up, they sought out an opportunity to study in the United States, aided by generous loan programs, both from their home countries and from American sources. The number of Asian students in the United States grew tenfold between 1955 and 1980.[40]

For young Asians such as Bob Chen, whose family fled from China's Hunan province in 1947, the chance to study in America seemed like the fulfillment of a dream. In his early years in an overcrowded, impoverished Taipei, Chen recalled, "things only got better—meaning food got on the table—when American aid came." When the opportunity arose to take a scholarship at the South Dakota School of Mines, Chen accepted immediately, packed his suitcase and scholarship money:

> I had no idea where South Dakota was, but I was going to go. I was very lonely and was mistaken for an American Indian. The Indians didn't understand who I was at all.[41]

Like many students, Chen eventually found his place in the United States, choosing, like roughly 70 percent of his fellow Taiwanese, to stay after completing his studies.[42] Indeed, with South Asians, notably Indians and Pakistanis, also shifting their attention away from the United Kingdom and toward the United States, Asia supplied four of the top five immigration countries,[43] providing over four million immigrants, or two out of every five legal entrants, between 1971 and 1988.[44]

During the decade of the 1980s alone, the Asian population in the U.S. nearly doubled, to over seven million,[45] and by the turn of the century it is expected to surpass eight million. But the quality of this immigration may prove more significant than the numbers, with immigrants two and a half times more likely than natives to possess postgraduate degrees.[46] By the late 1980s Asian-born students accounted for both the vast majority of all foreigners earning doctorates in natural sciences and engineering in the United States[47] and the overwhelming portion of the total net increase in new American science and engineering talent during the 1980s.[48]

Nowhere has the impact of this mass migration of Asian brainpower proved more critical than in California, home to roughly two out of every three Asians in America.[49] At California State University—which educates the vast preponderance of the engineers for the nation's top high-tech state—Asians constitute more than one in every three engineering majors.[50] In addition, among the large number of foreign nationals studying engineering at the University of California graduate school, Asians account for nearly seven out of every ten students.[51] So great is the Asian dominance at UCLA that white students in math and science sometimes refer to their school as "the University of Caucasians Lost Among Asians."

Foreign-born, predominantly Asian technical workers also play a critical role in the management of America's technology companies. In Silicon Valley, Asians constitute as much as one fourth of the total work force and almost one in three engineers.[52] At such elite research institutions as IBM's Yorktown Heights facility, Asians account for one in four researchers; at AT&T's legendary Bell Labs as many as two in five.[53]

Taken together, Asians constitute arguably the most talented, commercially oriented large new group since the massive influx of Jews in the early part of the twentieth century.[54] And perhaps nowhere are the parallels more striking than in New York, a city whose economic history has been shaped by repeated waves of entrepreneurial newcomers. Much as it was in the 1920s, when two thirds of the people in New York were immigrants or the children of immigrants,[55] the city has become one of the leading destinations for Asians coming to the United

States today. During the 1980s, some 280,000 Asians immigrated to New York.[56]

From the Koreans, who have come to dominate much of small-scale retailing, including some fruit and vegetable markets, to the Indians and Chinese, increasingly critical in much of the once Jewish-dominated garment trade, Asians increasingly represent the city's emergent middle class. Indeed even as the city's economy declined in the early 1990s, that of the Asian communities continued to surge forward.

Perhaps most buoyant of all has been the city's burgeoning 300,000-strong Chinese community, which by 1988 in the Chinatown section of lower Manhattan alone accounted for nearly 600 garment factories with payrolls in excess of $200 million.[57] Although concentrated in the low-end "contracting" side of the business, some firms, notably from Hong Kong, are moving into design and final manufacturing. Other Chinese entrepreneurs were buying up factories in the mid-South and other low-cost American regions, using New York as the center for their design, marketing and other high-end operations.[58]

But the Chinese were not restricted to the rag trade. In Manhattan's crowded Chinatown district, over twenty-eight banks have concentrated, up from just six in the 1970s,[59] as well as another thirty-one in Flushing. Many of these banks boast direct ties to the cash-rich overseas diaspora for whom New York ranks second only to California as a favored place for investment.[60] At the same time, these banks tap the savings of immigrant Chinese, whose savings rates at times approach over 60 percent of net income.[61]

As new immigrants pour into the city each year, they carry with them the age-old problems of newcomers—crime, exploitation of labor, gangs, widespread poverty.[62] Yet despite these problems, they also have one of the best performances in education among the city's youth, low unemployment and, through their overseas networks, access to the most rapidly growing capital markets in the world. As New York regional economist George Sternlieb sees it: "There's nothing wrong with New York that a million Chinese wouldn't cure."[63]

PSYCHOLOGICAL DE-INDUSTRIALIZATION

For many immigrants, the return to the Anglo-American metropolis has come as those societies—which from afar once
seemed so invulnerable—have begun to lose some of their historical industrial power and self-confidence. As Tirath Singh
drives his Honda through the rolling Yorkshire countryside, he
sees not only great edifices of the industrial past but reminders
of a dimmer present, young men in rags wandering the half-
deserted streets, the run-down rows of council flats.

Singh came to England at age eleven in 1948 to join his father,
following the path of thousands of other Indians and Pakistanis
who had come to find work in the country's many textile mills.
Parts of a British system that until the last quarter of the nineteenth century accounted for one third of the world's industrial
output,[64] the factories of northern England still bustled with
economic energy. To a young man from the Punjab, it seemed
"almost a miracle" that so much could come forth from so small
a place.

Today the mills of Leeds are largely deserted. Inside his "cash
and carry" discount store, Singh greets his customers, working-
class Britons, most shabbily dressed, rummaging for bargains.
Unlike Singh, who owns two such stores, they found no decent
replacement for their old factory jobs. Yet for all his success—a
large house in a tree-lined suburb, three well-educated children,
a respectable business—Singh is disturbed by what he sees, by
what has become of Leeds, and of Britain:

> When I came here, we were impressed with all the industry, the
> power of the place, the way things worked. Now it's not so
> good. The mills, they were different then, lots of work and a
> chance to make it.
>
> Now I don't understand the English. There aren't any values
> left here.[65]

To Singh, this decline in "values" explains, far better than the
vagaries of economic policy, the decay around him. Yet the origins of this moral devolution lay in a time when Singh's family

was still farming the Punjab, at the far fringes of the world's greatest industrial civilization. Even then, as the new middle class and its Calvinist virtues triumphed over the world's markets, a second generation with inherited wealth was already eschewing what Weber called "the ethically colored maxim" of modern capitalism.[66] Hunts, leisure, and the spirit of noblesse oblige were beginning to overcome the very rough and pragmatic values that had lifted the British above all peoples. As early as 1863, Richard Cobden, one of the greatest spokesmen of the entrepreneurial classes, complained:

> We have the spirit of feudalism rife and rampant in the midst of antagonistic development of the age of Watt, Arkwright and Stephenson! Nay, feudalism is more and more in the ascendant in political and social life. So great is its power and prestige that it draws clear to it the support and homage of even those who are the natural leaders of the newer and better civilization. Manufacturers and merchants as a rule seem only to desire riches that they may prostrate themselves at the feet of feudalism. How is this to end?[67]

Had Cobden lived into the next century, he would have had his answer. The middle-class England where Samuel Smiles had proclaimed "everything was young, from its engineering to its institutions,"[68] had moved toward an ever greater conservatism and yearning after more gentlemanly pursuits. By 1909, one Hawick minister castigated the sons of local tweedmakers for their slippage from the old Protestant virtues: "We [have] had many men, chiefly in the founders, businessmen not afraid of hard work, keeping pleasure in its place, sticking fast to their posts. In the *second generation*, however, we have often seen a different spirit; sometimes a contempt for trades, an aping of the fine gentleman, an aspiring to be what they were not . . . love of ease, self indulgence and lack of grit and backbone."[69]

The cost of this change in attitude—to become evident eight decades later—was not immediately apparent even to the most perspicacious of observers. Max Weber, among a growing number of sociologists and economists, believed that "the technical and economic conditions of machine production" had obviated the need for the maintenance of the old "asceticism" that created the spirit of modern capitalism. Science, technology, the very mechanism of rational corporate life, would proceed without the support of the old values.[70]

Yet the experience of the ensuing decades has clearly demonstrated that it is precisely these *values*—whether in Europe, America or Asia—that form the only reliable cornerstones for flourishing commerce and industry. This has been nowhere more evident than in Britain. Stripped of the moral purpose that so permeated the mid-nineteenth-century manufacturers, the very intellectual bases of the industrial revolution—expansion, efficiency, the search for new markets—became denatured, codified and bureaucratized. Similarly, a shrinking of economic opportunity for ambitious newcomers within the society, which occurred only later and less thoroughly in the United States, slowed the replacement of the "old guard" with more aggressive entrepreneurs.

This devolution of the entrepreneurial environment and the rise of "aristocratic" values among the corporate and political elites, notes historian Martin Weiner, eventually undermined the very motive forces that in the nineteenth century had made Britain "the workshop of the world."[71] Over time, British industry—and particularly the engineering-oriented businesses—stood on the margins of society, becoming increasingly unfashionable with the official church,[72] the media, the intellectual elites and the brightest college graduates, a victim of what Weiner describes as "psychological and intellectual de-industrialization."[73] Instead of investing in British industry, London financiers exported hundreds of millions in capital even as industries such as shipbuilding, where as late as the 1950s Britain remained the world leader, withered for lack of new capital.[74] "Industry," summed up one exasperated British manufacturer of the times, "is a leper."[75]

These attitudes permeated deeply—even among Britain's presumptive industrial leaders, many of whom regarded their firms as little more than family heirlooms. By the 1930s most boards of directors, John Maynard Keynes noted, had come to represent a kind of "jobbery" for influential people, most notably those with titles,[76] who usually had little or no expertise in the firm's business.[77] Behind the elegant facades—even of companies as famous as Jaguar Corporation—lay deteriorated plants, antiquated equipment and poor labor relations. Entrepreneur Harry Solomon, whose Hillsdown Holdings has bought numerous old-line food-processing and -distribution firms during the 1980s, remarks:

> Businesses built up over many, many years had traditions that were more important than the business. We've bought companies where there were four different dining rooms—one for directors, one for executives, one for middle managers and a canteen for the workers. For the employees it didn't exactly accelerate communication. For the directors, they didn't really care. It was more important to be in the right club.[78]

This industrial malaise also has extended to the workers, not only in Britain but across Europe as well. In comparison with their Asian counterparts, British and other European workers generally rank among the least motivated in the industrialized world, with the highest number of sick days and the greatest resistance to adapting to new technologies. Not surprisingly, these countries, most notably Germany, have suffered from the slowest rates of growth in industrial productivity.[79]

A similar devolution in values has also afflicted the United States, where aristocratic traditions were weaker and the Calvinist impulse perhaps even more pronounced. By the 1980s, many American industrial firms, much like their British counterparts, were headed by a largely self-perpetuating privileged class that earned as much as 500 times what its assembly workers earned—compare that figure to an average of 10 times for its Japanese counterpart.[80] At the same time the rate of new investment in plants and equipment dropped, with annual increases ranging between half and one third those of Japan.[81]

At decade's end Japanese factories—largely run by engineers, as opposed to lawyers, accountants or MBAs—had surmounted the once huge American lead in productivity and quality, particularly in such key core industries as steel and automotive manufacturing.[82] As a result, Ohio and other regions of the industrial heartland found themselves incapable of coping with a series of outside threats—the growing encroachment of foreign producers, particularly from Asia; increased competition from less expensive regions of the United States; and a changing industrial structure more favorable to younger, more innovative firms.

Various reasons—Japanese wages, protectionist policies and reduced cost of capital—were offered for this poor performance. Rarely, however, did what sociologist Pitirim Sorokin called "the managerial aristocracy"[83] face the critical issue of its own devolution of values, which had leached from enterprise its sense of intrinsic meaning for owners, managers and, most especially, the employees. Little more was left than what Sorokin called a "sensate," mechanistic and highly impersonal relationship between man and enterprise.

> Stripping man of his divine charisma and grace, sensate mentality, ethics and law have reduced him to a mere electro-proton complex or reflex mechanism devoid of any sanctity or end-value. "Liberating" him from the "superstitions" of the categorical imperatives, they have taken from him invisible armor that unconditionally protected him, his dignity, his sanctity and his inviolability . . . Rarely, if ever, have cattle been treated with such cynicism.[84]

One quintessential example of this "electro-proton" mentality in management was the attempt by American corporations to solve their competitive problems through massive expenditures on new technology. In the 1980s General Motors spent a colossal $80 billion on modernization of its plants, yet its market share and the shares of other American automakers continued to diminish. The high-tech, heavily automated plants proved no panacea, as Japanese quality standards rose more quickly than those of even the most technologically advanced domestic plants.[85] General Motors's ambitious scheme, manufacturing expert W. Edwards Deming noted, resulted in nothing more than "poor quality at high cost."[86]

The reasons for Japanese success, Deming points out, lay not in technology but in the organizational commitment of both managers and workers to the production process. Indeed, among GM's most successful plants was its joint venture with Toyota in Fremont, California, which, although relatively technologically backward, used Japanese "team" approaches in its management of the plant.[87] The Japanese approach to factory work succeeds, Deming suggests, because it at least attempts to appeal to people's "intrinsic motivation." Fixated on maintaining the privileges of the "managerial aristocracy," the prevailing American system, he concluded, "crushes that all out."[88]

TOWARD AN ASIATIC STANDARD?

Cast against this background of industrial decline, the emergence of a full-blown Asiatic alternative to Western systems of management and production, epitomized most spectacularly by Japan, represents a key watershed—and not only for the Anglo-American tribe. For the first time since the beginnings of the industrial revolution, the superiority of Western standards of organization, production and technological development have been called into question by the success of a distinctly alien form of capitalism.

By the early 1990s, for example, Japan's technological prowess—particularly in commercially applicable areas—was ranked in polls of business leaders as consistently well ahead of Europe and, in some cases, ahead of the United States.[89] Among the American public, the perception of Japanese technological supremacy is even greater, with a 1990s survey showing two of every three Americans rating Japanese technology ahead of that of their own country.[90]

The reaction among some observers and industrialists in the West has been predictably paranoiac. In some circles, the Japanese have taken on the character of a sort of dark "master race" seeking control over the world economy. Within the United States, fears of looming "Japanization" have transformed Japan in the span of a decade from a well-regarded ally—with a GNP and manufacturing base roughly half that of the United States and a far lower standard of living[91]—into the country most feared by Americans.[92] By 1990 nearly seven out of every ten Americans felt there was "too much" Japanese investment in the country,[93] a sentiment reflected in a country-and-western tune by Ray Stevens called "Working for the Japanese," which concludes:

> *I ain't ever read* The Wall Street Journal
> *I ain't got no Ph.D.*
> *But this much I know*
> *We are all working for the Japanese.*[94]

In tones reminiscent of the early-twentieth-century Protocols of the Elders of Zion—which predicted a Jewish-directed global takeover—many American and European writers increasingly draw up conspiracy theories posing Japan as a nation whose clear and central purpose remains total world dominion. A well-connected Washington corporate lobbyist, in one particularly absurd case, described the Japanese as "a third political party " gaining overwhelming influence over the American political system.[95] Even trips by American teachers to Japan are seen as being able to "infect" hundreds, even thousands, of Americans with enthusiasm for the Japanese society and way of life.[96] Similarly, a proposed massive Japanese plan to build a futuristic research city in Australia has resulted in a backlash among those seeing it as "a Trojan horse" for a Japanese invasion of the island.[97]

In Europe, such views have become, if anything, even more common. European leaders see their only salvation in building a grand alliance against the Japanese, forming what a 1990 French parliamentary group called "a common front" against an impending "electronics Pearl Harbor."[98] Edith Cresson, former French prime minister and close associate of President Mitterrand, explained:

We have a feeling of the most extraordinary growth and expansion of Japan. Its will to conquer and move markets and block

others from technologies is unquenchable . . . We are not ob-
sessed with this but we must understand that Europe is our land
and we must protect it. The British should be interested in the
continent more than anything—the Channel won't protect them
anymore.[99]

Such trepidation toward the threat posed by Asiatic power
has rested within the Euro-American consciousness from the
days of Rome and Charlemagne through racist fears such as the
"yellow peril." In the late nineteenth and early twentieth centuries it led to the banning of Asiatic immigration to the United
States, Canada and Australia, and later culminated in the hys-
terical efforts of Adolf Hitler to unite Europe, despite his hypo-
critical alliance with Japan, for what he considered its destined
"struggle for survival against Asia."[100]

Yet for others, the rise of Japan suggested not a threat but the
presence of a new, and appealing, model of industrial organization, the presumptive leaders of a new global society. As one
enthusiast, Silicon Valley–based consultant Sheridan Tatsuno,
puts it, they are "the New Americans—pioneering at the edge,
fueled by self-confidence and enormous wealth."[101]

Among the Japanese themselves, this perspective has grown
as well. In some senses they reflect older notions popular in
prewar Japan among liberals, who envisioned their society as a
new kind of model for world society. Just as Japan had blended
Confucianism with native Shinto and Buddhist beliefs, they
predicted that the melding of those traditions with Western science and technology would create a new, highly enlightened
form of Asiatic society. As two Japanese academics, both former
teachers at the University of Chicago, observed in 1921:

That the present Japanese civilization is largely a product of assimilation by native genius of American, French, German and
English ideas is an established fact. It may be therein lies the
hope, as many Japanese thinkers cherish, of making Japan a
modern Alexandria, where centuries of human achievements in
Asia and Europe may be harmoniously woven together for the
realization of a more perfect fabric of civilization.[102]

With Japan's late-twentieth-century emergence, this idea of "a more perfect fabric of civilization" has taken on new meaning. Three decades of economic and industrial productivity growth twice that of their European or American rivals,[103] increased technological leadership, and accumulation of official cash reserves among the world's largest[104] have added plausibility to notions, particularly among those too young to remember the Second World War, of Japan as the ultimate model for all societies. As early as 1986, a panel of intellectuals sponsored by the Ministry of International Trade and Industry suggested that the Japanese should take world leadership in shaping global economic and technological progress, with financial aid and investment as the prime lever for persuading other nations to follow its lead.[105]

Shigekazu Matsumoto, executive director of the Institute of Developing Economies in Tokyo, sees the particular relevance of the Japanese model for the nations of the Third World. With the collapse of communism, he suggests, the critical question for the developing world has shifted from alternative economic systems to a choice between Anglo-Saxon capitalism and what he calls the "government-led developmentalist market economy" pioneered by Japan.[106]

In this sense, Japan now would serve the role once played by the Calvinist entrepreneurs and propagandists such as Samuel Smiles, who spread across the world their gospel of self-help and laissez-faire capitalism. Over time, thinks Kimindo Kusaka, a leading adviser to Japan's Long-term Credit Bank, even Westerners—faced with the obvious failures of their own system— will be forced to acknowledge the essential moral and ethical superiority of the Japanese approach. Kusaka, relaxing over coffee in his cluttered Tokyo office, suggests:

I think Japan's role is to make certain concepts prevalent in the world, [like] the custom of long-term cultivation of human relationships as the most important aspect of business. We want to be a teacher of concepts that can contribute to the prosperity of the world. We can move beyond hardware, instructing people in such things as a basic business relationship.[107]

Some enthusiasts in the West share Kusaka's assertions. Western writers such as Ezra Vogel, author of the provocative *Japan as Number One*, contrast American and European societies—with their rising crime rates, falling education standards, increased family dysfunction and lack of basic self-belief—with a Japan seen as prosperous, highly efficient, literate and socially cohesive.

The sheer expansion of the Japanese industrial might into the West has perhaps had the most profound effects on European and American perceptions. Where once the world followed British or American standards of production, by the 1990s in Britain, the birthplace of the industrial revolution, Japanese investment was seen as reviving old industries, such as automobiles and electronics, that had been all but demolished during the 1960s and 1970s.[108]

Even as European protectionists such as Peugeot chairman Jacques Calvert derided Britain for serving as "a Japanese aircraft carrier just off Europe's coast" and "Japan's fifth island,"[109] Japanese managers were being widely praised in the British press for making high-quality vehicles in a nation whose cars once seemed synonymous with poor quality and unreliability.[110] "In the European car industry there is resignation that Europe can't do it," boasted John Cushingham, production director of Nissan Motor Manufacturing Ltd. "That's not so. We've done it."[111]

Much the same experience has taken place in North America, the recipient of roughly half of all Japanese investment during the 1980s.[112] Initially after the war, Japan was essentially an American protectorate, the Far Eastern center of America's "strategic system."[113] Even into the 1950s Americans viewed Japan's economy as weak and barely capable of sustaining its population. Its competitiveness was considered so feeble that Secretary of State John Foster Dulles arrogantly told Foreign Minister Mamoru Shigemitsu that his nation's trade with the United States would "always" be in deficit.[114]

By the mid-1980s not only was the United States suffering a severe and seemingly unyielding trade deficit with Japan, but many American businessmen were looking toward the Japanese as saviors of their basic industries. In their new plants from California to Tennessee, Japanese carmakers produced cars more quickly and with fewer defects than their American rivals. By 1990 a million American-made Japanese cars were rolling off the assembly line, a number expected to double by 1995.[115]

At the same time, a gnawing reality that Japan was indeed winning the industrial war had spread across the breadth of American industry. In a 1991 survey of top American manufacturing executives, nearly three in five admitted U.S. quality standards were below those of the Japanese.[116] Acknowledging the superiority of Japanese methods, many American-owned firms have changed long-cherished ways of doing business in order to follow Japanese standards, including strict quality control, "teamwork" and continuous improvement.[117] "I had to give up my ego . . . and understand how to share decision making," admits Kevin Harris, a fabrication manager at Goulds Pump, a Los Angeles–area manufacturing firm that adopted Japanese "total quality management" to save its faltering business.[118]

Although Japanese firms rank lower in such conventional measures as profitability and return on investment, their ability to gain ever greater control over world markets already has undermined belief in the ultimate validity of the Anglo-American corporate standard.[119] By the early 1990s even in Silicon Valley, arguably the most durable bastion of Anglo-American capitalism, once haughty entrepreneurs and venture capitalists were seeking ways to mimic Japanese corporate structure. Some even talked of developing linked groups of companies, sharing information and resources for competitive advantage. One venture capitalist even proposed forming what he called "the Kleiner Perkins *zaibatsu*," composed of various companies financed by that firm.[120]

Such efforts suggest that, like the Asiatic societies over the past century, the West, and particularly the Anglo-Americans, has begun to learn that civilization, culture and technology can flow in two directions. To survive in the global economy, suggests Rakesh Kaul, a former senior executive with both Beatrice Foods and Shaklee Corporation, a firm purchased by Japan's

Yamanouchi Pharmaceutical, Western firms must shift their emphasis rapidly toward an Asiatic standard based more on consensus and long-standing ties.

Kaul, an immigrant from India, believes the tide has already become irreversible and reflects the ascendancy of Asian tribal values over those of the formerly triumphant West. In a high-rise office overlooking San Francisco Bay, the tall, elegantly attired executive explained:

> In the West we have been living under the technocratic imperative. We have believed in the supremacy of the individual ego. We forget that there are things bigger than the individual—such as the family, the tribe, company—and relationships which extend beyond the contractual to the charismatic. The Japanese, other Asians are not taking the Western contractual form of doing business. They have rejected it—and are changing it into something different.[121]

CHAPTER FIVE

DIASPORA BY DESIGN

YUKIO OHTSUBO is a teacher far from home. Dressed in a gray suit, he sits stoically on a wooden chair in the old gymnasium, a worn Japanese flag hanging limply behind him. It is late afternoon and only the twang from electric guitars—young Japanese jamming—breaks the quiet.

For an outpost of arguably the world's richest financial empire, the London Japanese School in Acton, a fading middle-class suburb, seems unimpressive. Yet to Ohtsubo, and to thousands of other Japanese also far from home, the old brick building, with its antiquated laboratories and fading paint, represents something as important as the banks, corporate offices and factories that have brought them to Great Britain, their largest colony in Europe,[1] home by 1990 to almost $16 billion of their over $40 billion of direct investment in the EC.[2]

For Britain's 40,000 Japanese, schools like this, Ohtsubo explains, play a critical role by teaching their young in the Japanese identity. Like Jews throughout history, the Japanese see an essential need to preserve their unique racial and ethnic culture, even as the tribe expands to virtually every corner of the world.

"We must adjust to this new culture, but our children must remain Japanese," explains Ohtsubo, a thin, stern-faced man with nearly twenty years of teaching experience back in Japan. "We have to come to foreign countries for our work, but we know that a Japanese here will come home eventually."[3]

From Japan's emergence as a modern nation in the late nineteenth century, its unique economic and demographic structure has forced it to look overseas. In some sense, the Japanese were like the Jews in their diaspora or the British of the nineteenth century, a people with resources inadequate to maintain their population. As a result, the Japanese developed practical skills and became highly dependent on international trade.

But even by the standards of other peoples, the Japanese vulnerability was extreme. Unlike trading states such as Great Britain, the Netherlands or even France, it could not fall back on a large imperial hinterland for captive markets. Because it lacked the natural resources of the United States, Japan was dependent on imports of industrial raw materials such as cotton and oil as well as food—imports of which more than tripled during the years from 1913 to 1925.[4] It also relied heavily on a narrow range of exports, particularly silk and cotton, which by the mid-1920s represented better than two thirds of Japan's outbound trade.[5]

But not only commercial concerns drove the Japanese overseas. By 1925 Japan's population density was three times that of Italy and Germany,[6] leading some observers to advocate mass immigration as their only hope for a better future. In 1931, a distinguished Oxford don named W. R. Crocker even suggested that Borneo or New Guinea be handed over to the Japanese to relieve the overcrowded islands.[7]

In a desperate attempt to free themselves from this debilitating vise, Japanese businessmen early in this century fanned out in search of new markets not only in their East Asian backyard but as far afield as the Middle East, South Africa and Australia.[8] Immigrants poured out of Japan, and by 1930 over one million had settled outside the main islands, concentrated mainly in its nearby Asia-Pacific sphere of influence—Hawaii, Peru and the Philippines—as well as California.[9] But this tribal expansion began to be cut off as early as the turn of the century by Europeans determined to limit access to both immigration and new markets.

The Pacific War represented an attempt by Japan's leaders to forcibly expand their sphere of influence in their underdeveloped hinterland in East Asia. But their defeat in 1945 drove them back, exhausted and at the brink of starvation, with the burden of an additional five million Japanese who had returned from the outreaches of a shrunken empire.[10]

Yet the triumph of their Anglo-American rivals also ultimately provided a new pathway for tribal expansion. Under the new economic and political order imposed by America, the world's markets opened for the Japanese, who were now able to expand dramatically without the necessity of building their own empire. Rather than rely on battleships and the mettle of the Imperial Army for their expansion, they could build their commerce on mechanisms forged largely by the Anglo-Americans—jets, modern telecommunications and open financial markets—to explore an ever-wider sphere of activities and countries.

In the process, the postwar Anglo-American liberal order facilitated the creation of a new kind of tribal empire, one that did not rely on permanent emigrant colonies but on emanation from a highly productive central core. With the world open to their expansion, the Japanese recycled and expanded their prewar networks, managed by rotating groups of corporate managers in three-to-five-year stints.

The expansion of this unique dispersion—a kind of diaspora by design—has been among the most remarkable stories in world economic history. In little more than three decades, these corporate samurai have built a global economic empire more powerful than that developed by the Jews over two millennia and far more widespread than that of either the Chinese or Indians. In the less than twenty years from 1968 to 1988, Japan's current account surplus—the combination of net trade in products and services as well as income from investment and other transfer payments—rose from the third to by far the largest in the world, more than the positive balance of the oil producers and Germany combined. Over the same period, Japan's net outward private investment and its overall net foreign investment income[11] were by far the largest of any nation on earth.[12]

To manage this vast expansion the Japanese have become the most commonplace and conspicuous of wanderers. Over the last three decades they have dispersed into such key cities as New York, Los Angeles, Bangkok and London.[13] In less than twenty years the number of these wandering Japanese has more than doubled to nearly 600,000,[14] most of them in two-to-five-year hitches. Similarly, the number of Japanese traveling overseas doubled between 1986 and 1989 to roughly ten million,[15] becoming a permanent and highly visible presence in the world's hotels, airports and vacation spots. By 1990 nearly nine in every ten Japanese newlyweds spent their honeymoons abroad.[16]

Yet even in dispersion the Japanese maintain their relative distance from other ethnic groups, remaining fully a part of what Harold Isaacs has described as "the truest nation on earth."[17] On a worldwide basis this separateness has been preserved through a network of specially constructed institutions. These allow Japanese executives abroad to stay in their own hotels or spas, play golf on courses owned by their countrymen, and send their children to places such as London's Japanese School—one of over 230 such institutions that educate over 40,000 students across the world.[18] Virtually every Japanese overseas settlement also boasts its own religious institutions, movie theaters, booksellers, restaurants, bars and markets.

Satoru Nakamura, an overseas manager with the giant Marubeni trading firm, lives on the London branch of this global infrastructure. Executives such as Nakamura are the lifeblood of companies like Marubeni, which has over 7,000 employees and over 450 offices worldwide.[19] From London, he helps coordinate activities in over twenty offices throughout Europe and the Middle East, trading such diverse commodities as oil, chemicals, machinery sales and gold.

Yet when decisions are made, he admits, it is as if he were still comfortably in Japan. Virtually all the key inputs come from within the reassuring confines of the tribe, the decisions shared almost exclusively among fellow Japanese. Finishing his lunch at a trendy sushi restaurant overlooking the Thames, Nakamura comments:

> We are not really with the others. Every morning, my manager says "Good morning," and at the end of the day "Good-bye" to the British staff but that's about the extent of it. In Japanese and with Japanese we talk about all our other interests.
>
> My family is mainly with other Japanese families. So, really, it's the same family life, the same business life as in Japan, except that now we're in England. In a sense, we are still in Japan.

THE GREAT BRITAIN OF THE EAST

The vast expansion of the Japanese, like the previous one of the British, is the story of a small island race that transformed itself into a global tribe of enormous importance. The first Asians successfully to adapt Western technology, the Japanese naturally long have thought of themselves as the natural leaders of that part of the world. As Baron Makino, minister of agriculture and commerce, observed in 1913: "Our ambition is to be to the East what Great Britain is to the West.[20]

Like the British, and perhaps even more so like the Jews, the Japanese tribe's ascendancy also fed upon a self-image asserting the intrinsic superiority of its own unique history and culture. Though made up of diverse groups—with likely Polynesian, Chinese, Korean and other roots—the Japanese, according to their Shinto traditions, were a race apart, the so-called Yamato people. In their own mythology they were not simply special— or, like the Jews, chosen—but the seed of the gods, forming "the root of the world."[21]

Equally important, again like the British or the Jews, the Japanese combined this powerful "vocation of uniqueness" with a passion for the acquisition and development of knowledge. As historian John Dower has noted: "The Japanese, much like the

British, were traditionalistic and conservative on the one hand, and progressive and cosmopolitan on the other."[22]

From their earliest contacts with the West to their present-day worldwide commercial empire, the Japanese have combined these two elements, stubbornly molding imported Western culture and technology to their own ends. This ability impressed Lafcadio Hearn, one of the earliest and most prescient observers of Japanese society. In 1896 Hearn noted:

> The adoption of Western civilization was not nearly such an easy matter as unthinking people imagined . . . Thus the appliances of Western industrial invention have worked admirably in Japanese hands, have produced excellent results in those crafts at which the nation has been skillful, in other and quainter ways— nothing more than the turning of old abilities into new and larger channels.[23]

But as Hearn also suggested, the roots of this emergence lay in "old abilities" whose genesis lay in centuries well before the Japanese knew more than vaguely of the existence of Western technology and culture. Within the core of traditional Japanese attitudes and social habits, in fact, already lay a disposition toward commerce and industry that made them uniquely well suited to the rigors of the modern world economy. In essence, the Japanese tribe was possessed with a mentality—although based on such clearly Oriental sources as Confucian familialism, Shinto traditionalism and Buddhism—that produced an effective Asiatic equivalent to the Calvinistic faith underlying the British commercial hegemony.

This cultural trait incubated many aspects of the economic culture that became the foundation for Japan's remarkable economic ascendancy in the following centuries. It was most particularly during the Tokugawa era—a period of almost 250 years of enforced isolation from the rest of the world—that Japanese business developed unique systems of production and commercial attitudes unmatched by any other global tribe.

Tokugawa society, in particular, saw the full flowering of an emerging class of commercially oriented outsiders who would create the mold for Japan's economic culture. As early as the seventeenth century, for example, Japanese artisans and *chonin*, or merchants, like their Calvinist equivalents, sought out educational opportunities on a mass level virtually unknown in the rest of Asia and much of the West as well. At the highly popular *terakoya*, or temple schools, the commercial classes learned many practical skills such as use of the abacus in addition to the Chinese classics. The remarkable achievement of literacy rates as high as 80 percent in the early Meiji period was in large part built on this early emphasis on mass education.

The importance of knowledge was also critical to the accumulation of specialized skills within the artisan industries. By the early Tokugawa period, there already existed well-developed networks of small production units, a highly skilled artisanal work force in the countryside and a sophisticated national transport and distribution system.[24]

Even when Japan emerged from isolation, its relative lack of either domestic resources or rich foreign colonies reinforced the tendency first to look inward, toward the efficiency of its own workers, for competitive advantage. Japanese managers, notes Shigeo Shingo, an industrial engineer closely associated with Japan's most efficient production systems, viewed their workers as "the only resource" capable of securing company success and national prosperity.[25]

Similarly, this scarcity of resources and centuries of isolation also fostered the development of high levels of commitment among Japanese company owners and their employees, customers and suppliers.[26] In contrast to the Anglo-American countries, where such relations tend toward the confrontational, or to India, where the caste affiliation was most critical, or to China, where familial values prevailed, in Japan economic culture emphasized instead the stability of durable units, or *ie*. Although usually tied to a family or clan, *ie* refers most strongly to the broader concept of a corporate household, with attendant obligations to serve customers, suppliers and employees by maintaining the appearance of family continuity rather than bloodlines. In Japanese society, sociologist John Pelzell has noted, corporate assets in family-owned companies are widely considered to be those of the *ie*, with the current family serving as "a trustee."

This notion, Pelzell argues, grows out of the common mythology of genetic homogeneity among Japanese, a critical element of their "vocation of uniqueness." For them, he writes, "genetic legitimacy is racial or ethnic . . . and is assured by the myth that all Japanese are descended from the gods." More important than bloodlines, he argues, is "the mystique of the durable house," to be preserved by any means necessary.[27] In Tokugawa times, this concept often led a succession of adopted sons, usually relatives or qualified employees, to control of firms if the eldest son was deemed unworthy.[28]

In modern Japan, this old tradition, "corporate familyism," lives today in different forms.[29] In many of Japan's most important corporations—including electronic game giant Nintendo, fax maker Murata Machinery Limited, tire manufacturer Bridgestone, Suntory breweries, Seiko Instruments and the Otani hotel chain[30]—"the durable house" remains, at least ostensibly, under the tutelage of founders and their descendants. In other firms, such as publicly owned firms founded since the Second World War, elaborate attempts are often made to document and foster a sense of corporate "tradition."

Finally, the Japanese economic system also offered those within these *ie* significant room for social mobility.[31] Indeed, rather than fitting the extremely hierarchical Asiatic stereotype, Japanese society was, even in those early times, similar to a wheel, an analogy advanced by Father Maurice Bairy of Tokyo's Sophia University, a leading scholar of Japanese economic and social life. At the center conformist instincts are strong and things change only slowly. Near the edge of the wheel, however, lie the innovators, eccentrics and entrepreneurs—the marginal forces who nevertheless often force change.[32]

This pattern of outsiders forcing change has existed deep into the Japanese past, notes Hidetoshi Kato, one of Japan's leading social theorists. For instance, Toyotomi Hideyoshi, the man who united Japan in the sixteenth century, was the child of unknown poor peasants. The architects of the modernizing Meiji period were largely lower-class samurai. Similarly, many of Japan's early entrepreneurs—the Mitsuis, Iwasakis, Sumitomos—also came from less than aristocratic backgrounds.[33]

Perhaps most remarkably, some Tokugawa-era samurai purposely eschewed their traditional status for the lower rank but greater opportunities offered by commercial life. In 1616, in a move of arresting prescience, Hachirobei Mitsui renounced his samurai status for the lowly rank of *chonin*. Starting off with a business brewing sake and soy sauce,[34] over the next two centuries the Mitsuis and other great commercial houses expanded their domestic trade and industrial networks, establishing their economic primacy.

By the seventeenth century, in fact, these various social and cultural factors had created one of the world's most dynamic, if insular, economic societies. Rather than having a simple medieval social structure based on an Asiatic feudalism, Tokugawa Japan was characterized by a sophisticated combination of crafts-oriented manufacturers and traders—forerunners of today's powerful industrial networks—matched by few countries. The Tokaido road between Osaka and Edo, the Tokugawa capital, which carried the bulk of this enormous commerce, ranked among the most heavily traveled roads in the world—more crowded, noted one German observer, than any in contemporary Europe.[35]

This heritage would later prove critical in the development of Japanese capitalism. It all suggests that the long-term commercial achievement of the Japanese derived not so much from any peculiar genius in corporate or government strategy but as a result of a peculiar tribal ethos that has consistently colored business decisions. In this sense, Japan's high rates of investment—which during the 1980s grew at more than twice the rate of the United States and Europe[36]—can best be seen as the result of cultural choices made by managers whose primary commitment grows from a sense of commitment to the *ie* as a means of maintaining a "durable house."

So even when Western commerce and trade forced their way onto the islands, the Japanese—more than any Asian or non-European people—could turn to their own particular value systems as the foundation for future progress.[37] Of course, the

Meiji Restoration of 1868 swept away the political structures and many of the outward trappings of the Tokugawa era. But the attitudes toward craftsmanship, the sophisticated networks of production and the ethos of the durable house remained firmly in place. As historian William Hauser, a scholar of the Tokugawa economy, observes: "To describe the modern experience of Japan as 'miraculous' . . . is to overlook the realities of the Japanese case."[38]

FROM IMITATORS TO YELLOW PERIL

The preexistence of a well-established economic system also proved to be one of the critical elements helping the Japanese to fight off the Western imperialism that overwhelmed so many other nations in Asia, Africa and other parts of the nonwhite world. Even as technical knowledge was imported from the West,[39] the Japanese ruling elites, supported by commercial classes, worked assiduously, as historian G. C. Allen later noted, to "protect their cultural history from the corrosive influence of the West."[40] Modernization was to occur, but it was to follow a distinctly *Japanese* form.

In other regions of Asia, such as China, as historian Dr. Hu Shih pointed out, contact with the West took place more naturally, leading to free association and the "gradual penetration of ideas and practices." Chinese, Indian and other Asian businessmen quickly assimilated not only European languages but also corporate standards and forms at a rapid rate. In contrast, the fundamental norms of business life were far less challenged and transformed by Japan's modernization process.[41]

Critically—in contrast to China, with its weak central government, or India, under the colonial yoke—Japan's government was capable of supplying the key organizational and financial muscle of early economic development, by the late nineteenth century accounting for at least two fifths of all domestic capital formation. In those first few decades of economic growth, government purchases and mandates protecting local industry from foreign competition[42] assured that economic development would evolve predominately to the benefit of firms with a Japanese cultural base.[43]

As a result, the Japanese global extension has taken place within a remarkably self-contained pattern. Determined to limit the penetration of Westerners into the Japanese economy, Japan's leaders welcomed Western "knowledge," like that earlier absorbed from the Chinese and Koreans, but once that knowledge was ingested by local firms the *gaijin* (foreigners) were largely kept from playing a critical role in the domestic economy. Other great world cities—such as London, New York and Hong Kong—were built on a financial foundation by diverse peoples; Tokyo, perhaps alone of the leading urban metropolises, decidedly was not.

This pattern of indigenization was most evident within the development of Japanese industry. Although initially dependent on British technologists brought in by Hong Kong's Jardine Matheson,[44] Japan's homegrown stock of technologists and scientists grew rapidly with a rapid increase in the number of new technical colleges throughout the islands.[45] Ultimately, the students from these schools played the leading role, as both founders of new firms and modernizing managers of older, existing businesses in critical industries such as petrochemicals and electrical machinery.[46]

The pressures on these new leaders—progenitors of the contemporary "diaspora by design"—were enormous. Soaring population growth rates and increased consumption sparked rapid increases in imports and a consequent need for new markets. Emigration, the key to reducing such pressures in Europe, was all but impossible, since by the early twentieth century Japanese immigrants had been banned from virtually all the principal lands of settlement, such as the United States,[47] Canada[48] and Australia. Only in Brazil, where by the late 1930s over 137,000 had settled, did Japanese find an even moderately benign welcome.[49]

Blocked from forging their own conventional global diaspora, the Japanese poured most of their efforts into other means of extending their influence in the world economy. Among the principal agents for this expansion were the *sogo shosha,* or trading companies. Some, such as the Mitsui clan, had grown from Tokugawa-era trading networks. Once trade with the outside was opened, the Mitsuis were among the first to send their people abroad. Within three years of the new order, they were sending both family members and promising employees for education offshore, including a handful to learn industrial arts at the textile mills of Lowell, Massachusetts.[50]

Initially, the move abroad was on a small scale and rather poorly coordinated. Lacking any overseas markets, the first foreign operations, those of Mitsui, were conducted out of the Japanese embassy in London. In many other locations, Japanese language skills and commercial contacts were so limited they had to employ Chinese middlemen who knew at least some English and could recognize some of the Chinese characters used by the Japanese.[51]

By the turn of the century, however, Mitsui and the other principal *sogo shosha*—including both Mitsubishi and Sumitomo —were sending their own emissaries to both the West and the principal Asian ports.[52] These giant firms with their industrial subsidiaries and financial units, known collectively as *zaibatsu,* controlled one fourth of Japan's corporate assets and three quarters of its industrial assets[53] and together spearheaded a remarkable threefold jump in foreign trade between 1895 and 1905.[54]

By the 1930s nearly a half million Japanese were living temporarily abroad as "birds of passage," including agents for the *zaibatsu,* independent traders and students.[55] At the top of this worldwide network stood a new breed of college-educated managers—such as Hikojiro Nakakamigawa of Mitsui, Heigoro Shoda of Mitsubishi and Saihei Hirose of Sumitomo—who helped transform the old-line family *zaibatsu* into modern international firms. Under their leadership, the *honsha,* or central houses, created a large network of related companies, often quite independent, whose products and services they could in turn finance and then distribute through their global network.[56]

But if the traders and *zaibatsu* chieftains represented the elite face of the diaspora, their growing international influence depended largely on an increasingly efficient industrial machine at home. This development was largely ignored at the time by all but a few Westerners,[57] most of whom wrote off the Japanese as an often imitative, almost comic force in the world economy. "Only persons of Western origin," G. C. Allen, who first arrived in Nagoya as a schoolteacher in the 1920s, later wrote, "it was then assumed, were capable of manipulating valves and levers."[58]

Yet in the face of what he saw as the "complacency" of Europeans and Americans, Allen observed that Japanese firms were already beginning to build their own economic model, dependent largely on small firms employing the skills and attitudes of the Tokugawa-era artisan culture.[59] Indeed, even at the height of the era of *zaibatsu* dominance, with the government encouraging and subsidizing the creation of large, European-style mills, most of the employment and production inside Japan remained in literally thousands of "mechanized village industries."[60]

Observing the flexibility and quick response of such industries, which often served as key suppliers to the larger companies, W. R. Crocker envisioned a new, distinctly Japanese path of industrial progress based on smaller production units and held together by a common ethos of mutual self-help. Japan, he predicted, was creating "an industrial order unknown to any contemporary society."[61]

Such firms also existed in the larger cities, thriving alongside the larger industrial companies. In the 1920s Allen was startled by the energy and diligence among Nagoya's smaller, artisanal companies. Five decades later, Allen would recall:

> Much of the work was done by hand and craftsmen used what were to me quite unfamiliar tools. As electricity was available everywhere, the employment of little electric motors to drive the small machines was already widespread. There were numerous small metal and engineering workshops filled with two or three drilling workshops equipped with two or three drilling machines or lathes. In all of them the work seemed to go far into the night.[62]

Such smaller artisanal firms would prove critical to Japan's larger companies as they tried to cope with the disasters posed by the Depression, which cut the exports of Japanese firms to less than half their pre-1929 levels. Forced to cut back costs and improve their products, these smaller companies, and their larger customers, did not go bankrupt or lay off their workers at anything like the rate seen in the United States or other Western countries.

In a now familiar pattern, these firms dealt with hardship by expanding their products from basic textiles to a wide range of ever more sophisticated goods, often offered at prices well below those of their Western competitors. Microscopes made in the United States and wholesaled at $7.50, for example, were suddenly challenged by Japanese versions of similar quality that *retailed* at less than $2.[63]

Even at the height of the Depression, with much of the world's shipping tied up, Japan's merchant fleet was highly active, plying the seas for raw materials and new markets. "Our enterprising traders of the present day," observed Ginjiro Fujihara of Oji Paper, "find their way into the remotest corners of the world. No matter how trying the climate might be, these modern pioneers go wherever they can to sell Japanese goods."[64]

Such efforts, accompanied by the steady improvement in the quality of Japanese products, soon overcame their leading competitors in such key industries as silk production.[65] European producers, most notably in Italy, long the center for high-fashion silks, complained, but, noted *Fortune* in 1936: "The Italian government, while its press screamed Yellow Peril and Social Dumping and Wake Up Europe, admitted the real reason why Japanese silks were selling in silk-making Italy might be that Japanese machinery and Japanese organization were better."[66]

QUEST FOR EMPIRE

Opposition to Japanese commercial expansion in North America and Europe as well as the West's colonial empires gradually forced a general realignment in Japan's economic strategy. Even as Japanese firms attempted to develop their Western markets, the prime focus of their economic expansion began to shift inexorably to East Asia, where commercial and political opposition was far less formidable.

As early as the 1880s, Japanese traders had begun their penetration of nearby regions, most particularly the Korean peninsula. By 1894 their agents had precipitated a revolt, providing a convenient pretext for seizure of that unhappy country from the tottering Chinese empire. Within less than a year, the Japanese gained control of the peninsula and, in treaty negotiations, won title to Formosa and the valuable Liaotung peninsula as well.[67]

The Japanese military's spectacular campaign against Russia in 1904 and 1905 removed Russia as their leading competitor for influence in Manchuria, a vast and resource-rich province under the nominal control of the Chinese empire. Militarists, nationalists and its commercial backers, who helped finance their efforts, saw in Manchuria a base for imperial expansion that alone could help make Japan an equal to the other great commercial powers.[68] As early as 1906, key figures such as Koki Hirota, a member of the secret imperialist Black Dragon Society and later prime minister, began propagating the notion of an "Asiatic Monroe Doctrine" that, effectively dividing the world into European, American and Japanese spheres of influence, would leave Japan in clear control of Manchuria and much of the rest of East Asia.[69]

With the establishment of the puppet state of Manchukuo in 1931, this Japanese Monroe Doctrine began to take shape in reality. Spurred by the development efforts of key *zaibatsu* such as Mitsubishi or Mitsui,[70] by the 1930s over a million Japanese subjects, most of them Koreans, lived in the province, where the population expanded thirty times in three decades.[71] In Fuschun, they built the world's largest open-pit coal mine while exploiting the large nearby iron deposits.[72]

The young empire soon became a breeding ground for critical new industries such as the manufacture of chemical fertilizers, desperately needed to feed Japan's growing population.[73] The natural resources of Korea and, later, Manchuria, most notably hydroelectric power, provided Japanese entrepreneurs with vast new opportunities to expand their operations and experiment with new technologies. China and Korea, in effect, became Japan's "frontier," its land of unlimited opportunities for new and vaster development.[74]

When the Western powers complained about the Japanese move, the conventional wisdom in Tokyo, observed one American in 1925, was that "just as she was getting good at the game of grab, the other Powers, most of whom had all they wanted anyway, suddenly had an access of virtue and called the game off."[75] The idea that the conflict over China was largely an economic one was conceded by at least one American, *Business Week* editor Milton van Slyck, who in 1942 described the ensuing Pacific War as "essentially one of minerals." The "have-not," resource-poor countries, notably Japan and Germany, had seized territories in Asia and Russia in order to even the score with the British-Americans, with their vast North American and colonial reserves.[76]

Although clearly driven by profit, the Japanese expansion into Asia also rested on a broader ideological rationalization. Many Japanese, both in business and government service, felt their country was destined to serve as the champion of "Asian roots and Asian cultural solidarity" against Western domination.[77] As early as the turn of century, Japan had indeed served as an important refuge and training base for Asian nationalists, including China's Sun Yat-sen.[78] Later, at the Versailles Conference, Japanese representatives battled against racial covenants.[79]

Many Asians also embraced, at least initially, Japan's self-appointed leadership role. As the first nonwhite society to achieve world power status, Japan held a special fascination among its neighboring countries. More important, the Japanese defeat of the Russians and, then, in the early 1940s, the Anglo-Americans and their allies aroused the support of such important nationalists as India's Subhas Bose, who fled to Japan during the war.[80] As former Indonesian foreign minister Mochtar Kusumaatmadjah put it: "An entire generation remembers the Japanese with gratitude. . . . It was the end of the white man when we saw them as prisoners of war."[81]

In this ideological setting, hundreds of thousands of Japanese settlers naturally saw migration into their expanding Asian sphere of influence as a matter of manifest destiny, no less than the Anglo-Americans inheriting control of Mexican-dominated Texas and California. If Japanese migrants felt, as most undoubtedly did, superior to the "natives," there was also, as occurred among some settlers of the American West, a feeling that they were simply shifting from one part of their nation's natural domain to another.

Ichiro Momosaka, whose family emigrated around the turn of the century from the southern island of Kyushu to Pusan, then a growing port in expanding Japanese-controlled Korea, never regarded himself as conqueror of a subject nation but as a pioneer settling in relatively underdeveloped new lands. Still vigorous and at the helm of a small import-export firm in the southern Japanese city of Fukuoka, Momosaka recalls fondly:

> I was born in Korea, like many Japanese, and I didn't feel they were inferior. They were my friends. We worked together. We went to school with them. We shared a common life and values. It didn't seem unnatural to me, and maybe not to them either.[82]

This Pan-Asian consciousness extended to the top echelons of the government and army. By the 1930s many Japanese leaders saw themselves—the Yamato *minzoku,* or Yamato race—as, rather than imperial overlords, a sort of Asiatic "chosen people" destined to free all fellow Asians from the bonds of Euro-American cultural and economic domination.[83] In many aspects their views were no less idealistic than those of the British, who eagerly took up the "White Man's Burden" along with the riches of conquest. In 1939, two years before the attack on Pearl Harbor, General Kenkichi Uyeda, commander of the Kwang-tung army in Manchuria, laid out the basic vision:

> I firmly believe that our power, which is the stabilizing factor in East Asia, must be further strengthened, so that a new original Oriental civilization all our own must be created to replace Western civilization and bring about a great spiritual change to be propagated among mankind throughout the world.[84]

To achieve these goals Uyeda talked of a "new order in Asia," which within a year would take shape as the Greater East Asian Co-prosperity Sphere. In the new scheme, the Japanese would forge all the lands from Japan to Southeast Asia into a single autarchic economic zone. By 1950, according to the Japanese Ministry of Health and Welfare, some 12 million Japanese would be settled throughout this region in countries from Korea to New Zealand.[85]

Much like the British and other European colonialists they reviled, the Japanese assumed the superior place in the new order of things. Outside the "family-nation" of Japan, other Asians were seen as younger brothers, or junior branches of the main family. Most were no more ready to be granted advanced education, the Japanese propagandists suggested, than kindergarten students. Even the elites, trained in Japanese and thoroughly Nipponized, were seen as having nothing to teach the Yamato race.[86] Indeed, new settlers in the countries of the Co-prosperity Sphere were expected by government officials to constitute the local elite, live in *Nippon-machi*, or "Japan towns," and avoid intermarriage.[87]

Such racist attitudes, which had turned the subject peoples against the Europeans, also eventually backfired on the Japanese. Some local elites, such as in Indonesia, who benefited directly from the Japanese occupation continued to support them, but millions of others—forced to labor in huge projects for the Japanese and made hungry by enforced requisitions of rice—turned angrily against their new masters.[88] Even some of the most devoted pro-Japanese Asians, like Burma's Ba Maw, ended up denouncing their "brutality, arrogance and racial pretensions."[89]

Perhaps the biggest miscalculation came from the assumption, common among Japanese intellectuals and militarists, that the American and British forces, once defeated, would meekly accept Japan's self-proclaimed "new order in Asia." Instead of coldly assessing their opponents' strengths, many Japanese leaders chose to focus on the superiority of their national spirit against the materially better endowed Anglo-Americans. As late as the summer of 1944, one Japanese admiral suggested that "determination takes precedence over strength in an operation."[90]

Prisoners of their own rhetoric, the Japanese leadership—drawn largely from military and far-right ideological circles—simply lacked the information and the analytical skills to comprehend the nature of the enemies whose wrath they had inspired. As a traditional Japanese saying puts it: "The frog in the well knows nothing of the ocean."[91]

THE RENEWABLE MIRACLE

The war shattered the dreamworld of Japan's old leaders and expended roughly one quarter of its national wealth.[92] But it did not destroy the more crucial cultural factors that lay at the core of Japanese success in the past—the aggressive development of skills, maintenance of cultural uniqueness, an economic culture characterized by *ie* and sophisticated business networks.

In fact, in some ways, the architects of Japan's postwar success were forced by circumstances and limited resources to rely on these cultural factors to an even greater extent than the imperialists of the 1930s. Yet although they eschewed violence, the new leadership shared the traditional Japanese desire to maintain, at all costs, their nation's independence from foreign encroachment and domination.

Nowhere was this more evident than in the policies of the Ministry of Finance. Although critically short of capital after the Second World War, government bureaucrats and corporate leaders—playing on traditional fears of foreign domination—refused to allow anything like the massive overseas investment that helped revive the European and, later, other East Asian economies after 1950.

Instead, Japan's leaders developed a unique financial system that, as economist Masasuke Ide of the Nomura School of Advanced Management has pointed out, allocated capital overwhelmingly to drive industrial development. It also promoted the development of what Ide calls "relationship investors"[93] and issued regulatory incentives that allowed for levels of earnings less than one third those of their Western competitors.[94]

The existence of this system allowed Japanese firms to engage, Ide suggests, in what from the Western perspective would seem "predatory" policies, such as absorbing losses in foreign markets as a means to maintain market share and plowing large amounts of capital into new products and innovations almost irrespective of short-term financial conditions. Low allowable levels of profitability, he suggests, played a key role in creating Japan's unique "efficiency-oriented management" and allowing for the tribe's enormous outward expansion.[95] By the late 1980s it also served to boost the price of Japanese assets to a point where, even with a substantial liberalization, the economy remained by far the most effectively closed to direct foreign investment of any major industrial power, with average inbound direct investments of roughly one fourth those of Germany, one tenth those of France and one twenty-fifth those of the United Kingdom.[96]

But these policies hardly suffice to explain Japan's economic progress. In the past half century many governments—as diverse as Argentina, India, Mexico and even France—have sought to promote economic growth through financial controls and, in some cases, far more interventionist industrial policies. But none has had even remotely the global success enjoyed by Japan.

Instead the secret behind this remarkable emergence lies not so much in governmental bureaucracy, but through the reinvigoration of Japan's historic economic culture. As in the Tokugawa era, in the Meiji period—and again in the years leading up to the Pacific War—the Japanese found a way to reinvent their economy to fit the new challenges before them.

As has occurred at various points throughout Japanese history, many of the companies driving this process in the postwar era originated at the fringe of Maurice Bairy's wheel, often from the lower artisan classes and the ranks of subcontract manufacturers. Like many Meiji-era entrepreneurs, some of these new industrialists came from the countryside and possessed only minimal educations; most casting company entrepreneurs in 1955, noted one Harvard University study, came from agricultural backgrounds or from the ranks of traditional artisans.[97]

On the other hand, the former *zaibatsu* were not in a position to lead this resurgence. Many of their leaders—including the directors of 245 leading Japanese companies—had been purged from leading political and economic positions by the American occupation authorities.[98] At the same time, their great capital investment in factories, their subsidiaries in the former empire, upon which they had depended increasingly in the 1930s and 1940s, lay in ruins.[99]

"The dissolution of the *zaibatsu*," comments Hitotsubashi University economist Ken-ichi Imai, "created a competitive market system in Japan." Even as the old groupings began to coalesce, the new leaders were younger, more flexible and less centrally controlled. The new "democracy in the economy," Imai notes, saw the formation of the smaller units and more flexible, less hierarchical arrangements critical to the nation's postwar economic takeoff.[100]

Imai's thesis challenges some of the more conventional notions about modern Japan's development. For many observers —such as former U.S. trade official Clyde Prestowicz or author Karel van Wolferen—Japan's recent economic ascendancy grows out of a closely monitored cooperation between its giant businesses and a highly powerful government bureaucracy, most particularly the Ministry of International Trade and Industry (MITI). "The authentic entrepreneur," says van Wolferen in his monumental *The Enigma of Japanese Power*, is "peripheral," overshadowed by the giant industrial groups, the governmental bureaucracy and leading financial institutions.[101]

Yet contrary to this perception, the postwar era did not

marginalize the smaller producers, but provided them with new and unprecedented opportunities. Certainly such activities as textiles, the steel industry and shipbuilding —the core industries—remained largely dominated by the remnants of the old *zaibatsu*. But even as the giants gravitated to these more traditional, capital-intensive fields, independent firms[102] such as Sony ventured into new, more technically advanced arenas. Indeed, rather than the old giants, the real shapers of postwar Japan's ascendancy were frequently more marginal men, such as a virtually unknown Toyota subcontractor from the Shizuoka countryside named Soichiro Honda, who spearheaded Japan's technical dominance first in motorcycles and later in automobiles, or the eccentric Osaka entrepreneur Konosuke Matsushita, founder of one of the world's largest consumer electronics companies.

As independent businessmen with limited ties to the traditional groups, they did not fit the hierarchical, centrally planned models largely favored by government bureaucrats, many of whose habits of mind were shaped by their experiences managing Japan's wartime mobilization.[103] Yet entrepreneurs such as Honda, whose efforts to expand his motorcycle company after the war were described by one MITI official as having "bordered on insanity," overcame the determined opposition of the government bureaucracy, a conquest repeated again when officals attempted to block Honda's entry into the automobile market in 1960, arguing that the field be left to larger and more established Toyota and Nissan.[104]

In an interview a few years before his death in 1991, the old entrepreneur, who had begun as a Toyota subcontractor, grew visibly annoyed when confronted with the common Western notion of a Japanese economy skillfully raised by the MITI bureaucracy:

> The Japanese bureaucrats tried to block us at every turn. We would have been more successful had we not had MITI. MITI was incapable of making automobiles, but I was [capable].[105]

This dogged spirit of entrepreneurship characterized not only Honda but also an enormous sector of smaller, more specialized firms. In a system with origins in Tokugawa Japan, these smaller companies have constituted an essential part of their nation's unique economic system. Working with larger producers,[106] these smaller firms are at the root of Japan's highly sophisticated "network" economy. This system of cooperation between government and large and small enterprise defies characterization of Japan as having either a simple "command" economy of a semi-Socialist nature or a Western-style "free market." Instead, one observer noted, Japan's economic system more resembles a web without a spider, characterized by strong horizontal and vertical linkages but lacking a central controlling element.

As David Friedman suggests in his landmark *The Misunderstood Miracle*, such small company-dominated networks provided the critical edge for Japan in its competition with the traditional Western industrial powers. Between 1954 and 1977 the number of manufacturing firms in Japan with less than 300 employees grew from 430,000 to 720,000, while the number of such companies in the United States remained relatively stagnant. Indeed, as Japan's industrial economy soared, the size of its production units actually fell, and by the late 1980s their share of Japan's industrial value added rose to a level over 50 percent greater than their American counterparts.[107]

These smaller firms provided an essential element in helping Japan's large companies, such as automakers, achieve great flexibility and in particular an ability to modify products quickly.[108] Able to buy roughly 70 to 80 percent of their parts from outside suppliers, more than twice the percentage for General Motors, large Japanese car companies have been able to maintain relatively small and lean operations. Toyota, for example, in 1989 produced four million cars in Japan using 68,000 employees compared to GM, which manufactured five million cars with more than *seven times* as many workers.[109]

As Kuniyasu Sakai, an Osaka entrepreneur who owns several such smaller industrial companies, explains:

industrial companies are not what they appear to be. They do not develop their own product line, nor do they manufacture it.

In reality these huge businesses are more like "trading companies." That is, rather than design and manufacture their own goods, they actually co-ordinate a complex design and manufacturing process that involves thousands of small companies.[110]

Although some of the companies described by Sakai have remained essentially captive subcontractors, many smaller Japanese industrial firms have developed enormous technological expertise. Many of these more competitive smaller industrial companies, notes Banri Asunama of Kyoto University, increasingly develop their own blueprints and thus have greater control over their production as well as higher profits.[111]

Even as many of the exterior key advantages of postwar Japan—low yen rates, relatively cheap labor and cheap capital—have forced larger firms, and many of their subcontractors, abroad, such smaller firms have continued to expand as a portion of Japan's industrial work force. Between 1975 and 1988 the numbers of industrial workers in firms with under 300 employees grew at a 50 percent faster rate than those in their larger counterparts, while their share of Japan's value added from manufacturing jumped from less than half to nearly three fifths.[112]

These emerging industrial firms dramatically increased their concentration in high technology over the 1980s,[113] notes economist Tadao Kiyonari. They will increasingly spearhead Japanese technological development into an era characterized by small production runs and fragmented market niches. "The era of mass production is over and that will transform the whole nature of our industrial system," predicts the white-haired Kiyonari, himself a longtime adviser to Japan's Ministry of International Trade and Industry. "The trend is towards a very special kind of specialized artisanal company. The key Japanese company of the future will have less than 100 to 150 employees with very specialized products and technology."[114]

By the beginning of the 1990s the system of interlocks between innovative smaller firms and the more familiar larger firms represented Japan's cutting edge, its most distinguishing competitive global advantage. Even as other countries seek to adopt Japanese production methods and even leverage their lower labor costs, they frequently find themselves dependent on Japanese firms for critical components. By the mid-1980s, Korea, for example, was importing fully one third of its electronic components, with nearly 75 percent of the cash value, from Japan.[115]

At firms like Fuji Electronic Industries, business with the newly industrializing nations of Asia, such as Korea and Taiwan, boomed in the early 1990s. Even as assembly line jobs migrate to producers in these and other regions, company president Ryonosuke Kirishima remains supremely confident of preserving the lower-cost regions as customers for highly specialized parts such as clip contacts used in the fastening of sophisticated electronic components in products such as faxes, video cameras and small computers.

Over the past two decades, Fuji continually has found ways to shrink its components as appliances and other electronic devices became smaller. By investing heavily in new technology, the firm—with technical advice and financial backing from the Sumitomo group, a major *keiretsu*, with strong interests in both metals and electronics[116]—has created parts that literally no one else can currently manufacture. Fuji, for instance, is among the very few companies capable of producing electronic contacts for products such as the Walkman, whose sales increased fivefold during the 1980s.[117] Protected by their technological edge, even the "shock" from rapid appreciations in the yen could not slow down sales, which between 1987 and 1990 doubled to $16 million.

Over green tea in a conference room decorated with recent products, the gray-haired Kirishima, dressed in a plain blue smock, explained that only in Japan existed the skills, the special thoroughness, to make such products. Holding up a gold-colored sample of connectors welded together like a fine necklace, he explained:

> Regardless of the high yen, these goods cannot be produced by anyone else in the country. No matter how much the price, they have to buy it. People can assemble goods anywhere, but so far

no one can make this kind of product outside of Japan. The materials, the machining they can only find here.

Japanese have a sense of doing fine and precise work. In the West, you get these great ideas. But Japanese firms have the guts to challenge the little things that no one can challenge. That's the difference.[118]

PACIFIC DREAMS

Driven by relentless industrialists such as Kirishima, the Japanese have achieved an ascendancy on a scale unimaginable even to the militarists of the Second World War. Without the benefit of great fleets or armies, Japanese economic influence has spread across every continent and earned the admiration of peoples across the world.

Yet at the same time the very enclosed nature of the Japanese economic miracle—dependent on intimate ties between the various tiers of producers and suppliers—may prove the most critical limitation on the tribe's future expansion. For thirty years a resident of Japan, Mohammed Raees is among those foreigners who has witnessed this enormous industrial expansion from the inside. An unabashed admirer of their achievements and their cultural strengths, Raees, a Pakistan-born biochemist, has worked as an executive in some of Japan's most celebrated companies and has written and lectured widely throughout the home islands.

Yet as he walks through the streets of Kobe, long one of the most cosmopolitan of Japanese cities, Raees revealed a profound sense of alienation toward his adopted home. In contrast to his brother, who has acculturated easily to life in Maryland, Raees says he still feels utterly an outsider in Japan, in a society that, to him, seems fundamentally incapable of accepting the *gaijin* as a true equal. As Raees explained:

I think in Japanese, I write in Japanese, but I could never be accepted as Japanese. Internationalization inside Japan is bullshit. The Japanese are expert at Japanization, not internationalization. They will accept anything from abroad—anything, that is, but a human being. At that level, there's a wall.[119]

Most Japanese, Raees believes, live by two distinctly differing standards: one for Japanese and another for everyone else. In dealing with each other, Japanese can be infinitely understanding and build remarkably cooperative relations. In contrast, he notes, Japanese views of foreigners—even those steeped in their language and culture—remain highly solipsistic, relying largely on stereotypes packaged by teachers, the media and other interpreters.

In this respect, notes scholar Masao Yamaguchi, Japanese still mirror many of the basic characteristics of Japan's ancient "village culture," with its traditional narrow-minded prejudice that classified even people from a neighboring town as "the outsider."[120] The problem for Japan, however, lies in the fact that it is no longer a nation of villagers but a global tribe, and its traditional ethos, however effective at home, can prove highly self-destructive on a worldwide stage.

The persistence of this "village culture" demonstrates the important ways in which the Japanese experience differs markedly from that of the other prominent global tribes. Unlike the Jews and British—and later the Chinese and Indians—the Japanese achieved their global prominence without any prolonged and intimate exposure to other peoples. Unlike the Jews, who have spent over two millennia interacting with other cultures, and the British, widely spread over the globe and mingled with many other races, the Japanese still confront global society largely from the context of a peculiarly narrow tribal experience.

During much of Japan's history this separateness was produced largely by its geographic isolation. This was further exacerbated by the enforced seclusion of Japan under the Tokugawas from the seventeenth to the mid-nineteenth century, a policy based largely on fear of contamination by Western ideas, particularly Christianity, and domination by European arms.[121] Europeans, the xenophobic officials of the shogunate told their people, were little more than "barbarians" who came from "a land of beasts who merely look human."[122]

Although softened in the Meiji era, such sentiments were revived during the prelude and duration of the Pacific War. Americans were referred to as, among other things, "misguided dogs," brutes, wild beasts, demons and devils. As a race, they were seen, notes scholar John Dower, as "mercenary, immoral, unscrupulous, vainglorious, arrogant, luxury loving, soft, nauseating, superficial, decadent, intolerant, uncivilized and barbarous."[123]

This basic antipathy—driven deeply into the consciousness of wartime Japanese—persisted even after the war, and by some accounts has even intensified in recent years. Increasingly, Japanese leaders, for example Prime Ministers Kiichi Miyazawa and Yasuhiro Nakasone, have derided Americans as essentially lazy and lacking in strong values.[124] Nakasone, a firm believer in Japanese superiority and "the eclipse of the European races," has suggested racial mixing as an explanation for some of the West's decline, particularly the United States. "The Japanese have been doing well for as long as two thousand years because there are no foreign races," he maintained.[125] By 1990 such sentiments were shared by as many as two in five Japanese, who trace American problems to the presence of too many minorities.[126]

As long as such attitudes remain commonplace, even the expansion of Japanese operations abroad, once seen as a solution to the nation's chronic surpluses with its key trading partners, will serve largely only to exacerbate tensions. Along with their often excellent production methods, notes author Hiroshi Komai, Japanese firms also often carry abroad with them the less attractive baggage of "corporate egoism" and "corporate groupism," producing a double standard that works against foreigners. As the Japanese expand their economic empire, Komai argues, "Japanese society characterized by exclusionism and group egoism springs up in clusters around the world."[127]

One reflection of this is the marked favoritism for domestically produced goods among overseas Japanese subsidiaries. One 1988 Australian survey, for example, found that Japanese firms purchased at least four fifths of their equipment exclusively from Japan, far more than either their American or European counterparts, who tended to be more partial to local or third country suppliers.[128] Another report, issued in 1991 by the President's Council of Economic Advisers, found Japanese firms in the United States eight times more likely to import equipment than American multinationals.[129]

The culture of "exclusionism and corporate egoism" extends as well to the daily operations of such subsidiaries, even in the most advanced countries. Japanese firms, for example, generally employ expatriate Japanese managers at a rate ten to twenty times greater than that of their rivals from Europe or North America.[130] In many cases, Japanese executives seem to view foreigners as barely capable of performing the most basic managerial tasks, with even supposedly high-ranking executives frequently overruled by Japanese "shadow managers," who actually exercise control over critical decisions[131] and in some cases are even prohibited from contacting Tokyo without consulting a Japanese staff member.[132] As Bruce Fane, a former top official at a Los Angeles bank purchased by the Mitsui group, recalled of his days under Japanese supervision:

> There was absolutely a sense they thought they were better—I saw it in the virtual exclusion of Americans from decision making. Nobody ever said we were stupid, but there was in the air a feeling that the Americans had to be watched and their judgment was not to be trusted.[133]

In the worst case, such contempt can even spill over into a sort of mean-spirited and ill-contained racism, particularly when applied to Asians, who many Japanese consider intrinsically inferior to Euro-Americans. For generations, Koreans, for example, both those living inside and outside of Japan, have been treated as inferiors, often as slave laborers in mines and at other hazardous jobs, have been denied citizenship rights—and even barred from competition with Japanese children in local high school sports events.[134] An attempt to erect a memorial for Korean workers killed at Hiroshima was quashed by local authorities—although a similar plaque commemorating martyred pet dogs remains prominently displayed.[135]

Nor do the vast majority of Japanese seem anxious to allow

any more Asians into their country, although economic necessity caused by shortages of labor virtually assures that foreign
workers—estimated to have been as many as 300,000 by 1990[136]
—will continue to dribble into the country.[137] "They could destroy the harmony of our society," argues author Hajime Yamamoto, one of the leading critics of the new immigration. "Low
crime rates and little social disorder have been the pillars of our
society. Can we still maintain those standards?"[138]

Such ethnocentric attitudes often color the views of the Japanese toward neighboring Asian nations. Much like their predecessors earlier this century, Japanese nationalists such as
Shintaro Ishihara consider the region as "Japan's franchise"[139]
and natural sphere of influence. They point to Japan's leading
role as the largest national source of aid and investment[140] in
the region—up sixfold between 1985 and 1990, three times that
of America—as proof of their growing domination. Indeed, an
official at the Japanese Economic Planning Agency told one reporter that he envisioned the various Asian economies "like a
flock of geese" following the guidance of an Asian "brain"
based in Tokyo.[141]

Few Asians, however, with the notable exception of those in
the Malaysian government, seem likely to accept such a conde-
scending notion of Japanese "economic leadership."[142] To
Mohammed Raees, Japanese attitudes are simply too ethnocentric to allow any genuine solidarity with other Asians. He recalls, for example, how his colleagues—at home often quite
polite in their treatment of subordinates—were instructed by
their superiors upon arrival in Bangladesh to use a commanding tone with the *mushikera,* or "worms," as they described the
locals.

When Raees attempted to get his superiors to treat at least
educated Bangladeshis with respect, he was told this was
counterproductive and even dangerous to the maintenance of
the Japanese aura of superiority. Not surprisingly, Raees reports, the Japanese he worked with were "hated due to their
attitude" by most of the Bangladeshis under their supervision.[143]

Japanese firms in Asia, although not always so brutal, seem

at least as reluctant as those in the West to bring the indigene-ous population into their core management. At Yaohan Corpo-ration, a firm that prides itself on its long-term commitment to Asia, Hiroshi Takahashi, the managing director of operations in Kuala Lumpur, complains openly of the tremendous problems with training employees at his showcase stores, starting with the recitation of the company song. Even customers, he sug-gests, had to be trained to behave in a modern Japanese-style superstore. In his spartan office within the sprawling Yaohan complex, the affable Takahashi recalls the preparations for the store's opening in 1987:

> We had to teach people everything. We had to teach them how to use the escalators. We had to take them by the hand and ride up and down the escalators. We had to train people how to use the shopping baskets and the checkout counters.[144]

Not surprisingly, Takahashi doesn't believe that the locals are ready to take a leading role in management. Although strict visa policies by the Malaysian officials have limited Yaohan to 15 Japanese employees out of a work force of 1,400, virtually all the key positions remain in their hands. Not even its joint ven-ture *bumiputra,* or Malaysian, partner has much say. "The man-agement of Yaohan Malaysia is 100 percent Japanese," he admits, adding, "The *bumi* partner just takes some of the money."

At the same time, although lower-level workers seemed rea-sonably satisfied with such a stance,[145] surveys by the Asian Productivity Center in the late 1980s found high levels of frus-tration among the more educated, managerially oriented em-ployees, who saw little chance of promotion within the Japanese organization. Most, including those still working for Japanese firms, saw American or European firms as far more open to local executives. According to a 1990 Mitsui Bank Re-search Institute study, it took twelve years for a typical local manager to be promoted to even a junior position, three times the average for other foreign or locally controlled firms.[146] Even after over three decades in the country, for instance, Toyota

Motors' top Thai employee remained an associate director, four layers from the top.[147] As one college-educated Thai woman in her mid-thirties complained:

> I have a lot of friends who work for joint ventures with Japanese firms. Most of them are frustrated because they do not get promoted even though they are very talented. It is only the Japanese who get promoted to executive positions.[148]

Many Asians regard such attitudes as reflective of a self-centered and rather imperialistic approach to the region.[149] Throughout Asia, Japanese subsidiaries tend to be concentrated largely on low value added products, employing the lowest possible level of technology and lowest development of local skills.[150] They point out the general reluctance of Japanese firms to establish research and development facilities in their countries[151] as well as their refusal to transfer anything but the most outmoded technologies.

Resentment toward this approach is most pronounced among those Asians, such as overseas Chinese and Koreans, who increasingly see themselves as potential global competitors with Tokyo. For these groups, with their own considerable financial and technological resources, Japan's self-appointed championship of itself as Asia's "brain" seems nothing more than a repeat of past imperial arrogance.

This perception of Japanese economic expansionism as essentially closed, stingy and self-centered has been further intensified by the relative inaccessibility of Japan's markets to even East Asia's most internationally competitive products such as bicycles, furniture, toys, tape and silicon wafers.[152] By the 1990s these economies—effective exporters to the rest of the world—suffered among the most lopsided and fastest growing deficits of all of Japan's partners.[153]

As a result, many Asians in the early 1990s began to shift their emphasis away from seeking Japanese partners and toward what appeared to be more promising opportunities with the more flexible American and European firms. In cutting-edge industries such as semiconductors and computers, Taiwanese firms usually found American companies more innovative, straightforward and open to buying Taiwanese products than their more closed Japanese competitors.[154] As Cyrus Hui, a leading Chinese venture capitalist, explained at his Hong Kong office:

> The Japanese are not willing to accept people from another cultural background. . . . It seems in Japanese society everything is built around a code—there's no such thing as a real friendship as a Westerner or Chinese may know it. If they can't deal with us as people, how can they deal with us in business?[155]

In the coming decades, such suspicions among Asians may well represent a greater barrier than any potential Western competition,[156] as the strongest economies in Asia—most notably the Koreans and the overseas Chinese—seek strategies designed to fend off any perceived Japanese hegemony. When Korea started opening its financial markets in 1991, for example, Japan's four major securities markets were purposely excluded, while American, British and Hong Kong–based firms were invited in.[157]

Similarly, the 1990 attempt of Hong Kong's Mass Transit Railway to add Japanese, along with English and Chinese, to its train announcements, stirred a howl of protest from local commuters. As a railway official in the colony, the second largest and one of the fastest-growing recipients of Japanese investment,[158] explained: "People said that Hong Kong is not a Japanese community and we shouldn't cater to a minority, or upgrade the status of Japanese people."[159]

CAN JAPAN BE NORMALIZED?

By the early 1990s the perennial trade surpluses with virtually all its major trading partners, the closed nature of its management system and a growing sense of ethnic superiority were driving the Japanese tribe to the brink of global isolation. Some leaders in Western countries—having seen the collapse of their longtime Soviet enemy—have begun to accept the contentions of the "revisionist" school of scholars who argue that "the Japanese paradigm" now represents the single greatest threat to Western civilization.[160]

In a manner reminiscent of other attempts at racial stereotyping—such as those against the Jews in Europe and Anglo-Americans and Japanese during the Second World War—the revisionists, meeting in 1991 under the auspices of the American Central Intelligence Agency, portrayed the Japanese as a "highly directed culture" working toward a common goal of overthrowing the West, and most particularly the United States, in order to become hegemons of the global community. Only a full mobilization of all the Western countries, they suggested, could hope to contain such a determined foe.[161]

Only belatedly have some Japanese come to recognize the validity of some of these criticisms and begun to ponder the critical nature of their problems with the West. Sony founder Akio Morita, one of the most fervent apologists for Japan, admitted after an extended 1992 trip to the West:

> Japanese companies should be aware that European and U.S. tolerance of the state of affairs is reaching its limit. . . . Japanese companies should realize that they will no longer be allowed to continue their single-minded pursuit of economic efficiency and success in the market.[162]

The resistance building to the threat of Japanese hegemony in Asia, as well as in the West, poses profound questions for Japan's long-term expansion; a nation that fundamentally dislikes working with others can only be confounded as it is forced, by political and economic factors, to rapidly increase its presence abroad.[163] In essence, the Japanese tribe can take one of two basic courses. It can either attempt, as some ultranationalists suggest, to impose a sort of global economic hegemony against enormous hostility, or it can seek out some method of normalizing its relations with the rest of the world, in the process accepting an important but far from dominant role in the evolving global economy.

One direct impetus for following a course of normalization lies in the challenge posed by other Asian peoples, notably the Chinese, who have become the second major global tribe to enter the world economy imbued with Confucian attitudes of work and family obligation.[164] But the Chinese enjoy far superior networks of information based on permanent settlements throughout not only East Asia but North America as well, plus powerful natural ties to mainland China. By the early 1990s the overseas Chinese were employing all these factors to tremendous effect, already surpassing the Japanese "diaspora by design" as the largest investors and owners of business assets throughout the burgeoning East Asian region.[165]

There are other clear signs that Japan's global extension may well have reached its furthest limits. The early 1990s witnessed the first significant withdrawals of Japan's leading financial institutions—portrayed both by nationalists such as Shintaro Ishihara and Western observers[166] as on the road to world dominion[167]—from overseas markets both in Asia and in the West.[168] From a late 1980s annual average of $100 billion in outward investments, Japan in 1991, for the first time in over a decade, experienced a shocking $36 billion net capital inflow.[169]

This financial crisis, moreover, revealed a deep-seated weakness within the highly insular Japanese economy. Through formal restrictions and later subtle discrimination against foreign investors and even outsiders within the country, the tightly knit Japanese business community had long been able to bid up the price of its assets to astronomical levels. For a period, these enormous assets made Japan seemingly immune from the shocks and turbulence that afflicted most capitalist economies.

But by the early 1990s this idyll began to break down as international market conditions—such as forcing banks to more adequately cover their capital costs—began to impose new disciplines on the Japanese financial system. With bank and other financial stocks hurting, the Nikkei average fell precipitously along with property values.[170] Previously able to thrive despite what one study called "appallingly low relative" return on assets and equity compared to their main international rivals,[171] Japanese banks no longer could provide their domestic customers with cheap and inexhaustible credit, long a critical element in their global expansion.[172]

Yet the erosion of their financial position may not constitute the greatest challenge facing the Japanese. Perhaps more critical are the changing attitudes among the Japanese themselves, most particularly the young. Some revisionists, of course, reject the very possibility that the Japanese may be evolving away from the notion of a uniformly militant and aggressive people. Japan, according to the authors of the *Japan 2000* report, "is virtually impervious to change, and probably will remain so."[173] Revisionists and many other Japanologists flatly reject the idea that either Japanese "baby boomers" or Japanese in the under-thirty generation—known popularly as the *shinjinrui*, or "new race"—are in any significant way fundamentally different from their parents. To believe so, author Ezra Vogel insists, is nothing more than "public relations" designed to please foreigners.

This is also the hope of many of the old-line nationalist Japanese, who believe rigorous training and school-induced discipline will erode any future sign of different ways of thinking. "Put the *shinjinrui* in a suit and keep him in the company for ten years," Honda Motor Corporation chief executive Nobuhiko Kawamoto believes. "He becomes just like the old breed."[174]

Yet the reality remains that Japan—particularly in its new generation—increasingly no longer resembles the nation of aggressive workers depicted by the CIA-sponsored *Japan 2000* report as "driven by pride, nationalism and downright irrationality." One 1991 MITI survey, for example, found the contemporary generation of Japanese the *least* ready to die for its country among its counterparts in ten major countries—and also the least likely to express pride in its country's companies.[175]

These postnational sentiments are most deeply felt among Japan's young, a group largely outside the purview of most Western journalists and intellectuals. The first generation of Japanese to grow up in affluence, they are also the group who must cope with what Takeshi Umehara, director general of the International Center for Japanese Studies, has called a "culturally empty prosperity" that offers little to either the rest of humanity or to posterity.[176]

One clear sign of this has been a diminishment in identification with the Japanese nation-state. Few young people, for example, want to serve their country in the Self-Defense Force; out of 70,000 letters sent to prospective recruits in 1990, according to a chief recruiter, there were virtually no replies.[177] In a good month, a Tokyo-based recruiter said, he might get four or five recruits, mostly high school dropouts.[178]

In addition, recent developments in their society, notably a seemingly ceaseless spate of scandals involving prominent businesses and political leaders, have led many Japanese, again most notably the young, to reject many of the basic aspects of Japan's postwar political economy. Their parents might have endured low living standards without complaint even as Japan's corporations became the world's wealthiest; but a vast majority of Japanese between the ages of twenty-six and thirty-five, according to a survey by the Dentsu Institute for Human Studies, described their society as one where "only companies are rich" and feel that honesty and hard work do not pay off.[179]

This change in attitudes has been largely ignored, in part because it is, in essence, apolitical, a logical response to an essentially one-party state dominated by corrupt, entrenched and elderly politicians. "The individualism is a product of the changes in the society," notes marketing expert Yohko Abe, who has done major research on youth attitudes. "They are less in rebellion against society, as they are representative of a change in the stages of our development. It's less dramatic, but maybe more lasting a change because it deals with the basic values."[180]

Nowhere is the difference in "basic values" of the two generations more profound than in attitudes toward work. To a large extent, many young Japanese simply seek many of those things —such as satisfying work, time with family and friends—that had been denied their parents. Most particularly they tend to detest the stifling workplace conditions that have made Japan's workers, according to a 1990 Asian Productivity Council survey, among the least satisfied of any group in an advanced industrial country.[181]

Tsunehiro Suzuki's own father was a classic Japanese of the old school, a manager of a small firm that manufactures screws in Kanagawa Prefecture, about an hour's train trip west of Tokyo. Family life, such things as spending time with his son, seemed to mean almost nothing to the senior Suzuki. "Unfortunately, I never talked to my father," the handsome, well-dressed twenty-seven-year-old says a little sadly. "His hobby was working."[182]

The reaction to such experiences among many young people such as Suzuki increasingly is to question the monomaniacal addiction to work and company so characteristic of their parents' generation. In 1979 Japanese youngsters, according to a survey by the prime minister's office, regarded work as the center of their life by a margin of two to one over their American counterparts.[183] But by 1990, young Japanese—in sharp contrast to previous generations—were arguably less work-oriented and more self-oriented than their counterparts in the United States. Asked by Dentsu to identify their purpose for living, fewer Tokyoites under thirty named work than did their counterparts in either New York or Los Angeles. In contrast, self-improvement, the supposed be-all of Southern California's "me"-oriented society, was named twice as frequently as a top priority by young Japanese.[184]

Inevitably some Japanese see the "new race" as a product of insidious Western, and particularly American, influence. Soswke Kato, an owner of a a small culinary academy in northern Japan, for example, complained that his students—mostly from working-class families—lack the "Confucian values" that underlie the legendary Japanese virtues of loyalty, hard work and respect for elders. "The young people today are getting the wrong information from the U.S.A.," the sixty-three-year-old said bitterly. "Being lazy, having fun, enjoying life—that these are good things and that to sweat and work are not trendy."

Yet, in reality, the new attitudes are not so much a product of foreign influence as they are phenomena of Japan's own peculiar history and its pattern of postwar economic development.

Growing up amidst the rubble of defeat, the current ruling class in Japan entered the workplace at the dawn of the nation's postwar economic ascendancy. The Japanese value structure of the time placed the country first, then the company, followed by family and, last, the individual. Most important, work was scarce and people were happy to find any means of making a living.

In contrast, the current generation has been dealt an almost opposite set of conditions, most particularly a critical labor shortage in Japan that is likely to get only more severe in the near future.[185] In 1990, there were roughly two positions for every high school graduate and three for every male college graduate in Japan and the projected gap for research and development technicians alone was projected at 200,000.[186]

These new conditions allow young Japanese to indulge in such hitherto rare luxuries as job-hopping. A 1990 survey of students by the Economic Planning Agency, for instance, found only 15 percent of college seniors planned to follow the traditional pattern of lifetime employment after graduation.[187] Among employees of small and medium-size companies, people under thirty were found to be two to three times more willing to switch jobs than workers over forty.[188]

Equally revealing, many younger Japanese also expressed reluctance to enter careers in traditional mainline Japanese industries, including electronics and automobiles, with large numbers looking for more "creative" opportunities in the arts or media.[189] All these new attitudes, suggests Mitsuko Shimomura, one of Japan's leading social commentators, seem likely to shift Japanese society away from its current monomaniacal obsession with economic growth and expansion. Products of the huge social distortions on the Japanese family caused by the frenetic postwar economic boom, the next generation of Japanese, particularly the males, Shimomura suggests, lacks the basic psychological fortitude of its predecessors, who challenged the world and willingly suffered enormous hardships in the process.

Deserted by their husbands, Japanese mothers—who traditionally shared such duties with men—took solitary control over the upbringing of their youngsters, creating a generation of what Shimomura calls "mother-obsessed neurotics." As she puts it:

> Unfortunately the ever present mother is not a myth. She's there all the time—it's too much! The mother not only focuses all her energy, but she vents all her frustration on the kids. She sticks to them day and night. Mothers use kids as a replacement for their husbands who are always working.[190]

The result, Shimomura maintains, has been to create a generation ill suited for dealing with the stresses that come with corporate life in an economic superpower and a deep yearning for escape from responsibility. In the workplace, they tend to be indifferent and passive; one former manager at IBM Japan calls them "the goldfish generation" because they have to be hand-fed everything.

"I notice that many of my [young] male colleagues can't make decisions. They're brilliant, they are enormously talented and well educated; they just can't put it together and conduct their own lives," observes Shimomura. "They're so used to everything being handed to them before they ask, they can't even dig up a source or find an alternative if the person they ask for an interview says no. They just give up and don't know what to do next."

Perhaps most important, she notes, the new generation may also prove reluctant to take on the hardships and risks, particularly in terms of international assignments, that made possible the earlier expansion of the "diaspora by design." Used to the comfortable, largely ersatz cosmopolitanism of Tokyo or Osaka, many younger Japanese seem to regard overseas assignments as more of an inconvenience than an opportunity.

In this sense, noted Tsuneo Iida, professor of economics at Kyoto's International Institute for Japanese Studies, the soldiers necessary to operate and direct any future global conquest are likely to be missing in action. The corporate samurai of the 1980s, he suggested, were slowly being transformed into the consummate consumers and tourists of the 1990s.

When I was young, Japan was very poor, so we wanted to go outside and go to the United States and Europe. Ten or twenty years ago being posted abroad was an elite course, but now it's not so. . . . The young Japanese see the world as a place to vacation, not work.[191]

To some Japanese these changes seem a sign that the tribe has become exhausted and is perched upon the precipice of a major decline. But author and venture capitalist Hiroshi Kato views this transformation as critical for Japan's gradual acceptance into the cosmopolitan world economy, a necessary correction from a culture that has been distorted by its almost single-minded quest for economic expansion. By seeking a return to more traditional values of family and other nonpecuniary aspects of life, Kato sees the first stages of a normalization critical for a global tribe that likely has achieved its furthest possible extension.

Kato envisions, in place of the much-feared hyperindustrialized Japan, the development of a more well-rounded, affluent nation, transforming the world's most fearsome economic power into a respected contributor to the world society. With their traditions of artisanry and their unsurpassed industrial networks, Kato believes, the Japanese can remain assured of their continuing importance even as the other Asian tribes—most notably the Chinese—begin to assume central stage.

The critical issue, he suggests, is that this normalization be carried out quickly and effectively, before stubborn nationalist pressures turn them into a pariah race, outside the pale of both Asia and the West. "We must become a normal country. A country that has accumulated money like England in the 1950s," Kato said as he looked at the squat Diet building across from his central Tokyo office. "The work ethic will be more normal, the savings rate more normal. Maybe the kids are telling us Japanese enjoy happiness and home and the decreasing of money. There's nothing wrong with that."

CHAPTER SIX

THE SPACEMEN HAVE LANDED

OVER LUNCH in a squat office building behind the Holiday Inn in Torrance, California, Denny Ko shares his vision of the next great Asian economic empire. Over the last decade of the twentieth century, Ko sees the emergence of a new Chinese-run network of technology companies nurtured amidst the elite universities and high-technology laboratories of California, an empire capable of challenging, and ultimately overcoming, the Japanese quest for global dominance.

Since 1976, when he founded his own consulting firm, Dynamics Technology, the American-educated engineer has built upon his vision, covering technologies as diverse as electronic imaging, microwave transmissions and, in 1991, a bid to buy into McDonnell-Douglas's California-based commercial aircraft operations. Ko, a fifty-one-year-old graduate of Berkeley and the California Institute of Technology, explained the role of his adopted home state in the emerging Chinese-based economy:

California is the starter for the barbecue. You come up with ideas
and heat the coals and when it's already heated, then you move
it to another spot. And then you light the starter again with
another idea.[1]

Chinese like Ko constitute only one small portion of the
emerging Chinese economic network. Spread among over a
dozen countries around the Pacific, the overseas Chinese control an "empire" that is multinational by nature, essentially an
archipelago of critical nodes ranging from centers throughout
Southeast Asia to Taiwan, Hong Kong, and the coastal provinces of China as well as overseas outposts in such places as
Canada, California, New York and the United Kingdom.[2]

Taiwan, the source of most of Denny Ko's financial backing,
represents arguably the strongest center of this economic empire. A tiny island with only 20 million people, Taiwan has
emerged as one of East Asia's most successful and technologically advanced states. Seen as recently as the late 1970s as
largely a center for low-wage, low value added production, Taiwan is rapidly emerging as a new epicenter for design, high
technology and science. Today Taiwan ranks sixth in the world
in, and stands as Asia's second largest producer of, computer-
related products.[3] In personal computers, according to some
estimates, Taiwan ranks among the top three producers.[4]

This enormous productive power has helped make Taiwan
one of the world's wealthiest nations; with foreign currency
reserves estimated by some analysts as second only to Japan's,
Taiwan is rapidly emerging as a financial powerhouse of the
first order.[5] But Taiwan represents only one component of this
mounting Chinese economic power. The wealth of the Chinese
in Southeast Asia and Hong Kong alone is estimated as high as
$250 billion, which is equally daunting. With American, Euro-
pean and Japanese banks under severe strain as they entered
the 1990s,[6] the cash-rich Chinese seem uniquely well positioned.

By the early 1990s Hong Kong, Singapore and Taiwan—the
most developed centers of the Chinese diaspora—taken together were emerging as fast-growing Southeast Asia's largest

foreign source of capital, several times larger than the Americans and ahead even of the hard-charging Japanese in many of the key nations such as Indonesia, Malaysia and the Phillipines.[7] Chinese also have become the largest investors in Vietnam, which could emerge over the next decade as another Asian "dragon."[8]

Throughout this region, the world's fastest-growing consumer market,[9] Chinese-owned firms have established powerful presences in fields as diverse as business services, food products and toys and increasingly challenge the Japanese in televisions, telecommunications and computers. Similarly, firms from Hong Kong, Taiwan and other diaspora centers represent easily the largest source of foreign investment within mainland China, itself both an enormous source of inexpensive labor and raw materials and a huge potential market.[10]

The Chinese expansion also extends beyond Asia. Seeking markets, as well as potential safe havens, Chinese-based investors have been increasingly active in some Western developed countries, most notably the United States, Canada, Australia and the United Kingdom. By the early 1990s Chinese entrepreneurs, largely from Taiwan and Hong Kong, also were expanding their activities in Latin America, including such countries as Panama, Guatemala, Costa Rica, Honduras[11] and, most important, Mexico.[12]

The pattern and fundamental character of the Chinese global extension differ dramatically from those of the Japanese. In contrast to the exceedingly close ties between the Japanese *salarimen* abroad and their home islands, the Chinese global network possesses no fixed national point of origin, no central "brain." The industries now heavily under Chinese influence— such as garments, toys, watches and, increasingly, computers[13] —are controlled by executives whose residences can range from Thailand and Indonesia to Taiwan, Hong Kong or California.

Instead of following the strategic decisions of large institutions, Chinese capital tends to be in the hands of private investors and circulates freely from country to country, often handled by various branches of the same family. Funds invested one week in Malaysia find their way to Thailand or Canada the next, often disguised under corporate fronts that make tracing the money trail virtually impossible.[14]

Equally important, unlike the Japanese, whose managers come and go much like missionaries devoted to their corporate Vatican, the Chinese often choose to settle permanently in the regions where they conduct business. California, for example, with roughly one million Chinese,[15] represents the largest diaspora settlement outside of Asia. Like Denny Ko, many of the state's top engineers and scientists—at least as many as 12,000 in Silicon Valley alone[16]—are of Chinese descent.

Nor is their presence likely to shrink in the years ahead. By 1990 the number of American university doctorates in science and engineering granted to students of Chinese descent more than tripled, accounting for one third of the foreign total, far more than any other single ethnic group.[17] At the elite University of California they account for two in every five foreign engineering and science graduates.[18]

Increasingly, these engineers are more than mere technological fodder for American companies. Hundreds of them, much like Denny Ko, have formed companies, often with financial links and production facilities within the Chinese-dominated economies of East Asia and mainland China. Constantly traveling between North American centers such as Los Angeles and their various Asian bastions, these transpacific nomads— known in Taiwan as *tai kung fei jen,* or "spacemen"—represent a unique new breed, a modern-day variant of the "wandering Jew" of the European past, living their business and personal lives in numerous venues.

To Chinese spacemen such as Denny Ko, such a bifurcated existence suggests no test of divided loyalties. Like Ko, many spacemen are themselves products of previous migrations. Ko's father, a rich landowner from Fukien province, had moved during the Japanese invasion of China to Hong Kong, where Denny was born. Shortly after returning home, the Ko family was on the run again, this time escaping the Communists. Broke upon his arrival in Taiwan, Ko's father struggled to put his children through school, mostly in the United States. With an ancestral home in China, birthplace in Hong Kong and a boyhood spent in Taiwan, Ko then lived the bulk of his adult life and raised his family in California.

Their background leads spacemen such as Ko to think not so much in terms of nations or states but of a seamless global network connecting communities nevertheless united by a common ethnic identity. To him, choice of residence, work and investment remains largely a matter of pragmatic considerations. Taiwan may remain the preferred locale for making money, and directing business affairs, but not for raising a family. As Ko explains:

> Once you know the difference in quality of life, you want to live in California. I know very well. Maybe one in ten who comes here goes back permanently. They say they live in Taiwan while doing business, but they live their personal lives here.

Such seemingly disingenuous sentiments, Ko insists, actually represent a key asset in the struggle of the Chinese against their Japanese rivals in Asia. As residents and citizens of various countries, he asserts, the Chinese spacemen learn far more than the rotating Japanese *salarimen* about their countries of residence and naturally adopt a more cooperative, flexible approach in dealing with partners. U.S.-based research and development operations—critical to all but a few Taiwanese technology companies—are run by American-educated executives, sometimes family members, fluent in English and with long experience living in the United States.[19] Japanese firms, on the other hand, are largely outposts manned by rotating executives whose only true standards are those of the home islands and whose foreign minions are largely consigned to irrelevance.

Indeed, much like the great Jewish businessmen such as the Rothschilds, whose family settled in numerous European cities, Chinese entrepreneurs remain, in essence, arbitrageurs, their widespread dispersion a critical means of identifying prime business opportunities and developing the means to exploit them. It is the diaspora itself—not any nation-state or group of corporate entities—that underlies the emergence of Chinese economic power. As Denny Ko observes:

The Chinese are a closely knit community, wherever you find them; over the last forty years, they have established ties with each other. Sometimes it seems like everyone's related. I know someone in Taiwan, and he knows someone else in Hong Kong, and you link them together and you have this network, and you find this opportunity. That's how it works.

THE JEWS OF THE EAST

From the time Europeans began to penetrate the markets of Southeast Asia, they quickly noted the presence of a race, not native to the region, that had gained economic preeminence while retaining its cultural distinctiveness. As early as 1621, Sir Thomas Herbert, a British traveler, described the local Chinese merchants as "Jew-like," making their living by "gleaning here and there" to make profit under the most difficult circumstances. In the late eighteenth century, a Dutch admiral, Johan Splinter Stavorinus, noting the Chinese control and management of sugar refineries in Java, also was reminded of the business activities of the Jews in his native Holland.[20]

The Chinese movement into Southeast Asia had begun even before Jews were forced from their devastated Palestinian homeland by the Romans. But unlike the case of the Jews, who were essentially refugees, what one writer called "China's march toward the tropics"[21] began as an expression of imperial ambitions rather than an escape from persecution. Encouraged by expansion-minded emperors, Chinese traders established posts as far away as Afghanistan, and their silks were well known among the Roman upper classes.[22] Later on, Chinese political and economic influence expanded to locales as remote as Vietnam, Malaysia, Cambodia and Java.[23]

Yet, until the sixteenth century, the Chinese had left behind only a few small colonies in a wide arc of Southeast Asian lands,[24] their influence restricted largely to local middlemen who had established themselves in Sumatra, Java and the kingdom of Siam, where a handful of Chinese gained positions as government officials.[25] Culturally, the influence of India, notes historian Victor Purcell, remained far more important.[26]

But with the onset of the seventeenth century the migration of Chinese began to accelerate. Seeking to escape Manchu repression as well as increased poverty, millions of Chinese sought better fortune in the newly European-dominated regions of Southeast Asia.

Like the Jews in Poland and elsewhere in Europe, the Chinese in Southeast Asia dominated many critical commercial niches as traders, artisans and skilled workers, often filling the "middleman" role between the dominant elite—made up of European merchants, plantation owners and colonial officials—and the masses of native agriculturalists. Cut off from their native land, much like the Jews, they had little alternative but to engage in such activities as trading and money lending. As Rustam Sani, a senior fellow at the Malaysian Institute for Strategic and International Studies, explains:

> They had no choice but to become active in business, in trade. Malays could retreat to the land because they owned the land. They could go back to the villages. But the Chinese had no choice except in business. . . . They became well entrenched.[27]

The Chinese in Malaysia, whom one British official described as "indefatigable in the pursuit of money,"[28] became so "entrenched" that they seemed to force the native people—the *bumiputras*, or "sons of the soil"—into the economic background. "I have written a great deal about the Chinese and very little about the Malays, the nominal possessors of the country," noted British author Isabella Bird, "but the Chinese may be said to be everywhere and the Malays nowhere."[29]

By the late nineteenth century the Chinese role in the Nanyang, as they called Southeast Asia, extended from petty trading and the management of European estates to providing agricultural credit.[30] Far more than the native Malays or Thais, the Chinese quickly adapted to the new conditions brought on by the European ascendancy, learning the languages, customs and standards imposed from the West. Although their relations with the Europeans were often marred by racial prejudice and occasional violence, many colonial authorities regarded the Chinese as a key commercial asset for developing their possessions.

In 1920 British colonial officer Frank Swettenham, stationed in Malaysia, observed of the Chinese:

> Their energy and enterprise have made the Malay States what they are to-day, and it would be impossible to overstate the obligation which the Malay Government and people are under to these hard-working, capable and law-abiding aliens. . . . They brought all the capital when European feared to risk.[31]

Such an admiring disposition often was not shared among the native inhabitants, who frequently felt exploited and displaced by the Chinese. When the king of Siam, Rama VI, first labeled them "the Jews of the East" in 1914, it was not meant as a testament to their intelligence or industry but to point out their less positive, allegedly "Jewish," characteristics such as overcompetitiveness, greed and double-dealing.[32] The Chinese, the king complained, "lived like rats" and ate "food not fit for human consumption" in order to undersell and undercut their competitors.[33]

Even worse, Rama and others complained, the Chinese, even if naturalized citizens, remained loyal only to themselves and their native land.[34] They were thus willing to cooperate with European colonialists or anyone else, no matter how unsavory, who promised them the lure of economic gain. As one Asian proverb put it: "The Chinese do not care who holds the cow so long as they milk it."[35]

The Chinese communities, like those of the Jews in Europe, certainly remained separate from others, choosing to maintain their own subeconomies, community associations and community leaders, as well as the inevitable criminal rings. In many cases the vitality of this parallel society often seemed greater than that of other groups. James Lyng, a lieutenant in the British army serving in the colony of New Britain in New Guinea in 1919, described Rabaul's Chinatown:

> It is as if a little East-Asiatic township, by some magical power, had been transplanted to New Britain. . . . There are a half

dozen stores there, several restaurants, tailors, laundries and bookmakers; butchers, bakers, carpenters, mechanics, etc. . . .

Over and above all, Chinatown is Rabaul's busy, unruly corner—where people rise early—are always on the move—and go to bed late. While after sunset the European corner becomes quiet, and the streets look empty and desolate, life in Chinatown moves on—intense—rapid—and wicked.[36]

These communities, if not exact replicas of mainland China, preserved a strong sense of ethnic identity. In virtually every country of settlement—from the wilds of Borneo to the burgeoning commercial port of Singapore—Chinese schools, like the religious institutions of the Jews, sought to make sure that the next generation would not forget its origins and critical cultural values espoused in the writings of Confucius. The ideal, noted sociologist D. Stanley Eitzen, was to shape good *Chinese* —and then good residents of the land of settlement.[37]

Some predicted that the Chinese would soon lose their distinctiveness in their dispersion,[38] much as had been repeatedly said about the Jews. But not only did they retain their identity through the centuries, the late 1980s actually saw a resurgence of interest in Chinese culture in areas such as Singapore and Thailand, where previously assimilationist tendencies had been most marked. Confucianism in particular, once derided by Chinese and Westerners alike as a source of backwardness and superstition, has enjoyed a renaissance, being credited in large part for providing the ethical foundation for contemporary success among Chinese, as well as Koreans and Japanese.

Singapore's Chinese-dominated leadership, which long has promoted English over their native language, in 1990 even launched a Speak Mandarin campaign with the slogan "If you are Chinese, make a statement in Mandarin." Some non-Chinese Singaporeans complained,[39] but Ow Chin Hock, a young member of the ruling People's Action party, defended the new cultural drive by explaining: "People will respect someone only if that person respects himself and his own culture and language."[40]

It is the adherence to these cultural factors—to language, heritage, a sense of values—that most strongly defines the Chinese. The great revolutionary leader Sun Yat-sen might have sought to define the Chinese as a "single race with common blood," but in reality this is no more true for them than for the English, the Jews and the Japanese; their diversity of racial ancestry can be seen in how Chinese differ markedly from region to region in height, color and bone structure.[41]

At the same time, the Chinese attachment to their "vocation of uniqueness" differs radically from that of the Jews. A people from a small, rather politically insignificant country, the Jews derived their specialness largely from their unique religious and historical experience in diaspora. In contrast, the Chinese tribe's inspiration stems from the enormous *material* accomplishments of what may arguably be considered the world's greatest imperial tradition. The Jews claimed to be the "chosen people" of Abraham, Isaac and Jacob, all religious figures, but Chinese mythology stems from essentially political leaders, such as the "Yellow Emperor," Huang Ti, the mythological founder of the first Chinese dynasty, whose consort was credited with the development of the practical art of silkworm breeding and the weaving of the fabric.[42]

But China is not merely a country, like France, Germany or even Britain. It is also, as historian Maurice Freedman pointed out, *t'ien hsia*, "all-under heaven, a civilization (*the* civilization in its own estimation) embracing its neighbors without imposing its culture on them."[43] This self-confidence reflected, to a large extent, the long-standing status of what the Chinese called "The Middle Kingdom" as among the most stable, largest and most powerful realms on earth, and also arguably the most technically advanced. In everything from agriculture to medicine, from the invention of paper and gunpowder to the early designs for steam engines, China held a significant lead over most other societies.[44] Its cities, noted Marco Polo, the Venetian traveler of the late thirteenth and early fourteenth centuries, included "without doubt the finest and most splendid in the world."[45]

Unlike the Japanese, whose attitude toward the outside world has oscillated between defensiveness and aggression, the

Chinese generally have assumed the centrality and intrinsic superiority of their civilization. This self-confidence and an overwhelming desire to maintain their cultural continuity stand at
the heart of their "vocation of uniqueness." As Harold Isaacs
once observed:

> The Chinese are also possessors of a Great Past, indeed, in what
> is often the not-very-humble opinion common among them, the
> Greatest of all Pasts. . . . Indeed they see themselves as without
> peer, above all the peoples on the earth, far above, for example,
> the Japanese, whose tradition they see as junior and derivative
> from the Chinese in all its important beginnings.[46]

THE NEW CHINESE

This powerful sense of shared communal identity worked directly for centuries as a barrier to any mass migration, particularly with the growth of anticommercial, neo-Confucianist
tendencies in the late Ming and early Manchu periods.[47] Even
as tiny European nation-states such as Portugal and Holland
began to assert themselves on the periphery of Asia, the tradi-
tionalist revival led the Chinese administrations to haughtily
reject contact or trade with the newcomers.[48]

The inward-looking Mandarins also hoped to isolate their
people by essentially locking Chinese inside their country. By
the mid-seventeenth century the Ch'ing dynasty forbade migration for either trade or settlement, and in 1712 it ordered all
Chinese living overseas to return home.[49] These measures also
played upon traditional Chinese values, particularly ancestor
worship, which obligated, among other things, the constant
maintenance of family tombs, making emigration rather unap-
pealing.[50]

As a result, the vanguard of China's expansion into Southeast
Asia and beyond—the eventual shapers of Chinese capitalism—
developed among those living on the periphery of their tottering empire, where imperial interests and influence was weakest.
From the beginning of Western settlement, starting with the

Portuguese in Macao in 1519,[51] Chinese officials endeavored to keep commercial relations with the West restricted to regions, mostly in the southeastern coastal region, largely seen as expendable enough to suffer direct contact with the *kweilos* (foreign devils). Many of these areas had not even been settled by Chinese until after the third century B.C.[52] and seemed barely civilized compared to the older settled regions north of the Yangtze River.

Even less in the mainstream of Chinese culture was Taiwan, which in the third century was referred to as *I-chou*, or "Barbarian Island," and had initially been populated largely by Malays. Chinese settlement, mostly from nearby Fukien province, began in earnest in the sixteenth century—and even then it was barely considered part of the Chinese empire.[53] So unimportant was the island that when others, notably the Portuguese and the Dutch, established colonial outposts on it, there was barely a protest from Peking.[54] Only with the overthrow of the Ming dynasty in 1644 by the Manchus did China establish a hold on Taiwan; even then it remained the scene of continuous social turmoil, lawlessness and unrest until shortly before being ceded to the Japanese in 1895.[55]

For their part, the southern Chinese often took advantage of the surrounding chaos to defy the rules and regulations of the northern-centered imperial state. In the face of imperial edicts, they profited from illegal trade and even settled abroad at times when being an immigrant, or *hua qiao*, was tantamount to being "an enemy of the state."[56] Later on, as Chinese immigration increased, the southerners supplied over three fifths of all emigrants to Southeast Asia as well as the bulk of those moving to North America and Oceania.[57]

The new cities settled by these ill-regarded southerners and coastal dwellers—Hong Kong, Singapore, Shanghai—provided the setting for what Singapore-based investor Ong Beng Seng has called "the transformation of Chinese peasant-entrepreneurs into an urban people."[58] Under the influence of the latest technologies and business trends from Europe, Japan and America, "a new kind of Chinese" arose, notes historian Rhoads Murphey.[59] These new Chinese were cosmopolitan, commercially sophisticated, yet still wedded to the intrinsic tribal identity.

These Chinese were also the first to abandon old ways of thought, cut off the queue (symbol of subservience to the hated Manchus) and don Western dress.[60] Equally important, as sociologist Ambrose King has observed, these new Chinese—far from the traditional centers of the "great Confucian tradition" —began to change some of their traditional belief systems.[61] In the crucible of the new Chinese cities, observes King, Confucianism evolved into something he describes as "the culture of rationalistic traditionalism," a combination of traditional filial and group virtues with a pragmatism shaped by the conditions of a new competitive environment.[62]

Critically, in sharp contrast to their Japanese counterparts, whose Meiji-era modernization left them still largely insular in their attitudes and customers, these new Chinese developed along highly cosmopolitan lines. Unlike their Japanese rivals, Chinese could never rely on a large and protected home market.[63] They could not, like the Japanese, develop their domestic market first and then expand outward from the established commercial centers such as Osaka or Tokyo.

Instead, like the Jews in their European diaspora, the Chinese, without firm roots in their lands of settlement, remained both flexible and geographically mobile. Like the Russian or Polish Jews, they also tended to embrace Western European technology or philosophy more quickly than the indigenous people surrounding them, allowing them to benefit more decisively from the spread of Western capitalism.

The early phases of Chinese global extension, notes Japanese economist Yoshihara Kunio, relied almost exclusively on the pathways created by the European powers, most notably the British. European capital, technology and what Kunio calls the "institutional-legal order" permitted the overseas Chinese to advance in ways all but impossible for their counterparts back home, who were forced to endure a succession of horrendous political conditions—from the reactionary and often arbitrary Ch'ings, to the chaos of the civil war and Japanese occupation, to the accession to power of the Communists.[64]

The rise of the Chinese, however, was based on more than a blind acceptance of Westernization; it also involved the application of traditional values in a radically new situation. Confucian values that emphasized learning, for example, served the Chinese much as the Talmudic tradition had aided the Jews in Europe—by providing a cultural predisposition toward scholarship and academic achievement. As Chinese philosopher Tu Wei-ming points out, Confucianism placed enormous value on the search for knowledge and self-improvement, even in the most difficult conditions.[65]

> . . . if the body politic is not yet in order or if peace has not yet pervaded under Heaven, the effort of self-cultivation should not be interrupted. Learning [*hsueh*] . . . requires an ultimate and a continuous commitment.[66]

In the Westernized parts of Asia, notes Ambrose King, the new Chinese simply shifted their emphasis of education from a means of achieving higher social position to a "perquisite for material wealth."[67] A traditional emphasis once focused on the tribe's classical tradition became diverted into the more modern channels of local trade schools, colleges and universities.[68]

The emergence of this new technically sophisticated Chinese tribe became evident early in Singapore and Penang, where by the 1830s the Chinese constituted an absolute majority of the population.[69] From their inception, the Straits Chinese developed close ties with British interests and quickly appreciated the importance of using English language and standards. By the late nineteenth century Singapore's emerging Chinese middle class was already sending its children to the local Raffles Institution—and even on to Cambridge.[70]

This rising Chinese class possessed what historian Michael Godley has described as "an amazing willingness to split their personalities" between British and Chinese characteristics. Some, like the tycoon Foo Choo Choon, managed to be both British subjects and Ch'ing officials at the same time. Another of these "Anglo-Chinese gentlemen," Singapore businessman Lee Bok Boon, returned home to China in order to use his wealth to purchase a rank in the Ch'ing bureaucracy[71]; yet arrangements were made for an English education for his son, left behind in Singapore.[72] By the 1960s Lee's great-grandson, Lee Kuan Yew, had emerged as the leader of the newly independent Singaporean state. Highly educated in European languages, customs and culture, Lee, a graduate of Cambridge with an outstanding record, boasted that his fine British education made it possible for him to speak "as equals" with top British leaders such as Prime Minister Harold MacMillan.[73]

Later, the United States replaced Britain as the training ground for the Chinese. By the end of the 1980s the number of Chinese-speaking students in the United States was about 90,000, easily the largest number of any ethnic group.[74] At that point the Taiwanese alone accounted for roughly one in every four candidates for doctorates in electrical engineering in the United States.[75]

Over time, this passion for education and exposure to foreign influences forged a remarkable new elite class among the Chinese, increasingly self-confident in their dealings in the world economy. Far better acquainted with the indigenous cultures than the Europeans, they began to challenge Western economic power, particularly in the aftermath of the Great Depression.[76] With America's financial and corporate system in disarray, for example, the burgeoning Chinese community in the Philippines by 1932 controlled as much as four fifths of the colony's retail trade and internal commerce.[77]

Observing these developments, Arnold Toynbee predicted by the early 1930s that the Chinese would soon dominate Southeast Asia's "weaker and less efficient peoples" and gradually supplant the Europeans as well. At the time the overseas Chinese numbered roughly eight million, and most were still petty traders, laborers and artisans,[78] yet from Singapore to the jungles of New Guinea, the smaller European traders were already being squeezed out by "John Chinaman."[79] Toynbee's observation proved prescient.

Today the *hua qiao*—worldwide numbering over fifty million strong—dominate the economies of Southeast Asia, controlling, for example, up to two thirds of the region's retail trade with less than 10 percent of the population.[80] In Thailand, where they make up less than one tenth of the total population, the Chinese control the majority of corporate assets; in Indonesia, where they constitute a mere 5 percent of population, they hold sway over a remarkable 75 percent of assets,[81] with one Chinese conglomerate, the Salim Group, accounting for 5 percent of total GDP.[82] The five billionaires in the two countries are all of Chinese origin.[83]

Even in Malaysia, in the face of a policy of active racial discrimination, the Chinese, who represent slightly more than one third the population,[84] by all accounts dominate the nation's emerging business and technical elite. And they will clearly command that country's high-tech future; although roughly equal to Malays in numbers at the country's universities, by the late 1980s Chinese outnumbered the native *bumiputras* eight to one in science and fifteen to one in engineering.[85]

In business the Chinese often use subterfuge to keep their control over the economy, cleverly employing Malay frontmen, a practice referred to as "Ali-Babaism," to help gain the necessary permits and requisite political influence.[86] As a result, despite the strenuous efforts of the government, Chinese incomes remain twice those of the average Malay, and Chinese control of corporate assets is estimated to be at least six times greater.[87] As Malaysian Prime Minister Dr. Mahatir bin Mohammed once admitted frankly: "Whatever we could do, the Chinese could do better and more cheaply."[88]

THE REFUGEE MENTALITY

Over the past century, the remarkable success of the Chinese diaspora, like that of the Jews, has sparked repeated persecutions. In virtually every land of settlement they have faced discriminatory restrictions, political repression and, at times, pogroms. Even after one hundred years in residence outside China, notes scholar David Wu, the diaspora's circumstance, more often that not, has remained "that of utmost uncertainty."[89]

This condition of "utmost uncertainty" worsened with the passing of the European imperial regimes from Southeast Asia. In occupied Malaysia, Singapore, the Philippines and Indonesia, the Japanese and their native allies denounced the Chinese both for their ties to China and their long-standing economic links with the Europeans. Suspected pro-Ally leaders were singled out for brutal treatment and selective execution.[90] Even so, the British, who worked assiduously to save local Europeans, did little to evacuate the Chinese before the Japanese took control.[91]

Japanese views of the overseas Chinese mirrored European stereotypes of Jews as thoroughly amoral people who warranted exclusion from any healthy society.[92] This perspective echoed the postwar sentiments of many of the indigenous peoples, who continued to confiscate property of and threaten Chinese residents. In Burma, Indonesia and Vietnam the Chinese were slaughtered or forced to flee[93]; nearly half a million returned to the impoverished but at least welcoming mainland.[94]

Emigration, both of capital and people, has remained a constant for the Chinese in the Nanyang. Even in Singapore, the authoritarian nature of the regime, partially as a reaction to fear of invasion from neighboring Muslim states, has created an annual demand for emigration visas that reached over 14,000 by 1989.[95] For Chinese still living in the Islamic states of Asia, fear of expropriation[96] has compelled some prominent businessmen —such as Robert Kuok, leader of arguably the most important Chinese entrepreneurial family in Malaysia[97]—to shift money and companies to other locations, particularly in North America, Oceania and, at least temporarily, Hong Kong.[98] Strict quotas on admission to Malaysian universities also forced most middle-class Chinese there to send their children abroad for higher education.[99]

After centuries of settlement, many Southeast Asian Chinese still live a sort of nether existence, part of the local scene but not fully accepted. Cheah Kean Huat, manager director of Hewlett Packard's Malaysian operations, the grandson of an immigrant from south China, explains:

As Chinese, we've accepted this reality as a living condition in Malaysia. We know there will never be a Chinese Malaysian prime minister. That is a condition of our existence here. . . .

The underlying emotion here is that the Malays are the natives and they have a right to all the wealth. They ask why a stranger has a right to come to the country, a right to own it.[100]

An even more intense sense of insecurity envelops those who live closer to mainland China, including the generally well-heeled population on Taiwan. The "return" of an estimated 500 Chinese entrepreneurs to Taiwan between 1985 and 1991 attracted massive attention from the Western press,[101] but an estimated 50,000 Taiwanese a year during the same period emigrated abroad, mostly to the United States, Canada and Australia. As many as one in ten middle-class residents of the island, according to one 1991 survey, were contemplating emigration.[102]

To some extent, this emigration stems from a desire by some Chinese to escape Taiwan's overcrowded, heavily polluted environment, as well as a rising crime rate that led the *Commercial Times* to describe the island as "a haven for making money" but a "hell for living."[103] But Pi Cheng Wang, the vice chairman of *United Daily News* and eldest son of Tih-Wu Wang, the paper's founder and Taiwan's dominant newspaper publisher, argues that this continuing exodus reflects not so much an outright rejection of Taiwan but a conditioned response to deeply held fears. Wang, who himself holds a degree in chemical engineering from the University of Tennessee and once worked for General Motors, explained in his elegantly appointed Taipei office:

The passport is a tool to help you if we get into a problem. Every person wants to help China but even my senior employees, they know how cruel the Communists are—they still feel unsafe. They still want to go to the U.S.[104]

In Hong Kong, such sentiments are even more palpable. In 1989 alone, nearly $5 billion—roughly $1,000 per man, woman and child—left Hong Kong for safer havens. By 1991, even Chinese mainland corporations, fearful of the consequences of their own government's takeover of the colony six years hence, similarly started to ship billions more overseas, particularly to the United States.[105]

More important, however, have been the hundreds of thousands of Hong Kongese who simply picked up and moved, with the annual rate of emigration running at 50,000 annually by 1990.[106] Nearly four in ten people and over half the colony's professionals, according to one survey, were planning to emigrate.[107] In some cases, desperate measures have been taken in order to procure citizenship from investment-hungry Eastern European countries[108] or Third World countries, including one South Pacific state called Corterra, which, its promoters failed to mention, does not exist.[109]

Another popular ruse to gain foreign nationality is for Hong Kong mothers to travel to North America to give birth. "In Hong Kong, when you ask where you are going to have your baby, they don't mean which hospital," noted local columnist Frank Ching. "They mean which country."[110]

But most Chinese—whether in Hong Kong or Taiwan—do not see emigration as cutting off ties with home, any more than Israeli wanderers view their move to America as an end to their being Jewish. Many Hong Kong residents, in an expression of their extraordinary spirit of opportunistic ambivalence, often return home once they have secured an alternative passport, in order to stay close to family or simply to make money; this includes many of the estimated 35,000 to 40,000 "Canadian" citizens resident in the colony in 1991.[111] Even the individual retained by the British administration to compile the out-migration statistics was "the perfect Hong Kong man"—born in China, educated in Hong Kong, a citizen of New Zealand and now a permanent resident of the Crown Colony.[112]

This quest for a passport—or a safe refuge—is more than an exercise in paranoia. For the entrepreneurial classes in particular the Communist takeover of China was an enormous catastrophe, carrying in its wake the destruction of property and businesses developed, in some cases, over hundreds of years. For many of China's most successful families, such as Denny

Ko's, the advent of communism meant a wrenching shift from affluence to destitution, with families suddenly forced to scramble for a living in an overcrowded, impoverished Taipei. Over forty years later, Ko remembered:

> We went from one extreme to another. We had six kids, with nannies, with everything. We saw our parents once a week. Then we had nothing.
>
> Mother took it worst of all that we lived a minimum standard. We had seven people to a room. It was very primitive and mother didn't even know how to boil water—she couldn't make tea.

As a result of this exodus, Hong Kong, which was inundated with over 100,000 refugees a year during the first two decades after the revolution, saw its population swell from only 800,000 before the Second World War to over three million, half of them refugees.[113] Among them were nearly 50,000 homeless and orphaned children.[114]

The squalor of the Chinese refugee communities led most Westerners, including the British authorities, to despair about their future. But James McGregor, then a minor official with the colonial Department of Trade and Industry in Hong Kong, marveled at their resiliency in the face of hardship. They may have lived in shacks or on dilapidated boats, McGregor recalls, but the Chinese almost immediately upon arrival began opening small shops and factories, seeking any opportunity to eke out a living. McGregor, subsequently the head of the Hong Kong Chamber of Commerce and thereafter a top executive at a local Chinese-owned bank, remembered:

> The place fascinated me. We had one and a half million refugees living here. They were on the hillsides and the rooftops. We couldn't stop them. We had a scene of desperation, yet the Chinese did what they could by themselves. I saw the capabilities of the Chinese. They could get around all the petty corruption. Here were people who could do anything if you gave them a chance.[115]

Amidst this ramshackle sprawl lived a young doctor from Canton named P. S. Hui, who in 1957 had fled the Communist regime with his five children. Initially unable to practice medicine because the British considered his Chinese degree invalid, he studied for his British diploma at night while serving as a "consultant" for patients in the run-down Kowloon slums.

After two and a half years he gained an equivalency medical degree from the University of London and was able to practice again. His son Steve later recalled that conditions soon improved for the family. But the experience of being uprooted from their home in China and forced to begin life again created what Steve Hui calls "the refugee mentality." Now president of Everex Systems, a San Jose, California, manufacturer of personal computers, the younger Hui, who emigrated to California in 1975, explains:

> The way I was brought up I feel there is opportunity in hard times, that if we can be tougher and more durable we will come out ahead. This is how you look at life if you are uprooted. There are no failures in this life, just setbacks.[116]

Rather than seek support from the state or from the society at large, Hui notes, families such as his accepted difficulties as a natural part of life, something to be overcome by themselves, their families and kinsmen. Conditions of chronic insecurity, much like those facing the Jews in Europe, led the overseas Chinese to treasure the instruments of self-reliance—whether in the form of a business, a hoard of cash or gold, real estate, or simply the money to pay for their children's education, so they might then develop economically useful skills.

Such attitudes dominate the economic behavior of overseas Chinese around the world. Taiwan, for example, boasts one of the world's highest savings rates, ranging on average around 30 percent of gross income.[117] When asked for the reasons for their success, according to researcher Bernard Wong, old-time New York Chinese constantly repeated the saying *"Kan kim hay ka,"* or "Frugality is the key to success," certainly an apt parallel to the dictums of Samuel Smiles or Benjamin Franklin.[118]

Even in California's Silicon Valley, where Porsches fill the parking lots of start-up firms, Chinese entrepreneurs such as Steve Hui try to live by the old credo. President of a company with 1,700 employees in the United States and 2,700 worldwide, Hui refused to hire an assistant and insists on flying coach, even on long transpacific hauls. And in 1991, when a plunge in computer sales drove once high-flying Everex to its first losses ever, Hui characteristically refused to scale back research and development funding, preferring instead to cut his own salary 50 percent, allocating the remainder to pay for the expenses of those laid off in the downturn.

"The difference [between Chinese and Anglos] is not so much dedication as mentality—we come from a culture that's hard on yourself," said Hui as he rapidly gulped down a noodle lunch. "The tradition in the Chinese culture is that if you want to be successful you have to be trained under the worst conditions for a long time."

THE EMPIRE OF GUANXI

Emigrants, colonials or residents of small isolated states such as Taiwan or Singapore, the overseas Chinese have developed a unique transnational economy based largely on a personal sense of responsibility and obligation. Eschewing both Western capitalism, with its finely crafted contractual system and well-developed welfare state, and the "companyism" characteristic of the Japanese, the Chinese-based economy relies largely on self-generated informal ties among its disparate members. As one Western observer, Catherine Jones, has put it:

> Economic success stands as the prime objective, indeed the rationale, for everyone's sake . . . there is no mystique attached to the concepts of the welfare state or social service per se; quite the reverse. It is the pursuit of prosperity which here calls for discipline and duty no less than family ambition.[119]

The Chinese businessman's progress in this system revolves largely on his ability to gain the confidence of others who can provide connections, or *guanxi*, in the broader society. Like the Jews in their dispersion or the Calvinist entrepreneurs of nineteenth-century Britain and America, the Chinese rely heavily on mutual support networks, usually consisting of friends, relatives and business associates who provide capital and other assistance for launching their entrepreneurial ventures.

Steve Hui, for example, found his key financial support from the Wong's Group, a family-owned electronics conglomerate that started with ten employees in a tiny Hong Kong factory in 1962 and by 1990 had sales that surpassed $200 million. Michael C. Y. Wong, second youngest of four sons of founder Wong Wah San, met Hui in 1973 when he was a salesman for an electronics distributor. Convinced by Hui's apparent sincerity and drive, Wong persuaded the family several years later to help finance Everex. In a brightly lit office above a gray, menacing and litter-strewn back street in Kowloon, Wong explains:

> His personality and character—the way he was doing his business—this impressed me. I trust him entirely. In the early stages he worked eighteen hours a day, slept on the factory floor. He may have been doing business in America, but he had the right Chinese people's character.[120]

Over the past hundred years such informal and subjectively derived financing has played a leading role in the creation of Chinese capitalism. For many smaller firms, such capital is funneled through communal *huis*, or credit associations, based on informal relationships of kinship, friendship and patron-client relationships. Often these groups require a small investment from each of their members, who then collectively lend the funds to those in need of capital, particularly to launch or expand an enterprise.[121]

Such financial vehicles grew largely as a response to conditions in many of the lands of settlement. In North America, some banks refused to do business with the Chinese,[122] forcing entrepreneurs to look toward the community for support. Similarly in the developing countries of the Nanyang, alternative financial systems were poorly developed at best and governments were frequently corrupt, making the securing of funds by conventional means less palatable than relying on *guanxi* with established Chinese capitalists.

Such intratribal systems have often been supported by more formal organizations such as chambers of commerce and trade associations in the various lands of settlement. As early as 1851 Chinese immigrants in San Francisco set up the Chinese Company, an organization whose purpose was to greet newly arrived immigrants, protect them and find employment for them; it was similar in purpose to the groups organized for Jewish immigrants in America and later in both France and Palestine.[123] Even in such cosmopolitan Western cities as New York, London and Los Angeles, such associations still try to play an intermediary role in helping newcomers interface with the local community.[124]

Regional networks based on accent and place of origin also play an influential role. Some networks, such as those of the Hokkiens or Yunnanese of south China, are linked across national borders, connecting Indonesia, Singapore and communities on the other side of the Pacific.[125] But easily the most important of these networks comes from within the family group itself, long the basis for Chinese society.

In this system—what author Siu-kau Lau calls "utilitarian familism"—concern for the family, and its long-term assets, not company or country, stands at the apex of priorities. In one 1980 survey, for example, Hong Kong Chinese ranked their families more important than society by a margin of better than five to one.[126]

This reliance on family, however, not only reflected traditional values but also fulfilled a practical need for reliable, motivated and trustworthy workers and managers, particularly in an atmosphere characterized by relentless uncertainty.[127] Even by the 1980s as many as three fifths of Hong Kong's larger and half the smaller industrial firms had relatives on the work force, with many others coming from similar linguistic and regional backgrounds.[128]

This family orientation has led the Chinese to look for entrepreneurial opportunities as means of securing assets for their closest relations. Like the Talmudic injunctions favoring self-employment and self-sufficiency, the overseas Chinese culture also emphasized the importance of proprietorship, as reflected in the popular saying "Better the head of a chicken than the tail of an ox." Hong Kongese, for example, in 1980 started businesses at roughly twice the rate of Americans, most of them with under one hundred employees.[129] And with a population less than half that of South Korea, Taiwan boasted nearly ten times as many trading companies and three times as many firms, all but a few family owned or controlled.[130] Conversely, South Korea accounted for eight of Asia's hundred largest companies compared to only one Chinese-owned company.[131]

Even the most globally influential contemporary Chinese capitalists still follow this general pattern of enterprise. Most of the tribe's most powerful economic entities remain largely in the hands of family networks, such as the Kuoks of Malaysia, the Riadys of Indonesia, Y. K. Pao and Li Ka-sheng of Hong Kong, Y. C. Wang of Formosa Plastics and the Wang global publishing empire.

Perhaps in no other segment has the effectiveness of this family-based form of enterprise been more evident than in the garment industry. In Chinatowns around the world garment manufacturing is now referred to, along with laundries and restaurants, as *Wah Yan Sam Yong,* or the "trades of the Chinese." This was natural to some extent since, like the Jews who arrived in New York and London during the late nineteenth and early twentieth centuries, the Chinese also possessed a long-standing tradition of garment production, most particularly in the silk industry.[132]

The Chinese role in garment production was greatly spurred by the influx of capitalists into Hong Kong, Singapore and other diaspora centers following the Communist takeover of the mainland in 1947. These capitalists, including many from more sophisticated heavy industry backgrounds, lacked the capital to revive their old businesses. They gravitated to garments for many of the same reasons—low capital requirements and a large supply of cheap, disciplined labor—that earlier motivated the Jews who crowded into turn-of-the-century New York.

Typical was the case of C. Y. Tang, once owner of one of

Shanghai's leading textile factories, who lost virtually all his physical assets to Communist takeover. Although virtually penniless, he still retained many of the essentials—a knowledge of the market, entrepreneurial flair and a bit of *guanxi* with old friends among the exiled Shanghaiese, who at that point represented as much as one fourth of Hong Kong's population.[133]

At its inception in the 1950s, the family business was on a "primitive" level, restricted mostly to weaving fabric and yarn, Tang's grandson, Henry Y. Y. Tang, explained. But the second generation, represented by Henry's father, Winston Tang, began to move more aggressively into the garment trade, expanding into finished goods. By the 1990s the family textile and garment empire had sales over $300 million annually and had expanded far beyond the confines of Hong Kong, with new factories in the United Kingdom, California and, most important, in neighboring Guandong province.

Tang maintains that Chinese family-owned firms in the fashion industry possess unique advantages. With family members living in the United States, educated in various countries, they enjoy the advantages of cosmopolitan information networks without the burden of corporate bureaucracy. In his office in a menacing gray industrial district, the elegantly attired Tang observed:

> This may change in time, but in this business the Chinese way has its advantages. As a family we can be more reactive and flexible because one person can do it. Nobody else is right—only I am right. You do what you have to do to survive. And it works.[134]

In fact, the garment and textile industries have become the first case where the Chinese model of family-based, widely dispersed enterprise has achieved global preeminence. As early as the 1970s, Hong Kong alone had surpassed Italy as the world's largest exporter of clothing.[135] In textiles, Chinese-based production centers taken together—in China, Taiwan and Hong Kong—equaled the combined exports of Germany and Italy, the postwar world's leading manufacturers, and were triple those of Japan or the United States. More important, the Chinese-based economy's market share was growing far faster than any other, more than doubling its percentage of the market between 1982 and 1988, a trend expected to continue well into the next century.[136]

Chinese producers—who are rapidly extending into other countries from Ceylon and Thailand to Indonesia—also benefit from Asia's emergence as the world's fastest growing market for clothing.[137] Increasingly, European-based garment and textile firms can rely for advantage only on their historical strengths in design and marketing. But even here the Chinese are slowly coming up with their own name-brand designers, such as Hong Kong's Eddie Lau[138] or Taipei's Jenny Su.[139]

But perhaps the future center for the new Chinese designers lies at the diaspora's eastern edge, particularly in such emerging garment centers as California. Spurred by mass migration, Chinese and other Asians—including Vietnamese, Filipinos and Koreans—by 1990 accounted for nearly three fifths of all sewing contractors in the state,[140] which at that juncture had surpassed New York as the largest center of American garment production.[141] Chinese also increasingly dominated California's growing fashion industry, by 1990 accounting for the largest ethnic group among students in the design department at the Los Angeles Fashion Institute.[142]

For a new generation of Chinese garment entrepreneurs, these California designers could prove the critical element in breaking down the last bastions of European fashion. By the early 1990s many of the leading-edge producers from California, such as PCH and Bugle Boy, owned by Chinese entrepreneurs, employed a network of production facilities, designers, shippers and agents around the Pacific Basin and California.

Bugle Boy founder Bill Mow, the son of a Nationalist Air Force general who chose to settle with his family in New York after 1949, sees the huge productive potential of mainland China, which in 1990 provided 20 percent of his goods,[143] coupled with a highly skilled network of manufacturers throughout East Asia and the design resources of California, as providing firms such as his with an almost insurmountable advantage over European producers. Relaxing in his ultramodern headquarters complex in the Los Angeles suburb of Thousand Oaks, Mow, who founded Bugle Boy in 1975 and owns virtually all of it, with 1990 sales in excess of $500 million, explained:

> Everyone you meet in Southeast Asia in apparel is Chinese. If they are not Chinese, they are not in business. The Chinese have the affinity for this business—here and there. . . . People may look to Europe, but the inspiration is shifting here and we also have the work ethic and those with the work ethic will win.[144]

THE RECONQUEST OF CHINA

For Bill Mow, however, the mainland represents far more than a business opportunity. Even for assimilated Chinese like him, the mainland remains the repository of virtually all the cultural heritage of the tribe.

This emotional tug has remained a constant in the history of the Chinese diaspora. For centuries imperial officials dismissed the overseas Chinese as potential subversives or *yu-min*, unproductive vagabonds who would not be missed,[145] but emigrants usually remained stubbornly attached to their homeland. "Generally speaking," wrote one British observer in the 1880s, "no Chinese leaves his home not intending to return. His hope is always to come back rich, to die and be buried where his ancestors were buried."[146]

Even the most successful immigrants have kept an eye looking for an opportunity to go home. One New York venture capitalist, son of a Chinese immigrant who arrived illegally in the Philippines during the 1920s, recalls how his father refused to buy property there, even after three decades as a successful merchant in Mindanao: "He never bought real estate," the son explained. "A coconut tree has deep roots, and if you buy it, you never go back to China."[147]

Despite such strong feelings among its progeny, China's imperial state only began to acknowledge its ties to its growing diaspora late in the nineteenth century. Imperial consulates opened in diaspora cities such as Singapore, San Francisco, Manila and New York,[148] and some attempt was made to defend the rights of the often abused wayward Chinese.[149] Similarly, the government began to tap the overseas community for its expertise and capital, asking its members to return in order to develop local industries such as winemaking and mining[150] free of control from the hated *kweilos*.[151]

But if some overseas Chinese were willing to help the Ch'ings modernize, others maintained that this modernization could be accomplished only by overthrowing the imperial system itself. Forced to flee from the imperial authorities, the premier revolutionary figure, Sun Yat-sen, spent much of his career winning adherents and raising money among overseas communities from Hong Kong, Malaysia and Yokohama to Hawaii, California and New York. Like the Zionist organizers in the first part of the twentieth century, the Chinese diaspora incubated the revolutionary movement. "Wherever I went," Sun wrote in 1903, "the overseas Chinese gave me a hearty reception."[152]

Sun traveled widely in the United States, staying in such cities as Los Angeles, San Francisco and Sacramento,[153] all of which had flourishing revolutionary support groups. When the revolution initially broke out in 1910, Sun himself was at the Brown Palace Hotel in Denver raising funds.[154] "The diaspora," he later claimed, "is the mother of the revolution."[155] Lilli Lee, a Los Angeles realtor, recalls how her grandfather, who owned an herbal shop in the city's Chinatown, thought it natural to support Dr. Sun:

> When Dr. Sun came to Los Angeles my family helped him raise money and so the Imperial authorities could not find him in LA's Chinatown. It is natural for Chinese to help other Chinese, even if we live in California.[156]

The aftermath of the revolution—the ensuing civil strife, the Japanese invasion and the Communist takeover—shattered much of the solidarity so evident in Sun's time. Overseas Chinese were soon divided among supporters of the Nationalist regime on Taiwan, backers of the Communists and, probably the largest group, those who simply sought to make their way wherever they had settled.

The fall of the Maoist hard-liners in China during the late 1970s opened a new process of reunification both among the dispersed Chinese and between them and their brethren on the mainland. Members of the overseas community, which had previously been regarded as hopelessly corrupted by Western capitalism, suddenly found themselves welcomed back as brother Chinese and as citizens of newly friendly countries such as the United States.[157]

For the mainland Chinese the appeal of the diaspora was pragmatic enough; Maoist economic policy had left the country impoverished, underdeveloped and without a modern infrastructure. The overseas Chinese possessed the cash, the technology and the business acumen to jump-start the economy without the threat, posed by the Japanese and Westerners, of establishing a new form of neocolonial control by ethnic outsiders.

The diaspora, as well, had numerous reasons to invest in China. In each of the major overseas Chinese centers—Hong Kong, Taiwan and Singapore—problems of excessive wealth and lack of a coherent belief system were beginning to erode the very work ethic that had created their economic miracles. People no longer seemed as willing to work long hours in dreary factories and save a huge portion of their incomes in a society where soaring stock or real estate markets seemed to promise easier riches. "The majority of stockholders in Taiwan seek immediate wealth," complains Emily Shen, a vice president at Yangming Resources, a Taipei import-export firm. "The Chinese people were once the most diligent in the world. Today it seems that all the diligent people have disappeared."[158]

As with Japan's *shinjinrui*, the changes of attitudes among the current generation of Chinese in places like Taipei and Hong Kong reveal a growing moral crisis brought on, at least in part, by a growing affluence unleavened by a strong moral or political ethos. As Paul Hsu, an attorney from one of Taiwan's most politically influential families, admitted at his Taipei office:

You see the money. You see clothes and jewelry, but if we don't replace what we have lost with something, if we don't reach for

a higher principle, for a nonmaterial sense of value we're lost.
. . . The wedding party I was at last night was like Shanghai in
1937, the last days of the Roman Empire.[159]

To Hsu, best hope for a "nonmaterial sense of value" may lie
in linking up with the impoverished mainland, thus reasserting
the central unity of the Chinese culture and economy. "This
would be something new, a pioneering effort," Hsu maintains.
"The old government ideology of nation-states will be outmoded. . . . The government won't lead this effort. Until the
late 1970s the government took the lead, but now the private
sector is leading and creating this new thing, this Chinese-based
economy."

If it is to come to pass, more pragmatic economic considerations—not any inward search for meaning—may well provide
the prime impetus for the creation of Hsu's "Chinese-based"
economy. Both political leaders and entrepreneurs in the leading Chinese states see such a tribal alliance as the prime means
of avoiding relegation into secondary status in a Japan-domi-
nated "yen bloc." To prominent Taiwanese business leaders
such as Sampo chairman Felix Chen, mainland China offers
Taiwanese and other Chinese diaspora economies the elixir they
need—access to inexhaustible labor supplies, natural resources
and a potentially huge market. As Chen sees it:

> It's as simple as this: Asia will be dominated by Japan for thirty
> to fifty years, unless China wakes up. China is most of this conti-
> nent. If we have policies in Singapore, in Malaysia, Hong Kong,
> Taiwan to work together, we could be the next power.[160]

The powerful synergy of this emerging "next power" is already evident in some labor-intensive industries such as toys,
garments, clocks and shoes. For shoe manufacturer Chin Hsien
Tang, for example, a move to China was about the only way to
preserve his business, started by his father in 1969 with ten
workers. Taiwan's economic boom and growing labor shortage,
as evidenced in 1990 by a less than 2 percent unemployment
rate,[161] were driving costs up 10 percent annually at his factory

in Tachiya, a small town in the foothills of Taiwan's Paukau Mountain.

Faced with the prospect of losing the family business, Chin, who has no relatives in China, invested $2 million in a new factory outside Canton. With wage rates one tenth those of Taiwan, the China plant can compete with plants in other developing countries as well as give him access to a large potential market. As Chin explained at his modest Tachiya office:

> Labor costs and the shortage of workers—no one in Taiwan wants to work for their money, particularly in a shoe factory. But when you go to China, the customs, language, tradition is the same. For me, it's like Taiwan again—but it's now.[162]

Even after the Tiananmen massacre sparked widespread fears among Communist authorities in Beijing about the corrupting influence of overseas Chinese, many of whom had openly supported the democracy movement, this pattern of collaboration continued to accelerate. American and other foreign firms might have pulled back in horror from the brutal regime, but the overseas Chinese, including as many as 3,000 Taiwanese entrepreneurs,[163] actually accelerated their investments.[164]

Virtually illegal at the beginning of the 1980s, trade with the mainland grew to as much as 10 percent of all Taiwan's "foreign" trade and accounted for nearly *one third* of its total worldwide surplus.[165] In China, particularly in the burgeoning southern coastal region, local officials increasingly seemed to place greater priority on cultivating their overseas capitalist brethren than pleasing their masters in faraway Beijing. "I don't worry about it," explains S. C. Ho, president of Yuen Foong Yu Paper Manufacturing, one of Taiwan's leading conglomerates. "The people in Guandong just say, 'Beijing issues the regulations, but we interpret them.' "[166]

Overseas Chinese such as Ho—who in 1990 accounted for *ten* times as much of China's new foreign investment as did the Japanese[167]—already have transformed the mainland's southern coastal provinces of Guandong and Fukien, the ancestral homes of most Chinese abroad, into arguably the world's most rapidly growing economic region. Capitalists from Hong Kong employed over two million workers in Guandong alone and nearly one third of the colony's currency has already circulated there. With economic growth averaging better than 12 percent annually in the 1980s, exports more than tripled. Per capita output reached to as much as four times the national average.[168]

Besides absorbing roughly half China's foreign investment, Guandong, with over seventy million people, also has developed its own network of smaller private companies, which has helped reduce the share of the economy responsive to central planning to a mere 15 percent. "Does socialism exist there now?" asked Martin Barrow, a director at Jardine Matheson, the old Scottish trading firm. "South China has a life of its own."[169]

By 1992 Overseas Chinese Affairs Committees, eager to share in this windfall, had sprouted up in twenty-seven other provinces, with scores of county and city branches, each busily competing for investment and technical assistance from the diaspora. In some cases, following the long-standing traditions of patronage, overseas Chinese have used their financial power to boost the status of their mainland relations, appointing them to management positions in their new China-based companies.[170]

By the early 1990s there were even attempts by some Chinese to formalize these growing transnational linkages. One group of economic experts from China, Taiwan and Hong Kong, meeting in Hong Kong in 1992, proposed the formation of a "Greater Chinese Economic Zone" among their countries. Such a bloc— including China, Taiwan and Hong Kong, as well as Singapore —would boast combined foreign currency reserves roughly two and a half times those of Japan and would rank second only to that island nation as Asia's leading industrial power.[171]

This slow process of economic integration with their capitalist cousins could over time do more damage to the Communists than the democracy movement itself. China's economic emergence of the 1980s, for example, also saw the precipitous decline of its socialist structures as the state-owned share of industry nationwide dropped from over four fifths of industrial production to barely half. In 1990 non-state-owned factories accounted for 70 percent of all industrial growth; the output from factories involving foreign, mostly Chinese, investors grew at nearly twenty times the rate for government-owned plants.[172]

The increasing personal contact between mainlanders and their diaspora brethren could prove equally corrosive to the Communist order. With over 300,000 Taiwanese alone visiting the mainland every year,[173] increasing numbers of mainlanders have become aware of the enormous strides taken by Chinese in places like Taiwan or North America, whose governments generations of mainlanders have been brought up to revile.

"It's a long process but we're making the channels to mainland China here," notes Steve Lu, a Taiwanese engineer, part of a California-based group that uses business and technical ties to spread anti-Communist information. "When the time comes [to overthrow the regime], we'll have the direct contact. And direct contact is the Achilles heel of the Communists."[174]

Critically, once-huge cultural differences—in attitudes, work ethic, even appearance—between mainlanders and overseas Chinese have begun to fade. Industrialist M. C. Tam has been struck by the rate of change at his own small plant in Shekou, an hour's boat ride from Hong Kong, since he opened it in 1985.

A native of Macao, one of the oldest outposts of European imperialism, Tam faced numerous frustrations in the initial phases of opening his plant. A former executive with California-based Ampex Corporation, Tam tried to make his plant, which manufactures components for computer disc drives, work to Western or Hong Kong standards. But he found the work force, long used to Communist labor practices and low quality standards, both lazy and poorly motivated.

But by 1991 the once-enormous gap between the Hong Kong standard and his China factory had all but disappeared. With his factory employing 2,000 workers and his sales reaching upward of $100 million, Tam considers his Shekou operation the equal of any on Taiwan or in Hong Kong. As he walked through the clean, modern facility, Tam observed his workers, mostly young women, with an air of amazement:

When we first started here, the efficiency was very low. They'd go to sleep after lunch. Sometimes they'd be asleep under the worktable.

Now they work effectively. They wear makeup. You can't tell the difference anymore between the Hong Kong girls and them.[175]

China's potential, Tam believes, extends far beyond providing a source of cheap, disciplined labor. China also now provides his factory, and others in the burgeoning coastal region, an ever-larger cadre of skilled workers, scientists and engineers. Once shattered by Maoist excesses, China's graduate enrollment has been soaring, increasing fivefold between 1980 and 1986,[176] when China graduated more scientists and engineers than Germany and France put together.[177]

China also sent more new students to the United States, the penultimate training ground for technology, than any other nation. As occurred previously with the Taiwanese, roughly two out of three of the estimated 80,000 mainland Chinese students and scholars in the United States, most of them in science and engineering, failed to return home.[178] "There are two kinds of people in China these days," one Chinese mainland student in his twenties explained. "First there are those who simply want to go to the United States; and second, there are those who are already well along in their preparations to depart."[179]

But at the outset of the twenty-first century, even such a massive migration can be seen not so much as a debilitating "brain drain" but as yet another extension of Chinese influence. Drawn together by a common identity, these Chinese will only swell the ranks of those spacemen, such as Denny Ko, who are tying together California, Southeast Asia and the mainland into a new and powerful global high-technology network.

Perhaps nowhere is this effort more consciously conceived than at Hong Kong's newly established Chinese University of Science and Technology—which garnered over $1.5 billion support from Chinese in Singapore and San Francisco as well as on the mainland and in Taiwan. No matter how many people emigrate to America, argues university president Dr. Chia Wia

Woo, the Chinese, with their rapidly growing population of engineers and scientists, have the means to more than fill their future technological needs.[180] As an imperial Chinese viceroy once said when warned about the risks of sending students abroad: "When the emperor rules over so many millions, what does he care for the few waifs that have drifted away to a foreign land?"[181]

In his Hong Kong lair, Woo shares the viceroy's views about Chinese leaving the homeland. A native of Shanghai whose family emigrated to Hong Kong and who later became president of San Francisco State, he sees his new school as connecting the Chinese—both within the mainland and outside—to the flow of the world's technology. "The issue in history is not the brain drain but the shortage of brains," Woo noted in his unaccented Californian English.[182]

To evolve, Woo acknowledges that his tribe must continue to seek out new technology and opportunities on a global level. Unlike the Japanese, insular and anxious to defend themselves from encroachment, the Chinese, Woo believes, will find their future shaped by more cosmopolitan attitudes, largely because so many of their people possess such long experience with and exposure to other cultures.

If it is willing to capitalize upon this global experience, the Chinese tribe has a potential to develop a worldwide presence —in terms of permanent settlement and global network—not seen since the hegemony of the British. With their enormous human resources, historic flexibility and entrepreneurial skills, the Chinese could prove the best positioned of all ethnic groups in the coming century, and their emergence the most momentous contemporary movement in the ongoing history of global tribes.

CHAPTER SEVEN

THE GREATER INDIA

AS THE DRIVER STEERED the Rolls-Royce through the tree-lined streets of Kensington in the damp early morning, Gulu Lalvani looked out through the now-familiar streets of fashionable West London. When he first arrived in the country over three decades earlier, the seventeen-year-old son of a Sindhi businessman, it was to decidedly less elegant surroundings in the worn industrial town of Leeds.

Like millions of other Indian emigrants, Lalvani never went home. Shortly after arriving in Leeds, he met a pair of Jewish brothers named Rosenbaum who were selling costume jewelry and seemed to be making good money at it. Intrigued, Gulu and his brother Pratap took out a loan and bought some ersatz pearl necklaces through family contacts in Hong Kong, which they sold to the Rosenbaums at a handsome profit. Soon the Lalvanis were selling to the Jewish wholesalers down in London, taking in orders of up to 60,000 pounds at a single swoop.

The brothers went on making money until 1960, when costume jewelry suddenly fell out of fashion. Stuck with over 200,000 pounds' worth of stock in Hong Kong and more on order, Lalvani sold off his old inventory and rushed back from the crowded Crown Colony with a host of new products, including toys, watches, cutlery and pocket radios, which he was quickly able to sell. By then, Lalvani realized, an industrial revolution of mammoth proportions was in the offing in East Asia, a revolution whose products had huge potential markets in the United Kingdom and Western Europe.

In contrast, India, his homeland, its industrial infrastructure and trade strangled by government regulation, was a traders' nightmare, with little such opportunity for either production or consumption. As the sun began to rise over a sodden British sky, Lalvani explained what sealed his permanent change of abode:

> India is not a place for business. Too much government. You can't make components and you can't bring them in. So all the production goes on in Asia and we look elsewhere for markets.
>   . . . I have become an international person, I suppose. I like going to India—once a year.[1]

Lalvani's London-based company, Binatone, became the *first* British-based consumer electronics firm to develop a Far East network. Three decades later, Lalvani's prescience had paid off as he became a prominent member of a growing fraternity of transnational Indian multimillionaires, including at least 300 based in Britain.[2] Increasingly at home, these Indians had risen to prominence in Margaret Thatcher's "enterprise society" and, if not totally accepted by the sometimes xenophobic British elites, found a comfortable place within the former heart of the empire that ruled their homeland.

Yet if he admired England, its lifestyle and its well-developed civility, Lalvani was also quick to understand its weaknesses. From his first small-scale purchases of Far East Asian goods in the mid-1960s, he recognized that Great Britain's days as a power in electronics were over. Even as he worked onto the Continent, examining the supposed achievements of German industry, he saw nothing in terms of price or quality to compete with the product coming from Japan, Hong Kong, Taiwan and Korea.

Arriving at the modest brown-brick office building that serves as the headquarters of Binatone, now one of Europe's largest distributors of consumer electronic products, Lalvani walked up the stairs and into an old conference room, once the headquarters of a British firm that long ago had passed into oblivion. Sitting back in his chair, he observed:

> We were in the U.K. at the time when there was a gap in the market. The British companies dominated the market along with the Germans and Dutch. Now they all are hardly in the business, except for Phillips. It was all run as if it had such "high technology" that nobody could get in. But in the 1960s the technology changed in the Far East.

For Lalvani, the critical break came with the transistor radio. Few in Britain or on the Continent took seriously the little devices pouring off the Japanese assembly lines. Yet, like other immigrants to the advanced countries, Lalvani seized an opportunity that the long-entrenched former colonial "masters" failed to recognize. "No one else was doing it for some stupid reason," he recalled, still amazed. "They didn't want to disturb their works. I guess they had gotten used to pushing things on their colonies so they were lost when the colonies weren't there."

Here, Lalvani decided, was a perfect opportunity for a former "colonial." The Japanese had the product, but they also had problems with language, market access and distribution. Lalvani, and his network of Sindhi friends across the Continent, who had been selling everything from pearls to garments, knew the markets. The Japanese made the goods, the Indians provided the channels, and they both made money selling European consumers the product.

Over the ensuing decades Lalvani, unlike many of his British competitors, kept moving, constantly innovating, seeking new sources of advantage. When Japanese firms developed their own strong marketing channels, for example, Binatone moved more of its production of stereos, video recorders, televisions and telecommunications equipment to Korea, Hong Kong and, in the late 1980s, to mainland China in order to keep costs down and maintain control over product supply. Moreover, Binatone increasingly designs, develops and manufactures its own products, searching incessantly for "price points" and weak markets, an effort so successful that the company now sources products for such major firms as Panasonic, Canon, Pitney Bowes, and Hong Kong Telecom.

Through such adept vertical integration, Lalvani has developed a worldwide electronics empire with 1991 sales of approximately $150 million. Although most key management decisions have remained within the family and the tight-knit largely Indian management group, Binatone also developed into a genuinely multinational business, with the bulk of its key technical and manufacturing talent concentrated in Hong Kong. To keep up with the latest Japanese advances, Lalvani hired Takashi Morio, one of Japan's best-connected design and development gurus, who has provided Binatone with access to a network of small, highly flexible Japanese design and production houses. And in line with his largely European customer base, he has entrusted marketing largely to a British staff based at the Wembley headquarters.

INDIANS ABROAD

Indians are the most recent to emerge of the modern global tribes. Although their cultural influence has been felt in Asia for millennia, their global extension has developed in only the last century and reached significant levels during only the last few decades. As recently as the early 1960s the total number of Indians living abroad stood at barely five million[3]; by the early 1990s their numbers were estimated to have jumped to fifteen to twenty million strong.

Additionally, perhaps more than any other dispersed group,

as the success of Lalvani exemplifies, this new tribe has developed along remarkably cosmopolitan lines. Unable to flourish in their homeland, they have established beachheads in a staggering array of places, ranging from Africa and North America to Japan, Southeast Asia and northern Europe.

The movement of Indians abroad does not fit comfortably into the pattern of other Third World migrations, such as those of the North Africans or Turks in Europe, who also live at the fringes of advanced industrial societies. In contrast, the Indian immigrants have made a generally quick and successful adaptation to life in advanced countries. Virtually wherever they have settled, they rank among the most professionally and economically mobile of all groups.[4] In settings as diverse as Malaysia,[5] the United Kingdom[6] and North America[7]—Indians, most particularly Hindus, consistently display higher than average levels of education, most notably in technical areas.

In a manner perhaps most reminiscent of the Jews before the establishment of the state of Israel, the Indian diaspora has concentrated on those fields where global extension, a solid ethic of hard work and communal self-help, and the ability to think and adapt quickly to changing economic conditions are critical advantages. To a remarkable extent, they have flourished in many of the very niches—garments, real estate, trading, finance, entertainment, and diamonds—where Jews have traditionally found their greatest success.

To a large degree, the peculiarly fractionalized nature of Indian society—with its vast array of castes and ethnic and religious groups—also has created not one diaspora but many, tied together as much by small intragroup relations as by a common Indian identity. In this sense, the Indians are best understood, at least to date, as a series of "tribes within tribes," where the primary loyalties and networks often follow narrow sectarian lines rather than a single overarching Indian identity. There is, among Indians, no direct equivalent to the sense of a single racial and historic heritage that exists among the British, the Jews or the Chinese, much less anything approaching the fixation of the Japanese upon their identity as the Yamato race.

Lalvani's "tribe" is the Sindhis, largely refugees from the province of Sind in what later became Pakistan. Their one-million-member diaspora[8]—spread across Asia, Africa, Europe and the Americas—tends to "cling together" even more than most Indian entrepreneurial groups,[9] with even the wealthiest families living together in large communal houses. Much like the Chinese spacemen, they are inveterate wanderers, shifting their locale in search of opportunity. As one Sindhi merchant put it: "When you land on Mars, there'll probably be a member of a Sindhi family already selling there."

Another outstanding example of this sort of diaspora-within-a-diaspora involves members of the four-million-strong, highly ascetic Jain sect,[10] who in less than two decades have grown to be second only to the Jews in the worldwide diamond trade. Using their cut-rate stone-cutting operations in Palanpur, 350 miles north of Bombay, Jains have established commercial colonies in such diamond centers as Tel Aviv, Antwerp and New York, and by the late 1980s accounted for roughly one third of all purchases of rough diamonds.[11]

The Jain diamond merchants rely on their interethnic ties to keep their highly scattered, specialized and intrinsically high-risk businesses intact. Sitting in his office in the New York diamond district, Sheyras Mehta, part of a far-flung diamond-trading family, explained:

> We Jains are very close and everyone knows everyone. In a business like ours this is very important since you are entrusting people all the time to carry small packets of merchandise that could be worth hundreds of thousands of dollars. It's why Orthodox Jews are good in this business. If you break the rules, you risk being cast totally out of the group.[12]

Other groups, such as the Muslim Ismailis, also known as *khojas*, and Gujerati Hindus, employ their long-standing traditions as traders and middlemen through much of the developing world, particularly in East Africa. Before the "Africanization" campaigns of the early 1970s, both groups played prominent roles in the commercial lives of many East African countries, where they numbered over 76,000 and wielded dominant influence over both the professions and the communities of trade. By 1969, for example, two thirds of Kenya's Indian community of nearly 200,000[13] was classified as white-collar, including a large number of managers or college-educated professionals.[14]

The value, for instance, of the Indians as both businessmen and professionals to developing African societies became most obvious upon their departure. With their exodus, the Indians carried off with them their well-developed family-based global networks, leading to immediate and massive increases in the prices of basic commodities. Shortages of doctors, skilled office workers and other professionals grew increasingly acute.[15]

Eventually some of these countries, notably Uganda, once the most virulently anti-Indian state, were sending missions to Britain asking their productive former countrymen to return home.[16] But by then many of these same Indians had successfully resettled, largely in Great Britain, achieving a disproportionately important role in the commercial community. Many, like Lakhani Noor, an Ismaili Muslim trader who left Tanzania in 1972, used the assistance of friends from his community, which has a centuries-old tradition of communal self-help, to set up a new store in Britain.[17] As he straightened the shelves of his clean, well-organized store in London's multiethnic Golders Green section, he explained:

> Just like the Africans back home, the Britishers wouldn't work these kind of hours. They don't see the point of it, I guess. They see us coming in early, working late, giving personal service. . . . It's something to do with the culture. Before us the Scots were here, then the Jews. After us, maybe the Chinese will come.[18]

Perhaps one of the most unusual cases of Indian success abroad has come amid the rich farmlands surrounding Yuba City, California, a town roughly one hundred miles northeast of San Francisco. With the first settlement early in the century, Sikh farmers in the region, working first as day laborers, have developed one of the last successful bastions of family-owned farming in a state dominated by large-scale agribusiness. Many Anglo small farmers have gone out of business, but the state's Department of Agriculture officials could not identify *one* Sikh-owned farm that has gone bankrupt in twenty years.

By 1989 the Sikhs, roughly one tenth of the area's 30,000 residents, not only accounted for 55 percent of the region's peach crop but also many of the area's doctors, realtors and other professionals, as well as over one third of the local high school's honor roll students. Northern Californian Sikhs credit their success largely to their values, notably frugality, and their willingness to pool savings.[19] "We work hard," explains Suki Bains, a 36-year-old peach farmer, his fingers balled into a fist, "and we stick together like this."[20]

Other Indians and Pakistanis moved aggressively into other fields, most notably in hotels and motels. In the United States alone, where the Indian population has soared from 32,000 in 1970[21] to at least 800,000 in 1990,[22] Indians own close to 40 percent of all small motels.[23] Much like the Jews in Europe, these hotelkeepers have been painted in some cities, such as San Francisco, in the unflattering colors of "close-knit and secretive" slumlords who pinch pennies and are often coldhearted toward their mainly destitute tenants.[24]

But increasingly Indian investors have begun—much like the descendants of former Jewish slumlords—to shift into more upscale properties. Los Angeles–based Shashi Jogani, the American-educated son of a Jain diamond merchant, took $4,000 in diamond profits and leveraged them over the 1980s into a real estate empire that at decade's end included 6,500 apartment units worth an excess of $400 million.[25] By 1989, according to estimates by Prakash Shah, a New Jersey–based investment banker, the combined overall global real estate investment of overseas Indians totaled some $100 billion.[26]

Similarly, Indians, to an extent perhaps greater than either the Japanese or the Chinese, were entering the mainstream of Western corporate life. One 1990 report on fifty British-based Indian entrepreneurs estimated their combined net worth at roughly $5 billion. Their business interests extended to such high-priced corporate assets as luxury hotels, shipping lines and steel mills.[27]

These Indian businessmen have made London arguably the central focus of their diaspora, playing much the same role that Hong Kong plays among the overseas Chinese. The wealthiest Indians in London, the Hindujas, already rank as Britain's eleventh wealthiest family and control a worldwide empire that includes everything from film production in Bombay to sales of commodities in Tehran, as well as alleged widespread arms dealing.[28] Like many other Sindhis, they initially made their money largely outside India, in their case mainly in Tehran, but have since shifted their main offices to the safety of London, although family members maintain residences in Switzerland, India and New York.[29]

The Indians have also been establishing beachheads in such fields as music, the movies and book publishing, where their familiarity with English has made for a quicker ascent than that of other Asian immigrant groups.[30] Writers such as Britain's Hanif Kureishi or America's Bharati Mukherjee have used this facility with English to express themselves in remarkably indigenous, yet still distinctly South Asian terms.[31]

"She wants to be American," New York–based Mukherjee says of her main character in *Jasmine.* "Not like a nineteenth-century Anglo-Saxon but living in the New World, with roots here. Jasmine always knows who she is and what she wants in the world. She does not malinger in the past."[32]

This self-knowledge and self-confidence have also been evident in the garment business, where Indians have begun to make significant strides in the once-European-dominated fashion end. In contrast to the Chinese, who have powered their way into the higher end largely through manufacturing muscle, Indians have relied more on familiarity with fashion—developed in places as diverse as London, Hong Kong and New York —to ascend in the design side of the business.

Shami Ahmed, the twenty-seven-year-old son of a Pakistani immigrant, is widely seen as one of the originators of the "north of Britain" fashion look. With his father, who turned a pushcart stall into a small jeans wholesale business, Ahmed launched his

Joe Bloggs line of designer casual clothes as part of his goal "to turn Manchester into the new Milan."[33] By 1991 his burgeoning business employed over 1,500 people sewing jeans, jackets and other fashion items, and was enjoying annual sales approaching $40 million.

Ahmed, like others of his generation, expresses a new kind of Indo-Pakistani identity comfortable in a highly cosmopolitan economic environment. As he walked around his main Manchester showroom, the slight, elegant entrepreneur explained:

> When you make it in the West, you don't lose your identity but get a new one. You become a new kind of person, looking to the past and the future. This is a new kind of Asian you are seeing. We are the models [for] where the Indians and Pakistanis fit in the world.[34]

THE GREATER INDIA

This emergence of the Indians as a sophisticated global tribe contradicts many stereotypes developed in the West, yet the roots of this international success lie deep in history. When the British imperialists imposed themselves over the huge Indian subcontinent, they assumed that Indian society was profoundly impervious to technical and economic progress. Hindus, living within a rigid caste system and following ancient traditions, seemed to authorities such as Lord Cromer as "people living on a lower plane,"[35] ill suited for the adoption of new industrial forms and technologies.[36]

Such sentiments came naturally to Europeans shocked by the political decay as well as massive and deplorable poverty of the society they now commanded. They did not reckon with an India that, in the years dating at least to the time of Alexander the Great, attracted the brightest minds of China, Korea and Arabia to study mathematics, medicine and philosophy.[37] Traditional European and American conceptions of India as a permanently backward and inwardly focused society, as historian

Milton Singer has pointed out, are considered inconsistent with this background, even among the most orthodox of Hindus:

> "If that [the Western conception] were true," they usually reply, "how could we have lived and done so many things—built temples, fought wars and organized agriculture, crafts and trade?" . . . Even the sacred scriptures recognize the need for rulers, administrators, traders and artisans, as well as priests, scholars and saints. Not everyone can be or needs to be an ascetic who renounces the world.[38]

In the industrial arts as well, particularly the manufacture of spices and textiles, India developed strong export markets as far away as the Roman Empire.[39] After the fall of Rome, Indians also established strong commercial ties with their Byzantine, Persian and Arab successors, forming a wide-ranging array of trading partners in Europe and, most particularly, the Middle East.[40] By the thirteenth century Indians also had developed world-class spinning wheel technology,[41] and some of their products, such as Kashmiri shawls, were prized even by the emperors of China.[42]

India's influence in Asia grew from early trading ties established by fourth-century Dravidians with southern China and much of Southeast Asia. These traders brought with them not only products but also irrigation techniques and cultural influence, first in the formats of Buddhism and Hinduism, and later Islam.[43] By 1500 an estimated 1,000 Gujerati merchants had settled in Malaysian Melaka, which emerged as a critical center for trade in spices, foodstuffs, handicrafts and textiles from Arabia to Indonesia and China.[44] By this time Southeast Asia, in at least cultural and economic terms, was essentially a part of a "greater India."[45]

But, as in the case of China, various forces—some political, some cultural—began to retard India's technological and economic progress. Under the Mughal empire, which came to power in 1526, the suppressed Hindu elites clung increasingly to the religious and caste system as a means of excluding the new rulers from dominant social institutions and maintaining their own superiority over other Hindus. "Although the Muslim ruled the infidels," notes historian Romila Thapar, "the infidels called them barbarians."[46]

The growing influence of the caste system sharply limited the progress of a market-based economy. High-caste Indians stayed largely outside the commercial sphere altogether and virtually every activity was broken down into ever more specialized categories.[47] Overall lack of mobility—an unwillingness even among Muslims to break the caste patterns—hindered the progress of many of the very classes such as artisans who in Britain, continental Europe and Japan played critical roles in commercial and industrial development.[48] Under the caste system, for example, even interest rates for the *vaishyas* (traders) and *shudras* (artisans) were set at twice or higher than rates for the Brahmins, who generally disdained new commercial ventures.[49]

The enormous relative wealth of India, as it did in China, also deflected interest in foreign trade, often a critical element in spurring both technical improvement and changes in the social order. The Mughal emperor, noted an Italian traveler in 1624, was indeed a "great and wealthy king"[50] whose tax revenues at the time of the great Moghul emperor Akbar were more than fifteen times greater than those available to Britain's James I.[51] Even as late as 1757, the British conqueror Lord Clive compared the silk-producing city of Murshidabad in Bengal, now little more than a small village north of present-day Calcutta, favorably to London in size, population and wealth of its merchant class.[52]

Again like China, India's loss of economic control began first at its periphery. European power grew, but Indian traders, lacking the aggressive backing of their state, were reduced to serving as middlemen for newcomers such as the Portuguese,[53] whose state actively promoted their activities[54] through both missions of exploration and direct military action.[55]

The European states also increasingly took advantage of their growing technological lead, sometimes improving upon innovations and knowledge originating in India. The very ships the Portuguese explorer Vasco da Gama used to circumnavigate Africa employed both Indian navigational technology and a pilot from Gujerat whose experience with sailing African waters exceeded that of his European counterparts.[56]

Perhaps even more critical was the widening gap in spinning technology. As late as the eighteenth century, India's textile industry, using the traditional spinning wheel technology, was still competitive enough to export products to Europe, as well as to serve a vast domestic market.[57] But by the early nineteenth century technological improvements pioneered by the manufacturers of Manchester—as well as new restrictions on the import of Indian textiles[58]—were bringing on the virtual annihilation of an entire class of native weavers, whose bones, the British governor general would report in 1835, were "bleaching the plains of India."[59]

The British hegemony, which started in the latter half of the eighteenth century, transformed India far more than such peripheral trading diasporas as the Dutch or the Portuguese. The empire needed modern ports and cities to service its expansion, and within a century British-developed cities such as Bombay and Calcutta had all but eclipsed the older centers of urbanization,[60] remaining the leading centers for Indian economic life to this day.[61]

British commercial dominance also overcame the last elements of influence held by Indian merchants throughout Asia, essentially detaching the subcontinent from direct access to its traditional markets.[62] Even more important, British imports, most particularly textiles, swamped Indian markets, devastating the huge village-based economy that, as recently as the early nineteenth century, had been *exporting* its products to England.

Soon one of the world's oldest trading civilizations, notes economic historian Dharma Kumar, had become little more than a "satellite" of Great Britain.[63] The imperial interest controlled major industries from jute to coal mining[64] and treated the Indians as if they existed purely to further British commercial advantage. Between 1834 and 1934, roughly thirty million Indians were sent out as indentured servants to work on the empire's plantations, in the mines and on other projects, often being subject to the most deplorable conditions.[65]

India's overall domestic economy received similarly one-sided treatment. Despite the favored position of British industrial products, India ran a huge trade surplus with the imperial metropolis and the rest of the world. By 1914, according to estimates by economist Susan Strange, these surpluses were essentially propping up the entire financial structure of the empire itself. British interests carried away the profits from India's vast natural resources and agricultural products ranging from cotton to opium. Bullion, earned in India, found its way into the coffers of London and from there was reinvested in the expanding British world economic network.[66]

IN THE FAMILY WAY

But even under British hegemony, new and aggressive Indian business groups already had begun to evolve on an increasingly impressive scale. This new Indian capitalism did not simply mimic the patterns of India's colonial masters, any more than did its counterparts among the Chinese or Japanese, but in a manner was profoundly derivative of long-standing traditional values.

Indian business has followed to a remarkable extent the model of the "joint family company" whose origins lie in India's earliest history, deriving largely from the economic and social patterns of agricultural village life.[67] Unlike Western societies, where the "rationalist economic order" and the division of property among heirs has dominated, property in this system is held in common, making each son, at least theoretically, an equal co-owner and inheritor.[68]

In the corporate world, the joint family can mean not just sharing in the ownership of the enterprise but living in the same house, with a common kitchen and family worship.[69] Increasingly, however, such family control has been exercised more subtly, through the elaborate use of subsidiaries, with essential control remaining in the hands of family members and kinsmen.[70]

Even into the 1990s, many prominent Indian capitalist enter-prises—the Tatas, Hindujahs, Reddys, Harilelas, Birlas—con-tinue to follow an essentially family-based model. This pattern has been further accentuated by the importance of particular subgroups, who in their own way have formed their own well-developed, family-based networks, sometimes on a global scale.

This pattern extends even to the Parsis, arguably the most sophisticated and cosmopolitan of all India's "tribes within tribes." Even the most powerful Parsi group, the Tatas, has re-mained—despite the increased use of professional managers[71]—largely in family hands, with a disproportionate influence by fellow Parsis in upper management and as directors.[72]

In many respects the Parsis, most notably represented by Bombay dynasties such as the Tatas, the Modis and the Wadias, have served as the vanguard of Indian capitalism. Followers of the Zoroastrian faith who migrated to the region near Bombay in the eighth century, fleeing Muslim persecutions, they were ideal agents for change, a tiny, highly cohesive community whose members had long made their living as merchants, arti-sans and money lenders.

More important still in the Indian context, their religion—far more explicitly than that of their Muslim or Hindu neighbors—stressed many of the classic "Calvinist" virtues, such as the order of nature, rationalism, the importance of knowledge, hard work, thrift and the maximization of material wealth. As one verse, repeated some sixty times through the Gathas, their holy book, explains:

> *The excellent Law immutable is prosperity; it is uprightness,*
>   *the Law immutable is weal for him who is for the excellent Law*
>   *immutable.*
> *In the name of God*
> *May the eminent glory of the prospering*
>   *Lord Ahura Mazda increase!*[73]

Their natural interest in prosperity led the Parsis early on to dispatch their young men to Britain for education and commer-cial training. These young British-educated Parsis helped their people develop successful industries, such as shipbuilding, at a time of general decline for most Indian manufacturers.[74] By the 1930s the Parsis were the most urbanized and by far the most literate in English group in India.[75] With less than .03 percent of the population, they accounted for nearly 7 percent of all engineering degrees and roughly 5 percent of all medical degrees.[76]

With their growing technical skill and sophistication, the Parsis, who inevitably earned the moniker "the Jews of India,"[77] played a disproportionate role in the subcontinent's commercial life, by 1800 accounting for a larger number of the largest Bombay firms than either the Europeans or the Hindus.[78] Concentrated in Bombay, center of the estimated 150,000 Parsis worldwide,[79] the group still accounts for fourteen of India's top one hundred companies.[80]

Although India has remained the base for Parsi power,[81] the Parsis were also pioneers in reestablishing Indian economic influence beyond the subcontinent. Much like the Chinese, they often followed the British flag in their search for new markets. Parsis were among the first, for example, to establish trading outposts in Canton and later at the newly acquired port of Hong Kong, joining there other Bombay-based traders including Ismaili Muslims and Jews; a Parsi businessman, Dooraji Naorojee, launched the Star Ferry, until the 1980s the primary means of public transit from Hong Kong Island to Kowloon. Three Parsis also sat on the founding board of directors of the Hong Kong and Shanghai Banking Corporation.[82]

If arguably the first of the subgroups to accommodate themselves to global capitalism, the Parsis were not the only Indians to take advantage of the opportunities provided by the British. As the empire expanded into Asia, Africa and elsewhere, Indians served prominently as clerks, lawyers, civil servants and police.[83] Other Indians settled permanently in the British dominions, sometimes achieving powerful positions in both business and the professions.

When the empire collapsed, these wayward Indians suddenly found themselves in many ways in an enviable position. Even as India itself was convulsed by post-independence violence and chaos, the withdrawal of British professionals, administrators and businessmen opened new vistas for former "colonials" who had been relegated often to secondary status.

Particularly attracted to the fresh opportunities abroad were an estimated eight million Hindus and Sikhs, including many Sindhis, who now found their homes part of the new Muslim nation of Pakistan.[84] Like the old Jews of Europe, these refugees suddenly were cast into the role of wanderers, seeking somewhere to make a living. For many young Sindhis such as J. R. Daryani, former colonies like Nigeria, where family members and other Sindhis had already established a small but increasingly prosperous community, seemed all but irresistible, full of unlimited promise.

As a boy, Daryani, whose father had served as an agent for the British textile house Total Brothers, had heard tales of the fortunes earned in Nigeria by other Sindhis. So rather than stay in India, Daryani on the eve of independence packed up and moved there, where he quickly found employment at Inlaks, a Switzerland-based Indian trading company specializing in the sale of dried Norwegian fish to the bustling West African market.

In Africa, Indians such as Daryani soon found themselves challenging the entrenched positions of other entrenched ethnic groups, including the residue of the English community and a large and prospering community of Lebanese traders. But without the support of the empire, Daryani found the Europeans surprisingly unprepared for doing business in the post-independence environment. Four decades later, in a small office cottage located behind his sprawling home in New Delhi, he recalled:

> We competed with them on overhead—small staff, lower salaries, not too much fat. They had lots of fat, particularly the Europeans. We eliminated the Lebanese and became their suppliers. We did it by dynamism. We were better connected, we had better networks, we had better control in Hong Kong, Japan, and the United Kingdom. We became dominant.[85]

By 1975, when Daryani returned to India, Inlaks under his leadership had extended its interests into textiles, rice and sugar. From his base in New Delhi he expanded the company's operations into industrial production, building one of Nigeria's first tomato paste factories, as well as other interests, including packaging plants and breweries. By 1990 the value of Inlaks' Nigerian operation stood at nearly $1 billion.

Although now retired from Inlaks, Daryani maintains close family and commercial ties to the roughly 7,000-member Indian community in Nigeria. He has established several new industrial plants producing pharmaceuticals, cardboard, auto parts and plastics. "Today in Nigeria industry is more in the hands of Indians than the Europeans," he says with unmistakable pride. "We are a very large force there. We are no longer just the traders—we are industrial powers."

These Indian family networks also proved effective in other regions, including some of the very Asian regions that, in earlier times, had been important trading partners with the subcontinent. As occurred in Africa, the process began under the aegis of the empire, with Indian businessmen carving out considerable economic spheres of influence in countries such as Burma[86] and Malaysia, which grew into the largest Indian settlement outside the subcontinent.[87]

As early as the 1920s these Indian entrepreneurs were already establishing strong ties outside the empire as well, most particularly in Japan and in the rapidly industrializing coastal areas of China, notably the Shanghai region. Indian traders, selling Indian products and raw materials, found a ready market in these Asian regions. Japan, in particular, offered a huge market for Indian cotton, jute and other raw materials.[88]

With the ascent of Japan after the war, these linkages became even more critical. D. R. Reddy's family trading firm, based in Madras, first went to Japan in the late 1930s, selling mica from its mines in Uttar Pradesh for electrical insulation. After the war, the family—led by four brothers—returned to a Japan devastated by bombing, its once wide-ranging commercial networks shattered. In an elegant Japanese restaurant overlooking Osaka, Reddy recalls:

> If you could believe it, this city was worse off than Bombay. Our
> Japanese partners were in trouble. They couldn't travel, they had

no contacts outside. But we Indians had people—we became the conduits to Africa, Middle East and South Asia. We were insiders everywhere.[89]

Over the years the Reddys and other Indian traders continually adjusted their business to rapid changes within Japan. As Japanese textile firms began expanding, they became their leading overseas agents; later, they shifted their emphasis to brokering both electronics and automobile components. And as Japan became a consuming nation once again, the Reddys started to ship seafood from both India and their own shrimp operations in Thailand to the burgeoning Japanese market. By 1990, the Reddys' operations were spread from Osaka, still the largest source of business, throughout Southeast Asia, Southern California, the Maldive Islands and back to India, with businesses spanning garment manufacturing to resort hotels.

Similarly in Southeast Asia, other Indian family networks have also achieved remarkable results. Although the estimated 20,000 Indians in Hong Kong constitute less than .4 percent of the colony's population, they control as much as 10 percent of its trade.[90] Like the Reddys' firm, most of Hong Kong's Indian businesses—from the tiny two-man operation to the giant conglomerate—fit the classical mold, with extended families providing the linkages between various national markets.[91]

Even the most influential of Indian business empires, such as the Harilelas, remains at heart a family enterprise dependent on kinship ties around the world. Family patriarch Lilaram Harilela, an obscure Sindhi trader, made his way as a middleman between Chinese and Europeans in Canton, Shanghai and Hong Kong in the 1920s. By the end of the decade, the business had grown sizable, only to collapse with the worldwide economic depression.

Lilaram's six sons, once the prospective inheritors of a prospering commercial enterprise, were forced to hawk newspapers and sell soap to British officers on the street. By 1940, they had scrimped together enough to start a silk-trading business, but were forced to scrap their plans during the Japanese occupation, during which they barely survived by selling rice and other items in violation of Japanese regulations.[92]

After the war, with the trading economy still in tatters, the family opened a small tailoring shop in the crowded Tsimshatsui business district. Soon off-duty English officers poured into the port city looking for new suits. With so many of their customers in town for only a short stay, the family came up with the idea of mass-producing custom-made suits by measuring them in the evening and sending them out to sewing shops for delivery the next morning. At the same time, the Harilelas managed to project a quality image by making their suits with the finest European fabrics, bought in huge volumes at reduced rates.[93] By the early 1970s the "made to order" industry had grown into literally hundreds of shops, many of them owned by other Sindhis, employing over 40,000 workers.[94]

Building on their success in the custom suit business, the Harilelas expanded into numerous unrelated fields, including hotels, contract electronics manufacturing and software ventures. Although their Hong Kong businesses alone have revenues in excess of $200 million annually, they retain the basic characteristics of an Indian "joint family" business, sharing a massive communal twenty-five-room mansion on the outskirts of Kowloon's central business district.

On Sunday nights, the family gets together in a setting of Moghul-like splendor: arched doorways, Indian antiques, carpets, even a small room set aside for the chanting of Hindu prayers. But at the table the picture is not one of high technology or global finance; it is purely a family occasion, with aging uncles, jet-setting daughters, assorted friends, all sharing a casual, rather simple dinner. Like Baron Rothschild, the seventy-year-old eldest brother and head of the family trading operations, George Harilela, credits his family's remarkable global success to its adherence to long-established religious and familial traditions:

> We have no real skill other than being traders and working hard. It's more our having something to believe in. If we have no belief, no wife taking care of things, then we would have noth-

ing. We work for our children. Without that, there's nothing. If not, why not drink? Happiness is one thing: working for them, for the future, for the family.[95]

PRISONERS OF THE THIRD WORLD

Even though often successful financially, the Indian abroad still sometimes finds himself in a largely precarious position. Even as others are welcomed back to Africa, thousands of Indians and Pakistanis in Hong Kong face the possibility of losing their residency rights when the Chinese reclaim the territory in 1997. Certainly, if the Communists remain in power, the prospects for this most remarkable of communities remain bleak. "They'd probably be just as happy to see the whole Indian community go," admits one top British official who has been negotiating with the Chinese.[96]

For decades overseas Indians have faced a consistent "citizenship" problem in Africa and elsewhere, their loyalties and ethics repeatedly questioned by nationalist leaders. Idi Amin, pointing out that only one third of Uganda's Indians were Ugandan citizens,[97] complained shortly before their expulsion: "Some members of your community have no interest in this country beyond the aim of making as much money as possible, and at all costs."[98]

Given this history, a return to India would seem the safest course. And certainly, with their capital, global connections and high level of education, the overseas community could provide an enormous boost to the homeland's development. Yet, for the most part, few Indians in Hong Kong, where they face the prospect of becoming "citizens of nowhere," seek citizenship in their historical motherland. Their choice, rather, has been Britain,[99] the United States or Canada.[100] Prime ministers, such as V. P. Singh, even as they mouth nationalist rhetoric, have been forced to explain why their sons chose to settle in Britain and America after their educations there.[101]

This continuing distance between the Indian diaspora and the homeland marks a unique departure in the development of global tribes. The Jews, Chinese and Japanese have maintained strong ties to a common point of origin, but for Indians the return home seems all too often a step backward to the Third World. Nilesh Shah, a thirty-five-year-old expatriate Indian who runs a family trading business above a crowded street just outside the Hong Kong financial district, explained:

> My long-term plan was always to take a product to India. Everything I see here, particularly in China, I ask why I can't make it in India.
>
> These are low-tech products. We have low wages and we are as smart as the Chinese. You ask why it can't happen in India. But in reality you look at the situation there, the situation they have gotten themselves into. It will take time to get out of this mess.[102]

The "mess" about which Shah speaks applies to virtually everything in the way business is conducted at home, particularly in comparison to standards found in Europe, America or East Asia. Almost from the moment of independence, he asserts, India has burdened itself with quasi-socialist economic policies that have blunted any move from the lower echelons of the Third World and all but forced the ambitious to emigrate.

Certainly India's towering post-independence figure, Prime Minister Jawaharlal Nehru, although a committed democrat, was no believer in free enterprise. Like many Third World intellectuals, he had been deeply impressed in the 1920s by the collectivist economics of the Soviet Union and saw among his chief goals the reduction of any continued encroachment of Western, increasingly American, corporate interests.[103] To this end, Nehru promoted both state-run industries and a complex system of licensing to limit the control of resources of both domestic private enterprise and foreign encroachment.

Although couched in socialist rhetoric, these policies also paralleled the special interests of many of India's larger firms, eager for a respite from outside competition. As early as the turn of the century, Indian industrialists had joined the nationalist movement in pushing for "discriminating protection" from foreign, mostly British, products, which they saw as strangling their country's indigenous industrial development.[104] As one Hindu poet, himself a small-town merchant, wrote:

> *Get up! Arise Brothers! Personally salute your nation.*
> *Today is for Manufacturer, tomorrow for opening factories.*
> *No more shall we export raw goods and receive foreign manufacturers.*
> *Now after "made in," "India" shall everywhere appear.*[105]

Years of contact with the British and their often insufferable sense of superiority further exacerbated nationalist and protectionist sentiments. Indian entrepreneurs such as G. D. Birla, the founder of the nation's premier industrial empire and key backer of the independence drive, bitterly resented examples of what he called "the racial arrogance" of the British during his early days in Calcutta. These included such indignities as being prohibited from using the same elevators as the British or sitting on the same benches.[106]

In its initial phases, the Nehru program greatly benefited the progress of the Marwari families such as the Birlas, who had come from the deserts of Rajastan and excelled in cities such as Calcutta as traders and agents under the British. With the opportunity to develop fully into major industrialists,[107] the various merchant castes of Rajastan, perhaps numbering one million persons at the most, by the 1960s accounted for as much as 60 percent of the assets of Indian industry.[108] In 1990, they remained the most preeminent economic group in the nation, accounting for fully one third of the country's hundred largest firms, more than twice the number for the second-place Parsis.[109]

But by the mid-1960s Indian industrial development began to show marked signs of stagnation, falling well behind not only that of the ultradynamic East Asian economies[110] but also such other developing countries as Mexico and Turkey.[111] In the ensuing two decades India's industrial output increased at a rate almost one third that of Korea, barely half that of Hong Kong or Indonesia, and even well below that of Pakistan.[112] By 1988 inbound foreign investment, a key factor in the development of many other Asian states, fell to levels roughly one seventh those in Thailand or Singapore.[113]

Perhaps most notable of all, India's share of the world export market—at a time when exports were driving the growth of many developing countries—shrank from roughly 2 percent in 1950 to barely one quarter that amount four decades later. Even in textiles, a natural field for a low-wage country that is one of the world's leading producers of cotton, production in the 1980s fell from one quarter to one seventh of China's and Hong Kong's combined world market share.[114]

India's relative inward-looking socialist policies also fell short in their basic objective to reduce the rate of poverty, particularly in comparison with most of India's Asian neighbors and many non-Asian developing countries.[115] Incomes in Hong Kong, the trade-dependent colony whose prospects seemed bleak in the late 1940s even compared to India's, by 1990 were twenty-five times higher. With a population four times that of the United States, India's GDP was roughly that of Holland, or Japan's relative backwater, the southern island of Kyushu.[116]

By the late 1980s India seemed increasingly, to both the over-seas community and those inside, to be a nation in eclipse, torn by its millennia-old divisions of caste, religion and region. Even in comparison with Communist China, the country was making little headway in either controlling its population or building infrastructure for trade with the First World. By the year 2000 India—which long has prided itself on providing the model for the Third World—could emerge with the dubious honor of having the world's largest and poorest population.[117] "India is not even a developing country anymore," observed Bombay industrialist Ajit Singh. "It's an advanced country that's in an advanced state of decay."[118]

For many younger Indian industrialists such as Singh, the greatest cause of this decay lies in India's bloated bureaucracy, which, unintentionally, has lived up to Lord Curzon's turn-of-the-century description of the Raj's elaborate British administration as "a mighty and miraculous machine for doing nothing."[119] This monstrous bureaucracy, however, is perhaps at its worst when active in carrying out what Deepak Lal, a former member of the Indian Planning Commission, calls its "dirigiste dogma."[120] By limiting competition both at home and from foreign producers through the process of granting "licenses" to favored businesses, the bureaucracy helped stifle the very entrepreneurship so evident among Indians abroad.[121]

Indeed, many regard the primary key to success in India to lie not with innovation or entrepreneurial verve but with the successful manipulation of an often corrupt bureaucracy.[122] In 1990, the Bombay-based *Business World* described the political skills behind the rise of Dhirubbai Ambani, head of arguably the most ascendant of the major Indian family groups in the late 1980s[123]:

> He is the arch manipulator of socialism. A man who has looked closely at the confused pattern of government by controls and discovered the lever to turn political dross into gold, both for himself and those around him. . . . He has no quarrel with controls. In fact, he thrives on them. Controls, and more controls, help him and his ilk.[124]

As long as such a corrupt economic ethos dominates India, the country seems unlikely to reverse its relative decline or retrieve its most talented progeny. Lakshmi Niwas Jhunjhunwala, founder of the Bhilwara Group, a world leader in the production of graphites and one of the few Indian companies competitive globally, sees the only hope in the creation of a new kind of Indian business culture, less dependent on protected markets or on the limited choices of hapless consumers among India's Third World allies.[125]

With the Soviet bloc destroyed and much of the Third World in disarray, Indian business must now face the reality of growing competition in those markets from other Asian countries whose economic virtues have been forged in the fires of open global competition. Sitting in his modest headquarters in Delhi, dressed in baggy traditional white cotton shirt, Jhunjhunwala observes:

> We shouldn't want to be a Third World country, identifying with the least successful countries. . . . I would rather people should

judge us against Korea, Hong Kong and Taiwan. They still have the desert virtues. They gained their respect.

. . . Indians at home somehow have lost that self-respect. The urge to compete, to regain our place is no longer there. We are a confused country and sometimes the complexes are just too great for us to want to succeed.[126]

THE NEW CASTE

In this struggle to regain India's "self-respect" and its competitive edge, perhaps the greatest hope lies with the Indians of the diaspora. Like the overseas Chinese spacemen or the diaspora Jews, these Indians have been transformed by their contact with other societies. They have accumulated new skills and talents and, perhaps most important of all, new attitudes that could help overcome many of their homeland's chronic problems.

It is in the diaspora, most decisively, that Indians have begun to make the gradual transformation from a narrower tribalism to a more cosmopolitan perspective. This new kind of Indian, much like the "new Chinese," had its origin in interaction with British imperialism and was forced to develop, among other things, an English-speaking educated class to rule a domain divided among some 180 language groups and more than 500 dialects.[127] As Karl Marx observed:

From the Indian natives, reluctantly and sparingly educated under English superintendence, a fresh class is springing up, endowed with the requirements for government and imbued with European science. . . . The time is not too distant . . . when that once fabulous country will thus be annexed to the Western world.[128]

Ultimately it was from this "fresh class" that the shapers of Indian independence, such as Gandhi and Nehru, arose.[129] The Congress party, the prime political expression of the independence movement, itself followed the secular liberalism of Octavian Hume, a Christian from Britain who helped found it in

1885.[130] "In a country like India," Nehru noted in 1950, "no real nationalism can be built up except on the basis of secularity . . . narrow religious nationalisms are relics of a past age and are no longer relevant today."[131]

Inside India, at least to date, Nehru's religious optimism proved no more prophetic than his faith in socialist economics. By the early 1990s a rising tide of Sikh, Hindu and Muslim fundamentalism had left much of the subcontinent, from the rich farmlands of Punjab to the mountains of Assam and the tropical lowlands of southern India, at the brink of chaos.[132] Equally ominously, with the Congress party losing its grip, caste conflicts have grown more intense. There has been a spate of self-immolations to protest new quotas favoring lower-caste Hindus and, in the countryside, lynchings of lovers from different caste backgrounds organized by village elders.[133]

Outside India, where many members of this "fresh class" had emigrated, the secularist notion of the Indian fared far better. Cast apart from the setting of his village and clan, the overseas Indian has begun to adopt a broader identity that increasingly cuts across traditional sectarian lines. As historian Frederick Teggart has observed:

> If wandering, considered as the liberation from time and space, is the conceptual opposite of fixation at any point, then surely the sociological form presents the union of both specifications. . . . He is the freer man, practically and theoretically. He views his relations to others with less prejudice; he submits them to more general, more objective standards, and he is not confined in his actions by custom, piety or precedents.[134]

Certainly, as historian Robert Goldman has pointed out, most Indians emigrate primarily as members of their subgroup—as Gujeratis, Jains, Sikhs or Muslims—and initially find it difficult to develop a common *Landsmannschaft*, or brotherhood, such as that which developed among Jews.[135] But in the overseas setting, they soon are forced to confront not only their differences but also those things that make them distinctly Indian as opposed to the general population.

"No matter where we are, no matter how small the community, we Indians stick together," explains entrepreneur K. Sital, president of Hong Kong's Council of Indian Associations. "We like certain foods; an Indian has to have his curry, where is he going to get it than if not with other Indians."[136]

This trend is evidenced by the growing number of pan-Indian associations around the world. Even though each subgroup maintains its own communal and religious institutions, on issues of interface with the wider non-Indian community— whether racial discrimination in Britain or citizenship rights in Hong Kong—there are now numerous pan-Indian organizations. In Singapore, for example, the political and business leaders of the "Indian" community speak not only for Hindus from the state of India but also for Pakistanis, Bangladeshis and natives of Sri Lanka.[137]

Often the most intimate contact among the groups takes place within the business life of the diaspora. Mohammed Khokar and Chattar Singh Hayre arrived in Britain thinking of themselves as distinctly different in their upbringing, values and sense of nationality. Khokar, a Pakistani from Punjab, had come in 1962 to study engineering at a technical college in the Midlands. Hayre, a Sikh, had moved to Coventry and on to Sheffield to finish his education in merchandising.

In 1970 Khokar left his job at Britain's General Electric Corporation to set up his own trading firm. In 1983 the two established a partnership called Northern Wholesale, importing electronics and other goods from the Far East to Britain, as well as India and Pakistan. Their list of suppliers and distributors draw from Muslim, Sikh and Hindu networks alike, helping boost their annual revenues over one million pounds annually. As Khokar explains:

> Personally we really have no problem with the Sikhs or Hindus. On the personal level, we get here to an area where most of the people are different and what gets us together—the food, the language, the way of dressing is basically the same.[138]

To the two businessmen, sitting in their store on a rain-swept dreary Sheffield street, the political fights and religious wars that so dominate politics back home seem remarkably distant, almost absurd except for their deadly effect. Over time, Hayre hopes this spirit of tolerance becomes something Indians over-seas—the new global caste—can carry with them back to the subcontinent.

This process is perhaps most evident today among members of the burgeoning technology community. In their embrace of science, and rejection of many traditionally sanctioned distinc-tions, Indian technologists represent the most natural advocates of a new definition of nationality and identity critical to the future of their homeland.

From the time they came into contact with European science in the late eighteenth century, Indians have displayed a remark-able interest in the rational systems brought by the newcomers. By the mid-nineteenth century new Indian scientific societies, concentrated in Calcutta and Bombay, flourished[139] with stu-dents crowding into the new schools and colleges founded by the British. By the time of independence, a new class of techni-cally competent Indians and a widespread passion for modern education had spread through large segments of the society.

Over the next four decades India's scientific and engineering talent developed into a major force on the world scene, account-ing for the second largest English-speaking technical work force in the world.[140] But as India's economy has stagnated, leaving as many as 400,000 engineers unemployed, many technologists have emigrated and now constitute by far the largest number of Indian professionals working abroad, including over 20,000 in the United States alone.[141] Particularly notable has been the ex-odus of students from the elite Indian Institutes of Technology, where half the graduates seeking advanced degrees emigrate abroad.[142] As L. S. Srinath, director of IIT's Madras campus, complains: "IITs have become like Indian art, raved and appre-ciated abroad, but seldom here."[143]

In the 1980s alone, the number of Indian students studying in the United States quadrupled to over 26,000.[144] By 1990 several hundred Indians in California's Silicon Valley,[145] many of them IIT graduates, had become millionaires, playing prominent roles in the founding of such firms as Sun Microsystems.[146]

In this new setting, as in Sheffield, Indians of different castes and religions have developed a unique kind of shared identity and an affinity for each other. Most still have arranged marriages within their subgroup, but increasingly they identify themselves not as Sikhs or Hindus, or by castes, but as part of a predominately middle-class, upwardly mobile Asian ethnic group,[147] facing often common problems of affluence and assimilation.[148]

From this new caste of Indians has come a handful of entrepreneurs and scientists who, like the Chinese spacemen, have begun looking back toward India and Pakistan as potential fields for expansion, particularly as sources of technical talent. One company that exemplifies this new approach is Mylex Corporation, a firm headed by Pakistani entrepreneur Dr. Akram Chowdry, with a largely Indian Hindu engineering staff. Mylex, a cutting-edge manufacturer of computer circuit boards, uses a Bangalore-based Indian design firm for its new product layout and even imports Indian engineers to work with its manufacturing staff in the United States.

Chowdry sees India's burgeoning supplies of technical talent as the basis for a revival in the subcontinent's economy, whether in his native Pakistan or in India. In his San Jose office, decorated with Muslim art, Chowdry, whose investors are largely from the Middle East and Southeast Asia, explained:

> In Saudi Arabia the comparative advantage is oil, you have to buy from them. India's oil is engineering—they have the language and the skill. If you can change the problems you have with the government, you'd have money there. If the Indians have money, they'd start to forget these problems about Hindus or Muslims. They could dominate the computer industry.[149]

The unleashing of this potential torrent of intellectual power, suggests Kiran Mazumdar, founder of Biocon, India's largest biotechnology company, is possible only if the country removes its entrenched system of regulation. Mazumdar, who was trained in Australia, doubts that more Indians abroad will invest as long as they have to deal with such obstacles as 100 percent duties on high-tech equipment or seemingly interminable waits for export licenses. "Things always seem to be stuck in Delhi," she complained, adding with obvious disgust, "Maybe I haven't found the right people to pay off."[150]

Yet it's not only the bureaucracy that people like Mazumdar are fighting. Indians, she suggests, also need to change fixed attitudes about the world economy, understanding the critical pragmatic opportunism so evident in other global tribes. They must learn to take from the West without overly fearing the loss of Indian values such as family or the importance of maintaining traditions.

The personalities needed to effect such a change, however, are not those of the traditional heroes of Indian lore—the religious saint, the military hero or the charismatic political leader. Against the power of narrow tribalism, only a perspective that reminds Indians that they must compete, scientifically and technically, with other people who, at this point, seem far better organized for global commerce can possibly effect the necessary change.

Anupam Saranwala may well represent this new kind of Indian. After a decade working as an engineer in California, the thirty-one-year-old Saranwala returned in 1991 to India to take care of his aging parents and help establish a new factory for Silicon Valley Technologies, a start-up firm founded by Anil and Sucheta Kapuria, a San Jose–based husband-and-wife team bankrolled by the Harilelas and other leading Indian trading families.

At Silicon Valley Technology's new factory—rising amid the dust and squalor of Bhangel, a small village in rural Uttar Pradesh—Saranwala and his collaborators are trying to develop not only new products but also a new consciousness among their employees. For one thing, he seeks to break down the traditional nationalist mentality of Indian countries—a sort of not-invented-here syndrome taken to the absurd. Instead, he has his Indian engineers and staff working closely with a Chinese manufacturing expert brought in from a Harilela-backed firm in Hong Kong to teach them how to use the latest Japanese and American industrial processes.

Animated by this new cosmopolitan spirit, Saranwala believes that India—which has managed to incorporate such concepts as democracy and the English language into the fabric of its national life—can yet correct itself with the right kind of foreign influence. "We can transfer the results-oriented culture of California to the time-oriented culture of India," he claimed as he walked through the crowded, preindustrial streets of Bhangel. "India has the people and the talent, what they need is the opportunity to perform. We know the Indians in America and elsewhere have done it. We know that model works. Then let India take off, inevitably, in its own direction."

Of course, given the massive problems facing India, with its impoverished population, its legacy of monumental misrule and corruption, it is easy to dismiss the likes of Saranwala as a hopeless dreamer, pushing against centuries of social and cultural inertia.

Yet the history of global tribes has revealed before the enormous possibilities for change unleashed by the experience of migration and the development of a truly global economy. In just the last five decades, a relative handful of diaspora Jews have reclaimed their homeland after millennia in dispersion; Japan has emerged from rubble to project its "diaspora by design" to virtually every corner of the world; China, the most populous of nations, has begun the process of reuniting with its own scattered progeny, likely forging the next great transnational superpower. In each case, a relative handful of members of the tribe changed the course of history through contact with the global economy and the subsequent acquisition of new technologies, skills and attitudes.

Today the spread of technology—satellite dishes, telephones and jet aircraft—further accelerates this process, telescoping the distance from Silicon Valley to Bhangel in a manner unprecedented in earlier dispersions. Given the new opportunities for future transformations, even among the poorest and least cosmopolitan of peoples, India's revival, led by its wayward sons, could yet shake the firmament of the coming century.

CHAPTER EIGHT

FUTURE TRIBES

THE RISE OF THE Asian diasporas suggests a new epoch in the history of global tribes. After the emergence of the British in the seventeenth century, the pattern of dispersion and global ascendancy has accelerated with the rise of the Japanese, followed currently by the Chinese and, perhaps soon, the emergence of the Indians and other groups as powerful global influences.

Yet if nothing else, the story of global tribes is a protean one, with new groups always emerging. Some of them have been involved in the world's economy for centuries, others only more recently. The ascendance of new tribes has been accelerated by three factors over the past four or five decades: the collapse first of Western and later of Soviet imperialism; a worldwide revival of interest in religion and ethnicity; and the increasingly transnational nature of the global economy, which has fostered the emergence of new and potentially powerful global tribes in parts of the world that had been considered backwaters.

With the rise of the East Asian economy, for example, long secluded and frequently oppressed groups such as the Koreans have begun to establish the beginnings of their own powerful global network in Japan, North America and even into parts of the former Soviet Union. Other Asian groups, such as Filipinos, have also begun to develop their own transnational networks as they have begun to disperse to North America and Oceania.

This interconnectedness of the new global tribes is further accelerated by advances in new technologies. Unlike previous waves of wanderers, the new diasporas have emerged in what Marshall McLuhan called "the age of acoustic space," where they can utilize modern communications and transportation technologies to maintain regular and initimate contact with both their homeland and other tribal colonies.[1]

But perhaps the most significant spur to the spread of ethnic groups around the world has been the emergence of truly global labor markets. Once the unregulated product of natural upheavals and mass migrations, or simply an expression of slavery, a mobile, transnational labor force emerged by the late 1980s as a multibillion-dollar industry. Worldwide, more than 25 million people work outside their national homelands as contract laborers, earning an estimated $25 billion a year.

Whole economies ranging from those in Bangladesh, India, Jordan and Yugoslavia to Egypt depend heavily on the remittances of this work force,[2] which the International Labor Organization predicts will expand even more quickly in the 1990s.[3] Today key economic sectors in advanced countries, such as agriculture and microelectronics in the United States, tourism in Switzerland, or even basic government services in Germany, have become heavily dependent on imported workers for everything from manual labor to the very highest level of engineering and management.[4] This growing dependence among regions upon each other's skills and laborers, combined with the new communication and transportation technology, virtually guarantees that new ethnic global linkages will accelerate in the coming century. In a manner far beyond anything that could have been imagined by the Jewish traders or Yankee mechanics of the nineteenth century, the world has become a single market for labor and talent, a market perfectly suited for the development of new global tribes.

TRAGIC CRUCIBLES

The chaos that has accompanied the end of the European hegemony and, more recently, the collapse of Soviet communism has engendered new wanderings and the creation of new diasporas—like the end of the Roman Empire or the Ming dynasty. Perhaps nowhere is this more true than in the Middle East, which at the end of the Second World War reemerged on the world scene after decades of European domination. Since then, it has been among the most embattled regions in the world, as Western interests, various indigenous nationalisms and the former Soviet bloc struggled for control of the "cradle of civilization," with its strategic value and huge oil reserves.

In the process, groups of Middle Easterners, most of them Arabs, fled the often violent instability of the region and thrust themselves toward a possible new global role through their dispersion. The chaos inside their country, for example, has driven many Lebanese into a far-flung series of ethnic colonies including West Africa and France, as well as North and South America. Much like the Jews, the Lebanese emerged in the early twentieth century as a strong, commercial-oriented class with a large professional community.[5] In some cases, akin to the Indians in East Africa or the Chinese in Southeast Asia, they often replaced European elites and, after independence, found themselves occasionally persecuted by new African-dominated regimes.[6]

Their experience in Western countries, such as the United States, has been happier, despite some discrimination. Overall, Lebanese and other Arabs in the United States boast levels of income and education considerably above the national average.[7] But with the possible cessation of the hostilities in their homeland and the recovery of their historic base in Beirut, the Lebanese diaspora of more than one million people around the globe could find itself particularly well positioned in any future Middle Eastern economic growth.[8]

Like the Lebanese expansion, the Palestinian diaspora grew out of the tragic crucible of the Middle East. Repeatedly displaced by the series of wars between the Arab nations and Israel, the Palestinians—in one of the ironic developments in the history of global tribes—have developed along transnational lines, with over half the world's five million Palestinians living in a global diaspora spread from the Middle East to England and North America.[9]

Although most Palestinians, particularly on the West Bank and in Jordan, live in poverty, they have managed to emerge as one of the best educated and most professionally oriented of all the major Arab peoples. Before the allied victory over Iraq in the 1991 Gulf War and the subsequent persecution of Palestinians by Kuwaitis, for example, Palestinians accounted for much of the professional and technical elite there, as well as in many other oil-rich Gulf states.[10]

Palestinians have done even better in the United States, where roughly 300,000 have settled. In cities such as Detroit, and more recently San Francisco, they have developed intricate networks of small local convenience stores, with their own ethnically based supply and credit systems. In the San Francisco Bay Area alone, Palestinians—many of them Christians from the village of Ramallah just outside Jerusalem—control an estimated 600 such businesses, which most regard largely as the base from which their children can go on to receive professional training. Sitting at the register of his little store on Fulton Street in San Francisco, Salem Mufarreh, who arrived from Ramallah in 1962, observes:

> We're just like the Jews, Greeks and Italians who came into this city. What else can you do but start a grocery and invest in education? Then our kids don't want the stores. They want to go to college and get a profession. Because of the tragedy we did everything for education.[11]

Although successful in their new country, Palestinians such as Mufarreh—like their American Jewish counterparts—have not forgotten the people left behind in their ancestral homeland. Many Palestinian businessmen and professionals, including several important financiers, have helped finance both the Palestinian Liberation Organization and such groups as the Welfare Association, which invests in hospitals and economic development projects, such as olive oil processing plants in the occupied West Bank.[12]

Like the diaspora Jews who started and later nurtured the state of Israel, many of these Palestinians hope to employ the wealth and organized pressure of their disapora to build their own independent state. Even if they have little intention of returning permanently to their native land, Palestinians such as American-educated engineer Mohammed Sassour see themselves as obliged to help spur the development of a prosperous new Palestine. Sassour, on a temporary assignment with the United Nations to help assist local businesses, explained over coffee and honey-dipped baklava in a small East Jerusalem home:

> There's a pool of talent among our people that wants to do something back home. We think we can be the Jews of the Arab world and redo the West Bank like the Israelis did. They took people from all over the world and they brought the talent to the country. We can do the same thing.[13]

In the early 1990s another set of historic changes—the collapse of communism—further accelerated the creation of global tribes. Under the Communists, ethnic identities had been systematically repressed; Karl Marx, for example, considered both families and their extension into tribes to contain within them "the germ" of slavery, serfdom and all the class ills from which mankind has suffered.[14] "Tradition and previous generations," Marx wrote, "weighs like a nightmare on the minds of the living."[15]

In the early years of Soviet rule in particular, and later in Maoist China, active attempts were made to break down this "nightmare." Yet with the collapse of communism as a global force, the critical importance of ethnic identity has become ever more obvious. By the early 1990s, for instance, the Chinese drive to create a transnational "Chinese-based economy" was already eroding the old boundaries thrown up not only by Maoism but by the rival Kuomintang as well.

Smaller transnational ethnic alliances also have developed in other former Communist states, such as the Baltics and Eastern Europe, where emigrant communities in such countries as France, Canada and the United States have taken on the role of advisers and financiers for the newly liberated states. Hungarians, Poles and Lithuanians from America, Ukrainians from Canada, and expatriate Czechs from Germany all have sought to nudge their homelands along on the transition to capitalism.[16]

But perhaps the most momentous developments may be those taking place within the former Soviet Union itself, which ultimately failed in its repeated, and at times bloody, attempts to eradicate family[17] and ethnic ties. Once cracked open by Gorbachev's *glasnost*, the entire edifice of the ersatz Soviet identity collapsed, with the various ethnic components of the former empire—Turkic, Ukrainian and Georgian among others—spinning off on their own. Almost immediately as well, outsiders with natural ethnic and linguistic ties to the various republics, such as Turks or Iranians in Central Asia, were being welcomed as allies and potential investors in the newly formed states.[18]

This "retribalization" of the former Soviet Union will have a profound effect on the future of this vast territory. In the short run, the mass exodus of some key populations, notably Soviet Jews, Armenians and Germans, represents a significant loss of Russia's store of skilled and talented people,[19] a process *The Economist* compared to Spain's "brain drain" after the expulsion of the Jews in 1492.[20]

Yet at the same time the return to sovereignty of long-oppressed minorities has furthered the evolution of at least one other global tribe, the Armenians. With the recovery of independence in 1991, the Armenians have, in some ways, repeated the Jewish historical pattern in recovering their ancient state, which had been under perpetual foreign occupation for virtually all its modern history except for a restoration of sovereignty for three brief years following the First World War.[21]

Like the Jews of the last two centuries, the Armenian identity has been shaped largely by a series of persecutions but sustained by dreams of a long-lost past, one that traces back to kingdoms formed in the ninth century B.C.[22] Repeatedly conquered by others, including the Persian and Macedonian empires, under King Tigranes the Great, the Armenians built an empire stretching from the Mediterranean to the Caspian Sea[23] and, in the fourth century A.D., became one of the earliest peoples to convert wholesale to Christianity.

The Armenians maintained this religious identification as well as other aspects of their culture against great odds, first under the Arabs and later the Turks, who ruled them for over four centuries.[24] Some Armenians even rose to prominence, largely as traders, bankers and professionals, throughout various parts of the expansive Turkish empire in the Middle East.[25] But by the late nineteenth century, Armenians—both those living in the expanding Russian empire and those under Turkish domination[26]—faced increasing persecution, culminating finally in a genocidal campaign launched by the Turks that resulted in roughly 1.5 million deaths, nearly half the entire Armenian population.[27]

The deteriorating conditions in their native lands sent large numbers of Armenians fleeing toward the United States and France as well as several surrounding Middle Eastern nations. In this newly expanding diaspora, the Armenians maintained an extraordinary ethnic cohesiveness by clinging to their ancient traditions, a process anthropologist Margaret Mead referred to as "change within changelessness,"[28] even within cosmopolitan Paris, Marseilles, or Southern California, where over 200,000 Armenians represent the largest settlement outside the former Soviet Union.[29]

The need to aid distressed countrymen, whether during the long decades of persecution or after the 1988 earthquake, has further buttressed the Armenian identity.[30] In this sense, the newly reestablished republic in Yerevan represents for many Armenians not just a former homeland but the center of their own identity and aspirations.[31] "I am a French citizen but first of all an Armenian national," explained a Marseilles-born Armenian activist over a glass of wine at an elegant French bistro.

"I am French for sixty-four years but an Armenian for two thousand."[32]

In addition to this strong identity, the Armenians entered the 1990s sharing many of the classic characteristics of global tribes. Virtually everywhere they have settled, the Armenians—much like the Jews—have built highly independent business communities with strong traditions of self-help and entrepreneurialism. "Never open your hand to the *odar* [non-Armenian]," for example, is one old Armenian saying, implying that one should never reveal weaknesses to outsiders.[33]

As in the cases of other global tribes, this principle has created both success and, at the same time, consternation among many in the majority community. By the 1930s Armenians in the United States were enjoying a standard of living that was not only higher than that for other immigrants but was higher than the standard of native white Americans as well.[34] Yet this did not make them particularly likable among the majority population; one social science survey in Fresno during the mid-1930s found Armenians widely accused of being "dishonest, lying and deceitful," even though their rates of incarceration and other legal troubles were far lower than average.[35]

As new immigrants from the Soviet Union, Iran, Lebanon and other places gathered in the new lands of settlement—notably the United States, Canada and France—Armenians continued to make notable, even extraordinary, progress, constituting one of the most well-educated and economically successful peoples,[36] with particularly strong influence in real estate,[37] entertainment, agriculture and textiles.[38]

Armenian entrepreneurs such as Khachig Darakjian cite the difficulties faced by the Armenians—much like the overseas Chinese or the Jews—as instilling a certain resiliency and opportunism particularly well suited for global business. Darakjian's own father, for example, owned a tannery in Ethiopia that was closed down by the Marxist regime that took power in the early 1970s. This forced him to try his hand at various enterprises, including the carpet business. In 1991 Darakjian himself opened a new enterprise selling software to the newly independent Armenian republic and other parts of the former Soviet Union. As he explained at his Paris offices:

In business we Armenians have always had to be so much faster than others because we've always ended up losing what we had. A Frenchman in my place would not do it. A man like me—who knows how to lose and lose honestly—is someone who is always coming back. Money goes and comes; for an Armenian it's just like knowing your name.[39]

THE GREAT REVIVAL

The Armenian revival, and other tribal reawakenings, however, reflect a far broader worldwide trend toward increased interest in ethnic roots and religion. For nearly 200 years the rationalist tradition envisioned a humanity marching toward a destiny where morals would become a "positive science," free from the bonds of historical ties.[40]

The concept of mankind liberated from religious and tribal constraints—a world without global tribes—captured the imagination of intellectuals from Marx to Auguste Comte and H. G. Wells.[41] The "secularization" thesis, which accompanied the development of twentieth-century social science, held that the very process of industrialization and modernization would eventually overcome religion and ethnic identity in the advanced countries.[42] The influential mid-twentieth-century sociologist Daniel Bell maintained that a "continuous decline" in ethnic and religious identity was all but inevitable. "The ethos of science," noted Bell, "is the emerging ethos of the post-industrial society."[43]

Today, with the end of the Cold War and the apparent victory of the Anglo-American world system, this universalist future once again excites intellectuals. In his influential *The End of History and the Last Man*, Francis Fukuyama writes that in place of the old human identities there is arising a new kind of enlightened society, with man's natural desire to project his *thymos*, or sense of personal self-worth, now the driving universal motivation.[44] On the other hand, many others have viewed the emergence of this postnational, technologically sophisticated world order as conducive to a new kind of human tyranny, depicted most aptly in Aldous Huxley's *Brave New World*, in which man ultimately surrenders to a tyranny of routine and organization "not unlike that of the ants."[45]

Yet the twentieth century has not brought to an end either human history, the religious impulse or the powerful human need to link with a tribal past. The "scientific" assertion that humanity—for better or worse—could be satisfied by the search for purely material or individualist ends belies the motivating forces that, over the millennia, have characterized global tribes.

In fact, rather than dying off with the rise of scientific progress, religious and ethnic sentiment remain, at the outset of the twenty-first century, remarkably resilient within the various branches of humanity. As two prominent Mormon sociologists have suggested, these impulses periodically "freeze" and "unfreeze." Now, they suggest, we might indeed be entering an "unfreezing" stage.[46]

To many observers, such an "unfreezing" of ethnic and religious power necessarily contradicts hopes for commercial and scientific progress. Yet, in reality, a powerful sense of historical meaning and order has been one of the most notable characteristics of such diverse world civilizations as the Babylonians, Indians and Egyptians of antiquity and the British and American Calvinists of the eighteenth century.[47]

Biblical stories provided the Jews with a "hidden coherence" and a "transhistorical" significance critical to their survival during centuries of persecution.[48] Even the most advanced societies retain a critical and natural human urge to identify with a heritage or mythology that provides both meaning and the context for contemporary existence.

Recent developments within the Soviet Union reveal the enormous persistence of this "transhistorical" perspective. In the early years of this century, Marxists—many of whom, ironically, were Jews—concluded that communism had finally solved the "Jewish problem" by eliminating the class system and religious superstition.[49] Yet over seven decades after the 1917 Revolution—and despite generation of determined atheistic and anti-Semitic propaganda—the state had clearly failed to eradicate the unique Jewish religious and cultural identity.

Even though most Russian Jews, as one recent Israeli immigrant admitted, knew little about their faith except they "cut off the penises of their boys and in spring they bake matzoh,"[50] the Jewish historical spirit revived among both emigrants and those who remained behind in the new Russia.[51] Shoshana Dworkina, the nineteen-year-old granddaughter of an old Bolshevik, who once dreamt of a career teaching Russian literature at a Soviet university, recalls how she was lured back to her ancient roots. During a break in her lessons at a makeshift Jewish school in a drafty Moscow apartment, the dark-haired, soft-spoken student, who grew up in the distant Volga city of Kuibyshev 600 miles to the southwest, recalled:

> When I was ten years old I came home crying, saying I don't want to be a Jew—because other kids yelled at me—I don't want to be a Jew.
> But when I entered the university, my Jewish friends took me to the synagogue with other young Jews—they knew only *Avenu Sholem Aleichem* but that's enough.[52]

Religious activity has also been revived in other parts of the former Communist world, with Christianity and Islam increasing in influence virtually everywhere in the former Soviet empire. Even at the farthest reaches of the former Marxist empire, Mongolia's monks—once virtually wiped out by Communist purges—are enjoying a new resurgence in popularity among other people, who despite enforced official atheism retained much of their traditional allegiance to Buddhism.[53]

The Socialists weren't the only ones who failed to obliterate the need to turn "chaos into cosmos," however. With a forcefulness that has terrified the West, enthusiasm for Islam is spreading across an arc from western Africa and Soviet central Asia to Indonesia, an area of nearly one billion believers. To date, the Islamic revival has been largely reactionary, as exemplified by the theocracy in Iran and the feudal regime in Saudi Arabia, and as such seems unlikely to usher in the emergence of an Islamic presence capable of competing on a global scale.[54]

Yet Islam clearly has within it the capacity to become a powerful modernizing force; once, during a period stretching from roughly 750 to 1500, it represented, in the words of historian Philip Curtin, "the central civilization for the whole of the Old World."[55] An archipelago of Muslim-dominated cosmopolitan cities stretching from Baghdad to Damascus, Cairo, and Córdoba in Spain carried on a traffic in products and ideas unsurpassed in its time.[56]

Whether this pattern of a new pan-Islamic civilization can be revived remains open to question. Certainly, the emerging, increasingly well-educated middle class has been heavily involved in the Islamic regimes of Iran and Sudan; former students in engineering, medicine and natural sciences have played prominent roles.[57] And despite their often backward-looking image, Islamic countries continue to develop their scientific and technological infrastructures,[58] with a marked growth in the numbers of new scientists and engineers, particularly in Egypt—a nation that alone produces 20,000 new scientists and engineers annually[59]—and Pakistan. As a source of standards and a tie to a mythic past in regions now largely outside the mainstream of the world economy, a cosmopolitan Islam may prove to be a consequential and reinvigorating global force.

But perhaps the most surprising revival of religious sentiment has been in North America, which since the 1940s had been one of the world's most technically advanced and spiritually bereft regions. In 1970, for example, surveys showed that only 14 percent of Americans saw religion's impact to be increasing; by 1981 that number had risen to 38 percent. Similarly, the percentage of those who believed religion had the answer to today's problems had grown from half to two thirds of the population.[60] Another survey, conducted in 1990, found less than 8 percent of all American adults described themselves as without a religion.[61]

Critically, although some evangelicals found their recruits largely among the more backward sections of society,[62] the new religious revival resonates well with the best educated and most affluent of North Americans across a spectrum that includes such diverse groups as Mormons,[63] Catholics, Episcopalians, Methodists, Baptists[64] and Jews.[65] Perhaps no other single development so contradicts the traditional analysis—dear to Marxists as well as to many in the West—that knowledge itself would necessarily quench the longing for "the opiate of the masses."

OUT FROM UTAH

Perhaps the most impressive example of this current religious "unfreezing" has developed among one of the newest of these faiths, the Church of Jesus Christ of Latter-day Saints, more popularly known as the Mormons. They boast the fastest growth in members within the United States of any Christian sect,[66] roughly twice that of the Southern Baptists and five times that of Catholics.[67] Founded in the eastern United States during the first decades of the nineteenth century, Mormonism epitomizes the old Protestant ethic of diligence, education, the attainment of skills and the maintenance of family ties. Jewish literary critic and philosopher Harold Bloom describes the faith as "a kind of Puritan anachronism . . . the most work-addicted culture in religious history."[68]

Like the Jews and Calvinists—or today's Asian global tribes —Mormons have focused their attentions on both the acquisition of practical skills and building a strong self-sustaining economy. Although often derided as belonging to a cult by outsiders,[69] the Mormons never shared the anti-rationalism of many new religions.[70] Perhaps as much as any religious group, they have commingled practical values with their messianism, a combination that proved invaluable during their decades-long trek westward from Ohio to the emergent city-state around Nauvoo, Illinois, and, ultimately, across the great desert to Salt Lake Valley.[71]

Yet, in the end, what distinguished the Mormons and offended their "Gentile" neighbors was a kind of clannishness, what one mid-nineteenth-century writer described as their Jew-like "separation from their great brotherhood of mankind."[72] From early in their history, the "Saints" cultivated as well traits of self-discipline and self-awareness. As Charles Dickens, encountering some 800 new Salt Lake–bound pilgrims on a ship from Britain to America, observed in the mid-nineteenth century:

> Nobody is in an ill-temper, nobody is the worse for drink, nobody swears an oath or uses a coarse word . . . these people are strikingly different from all the people in like circumstances whom I have ever seen. . . . A special aptitude for organisation had been infused into [them].[73]

As in the case of Calvinists, these values helped the Mormons, who were largely drawn from the partially educated lower middle class, to adjust brilliantly to the economic and technological challenges of modernity. The combined force of the religion's value structure and messianic faith helped transform Utah from a desert to an agricultural oasis. Even more than British Calvinism, Mormonism suffused practical works with a theological significance; work and a steadfast moral character held the keys to heaven and the Godhead itself. As the old Mormon saying has it: "As man now is, God once was; as God now is, man may become."[74]

By the late 1930s this emphasis on personal perfection helped make heavily Mormon Utah first among the states in its per capita percentage of graduate scientists as well as one of the leaders in education and other fields.[75] A half century later, this leadership continued, with Utah ranking first among the states in median years of education, college test results and overall literacy.[76] Once a pariah race, Mormons were playing prominent roles in virtually every key aspect of American life, and in 1990 accounted for both George Bush's national security adviser, Brent Scowcroft, and Roger Blaine Porter, Bush's chief assistant for economic and domestic policy.[77]

With growing wealth and sophistication, these increasingly well-educated Mormons[78] have provided a cutting edge for their attempt to spread their faith beyond its North American base. With over 44,000 active missionaries working at any one time in various parts of the world, the Mormons have developed one of the Western world's largest pools of executives and technicians fluent in such key languages as Japanese, Chinese, Korean and German; over 60 percent of Brigham Young University's 28,000 students have intense foreign language experience.[79] Home-grown bilingual workers, for example, have helped internationalize Utah firms such as Wordperfect Corporation, one of the world's leading word-processing companies, with highly organized sales and marketing operations across the globe.[80]

Through such business expansion, notes Chris Jensen, a thirty-five-year-old investment banker based in Japan, Mormons have gained a worldwide influence far beyond the borders of their traditional redoubts in America's intermountain West. Jensen, who learned his fluent Japanese on his mission, observed in his elegantly appointed Tokyo apartment:

> The story once was that Zion was Salt Lake City. Now we should instead establish God's place—Zion—in other communities. Now we are in the business of exporting Mormonism abroad like we can't do if we stay at home.
>
> I can go home to Salt Lake and be one of fifty men who's a bishop or I can stay here in Japan and have real influence. God gives us talent and we should use that talent to grow the Church into a global church.[81]

This vision of a new "global church" also draws upon aspects of Mormon theology, which links each "saint" both to the cosmos and to his own tribal past. In Mormonism, upon conversion, members are said to become part of the seat of Abraham. Thus, members not only are part of the faith but also belong to one of the twelve "lost" tribes of Israel.

However difficult this proposition might be for others to accept, this theology helps create a "vocation of uniqueness" critical for the transformation of the Mormons from a tiny American religious sect to an emergent global tribe. Similarly, the church's cohesiveness is further enforced through behavioral codes— first revealed to the prophet Joseph Smith as "Words of Wisdom"—forswearing the use of alcohol, tobacco and caffeine, practices that separate Mormons from "Gentiles" in a manner similar to the rules of purification and *kashrut* practiced among the Jews.[82]

These characteristics have proved invaluable in the expansion of Mormonism, particularly beyond its North American homeland. In Asia, South America and Africa, where populations are increasing most rapidly,[83] many upwardly mobile people see Mormon models of thrift, sobriety and family values as more effective than those of traditional faiths. Antonia Sims, a Mexican-American convert to Mormonism and now a professor at California State University in Northridge, explains:

> The church appeals strongly to people from Mexico and Latin America and the key is family values. The church brings you so much happiness because you're doing things like cutting out drinking—to the Latino that's a wonderful thing because it brings less misery.[84]

This growth of the church in the Third World has keyed the expansion of its membership from roughly one million in 1950 to over five times that number four decades later. By 1990 nearly one third of all Mormons lived outside North America, and by the year 2000, according to estimates by some Mormon demographers, nonwhites, only a tiny fraction of pre-1970 Mormons, will surpass Anglos as the largest group within the church.[85] Such explosive growth has led at least one prominent non-Mormon observer to predict that the church could gain hundreds of millions of adherents within the next few decades and ultimately emerge as "the next great world religion," following the global extension of such faiths as Islam, Christianity, Buddhism, and Hinduism.[86]

Yet like the growth of any global dispersion, the key for the future may not lie simply in the continued development of an elaborate and well-oiled missionary mechanism. Perhaps more critical may be the inculcation of increasingly cosmopolitan attitudes that could counteract a long history of Anglo-American ethnocentrism and outright racial prejudice, particularly toward Africans. The current rapid transition to a "multiracial model," notes Brigham Young University sociologist Jim Duke, provides intense difficulties for the many Mormons reared in the essentially homogeneous semirural communities across the American intermountain West.[87]

This challenge—maintaining an essential coherency amid a growing diversity and exposure to other groups—remains the critical issue for the Mormons, just as it continues to be for all globalized identities. But given the scale of the current religious revival combined with the formidable organizational resources of the church, the Mormons could well conceivably emerge as the next great global tribe, fulfilling, as they believe, the prophecies of ancient and modern prophets.

THE TRIBAL FRONTIER

The emergence of tribes such as the Armenians and the Mormons demonstrates the still-enormous power of ethnic and religious identity in the modern world. Yet as these groups cross national borders, such revivals of religious or ethnic sentiments also necessitate within each society a shift from the old idea of enforcing a society's homogeneity toward an approach that tolerates the harmonious coexistence of different cultural groups.

Nowhere has this process been more evident, and more bitterly struggled over than in North America, the world's preeminent destination for immigrants and the natural laboratory for the melding of different peoples and races. For much of its history, American tradition suggested that all ethnic groups "melt" into a new American collective culture, eschewing much of their traditional culture and values. As David, the young Jewish immigrant in Israel Zangwill's 1914 play *The Melting Pot*, exclaims:

America is God's crucible, the Great Melting Pot where all the races of Europe are melting and reforming! Here you stand, good folk, think I, when I see them at Ellis Island, here you stand in fifty groups, with your fifty languages and histories, and your fifty blood hatreds and rivalries. But you won't be long like that, brothers, for these are the fires of God you've come to—these are the fires of God. A fig for your feuds and vendettas! Germans and Frenchmen, Irishmen and Englishmen, Jews and Russians— into the crucible with you all! God is making the American.[88]

Yet this universalistic ideal belied a more ethnocentric reality, an unstated belief in the "myth" of "Anglo-Saxon dominance."[89] In America, even successful ethnics, such as New York Mayor Fiorello La Guardia, could expect to be routinely put in their place by their Anglo-Saxon betters. Quotas and barriers against Jews, Italians, and other ethnic minorities were an accepted part of society, and only by accommodating the WASP ideal could European ethnics hope to find respectable places in the national order.[90]

The first serious challenge to the "melting pot," however, came not from whites from Europe but from African-Americans, perhaps in part because, for them, "melting" was never really an option. In the early 1920s Marcus Garvey, an immigrant from Jamaica, boldly challenged the black masses to embrace their African roots. In contrast to those who preached accommodation with white society, he encouraged them to resist white cultural and economic dominance.[91]

Garvey envisioned black Americans as part of a global diaspora—much like the Jews or Chinese—with ties not only to Africa but to other areas settled by blacks as well, such as his native Caribbean, South America and Great Britain. This transnational identity, he suggested, would provide the sort of powerful "vocation of uniqueness" most evident to him in the Jews. "Remember always," he wrote, "that the Jew in his political and economic urge is always first a Jew."[92]

By the early 1920s Garvey had built his United Negro Improvement Association into the largest organization ever created by Africans abroad, with over a million members organized in eight hundred chapters across four continents.[93] Like the Zionists who sought to transform the Jews from passive victims into soldiers, Garvey urged Africans to depend not on the kindness of sympathetic whites but on their own institutions. Following the traditions of self-help and self-reliance already well developed among his fellow West Indian immigrants,[94] Garvey concentrated on developing black economic power through a network of factories, laundries, restaurants and printing presses.[95] "Let Edison turn off his electric light and we are in darkness in Liberty Hall," he observed. "The Negro is living on borrowed goods."[96]

In this respect Garvey, like his predecessor and early hero, Booker T. Washington, saw the acquisition of critical scientific, technological and commercial skill as the precondition for true liberation. Although Garveyism was eventually discredited and Garvey himself was forced into exile,[97] the movement's nationalist mantle was later adopted by other, more radical elements, most notably the Nation of Islam. To the standard pan-Africanist rhetoric, the Muslims added a bizarre mythology that placed blacks as the earth's original inhabitants, who were destined for mortal combat with inferior but cunning "white devils."[98]

Despite these fanciful theories, the Muslims also managed to create, albeit on a smaller scale than Garvey, a set of institutions, including bakeries, mosques and schools, as well as programs designed to help reform former drug addicts and criminals. In this sense, their results compare favorably with the inability of the mainstream civil rights movement to halt an accelerating slide toward mass criminality, social collapse and economic devastation within significant portions of the African-American community.[99] Later, one of their most brilliant converts, Malcolm X,[100] transcending the blind racism of the black Muslims, helped bring this powerful message of self-help and ethnic pride—the essential elements of ethnic success in modern society—to the mainstream of his community:

> . . . the gospel of black nationalism is not to make the black man re-evaluate the white man, but to make the black man re-evaluate himself. It is not necessary to change the white man's mind. We have to change our own mind . . . to do what's necessary to get this problem solved ourselves.[101]

As the 1990s evolved, Malcolm X's words and perspectives gained increased acceptance within diverse sectors of the African-American community, increasingly disillusioned with the emphasis of most black leaders on exacting concessions from majority-dominated institutions. Without their own base in economic power, noted Paul Cobb, a leading activist in Oakland, California, black political leaders remained "people in uniform," modern-day equivalents of the sleeping car porters, compelled to do the bidding of economically dominant whites.[102]

But the African-American drive for self-realization epitomized by Malcolm X proved equally important in helping encourage other ethnic groups to challenge the "melting pot." By the mid-1970s these groups included, ironically, many of the same ethnic groups—Italians, Czechs, Poles, Jews—who had lobbied so hard for Anglo-Saxon approval and who subsequently also resented the new assertiveness of blacks.[103] Similarly, other long-oppressed minorities—such as French Canadians and Native Americans[104]—across North America began to stir, demanding not only control of resources on their lands but a greater degree of cultural and political autonomy.[105]

In the 1980s, a massive wave of immigration—the largest since the early part of the century—further accelerated the gradual de-WASPing of North America. With a rapid infusion of new immigrants, mostly from Asia and Latin America, to the already large communities of ethnic whites and African-Americans, the essentially British racial makeup of society simply began to vanish; by the 1990s less than one quarter of all American children under the age of fifteen could be classified as WASPS, with two British-descended parents,[106] and more than one in four Americans could trace their forebears to someplace other than the European continent.[107]

This phenomenon was most notable in the three American regions—Southern California, greater New York and south Florida—that accounted for as much as half of all the new immigration.[108] These areas, as well as the Canadian cities of Toronto and Vancouver, have become a new sort of tribal frontier, where new combinations of cultures attempt, often uneasily, to coexist in a manner and on a scale never before seen.

"We are going to be different from anywhere," explained Marc Wilder, an urban planner and former city council member in Long Beach, California, a city with large Asian, African-American and Latino communities. "And we are going to do things differently because a Cambodian, a black, a Hispanic, and a Jew share the same space. . . . We will see new institutions—new kinds of cities—created by new kinds of people."[109]

Arguably the most critical element in this new frontier will be the burgeoning communities from the Caribbean and Central America, particularly in regions, such as the Southwest and south Florida, where they enjoy long historical ties. Already cities such as Miami, Los Angeles and San Antonio have become genuinely multicultural societies, with widespread Spanish-language media, Mexican and Cuban restaurants, and virtually independent subeconomies in each region.

At the same time, the new immigration has made these cities uniquely suited for conducting international commerce. Julia Tuttle, the symbolic "mother" of modern Miami, might have predicted as early as 1895 that her fledgling city would one day prove "the center of commerce of South America," but it was only in the 1960s and 1970s, with the mass immigration of Cubans to the region, that this dream became a reality. By the early 1980s the city controlled roughly one third of all U.S. exports to South America, and tourists from that continent increased their visits to the Florida city eightfold in less than a decade.[110] With the Castro regime facing bankruptcy and international isolation, the roughly 700,000 Cubans in south Florida and an estimated 300,000 others scattered elsewhere seem poised to emerge as a powerful new transnational force, at least within the Western Hemisphere.[111]

An even larger transformation is taking place within the huge region encompassed by the southwestern part of the United States and the northern provinces of Mexico. By the 1980s the border areas between Mexico and the United States had grown as rapidly as virtually anyplace in North America, with nearly 30 percent population growth along the border during the decade. Ethnic ties, and particularly growing economic links, were creating transnational cities, with culture and families as well as cash and commerce flowing both ways.[112] "We're more like Minneapolis and St. Paul than the U.S. and Mexico," observes

Peter Vargas, city manager of Laredo, Texas, "because we are the same people."[113]

Such massive movements of people, each with their own strong sense of identity, also presents an enormous challenge in each of these new transnational communities. The border boom, for example, places the Third World on the doorstep of advanced First World societies, with enormous environmental and social costs. In many of the most intense points of contact, the conflicts between assertive ethnic groups—Muslims, Koreans, Latinos and Africans[114]—have been marred by urban disturbances, most spectacularly in the racial conflagration that consumed Los Angeles in the spring of 1992.

For the foreseeable future, these and all other regions now undergoing the process of migration and ethnic change face what Harold Isaacs has described as "a time of confused and chaotic passage."[115] Many older, more established communities —both African-American and Anglo—will feel themselves overwhelmed and in some sense displaced by the energetic newcomers, both in the marketplace and, over time, in the political arena.

Yet despite such inevitable problems, it seems likely that these migrants will, over time, become permanently embedded in the economies and cultures of most major American cities. To some extent, this is simply a matter of demographics. Slowing rates of labor-force growth among white Americans will likely boost dependence on the newcomers and other nonwhites, both skilled and unskilled, in the decades ahead.[116] At the same time the natural process of integration through jobs, schools, media and the political process should, with a modicum of public wisdom, allow these newcomers, like previous generations of immigrants, to adapt to the prevailing Anglo-American standards that have made these societies so attractive in the first place. And perhaps most of all, this tribal frontier will be tamed because the only alternative is chaos, the total breakdown of civilized society.

EPILOGUE:
THE ROAD TO
COSMOPOLIS

RATHER THAN BEING a relic of a regressive past, the success of global tribes—from the Jews and British over many centuries to the Chinese, Armenians and Palestinians of today—suggests the critical importance of values, emphasis on the acquisition of knowledge and cosmopolitan perspectives in the emerging world economy. In an ever more transnational and highly competitive world economy, highly dependent on the flow and acquisition of knowledge, societies that nurture the presence of such groups seem most likely to flourish.

Although we are witnessing on a worldwide basis the denouement of nearly four centuries of Euro-American predominance in science, technology and commerce, all of these rising global tribes have built their ascendancy upon Anglo-Saxon standards of business, science and political economy. Just as Roman systems of law and government became the foundation of the major European nation-states and a broad range of Chinese traditions shaped the development of the Asian tributaries of the *t'ien hsia*, or "All-under heaven" empire, so the Anglo-American systems have been incorporated by the new players in the evolving global economic system.[1]

In the twenty-first century, we are likely to see the further development of this multiracial world order running along British-American tracks of market capitalism, political pluralism and cultural diversity. The collapse of the Soviet Union has marginalized Marxism, the most important ideological challenger to the Anglo-American order. At the same time, even strong attempts to replace the Anglo-American order with a narrower, more insular "tribalism"—despite the chaos of the post-Soviet era—also seem doomed to fail against the intense economic and technological competition from those ethnic groups with a more cosmopolitan spirit.

Indeed, the nation-state itself—for two centuries the world's dominant organizational principle—seems increasingly a regressive force, most prevalent in those regions of Europe, North America and Asia with the least sophisticated economic and political structures. Certainly the end of the Cold War has dissipated the nation's economic importance[2] by reducing the need for the maintenance of centralized warfare economy.[3]

In the new environment, different kinds of association based upon geography or shared historical roots seem far more logical as a means of operating within the world economy. A common cultural heritage, for example, has been one of the driving forces behind the various movements for European integration. As early as the late 1920s, many of Europe's leading figures—among them Winston Churchill, Aristide Briand, Walther Rathenau, and José Ortega y Gasset[4]—recognized the cultural commonalities among the diverse and perpetually squabbling Europeans as the basis for what Ortega y Gasset saw as "a mission, to give them their bearings, to allot them a destiny."[5]

With the collapse of the Soviet empire, the importance of a common, distinctly *European* cultural heritage has helped define the community's natural sphere of interest. Largely on this basis, the nations of Eastern Europe may become part of an expanded community, while "alien" nations such as Turkey—with far better developed links with European economy—can expect to be perpetually excluded.

Inspired by the European example, other transnational movements such as the Arab League and the Arab Maghrebian Union,[6] have attempted, with only mixed success, to meld a common religious, linguistic and myth-of-origin basis into a new kind of regional grouping.[7] Similarly, a shared Asian heritage, the ideological prop for the Japan-led Greater East Asia Co-prosperity Sphere,[8] has been used to justify proposals for a new East Asian economic union; both more practical and likely to emerge, however, will be a narrower "Greater China" economic entity, encompassing the mainland and the diaspora and based on the common origin of the world's largest single ethnic identity.

Even more persuasively the weakening of the old nation-state affinities has also engendered a trend among local regions or ethnic areas to supersede the power of their nation-states, a phenomenon that includes Europe's Catalans,[9] Scots and Lombards, French-speaking Quebecois, and even prefectures in Japan's Hokkaido or Kyushu.[10] With the military basis of the nation-state principle weakening, local concerns about specific economic or cultural issues now tend to take precedence even over larger regional perspectives.

For global tribes, the supplanting of nation-states with more localized authorities represents a unique opportunity. Ever since the Jews became the first fully transnational ethnic group, their natural home has been in the cosmopolis: "a community in which everyone would be free to develop his or her existence in perfect conditions."[11] Global tribes flourish in such cities, from Alexandria in ancient times to contemporary London, Hong Kong or New York. In contrast, when the power and prestige of the nation-state become central to society—as in Nazi Germany, Stalinist Russia or many post-independence Third World nations—the results for global tribes, with their all-too-obvious transnational affiliations, have often been disastrous.

In this respect an increasingly denationalized, intensely competitive world economy plays to the traditional strengths of global tribes. Indeed, even as officials in Washington, Paris and elsewhere rail against Asian, and particularly Japanese, investment, local communities—embracing what Kenichi Ohmae has called "global regionalism"—actively court the presence of those groups that can bring new technology, skills and capital. A region such as Puget Sound in Washington State depends heavily on trade and investment from the Far East; it naturally opposes, even ridicules, the crude anti-Asian biases of the national elite in the distant District of Columbia.[12] There, and increasingly elsewhere, commercial opportunism overwhelms the narrower economic nationalism of the past as the cosmopolitan global city-state takes precedence and even supplants the nation.[13]

The creation of such successful cosmopolitan communities presents, arguably, the greatest challenge facing all advanced societies, not only in traditional regions of immigration such as North America and Oceania but also in the European heartland itself. Since the 1950s, nonwhite immigrants have been arriving in Europe, largely to relieve severe labor shortages.[14] But by the early 1990s most European countries seemed to turn decisively against accepting more newcomers. Even in Britain, where foreigners had long been accepted and offered citizenship, more than two out of three residents opposed the emigration of either Hong Kong Chinese or Jewish refugees from Russia; four in five opposed the arrival of more Indians or Pakistanis.[15]

Similarly, the overwhelming majority of West Germans[16] and French objected to the new immigrants. Three quarters of Frenchmen, once thought to be among the most tolerant of European peoples, agreed there were "too many" North Africans in the country, and a quarter of them felt the same way about the nation's large Jewish population.[17] In both countries strong right-wing movements, capitalizing on anti-immigrant sentiment, were gaining strength.

Worried about the growing unease among the voters, many mainstream European politicians now increasingly reject even the idea of embracing a multicultural model. In 1990, for example, former French president Giscard d'Estaing openly declared that France should no longer serve as "a country of immigration" and suggested refusing citizenship to the millions of newcomers, most of them North Africans, already there.[18] "We are just not a multiracial and multicultural society," insisted former mayor Walter Momper of West Berlin, a prominent Social Democrat whose city's population was fifteen percent foreign.[19] "We are really a pure good German society with a German social and cultural heritage."[20]

As a result, the roughly ten million legal and illegal new immigrants, largely from the nations of Southeast Asia or North Africa,[21] who are crowded into such European cities as Paris, Rome, London and Berlin, now confront increasing restrictions that essentially exclude even their children from access to greater opportunities. In the western part of Berlin, for instance, Turks account for roughly one in five young people, yet only 7 percent ever attend *Gymnasium*, the secondary education level required for university admission. Barely 3 percent ever enter a university, less than half the level achieved by Latinos and blacks in America.[22]

But as is the case for the whites of North America, Europe's demographics may force attitudes to change. The advanced Western European societies have become some of the world's oldest societies, with the lowest birthrates and paces of population and labor-force growth in the world.[23] Europe held roughly 15 percent of the world's population in 1950; four decades later it accounted for a mere 9 percent, and by the year 2150 it will represent less than 4 percent. The Continent, notes French demographer Gerard-François Dumont, "is entering a demographic winter."[24]

But perhaps the greatest problem in turning back the newcomers lies not so much in relieving this demographic deficit as in the newcomers' ability to bring new energies and skills to aging regions of the world. As Europe enters the 1990s the shortages of employees—from skilled technicians to scientists—will likely accelerate, most notably in Germany.[25] Today Japan alone has more engineers and scientists working in research and development than the *entire* European community, and future trends seem particularly ominous. In 1990, for example, Italy, France and Belgium produced barely half the engineers required by their industries and educated barely as many engineers as South Korea.[26]

Unless Europe reverses its inward-looking course, notes

Sighart Nehring, a top scientific adviser for the German government, it will inevitably fall behind Asian nations and those that avail themselves of the Asian countries' enormous human resources. Without the movement of foreign workers—most notably from the huge skilled Chinese and Indian labor markets—Nehring suggests, European countries over the next decade will face "a decline in the stimulus for technological and economic growth," particularly in comparison with societies such as the United States that have large immigrant populations.[27]

Indeed, as the history of global tribes has revealed, policies of exclusion against outsiders, from sixteenth- and seventeenth-century Spain[28] to the late Turkish empire and the modern Stalinist-Maoist states, have almost always also dimmed the lights of commerce and technology. In contrast, the healthy migrations of populations, particularly those with unique commercial and technological skills, have been critical in the shaping of world cities, from whence economies have flourished.

In large part, immigrants are critical precisely because they come from circumstances that are fundamentally different from those of the host country. Whether Rome after the Augustan age, India under the Moghuls, or turn-of-the-century Britain, established and wealthier countries naturally often lose their drive and ambition. As an old Japanese proverb puts it: "The fortune made through the hard work of the first generation is all but lost by the easygoing third."[29]

Yet through migration even the oldest societies can gain new life, drawing upon the skills and knowledge developed elsewhere. In Alexandria, which Michael Grant has called "the first and greatest universal city,"[30] the fresh ideas of Greeks and Jews helped usher in a new period of prosperity and creativity for at least a section of venerable Egypt. Later, in Rome, Baghdad, Kaifeng or Canton, commerce and technological progress occurred wherever the aggressive and worldly arbitrageurs of information and of goods—essentially the global tribes—chose, or have been allowed, to convene.

The archipelago of cosmopolitan world-cities that now dominates both global economy and culture has its origins in the interactions between aggressive newcomers and established societies, between cultures with different skills and attitudes. The earliest emergence of Paris as the great city of northern Europe accompanied contacts with Jews, "Syrians" from Byzantium and traders from the frontiers of the north and east.[31] Amsterdam, Frankfurt, Berlin and, finally, Saint Petersburg also owed their early global emergence to their incorporation of newcomers.[32]

Over the past few centuries, London, the first city with truly global reach, flourished most through this continuous importation of outside talent. Itinerant Venetian and Lombardy bankers spearheaded the City's early financial emergence; later, traders and engineers[33] came from the Low Countries and northern Germany,[34] bringing London in the fourteenth century both new technology and access to markets from Novgorod to Lisbon.[35] Some historians trace the very name of Britain's currency —the sterling[36]—from one of the common names for these traveling German merchants: Easterlings.

Still later came the Dutch and French Huguenots, who in the late seventeenth and early eighteenth centuries lent the British government and the private sector the enormous sums needed for the establishment of the emerging empire.[37] Soon afterward came what French historian Fernand Braudel calls "a veritable Dutch invasion," including Jews,[38] a group that had been excluded from Britain since the late thirteenth century but now was valued for its business contacts in Asia and North Africa.[39]

By the start of the twentieth century, the great financial families of Jewish descent, including the Schroeders, the Hambros, the Kleinworts, the Montagus, and most important, the Rothschilds, stood at the very center of London's worldwide financial network.[40] In the fabled City, each of the various global groupings—Huguenots, Jews, Italians, Irish—employed its own set of international connections, with the result that London became the uncontested financial capital of the world.[41] As Henry James observed, London at that time represented "the biggest aggregation of human life, the most complete compendium of the world. The human race," he concluded, "is better represented there than anywhere else."[42]

As the empire spread, the British also spawned a host of other cities, each with its own "compendium" of differing ethnic groups. Hong Kong, Singapore, Bombay, Calcutta, Lagos and Capetown, among others, each became host to diverse groups, including Africans and Indians of every kind, Lebanese, Chinese, Jews and Arabs. Even today, London's greatness remains based largely on its service to these widespread ethnic networks, each of which retains its own strong base in the City and its institutions.

In more recent times we have witnessed the emergence of new, non-European tribes, each catalyzed by the power and energy of technological and scientific change, who have in turn spread their influence across the world. From a position of almost total economic backwardness less than 150 years ago, Japanese, Chinese and Indians have now broken forever the Euro-American lock on posterity. Behind them lie other groups, such as Mormons, Armenians, Palestinians and Latino-Americans, some of them only recently striding upon the stage of global commerce.

In the next century, as the old nation-state structures continue to erode, such global tribes will play an ever more important role in the emerging world economy. Their success—based on the foundation of cosmopolitanism, knowledge, ethics, religion and ethnic identity—suggests a shift in future debates about effectiveness in the modern world away from conventional obsessions with the technology, the "scientific" and the systematic.

To those who aspire for this more universalistic world order, expressed in rational utopias based on technological determinism or from the theories of Marx or Adam Smith, such a focus on global tribes may well seem a regression back to the instinctual, a celebration of the peculiarities and even the irrationality of our species. Yet only when we recognize that human beings cling to such imperfect and varied habits of mind can we begin to journey on the road that can lead, ultimately, toward a workable cosmopolis.

NOTES

Prologue: Global Tribes

1. Harold Isaacs, *Idols of the Tribe* (New York: Harper and Row, 1975), p. 25.
2. The term *tribe* is derived from the Latin word *tribus*, which referred to the threefold division of the people of ancient Rome according to their own ancient mythology. In the 1933 edition of the *Oxford English Dictionary* a tribe is described as "a group of persons forming a community and claiming descent from a common ancestor." Other, more pejorative uses of the term, as the American anthropologist Morton Fried has explained, grew with the rise of Marxism, which stressed the barbarous nature of tribalism, as well as with the tendency of Europeans to use the term to describe relations among nonwhite people in lands occupied by them. For further description, see Morton H. Fried, *The Notion of Tribe* (Menlo Park, Cal.: Cummings Publishing Co., 1975), pp. 4–7.
3. Girlal Jain, "And the Winner Is . . . ," *World Press Review*, March 1990, p. 80.
4. Hidetoshi Kato, "Essays in Comparative Popular Culture: Coffee, Comics and Communication," *Papers of the East-West Communication Institute*, East-West Center, Honolulu, no. 13, p. 37.
5. Max Weber, *Economy and Society*, eds. Guenther Roth and Claus Wittich, vol. 1 (Berkeley: University of California Press, 1978), pp. 494–99.
6. Max Weber, *The Protestant Ethic and the Spirit of Capitalism*, trans. Talcott Parsons (New York: Scribners, 1958), pp. 165–66.

7. Jonathan D. Sarna, "The Jewish Way of Crime," *Commentary*, August 1984.

8. Dr. Jonathan Seidel, Professor of Jewish History at Stanford University, has even accused some prominent Jewish financiers—including Michael Milken and Ivan Boesky—of unfairly using Jewish "networks" to enrich themselves. Yet others, who were not Jewish, also participated in these networks. Perhaps it is fairest to say that Jewish businessmen, being heavily represented in investment banking, were naturally also implicated in disproportionate numbers in the scandals that rocked the industry. David Pauleen, "International Business: The Jewish Legacy," unpublished paper.

CHAPTER 1:
THE MAKING OF GLOBAL TRIBES

1. From biography provided by M. de Rothschild to the author.

2. Interview with author.

3. Rabbi Alexander Feinslaver, *The Talmud for Today* (New York: St. Martin's Press, 1980), p. 71.

4. Richard Davis, *The English Rothschilds* (Glasgow: Collins Publishers, 1983), p. 82.

5. Ignatius Balla, *The Romance of the Rothschilds* (London: Eveleigh Nash, 1913), pp. 146–47.

6. Frederic Morton, *The Rothschilds: A Family Portrait* (New York: Atheneum, 1962), p. 219.

7. Interview with author.

8. "Diaspora," *AIM*, April 1991, p. 28.

9. Brinley Thomas, *Migration and Urban Development: A Reappraisal of British and American Long Cycles* (London: Methuen, 1972), p. 2.

10. Robert Ezra Park, *Race and Culture* (New York: The Free Press, 1950), p. 346.

11. W. H. G. Armytage, *A Social History of Engineering* (London: Faber and Faber, 1961), p. 22.

12. Gerhard Herm, *The Phoenicians: The Purple Empire of the Ancient World*, trans. Caroline Hiller (New York: William Morrow, 1975), p. 14.

13. Philip D. Curtin, *Cross-Cultural Trade in World History* (Cambridge, Eng.: Cambridge University Press, 1984), pp. 66–67.

14. C. R. Boxer, *Race Relations in the Portuguese Colonial Empire: 1415–1825* (Oxford, Eng.: Clarendon, 1963), p. 3.

15. Dr. Spencer J. Palmer, "The Japanese and the Jews: Two Peoples That Have Surprised the World," paper delivered at the Kennedy Center, Brigham Young University, February 27, 1986.

16. Oswald Spengler, *The Decline of the West* (New York: Knopf, 1928), p. 32.

17. Eliyahu Ashtor, *The Jews and the Mediterranean Economy, 10th–15th Centuries* (London: Variorum Reprints, 1983), pp. 89–91.

18. Cecil Roth, *The Jewish Contribution to Civilization* (London: Macmillan, 1938), pp. 169–70.

19. Thomas Sowell, "Cultural Diversity: A World View," lecture presented at the American Enterprise Institute's Annual Policy Conference, December 5, 1990, p. 9.

20. Mauricio Hatchwell Toledano, "History of Sepharad," unpublished paper, pp. 2–9.

21. Balla, *The Romance of the Rothschilds*, p. 170.

22. Karl Marx, *A World Without Jews*, trans. Dagobert Runes (New York: Philosophical Library, 1959), pp. 42–49.

23. Stephen J. Gould, "Science and Jewish Immigration," *Natural History*, December 1980, p. 16.

24. Ibid., p. 8.

25. Roth, *The Jewish Contribution*, p. 173.

26. Abraham Korman, *The Outsiders: Jews and Corporate America* (Lexington, Mass.: Lexington Books, 1988), p. 113.

27. Chart provided by Sergio DellaPergola. "Jewish and General Populations in Selected Countries According to Education, 1957–1987" (Jerusalem: The Institute of Contemporary Jewry, The Hebrew University, 1983 and 1988).

28. Chart provided by Sergio DellaPergola. "Jewish Population and Total, According to Country and Occupation, 1960–1980" (Jerusalem: The Institute of Contemporary Jewry, The Hebrew University, 1983 and 1988).

29. Lewis Mumford, *Technics and Civilization* (New York: Harcourt Brace, 1934), p. 152.

30. Ibid.

31. R. H. Tawney, *Religion and the Rise of Capitalism* (London: Hazell, Watson and Viney, 1926), p. 205.

32. Max Weber, *General Economic History* (New York: The Free Press, 1950), pp. 352–69.

33. Jacob Neusner, "The Glory of God Is Intelligence: Four Lectures on the Role of Intellect in Judaism," vol. 3, *The Religious Studies Monograph Series* (Salt Lake City: Brigham Young University, Bookcraft Inc., 1979), p. xviii.

34. Mark Casson, "Changes in the Level and Structure of International Production: The Last Hundred Years," in *The Growth of International Business,* John H. Dunning, ed. (London: George Allen and Unwin, 1983), p. 106.

35. Herbert Feis, *Europe: The World's Banker, 1870–1914* (Clifton, N.J.: Kelley, 1974), p. 23.

36. Bernard Bailyn, *Voyagers to the West* (New York: Vintage, 1988), pp. 24–25.

37. Brinley Thomas, *International Migration and Economic Development* (Paris: UNESCO, 1961), p. 32.

38. Rhoads Murphey, *The Outsiders: The Western Experience in India and China* (Ann Arbor: University of Michigan Press, 1977), pp. 18–22.

39. Thomas, *International Migration and Economic Development.*

40. Louis L. Snyder, *Macronationalisms: A History of Pan-movements* (Westport, Conn.: Greenwood Press, 1984), pp. 96–97.

41. Sartre quoted in Frantz Fanon, *The Wretched of the Earth* (New York: Grove Press, 1966), p. 7.

42. "Economic and Financial Indicators," *The Economist,* September 29, 1990, p. 114.

43. Tony Smith, *The Patterns of Imperialism: The United States, Great Britain, and the Late-Industrializing World Since 1815* (Cambridge, Eng.: Cambridge University Press, 1981), p. 57.

44. M. C. Madhavan, "Indian Emigrants: Numbers, Characteristics and Economic Impact," *Population and Development Review,* vol. 11, no. 3, September 1985, p. 460; Murphey, *The Outsiders,* p. 101.

45. Noboru Tabe, *Indian Entrepreneurs at the Crossroads* (Tokyo: Institute of Developing Economies, 1970), pp. 8–13.

46. Dharma Kumar, *The Cambridge Economic History of India. Vol II: 1757–1970* (New Delhi: Cambridge University Press, 1982), p. 565.

47. Murphey, *The Outsiders,* pp. 17–18.

48. Karl Marx, *Capital* (New York: Vintage, 1977), vol. 1, p. 878, note 3.

49. Armytage, *A Social History of Engineering,* pp. 233–34.

50. "World Trade Survey," *The Economist,* September 22, 1990, p. 7.

51. "Future Shocklet," *The Economist*, September 22, 1990; "Survey: Asia's Emerging Economies," *The Economist*, November 16, 1991, p. 1; "World Population, By Region," *The Economist*, April 11, 1992, p. 107.

52. F. Gerard Adams, "Economic Performance and Prospects: South East Asia and Latin America," in *Perspectives on the Pacific Basin Economy*, eds. Takao Fukichi and Mitsuhiro Kagami (Tokyo: Institute of Developing Economies, 1990), p. 32.

53. "Price of Speech," *The Economist*, July 6, 1991, p. 16.

54. *The Economist*, July 20, 1991.

55. *The Economist*, July 20, 1991.

56. "Viewpoint," paid advertisement by Commerzbank; "Air Transport: Deregulation Will Stimulate Growth," *The Economist*, October 20, 1990, p. 82. The statistics are based on estimates by the International Civil Aviation Association.

57. Milton Singer, *When a Great Tradition Modernizes* (New York: Praeger, 1972), p. 317.

58. Interview with author.

59. Highlights of CJF 1990 National Survey, published by Council of Jews Federation, New York, pp. 56–58. Nearly three quarters of American Jews, including a considerable majority of the third generation, consider themselves closely attached to Israel.

60. Jenny Phillips, *Symbol, Myth and Rhetoric: The Politics of Culture in an Armenian-American Population* (New York: AMS Press, 1989), pp. 2–3.

61. Mathis Chazanov, "Job Springs from Ethnic Roots," *Los Angeles Times*, November 3, 1991.

62. Interview in "Diaspora," *AIM*, April 1991, p. 29.

63. Arthur Hertzberg, ed., *The Zionist Idea* (New York: Doubleday, 1959), p. 455.

64. Phillips, *Symbol, Myth and Rhetoric*, pp. 39–43.

65. Morton H. Fried, *The Notion of Tribe* (Menlo Park, Calif.: Cummings Publishing, 1975), p. 7.

66. Percival Spear, *India: A Modern History* (Ann Arbor: University of Michigan, 1961), p. 33.

67. Lynn Pan, *Sons of the Yellow Emperor: A History of the Chinese Diaspora* (Boston: Little, Brown, 1990), p. 10.

68. John W. Dower, *War Without Mercy: Race and Power in the Pacific War* (New York: Pantheon, 1986), pp. 215–25.

69. Barbara Tuchman, *Bible and Sword* (New York: Ballantine, 1984), pp. 1–21.
70. Ibid., pp. 121–22.
71. Friedrich Nietzsche, *The Birth of Tragedy and the Geneology of Morals*, trans. Francis Golffing (Garden City, N.Y.: Doubleday Anchor edition, 1956), p. 281.
72. Walter Kaufmann, *Nietzsche: Philosopher, Psychologist, Anti-Christ* (New York: Vintage, 1958), p. 339.
73. Michael Grant, *From Alexander to Cleopatra: The Hellenistic World*, p. 75.
74. Michael Grant, *The Jews in the Roman World* (New York: Scribners, 1973), p. 30.
75. Hyam Maccoby, *Revolution in Judea* (New York: Taplinger, 1980), p. 53.
76. Martin Gilbert, *The Jewish History Atlas*, 3rd ed. (Jerusalem: Steinmatzky Press, 1975), p. 75.
77. Ibid., pp. 19–21.
78. Grant, *The Jews in the Roman World*, pp. 289–90.
79. Nachum Gross, Salo W. Baron, Arcadius Kahan, et al., *The Economic History of the Jews* (New York: Schocken Books, 1975), p. 22. The authors cite an old proverb: "He who buys a Hebrew slave acquires a master unto himself."
80. Ibid., p. 52.
81. Jonathan I. Israel, *European Jewry in the Age of Mercantilism*, 2d ed. (New York: Oxford University Press, 1989), pp. 202–5.
82. Josef Kastein, *History and Destiny of the Jews*, trans. Huntley Paterson (New York: Viking Press, 1933), pp. 404–5; Elkan Nathan Adler, *London* (Philadelphia: Jewish Publication Society of America, 1930), pp. 172–74, 218–20; Anka Muhlstein, *Baron James: Rise of the French Rothschilds* (New York: Vendome Press, 1982), p. 65.
83. David Kranzler, *Japanese, Jews and Missionaries* (New York: Yeshiva University Press, 1976), pp. 174–76.
84. Jacques Attali, *A Man of Influence: Sir Siegmund Warburg*, trans. Barbara Ellis (London: Weidenfeld and Nicolson, 1986), pp. 54–56.
85. Mark Rosentraub and Delbert Taebel, "Jewish Enterprise in Transition: From Collective Self-help to Orthodox Capitalism," in *Self-Help in Urban America*, Scott Cummings, ed. (Port Washington, N.Y.: National University Publications, 1980), pp. 194–97.
86. Muhlstein, *Baron James*, p. 216.

87. Interview with author.

88. Irving Howe, *World of Our Fathers* (New York: Harcourt Brace Jovanovich, 1976), pp. 163–64.

89. Dennis A. Leventhal, *The Jewish Community of Hong Kong*, rev. ed. (Jewish Publication Society of Hong Kong, 1988), p. 9; Attali, *A Man of Influence*, pp. 120–22; Morton, *The Rothschilds*, p. 286.

90. Vicki Tamir, *Bulgaria and Her Jews: The History of a Dubious Symbiosis* (New York: Yeshiva University Press, 1979), p. 229.

91. Arthur Hertzberg, *The Jews in America: Four Centuries of an Uneasy Encounter* (New York: Touchstone Books, 1989), p. 373.

92. Joel Bainerman, "Cut Off Aid to Israel and Watch It Thrive," *The Wall Street Journal*, July 23, 1991.

93. Interview with author.

94. Henny Sender, "Inside the Overseas Chinese Network," *Institutional Investor*, August 1991, p. 30.

95. Michael Twaddle, "Was the Expulsion Inevitable?" in *Expulsion of a Minority: Essays on Ugandan Asians*, ed. Michael Twaddle (London: University of London, 1975), p. 13.

96. American Immigration Institute, July-August 1990, "Melting Pot Still Works," in *Focus on Immigration*, p. 6; U. O. Schmelz and Sergio DellaPergola, "Basic Trends in Jewish Demography," *Jewish Sociology Papers* (New York: American Jewish Committee, 1988), pp. 17–24; "WASP Children Are Waning," *American Demographics*, May 1991, p. 21.

97. Steven M. Cohen, *American Assimilation or Jewish Revival?* (Bloomington: Indiana University Press, 1988), p. 180.

98. Hamid Mowlana, *Global Information and World Communication: New Frontiers* (New York: Longmans, 1986), p. 175.

CHAPTER 2:
THE SECRET OF THE JEWS

1. Interview with researcher Hal Plotkin.

2. Leventhal, *The Jewish Community of Hong Kong*, pp. 6–8.

3. Michael Pollack, *Mandarins, Jews and Missionaries* (Philadelphia: Jewish Publication Society, 1980), pp. 63–66, 309.

4. Ibid., pp. 324–25.

5. Ibid., pp. 180–82.

6. Thomas Timberg, "The Jews of Calcutta," in *Bengal: Past and Present*, vol. 93, January–April 1974, pp. 7–8.

7. Leventhal, *The Jewish Community of Hong Kong*, p. 1.

8. Kranzler, *Japanese, Nazis and Jews*, pp. 20–21.

9. Eze Nathan, *The History of the Jews of Singapore* (Singapore: Herbilu Editorial Marketing and Services, 1986), pp. iii–vii.

10. Ibid., p. 1.

11. Ibid., p. 187.

12. Herman Dicker, *Wanderers and Settlers in the Far East* (New York: Twayne Publishers, 1962), p. 138.

13. F. J. George, *The Singapore Saga* (Singapore: General Printing and Publishing Services, 1985), pp. 75–76.

14. Nathan, *History of the Jews of Singapore*, in Foreword by David Marshall; Chan Heng Chee, *A Sensation of Independence: A Political Biography of David Marshall* (Singapore: Oxford University Press, 1984), pp. 1–11.

15. Based on an interview with Hal Plotkin.

16. Raphael Patai, *The Tents of Jacob* (Englewood Cliffs, N.J.: Prentice-Hall, 1971), p. 4; "In the history of the Hebrews," Patai observes on page 6, "*Diaspora* came first, and nationality, country and sovereignty second."

17. Stuart A. Queen and Robert W. Halbenstein, *The Family in Various Cultures* (New York: Lippincott, 1974), pp. 170–72.

18. Grant, *The Jews in the Roman World*, p. 36.

19. Grant, *The Jews in the Roman World*, p. xi.

20. Gilbert, *The Jewish History Atlas*, p. 12; Grant, *From Alexandra to Cleopatra*, p. 78.

21. Grant, *The Jews in the Roman World*, p. 60.

22. Gilbert, *The Jewish History Atlas*, p. 12; Grant, *The Jews in the Roman World*, p. xi.

23. Ferdinand Toennies, *On Sociology: Pure, Applied and Empirical*, Werner J. Cahnman and Rudolf Herberle, eds. (Chicago: University of Chicago Press, 1971), p. 310.

24. Nachum Gross, et al., *The Economic History of the Jews*, p. 21–24.

25. Curtin, *Cross-Cultural Trade*, pp. 99–100, 105.

26. Philip K. Hitti, *The Near East in History* (Princeton: Van Nostrand Co., 1961), pp. 275, 280; Roth, *The Jewish Contribution*, pp. 81–82.

27. Yves Lequin, *La Mosaique France* (Paris: Librarie Larousse, 1988), p. 109.

28. Curtin, *Cross-Cultural Trade*, p. 112.

29. Georg Simmel, *Sociology of Georg Simmel* trans. and ed. Kurt H. Wolff (New York: Free Press, 1950), pp. 402–8.

30. Gross, et al., *The Economic History of the Jews*, p. 43.
31. Roth, *The Jewish Contribution*, p. 229.
32. Ellis Rivkin, *The Shaping of Jewish History: A Radical New Interpretation* (New York: Scribners, 1971), p. 140.
33. Leon Poliakov, *Jewish Bankers and the Holy See*, trans. Miriam Kochan (London: Routledge and Keegan Paul, 1977), pp. 173–74.
34. Werner Sombart, *The Jews and Modern Capitalism*, trans. M. Epstein (Glencoe, Ill.: The Free Press, 1951), p. 13.
35. Fernand Braudel, *The Perspective of the World: Civilization & Capitalism, 15th–18th Century*, vol. 3, trans. Siân Reynolds (New York: Harper & Row, 1984), p. 109.
36. J. H. Elliott, *Imperial Spain, 1469–1716* (New York: St. Martin's Press, 1964), p. 98.
37. J. H. Parry, *The Age of Reconnaissance* (New York: Mentor Books, 1984), p. 21; Roth, *The Jewish Contribution*, pp. 70–72.
38. Braudel, *The Perspective of the World*, p. 187.
39. Arnold Wiznitzer, *Jews in Colonial Brazil* (New York: Columbia University Press, 1960), pp. 9–11, 66–70, 128.
40. Poliakov, *Jewish Bankers*, p. 229.
41. Gross, ed., *Economic History of the Jews*, p. 52.
42. Statistics from *Handbook of German Joint Stock Companies*, cited in Sombart, *The Jews and Modern Capitalism*, p. 114.
43. Raul Hilberg, *The Destruction of European Jewry* (New York: Holmes and Meier, 1967), pp. 94–95.
44. Sarah Gordon, *Hitler, Germans and the Jewish Question* (Princeton, N.J.: Princeton University Press, 1984), p. 12.
45. Ibid., pp. 803, 826–27.
46. Thomas Sowell, *Preferential Policies: An International Perspective* (New York: William Morrow, 1990), pp. 178–79.
47. Sarna, "The Jewish Way of Crime," pp. 53–55.
48. Sombart, *Jews and Modern Capitalism*, p. 295.
49. *Highlights of the CJF 1990 National Jewish Population Survey* (New York: Council of the Council of Jewish Federations, 1991), p. 37.
50. Chart provided by Sergio DellaPergola, "Jewish Population and Total, According to Country and Occupation, 1960–1980," (Jerusalem: The Institute of Contemporary Jewry, The Hebrew University, 1983 and 1988); Geoffrey Alderman, *The British Community in British Politics* (London: Clarendon Press, 1983), p. 37.
51. Clifford Longley, "High Finance, Higher Ethic," *The Times*, (London) September 8, 1990.

52. Taken from Hillsdown Holdings Group Profile, 1989, p. 6.
53. Chris Blackhurst, "The Leader of the Pack," *Business*, January 1989.
54. Interview with author.
55. Interview with author.
56. Hertzberg, ed., *The Zionist Idea*, pp. 324–25.
57. Israel, *European Jewry in the Age of Mercantilism*, pp. 29–34.
58. Rabbi Alexander Feinsilver, ed. and trans., *The Talmud for Today* (New York: St. Martin's Press, 1980), p. 72.
59. Israel, *European Jewry in the Age of Mercantilism*, p. 120. He notes that Jews occupied "most . . . of the middle ground between the peasantry, on the one hand, and the nobility and clergy on the other."
60. Caroline Golab, *Immigrant Destinations* (Philadelphia: Temple University Press, 1977), p. 46.
61. Ibid., p. 51.
62. D. Stanley Eitzen, "Two Minorities: The Jews of Poland and the Chinese of the Philippines," *The Jewish Journal of Sociology*, vol. 10, no. 2, December 1968, p. 125.
63. Stanislav Andreski, *Military Organization and Society*, (Berkeley: University of California Press, 1954), p. 206.
64. Gross, ed., *The Economic History of the Jews*, p. 192.
65. Michael Marrus, *The Unwanted: European Refugees in the Twentieth Century* (New York: Oxford University Press, 1985), p. 27.
66. Gilbert, *The Jewish History Atlas*, p. 75.
67. Golab, *Immigrant Destinations*, p. 55.
68. Lloyd P. Gartner, *The Jewish Immigrant in England, 1870–1914* (London: Allen and Unwin, 1960), p. 85.
69. Ibid., pp. 85–93.
70. Potter quoted in Stephen Aris, *But There Are No Jews in England* (New York: Stein and Day, 1970), pp. 194–95.
71. Ibid., pp. 104–11.
72. Howe, *World of Our Fathers*, p. 82.
73. Liebman Hersch, "International Migration of Jews," in *International Migrations*, ed. Walter Wilcox (New York: National Bureau of Economic Research, 1931), p. 504.
74. Howe, *World of Our Fathers*, p. 154.
75. Hersch, "International Migration of Jews," pp. 517–19.
76. Thomas Sowell, "Cultural Diversity: A World View," p. 7.

77. James Traub, "Behind All of That Glitz and Glitter, the Garment Industry Means Business," *Smithsonian*, August 1985, pp. 32–34.

78. Howe, *World of Our Fathers*, p. 154.

79. Interview with author.

80. Traub, "Behind That Glitter," p. 36; interviews with author.

81. Interview with author.

82. Phil Patton, "Jeans in the Genes: Why the S.Y.'s Are Sportswear's Chosen People," *New York*, May 22, 1989; and Jim Schachter, "Marciano Brothers Time of Trial," *Los Angeles Times*, January 21, 1990, pp. 40–41.

83. Patton, "Jeans in the Genes," p. 41.

84. Gross, ed., *Economic History of the Jews*, p. 158.

85. Israel, *European Jewry in the Age of Mercantilism*, p. 139.

86. *The Memoirs of Gluckel of Hameln*, trans. Marvin Lowenthal (New York: Schocken Books, 1932).

87. Gross, ed., *Economic History of the Jews*, pp. 159–60.

88. Gedalia Yogev, *Diamonds and Coral: Anglo-Dutch Jews and 18th Century Trace* (Leicester, Eng.: Leicester University Press, 1978), pp. 83–90.

89. Ibid., p. 145.

90. Eric Rosenthal, "On the Diamond Fields," in *The Jews in South Africa: A History*, Gustav Saron and Louis Hotz, eds. (New York: Oxford University Press, 1955), pp. 105–18.

91. Gross, ed., *Economic History of the Jews*, pp. 160–61.

92. Michael Szenberg, *The Economics of the Israeli Diamond Industry* (New York: Basic Books, 1973), p. 20.

93. Gross, ed., *Economic History of the Jews*, p. 160.

94. Szenberg, *Economics of the Israeli Diamond Industry*, p. 20.

95. "The Shaping of the Industry," paper written for the Israel Diamond Exchange, n.d.

96. Erica Harel, "A Look Inside Israel's Diamond Industry," an Israel Diamond Industry Publication, 1989, p. 7.

97. Kim Murphy, "Cracks in the Boycott," *Los Angeles Times*, May 22, 1991.

98. "Import and Export of Diamonds," *The Israel Diamond Industry Facts and Figures, 1990*, Diamond Division of the Ministry of Industry and Trade, p. 15.

99. Interview with author.

100. Interview with Hal Plotkin.

101. Korman, *The Outsiders*, p. 88.

102. "The Richest Congregations," *American Demographics*, December 1991, p. 13. The average Jewish household income was estimated at $36,700. The second-place Unitarians were pegged at $34,800, followed by agnostics at $33,300 and Episcopalians at $33,000.— J.K.

103. Compiled from "The Billionaires," *Forbes*, July 27, 1991. Further research conducted by Hal Plotkin and Julie Chien.

104. Miriam K. Freund, *Jewish Merchants in Colonial America* (New York: Behrman Jewish Book House, 1939), pp. 30–34.

105. Joseph L. Blau and Salo W. Baron, *The Jews of the United States: 1790–1840: A Documentary History* (New York: Columbia University Press, 1963), pp. 2–4.

106. Ibid., pp. 810–11.

107. Elliott Ashkenazi, *The Business of Jews in Louisiana, 1840–1875* (Tuscaloosa: University of Alabama Press, 1988), pp. 5–6; *Jubilee Souvenir of Temple Sinai*, comp. Rabbi Max Heller (New Orleans: 1922), p. 1.

108. Leon Harris, *Merchant Princes* (New York: Harper & Row, 1979), pp. 157–60, 167–76, 210–36.

109. Sombart, *The Jews and Modern Capitalism*, p. 39.

110. Fred Rosenbaum, *Architects of Reform: Congregational and Community Leadership Emanu-el of San Francisco* (Berkeley, Cal.: Western Jewish History Center, 1980), p. 1.

111. Sombart, *The Jews and Modern Capitalism*, pp. 39–40.

112. Harriet Rochlin and Fred Rochlin, *Pioneer Jews: A New Life in the Far West*, (Boston: Houghton Mifflin, 1984), p. 56.

113. Rudolf Glanz, *The Jews of California: From Discovery of Gold Until 1880* (New York: Waldon Press and the Southern California Jewish Historical Society, 1960), p. 149.

114. Neil Sandberg, *Jewish Life in Los Angeles* (Lanham, Md.: University Press, 1986), p. 27.

115. Rochlin and Rochlin, *Pioneer Jews*, pp. 127–28.

116. Glanz, *The Jews of California*, p. 41.

117. Rosenbaum, *Architects of Reform*, p. 14.

118. Ibid., p. 43.

119. Max Vorspan and Lloyd P. Gartner, *History of the Jews of Los Angeles* (Philadelphia: Jewish Publication Society, 1970), pp. 37–39.

120. Ibid., pp. 41–42.

121. Rochlin and Rochlin, *Pioneer Jews*, pp. 69–73.

122. Ibid., p. 122.
123. Moses Rischin, *The Promised Land: New York's Jews, 1870–1914* (Cambridge, Mass.: Harvard University Press, 1962), pp. 133–34.
124. Ibid., p. 134.
125. *World of Our Fathers*, pp. 164–65, 213.
126. Ibid., pp. 556–58.
127. Neil Gabler, *An Empire of Their Own: How the Jews Invented Hollywood* (New York: Crown Publishers, 1988), p. 62.
128. Kathleen Neumeyer, "A New Promised Land," *Los Angeles*, June 1985, p. 200.
129. Gabler, *An Empire of Their Own*, p. 2.
130. Neumeyer, "A New Promised Land," p. 200.
131. Vorspan and Gartner, *History of the Jews of Los Angeles*, pp. 132–34.
132. Neumeyer, "A New Promised Land," p. 200.
133. *World of Our Fathers*, pp. 568–69.
134. Ibid., pp. 165–66.
135. *CJF National Jewish Survey*, press release, November 15, 1990.
136. *Highlights of the CJF 1990 National Jewish Population Survey*, p. 48.
137. George Cohen, *The Jews in the Making of America* (Boston: The Stratford Co., 1924), p. 262.
138. Gary Libman, "Los Angeles Jews Gain Clout as Power Shifts to West," *Los Angeles Times*, March 18, 1990.
139. Neumeyer, "A New Promised Land," p. 172.
140. Ibid., pp. 170–75.
141. Sheldon Teitelbaum, "A Tale of Three Cities: Los Angeles–Beverly Hills Battleground," *Present Tense*, November–December 1988, p. 24.
142. David Biale, *Power and Powerlessness in Jewish History* (New York: Schocken Books, 1986), p. 180.
143. Ibid.
144. Lisa Gubernick with Julie Schlax, "A Dinner with Liz Taylor," *Forbes*, March 4, 1991, p. 113.
145. Lisa Gubernick and Peter Newcomb, "The Richest Man in Hollywood," *Forbes*, December 24, 1990, p. 94.
146. Interview with author.
147. DellaPergola, *World Jewish Population: 1986*, p. 418; Hilberg, *The Destruction of European Jewry*, p. 1047
    NOTE: DellaPergola's number seems to be low, at least according to some more recent estimates. This is markedly true in the dias-

pora with, as he himself notes on page 414, the enormous problems of definition caused by out-marriages, divorce, mobility within the Jewish populations outside of Israel. His estimate of French Jewish population, for instance, seems at least 100,000 less than that given by Le Consistoire de Paris; in the United States, these differences are even more marked. According to the 1990 Council of Jewish Federations Population Survey, the American Jewish population estimate of "core" Jews is similar to Della-Pergola's, but the "ethnic" Jewish population, which includes many children of mixed marriages, etc., could be as much as one million larger.—J.K.

148. Schmelz and DellaPergola, "Basic Trends in Jewish Demography," pp. 419–25. As noted earlier, the Hebrew University estimates tend to be lower than others; for instance, their estimates for Argentina of 224,000 are considerably lower than those offered by Gilbert in *The Jewish History Atlas* (p. 124), where the Jewish population is given as 400,000.

149. David Vital, *The Future of the Jews* (Cambridge, Mass.: Harvard University Press, 1990), p. 42.

150. Gilbert, *The Jewish History Atlas*, pp. 58, 60, 93, 110.

151. "Les Juifs de France ont plus de mal à être qu'à être français," *L'Evénement du Jeudi*, July 6, 1989, p. 62.

152. Michael Marrus, "Are the French Anti-Semitic," in Frances Malino and Bernard Wasserstein, eds., *The Jews in Modern France*, (Hanover, New Hampshire: University Press of New England, 1985), p. 236.

153. Hertzberg, *The Jews of America*, p. 388. Hertzberg predicts "American Jewish history could end" without some sort of full-scale revival.

154. *The Jerusalem Letter*, The Jerusalem Center for Public Affairs, January 15, 1991.

155. Matthew Nesvisky, "Broken Promises," *Present Tense*, March 20, 1989, pp. 22–26.

156. "Letting Their People Go," *Time*, October 9, 1989, p. 43.

157. "The Richest Congregations," *American Demographics*, December 1991, p. 13. This is all the more remarkable since this measures household income and Jewish households are also among the *smallest*, meaning *per capita* Jewish incomes are particularly high.

158. "Brooklyn on the Volga," *The Economist*, June 9, 1990, p. 25.

159. Chaim I. Waxman, *America's Jews in Transition* (Philadelphia:

Temple University Press, 1983), pp. 197–200; "The Exodus from Israel," *Time*, January 12, 1981, p. 39; "Now It's an Exodus from Troubled Israel," *U.S. News & World Report*, August 4, 1980, pp. 31–32; "Israel: The Exodus of the Disenchanted," *Maclean's*, January 5, 1981, p. 21.

160. *Bank of Israel: Annual Report 1989* (Jerusalem, 1990), p. 82.
161. Josh Meyer, "Seeking Word on Israel," *Los Angeles Times*, January 20, 1991. In this article the Los Angeles Jewish Consulate estimate of Israelis in just the seven western states is given as 200,000.
162. Daniel Williams, "New Jersey Comes to Jerusalem," *Los Angeles Times*, November 8, 1989; *1987 Statistical Yearbook of the Immigration and Naturalization Service* (Washington, D.C.: Government Printing Office, October 1988), p. 4.
163. Sheldon Teitelbaum, "They Love America: Israelis in Southern California Have Finally Arrived," *Present Tense*, March–April 1989, p. 30.
164. Asher Friedberg and Aharon Kfir, "Jewish Emigration from Israel," *The Jewish Journal of Sociology*, June 1988, pp. 11–12.
165. Tom Tugend, "The Brain Drain," *Jerusalem Post*, July 4, 1989.
166. Hugh Carey, "Immigration Tide Demands Urgent Changes," *Financial Times*, September 14, 1990.
167. For a discussion of problems of the Israeli film industry, see Edna Fainaru, "Fleeing Film-makers Point Up Crisis of Israeli Pic Industry," *Variety*, July 22, 1987.
168. "6000 Émigrés Apply to Travel Abroad," *Northern California Jewish Bulletin*, August 16, 1991.
169. Interview with author.
170. Golda Meir, "What We Want for the Diaspora," in Etan Levine, ed., *Diaspora: Exile and the Jewish Tradition* (New York: Schocken Books, 1986), p. 190.
171. Georges Friedmann, "Jews as a Product of History," in *Ethnic Conflicts and Power*, Donald E. Gelfand and Russell D. Lee, eds. (New York: John Wiley and Sons, 1973), p. 135–36.
172. Ibid., p. 137.
173. Baruch Kimmerling, *Zionism and Economy* (Cambridge, Eng.: Schenkman Publishing, 1983), pp. 27–29.
174. Alex Keynan, "Science and Israel's Future: A Blueprint for Revitalizing Basic Research and Strengthening Science-Based Industry" (Jerusalem: Israel Academy of Sciences and Humanities, The Jerusalem Institute for Israel Studies, 1988), p. 5.

175. Kimmerling, *Zionism and Economy*, pp. 3–5.
176. Robert Loewenberg, "Why Prop Up Israeli Socialism?" *New York Times,* June 24, 1991.
177. Ibid., p. 99.
178. Loewenberg, "Why Prop Up Israeli Socialism?"
179. Ibid.
180. This is based on 1990 figures of an approximate U.S. trade deficit of $100 billion and an economy of roughly $5 trillion, making the trade deficit roughly 2 percent of GNP.
181. *Bank of Israel, Annual Report* (Jerusalem: Ahva Press, 1990), p. 166. The 1989 number for foreign residents' investment in Israel is $425 million.
182. Comparison is from *Handbook of International Trade and Development Statistics 1988* (New York: The United Nations, 1990), pp. 315, 319.
183. Ziv Hellman, "Free the Orange," *Jerusalem Post,* May 12, 1991.
184. Yossi Melman, "Struggling to Survive, Kibbutzim Lose Identity," *Los Angeles Times,* January 6, 1991; Tom Bethall, "Is the Kibbutz Kaput?," *Reason,* October 1990, pp. 33–37; Ziv Hellman, "Free the Orange," *Jerusalem Post,* May 12, 1991.
185. Interview with author.
186. Dan Williams, "To Shamir, Emigres, Zionism and Disputed Lands Tied," *Los Angeles Times,* January 20, 1990.
187. Daniel Doron, "Free Enterprise Hasn't Been Given a Chance," *Jerusalem Post,* May 17, 1991.

CHAPTER 3:
LEGACY OF EMPIRE

1. L.C.A. Knowles, *The Industrial and Commercial Revolutions in Great Britain During the Nineteenth Century* (New York: E. P. Dutton, 1921) p. 35.
2. Ibid., p. 3.
3. "World's Top Twenty Companies," *The Economist,* July 11, 1992, p. 100.
4. *World Competitiveness Report, 1991,* p. 213.
5. Ibid., p. 240.
6. *World Competitiveness Report, 1990,* p. 198.
7. "The Marshall Plan: Doing Well by Doing Good," *The Economist,* June 15, 1991, pp. 30–31.

8. Gale Eisenstat, "A Cozy Japanese Near Monopoly," *Forbes*, September 30, 1991, pp. 52–54.

9. John Huey, "What Pop Culture Is Telling Us," *Fortune*, June 17, 1991, p. 89.

10. Leslie Helm, "U.S. Described Ahead in Key Technologies," *Los Angeles Times*, July 22, 1991.

11. *World Competitiveness Report, 1990*, p. 158. By another measurement, the number of worldwide citations for scientific papers of the four main English-speaking countries—the United States, the United Kingdom, Australia and Canada—between 1981 and 1990 boasted twice the total output of all the leading European and Asian countries *combined* ("The Machinery of Growth," *The Economist*, January 11, 1992, p. 17).

12. Interview with author.

13. Richard W. Bailey and Manfred Gorlach, eds., *English as a World Language* (Ann Arbor: University of Michigan Press, 1982), pp. 2–3.

14. Hannah Arendt, *Imperialism: Part Two of the Origins of Totalitarianism* (San Diego: Harcourt Brace Jovanovich, 1968), p. 9.

15. Murphey, *The Outsiders*, p. 32.

16. Arendt, *Imperialism*, p. 4.

17. Ibid., p. 5.

18. Tony Smith, *The Patterns of Imperialism*, p. 35.

19. Alain Peyrefitte, *The Trouble with France*, trans. William R. Byron (New York: New York University Press, 1981), pp. 107–8.

20. Arendt, *Imperialism*, p. 4.

21. Colin Crisswell, *The Taipans: Hong Kong's Merchant Princes* (Oxford, Eng.: Oxford University Press, 1981), pp. 19–21.

22. Francis Moulder, *Japan, China and the Modern World Economy* (Cambridge, Eng.: Cambridge University Press, 1977), p. 91.

23. Anthony B. Chan, *Gold Mountain: The Chinese in the New World* (Vancouver, B.C.: New Star Books, 1983), p. 26.

24. Crisswell, *The Taipans*, p. 6.

25. H. J. M. Johnston, *British Emigration Policy* (Oxford: Clarendon Press, 1972), pp. 3–5, 11.

26. Karl Polanyi, *The Great Transformation* (Boston: Beacon Press, 1944), p. 14.

27. Compton Mackenzie, *Realms of Silver* (London: Routledge and Kegan Paul, 1954, reprinted 1979), pp. 5–7.

28. Author interview with Rodney Galpin, Chairman of the Board, Standard Chartered Bank.

29. *1989 Annual Report of the Standard Chartered Bank,* pp. 14–19.

30. "British Business in Hong Kong," Hong Kong, June 13, 1989; supplied by the British Trade Commission.

31. Mario Pei, *The Story of the English Language* (Philadelphia: Lippincott, 1967), pp. 153–54.

32. Peyrefitte, *The Trouble with France,* pp. 251–52.

33. Robert McCrum, William Cran, Robert MacNeil, *The Story of English* (New York: Viking Press, 1986), p. 20.

34. Glynn Mapes, "Polyglot Students Are Weaned Off Mother Tongue," *Wall Street Journal,* March 6, 1990.

35. V. G. Kiernan, "Britons Old and New," in *Immigrants and Minorities in British Society,* Colin Holmes, ed. (London: George Allen and Unwin, 1978), pp. 23–27.

36. Defoe quoted in J. W. Gregory, *Human Migration and the Future* (Philadelphia: Lippincott, 1928), p. 161.

37. Alan Davies, "Is International English an Interlanguage?," *Tesol Quarterly,* vol. 23, no. 3, September 1989, p. 455.

38. Pei, *The Story of the English Language,* pp. 153–55.

39. Braj B. Kachru, "The Pragmatics of Non-Native Varieties of English," in *English for Cross-Cultural Communication,* Larry E. Smith, ed. (New York: St. Martin's Press, 1981), pp. 17–22.

40. Ibid.

41. Davies, "Is International English an Interlanguage?," p. 455.

42. "We Want to Play the Game," *Nature,* July 12, 1990, p. 124.

43. Randolph Quirk, *The English Language and Images of Matter* (London: Oxford University Press, 1972), pp. 32–33.

44. Randolph Quirk, "The English Language in a Global Context," in *English in the World: Teaching and Learning the Languages and Literatures,* Randolph Quirk and H. G. Widdowson, eds. (Cambridge, Eng.: Cambridge University Press, 1984), pp. 1–6.

45. Terry Nichols Clark, "The Irish Ethic and the Spirit of Patronage," *Ethnicity,* December 1975, p. 305.

46. Nina McPherson, "Hong Kong's Choice: English or Chinese?," *International Herald Tribune,* February 16–17, 1991.

47. Kachru, "The Pragmatics of Non-Native Varieties of English," p. 33.

48. Ibid., p. 17.

49. M. L. Boonlua Debyasuvarn, "Will EIIL Succeed Where ESL and

EFL Fail?," in *English for Cross-Cultural Communication*, Smith, ed., p. 87.

50. John Dougill, "The Good Feeling of Fine," *English Today*, vol. 7, no. 2, April 1991, pp. 50–51.

51. "Japperish," *The Economist*, October 31, 1987, p. 64.

52. Brian D. Smith, "English in Indonesia," *English Today*, vol. 7, no. 2, April 1991, pp. 39–43.

53. "French-American Relations: Rapprochement," *The Economist*, March 16, 1991, p. 20.

54. Rone Tempest, "American Look Sells in Europe," *Los Angeles Times*, December 27, 1990.

55. "Europe's Film Industry: Sleeping with the Enemy," *The Economist*, October 26, 1991.

56. Brochure of Le Centre National de la Cinématographie, 1990.

57. Alexandra Tuttle, "Nativist Protection for Frog Crooners," *Wall Street Journal*, September 20, 1991.

58. "Pan Asian Television: Starry Eyed," *The Economist*, August 24, 1991, pp. 59–60.

59. Barbara Crossette, "India Foreign TV Monitor Sights 'Alien' Influence," *International Herald Tribune*, June 13, 1991.

60. Thomas R. Rosentiel, "TV, VCRs Fan Fire of Revolution," *Los Angeles Times*, January 18, 1990.

61. Michael Balter, "For Europe Professionals, English Means Business," *International Herald Tribune*, February 17–18, 1990.

62. F. Burgdorfer, "Migration Across the Frontiers of Germany," in *International Migrations, Volume II: Interpretations*, Walter F. Wilcox, ed. (Gordon and Breach Science Publishers, 1931), p. 386; estimates vary to a high of 110 million estimated by Dr. Manfred Heid of the Goethe Foundation, Munich; Pei, *The Story of the English Language*, p. 153.

63. Paul Christopherson, "A Bilingual Denmark," *English Today*, vol. 7, no. 3, July 1991, pp. 7–10.

64. Carol J. Williams, "In Hungary, Learning Russian Is Out of Style," *Los Angeles Times*, March 15, 1990.

65. "Hungarian Teachers Learn English By Teaching in U.S.," *Los Angeles Times*, December 10, 1989.

66. Figures provided by Peter Hilkes from the Osteuropa-Institut, Munich, October 9, 1990, survey.

67. Interview with author.

68. Knowles, *The Industrial and Commercial Revolutions in Great Brit-*

ain, pp. 98–99; P. T. Bauer, *Equality: The Third World and Economic Delusion* (Cambridge, Mass.: Harvard University Press, 1981), pp. 32–33.

69. Tawney, *Religion and the Rise of Capitalism,* pp. 21–39.
70. Ibid., pp. 104–5.
71. Christopher Hill, "Protestantism and the Rise of Capitalism," in *The Rise of Capitalism,* David Landes, ed. (New York: Macmillan, 1966), p. 45.
72. Tawney, *Religion and the Rise of Capitalism,* pp. 106–8.
73. Tawney quoted in Adrian Furnham, *The Protestant Ethic: The Psychology of Work-related Beliefs and Behaviours* (New York: Routledge, 1990), pp. 1–32.
74. Stephen Gill and David Law, *The Global Economy: Perspectives, Problems and Policies* (New York: Harvester, Wheatsheaf, 1988), p. 5.
75. Bauer, *Equality,* p. 189.
76. Weber, *The Protestant Ethic and the Spirit of Capitalism,* p. 53.
77. Ivan Light, "Immigrant and Ethnic Enterprise in North America," *Ethnic and Racial Studies,* vol. 7, no. 2, April 1984, p. 205.
78. Weber, *The Protestant Ethic,* pp. 48–49.
79. Based on charts derived from Maurice R. Davie, *World Immigration* (New York: Macmillan, 1936), p. 32.
80. Dudley Baines, *Migration in a Mature Economy: Emigration and Internal Migration in England and Wales, 1861–1900* (Cambridge, Eng.: Cambridge University Press, 1985), p. 10.
81. Wilcox, *International Migrations,* p. 219.
82. Davie, *World Immigration,* p. 32.
83. Smith, *The Patterns of Imperialism,* pp. 58–59.
84. Baines, *Migration in a Mature Economy,* p. 67.
85. Bailyn, *Voyagers to the West,* p. 152.
86. Rowland Berthoff, *British Immigrants in Industrial America* (New York: Russell and Russell, 1953), pp. 21–23.
87. Baines, *Migration in a Mature Economy,* pp. 139–40.
88. Charlotte Erickson, *Invisible Immigrants: The Adaptation of English and Scottish Immigrants in Nineteenth Century America* (Coral Cables: University of Miami Press, 1972), p. 30.
89. John H. Dunning, "Changes in the Level and Structure of International Production," *The Growth of International Business,* Mark Casson, ed. (London: George Allen and Unwin, 1983), p. 106.
90. Barbara M. Tucker, *Samuel Slater and the Origins of the American*

Textile Industry, 1790–1860 (Ithaca, N.Y.: Cornell University Press, 1984), pp. 44–45.

91. Ibid., pp. 25–51.

92. Ibid., pp. 89–90.

93. David I. Jeremy, *Transatlantic Industrial Revolution: The Diffusion of Textile Technologies Between Britain and America, 1790–1830* (Cambridge, Mass.: MIT Press, 1981), pp. 87–90.

94. Barbara M. Tucker, "The Merchant, the Manufacturer and the Factory Manager," *Business History Review,* vol. XIV, no. 3, Autumn 1981, pp. 298–99.

95. Jeremy, *Transatlantic Industrial Revolution,* pp. 54, 131–32, 251, 253.

96. Thomas, *Migration and Urban Development,* pp. 3–5.

97. Ibid., p. 12.

98. Foreign Direct Investment: Effects in the United States, prepared by the Subcommittee on Economic Stabilization of the Committee on Banking, Finance and Urban Affairs, 101st Congress, July 1989, p. 35.

99. Feis, *Europe: The World's Banker,* p. 23.

100. Thomas, *Migration and Urban Development,* p. 61.

101. Ron Chernow, *The House of Morgan: An American Banking Dynasty and the Rise of Modern Finance* (New York: Atlantic Monthly Press, 1990), pp. 3–16.

102. Ibid., p. 30.

103. Mira Wilkins, *The History of Foreign Investment* (Cambridge, Mass.: Harvard University Press, 1989), p. 613.

104. Fred A. McKenzie, *The American Invaders* (New York: Arno Press, 1976), p. 5.

105. Wilkins, *History of Foreign Investment,* p. 130.

106. W. S. Woytinksy and E. S. Woytinsky, *World Commerce and Governments: Trends and Outlook* (New York: The Twentieth Century Fund, 1955), p. 191.

107. Wilkins, *The History of Foreign Investment,* p. 141.

108. Smith, *The Patterns of Imperialism,* p. 42.

109. Frank Vanderlip, *The American "Commercial Invasion" of Europe* (New York: Arno Press, 1976), pp. 69–93.

110. McKenzie, *American Invaders,* p. 6.

111. Ibid., pp. 8–9.

112. Berthoff, *British Immigrants in Industrial America,* p. 134.

113. Martin J. Weiner, *English Culture and the Decline of the Industrial*

Spirit (Cambridge, Eng.: Cambridge University Press, 1981), p. 88.

114. *Statistical Abstract of the United States, 1990* (Washington, D.C.: Government Printing Office, 1991), p. 10.

115. Arnold M. Rose, *Migrants in Europe* (Minneapolis: University of Minnesota Press, 1969), pp. 24–27. In some years during the 1950s over 1,000 engineers, more than half Canada's yearly net output, emigrated, mostly to the United States. Between 1951 and 1967, the emigration of professionals reached 5,000 annually.

116. Alan G. Green, *Immigration and the Postwar Canadian Economy* (Toronto: Macmillan of Canada, 1976), p. 165. The development of the Free Trade Agreement may further exacerbate this movement, see Diane Francis, "New Concerns about the Brain Drain," *Maclean's*, February 26, 1990, p. 9.

117. Green, *Immigration and the Postwar Canadian Economy*, p. 165.

118. Figures for the United States come from *1987 Statistical Yearbook of the Immigration and Naturalization Service*, October 1988, p. 4; for Canada, see John Paxton, ed., *The Statesman's Yearbook: 1990–1991* (New York: Saint Martin's Press), pp. xxx, 272.

119. Compiled from *1989 Demographic Yearbook* (New York: United Nations, 1991), pp. 595–96, 588, 562; also Ian Castles, *Australian Year Book 1991* (Canberra: Australian Bureau of Statistics, 1991), p. 147; and *New Zealand Pocket Digest of Statistics 1991* (Wellington: 1991), p. 45.

120. Information from Gregory Staple and Mark Mullins, "Global Telecommunications Traffic Flows and Market Structures," *IIC Research Report* (London: 1989), p. 22.

121. Eduardo Lachica, "Seeking Bonanza from US–Japan Air Routes; Cities-Carriers Coalition Lobbies for Expansion," *The Wall Street Journal*, July 29, 1989.

122. *Britain's Overseas Trade* (London: Central Office of Information, October 1989), p. 4; James Beeler, "Exports: Ship 'Em Out," *Fortune*, Spring/Summer 1991, p. 58.

123. Steven Globerman and Maureen Bader, "A Perspective on Trilateral Economic Relations," in *Continental Accord: North American*, Steven Globerman, ed. (Vancouver: The Fraser Institute, 1991), pp. 155–56.

124. *Statistical Abstract of the United States*, "US Exports and Imports and Merchandise Trade Balance, by Continent, Area and Country: 1980 to 1988" (Washington, D.C.: Government Printing Of-

fice, 1990), pp. 806–7; "Top 25 US Markets," *Business America*, April 22, 1991, p. 5.

125. Paxton, ed., *The Statesman's Yearbook: 1990–1991*, pp. 110, 287–88, 924–25.

126. The U.S. numbers come from "The Perfidious Japanese," *The Economist*, April 20, 1991.

127. Joel Kotkin, "The Empire Strikes Back: UK Fights Financial Sunset," *Los Angeles Times*, July 22, 1990.

128. Kotkin, "The Empire Strikes Back."

129. Kan H. Young and Charles Steigerwald, "Is Foreign Investment in the U.S. Transferring U.S. Technology Abroad?," *Business Economics*, October 1990, vol. 25, no. 4, p. 28.

130. From projections of Central Statistics Office, London, September 1989.

131. Joel Havemann, "Europe Is Weaning Itself from U.S. Economy," *Los Angeles Times*, January 17, 1992. These numbers are estimates from the Confederation of British Industry.

132. Randolph Quirk, in *English for Cross-Cultural Communication*, Smith, ed. (New York: St. Martin's Press, 1981), p. 151.

133. Hamish McRae and Frances Cairncross, *Capital City: London as a Financial Center* (London: Eyre Methuen, 1973), p. 2.

134. McRae and Cairncross, *Capital City*, p. 7–8.

135. Smith, *English for Cross-Cultural Communication*, p. 21.

136. Curtin, *Cross-Cultural Trade*, pp. 252–53.

137. Thomas, *Migration and Urban Development*, p. 60.

138. Knowles, *The Industrial and Commercial Revolutions in Great Britain*, p. 313.

139. Curtin, *Cross-Cultural Trade*, p. 252.

140. Knowles, *The Industrial and Commercial Revolutions in Great Britain*, p. 166.

141. Susan Strange, *States and Markets* (London: Pinter Publishers, 1988), pp. 96–101.

142. "Central Banking in the 1920s: The Age of Monty and Ben," *The Economist*, December 23, 1990, pp. 113–14.

143. Harold K. Jacobson and Dusan Sidjanski, "The Continuing Evolution of the World Political Economy," in *The Emerging International Economic Order*, Harold K. Jacobson and Dusan Sidjanski, eds. (Beverly Hills: Sage Publishers, 1982), pp. 22–23.

144. Thorstein Veblen, *Imperial Germany and the Industrial Revolution* (New York: Macmillan, 1915), pp. 82–83.

145. Asa Briggs, *Victorian People* (Chicago: University of Chicago Press, 1955), p. 123.
146. *Academy of Accounting Professionals,* monograph, R. H. Parker, University of Exeter, England, 1986.
147. A. C. Littlejohn, *Accounting Evolution to 1903,* Ph.D. thesis (New York: American Institute Publishing, 1933), pp. 3, 14, 20.
148. Jill L. McKinnon, *The Historical Development and Operational Form of Corporate Reporting Regulation in Japan* (New York: Garland Publishing, 1976), pp. 118–19.
149. Philip Yuen-Ko, *A Study of Government Accounting in China: With Special Reference to the Sung Dynasty (960–1279)* (Urbana: University of Illinois Press, 1968), pp. 23–24.
150. Philip Yuen Ko Fu, *A Study of Government Accounting in China: With Special Reference to the Sung Dynasty,* Ph.D. thesis, University of Illinois at Urbana, 1968.
151. *The Memoirs of Edwin Waterhouse,* Edgar Jones, ed. (London: Batsford, 1988), pp. 18–19.
152. Ibid., p. 20.
153. Ibid., pp. 20–21.
154. Ibid., pp. 25–26.
155. Ibid., pp. 24–26.
156. Ibid., p. 33.
157. P. L. Payne, *British Entrepreneurship in the Nineteenth Century* (London: Macmillan, 1974), p. 35.
158. *Academy of Accounting Professionals,* monograph, R. H. Parker, pp. 6–8.
159. Ibid., pp. 5–7.
160. Ibid., pp. 12–16.
161. James A. Stewart, *Pioneers of a Profession* (Edinburgh: Scottish Committee on Accounting History, 1977), p. 30.
162. Samuel A. Cypert, *Following the Money: Inside Accounting's First Mega-Merger* (New York: American Management Association, 1991), p. 2.
163. McKinnon, *The Historical Development and Operational Form of Corporate Reporting Regulation in Japan,* pp. 118–19.
164. Yuen-Ko, *A Study of Government Accounting in China,* p. 16.
165. Letter to author from Jeremy Davies, partner, World Firm, London, June 18, 1990.
166. "British Accountants: Quis custodiet?," *The Economist,* June 8, 1991, pp. 81–82.

167. Interview with author.

168. *Price Waterhouse World Firm Limited*, listing provided by London office, 1990.

169. Interview with author.

170. Seiya Ikari, "American Know-how and the Miracle," *Japan Update*, October 1991, pp. 18–19.

171. Alfred D. Chandler, *The Visible Hand: The Managerial Revolution in American Business* (Cambridge, Mass.: Harvard University Press, 1977), p. 500.

172. "Survey: World Trade," *The Economist*, September 22, 1990, p. 36.

173. Anne B. Fisher, "The Ever Bigger Boom in Consulting," *Fortune*, April 24, 1989.

174. "Survey: The Advertising Industry," *The Economist*, June 9, 1990, p. 4.

175. "Japan Is Getting Too Small for Dentsu," *The Economist*, October 26, 1987, p. 62.

176. "Why London?," *The Economist*, May 4, 1991, p. 15.

177. "London Still Leads," *The Economist*, December 16, 1989, p. 28.

178. "Europe's Capital Markets Survey," *The Economist*, December 16, 1991, pp. 27–28.

179. Robert Gibson-Jarvie, *City of London: A Financial and Commercial History*, pp. 118–19; McRae and Cairncross, *Capital City*, p. 18.

180. "Land of Hope," *The Economist*, July 20, 1991, p. 69.

181. "An Unsettled Minority," *The Economist*, September 8, 1990, p. 64.

182. "The Japanese are Coming—And Thatcher Is All Smiles," *Business Week*, February 20, 1989, pp. 46–47.

183. *Bank of England Quarterly Bulletin*, November 1989, vol. 29, no. 4, pp. 516–19, tables 13, 14, 15.

184. At least four of the top ten British merchant banks, for example, in 1992 can trace their origins directly to their Jewish roots. See "London's Top Merchant Banks," *The Economist*, January 25, 1992, p. 63.

185. Interview with author.

CHAPTER 4:
THE NEW CALVINISTS

1. Interview with author.

2. Thomas, *International Migration and Economic Development*, p. 9.

3. Uma A. Segal, "Cultural Variables in Asian Indian Families," *Families in Society*, vol. 72, no. 4, April 1991, pp. 233–34.

4. Illsoo Kim, *The New Urban Immigrants: The Korean Community in New York* (Princeton, N.J.: Princeton University Press, 1981), p. 299.

5. Sowell, *Preferential Policies*, pp. 43 – 44.

6. Badr Dahya, "The Nature of Pakistani Ethnicity in Industrial Cities in Britain," in *Urban Ethnicity*, Abner Cohen, ed. (London: Tavistock Publications, 1974) pp. 97–98.

7. "Ethnic Origins and the Labour Market," *Employment Gazette*, March 1990, pp. 125 –37.

8. Interview with author.

9. "Britain's Browns: East Meets West," *The Economist*, October 28, 1989, pp. 21–23.

10. Ibid.

11. Robert Moore and Tina Wallace, *Slamming the Door: The Administration of Immigration Control* (London: Martin Robertson, 1975), pp. 107–8.

12. Ibid., pp. 112–15.

13. "Asian Residents in Australia Targets of Racist Attacks, Discrimination," *Japan Times*, November 26, 1990.

14. William McGurn, "Stirring Up Trouble in Australia's Melting Pot," *The Wall Street Journal*, October 5, 1988.

15. "Asia Calling," *The Economist*, August 24, 1991.

16. Hal Quinn and Thomas Lewis, "Empire of the Triads," *Maclean's*, March 25, 1991, p. 25; Tim Egan, "Prosperity from Asia Has West in Conflict," *New York Times*, May 8, 1989.

17. Joel Kotkin, "Fear and Reality in the Los Angeles Melting Pot," *Los Angeles Times Magazine*, November 5, 1989.

18. Joel Kotkin, "The American Way," *Inc.*, September 1991, pp. 96–102.

19. Alka Sabherwal, "Institutional Barriers Against Asian Indians in the U.S. Labor Market," paper written at State University of New York, Stony Brook, 1991.

20. Ivan Light, "Immigrant and Ethnic Enterprise in North America," *Ethnic and Racial Studies*, vol. 7, no. 2, April 1984, p. 206.

21. Ivan Light and Parminder Bhachu, "Immigrant Networks and Immigrant Entrepreneurship," *ISSR Working Papers in the Social Sciences*, Institute for Social Science Research, UCLA, 1989–1990, vol. 5, no. 1, p. 6.

22. Ivan Light, "Koreans in Los Angeles," in *Self-Help in Urban America*, Cummings, ed., p. 41.
23. Pyong Gap Min, "Korean Immigrants in Los Angeles," *ISSR Working Papers in the Social Sciences*, Institute for Social Science Research, UCLA, 1989–1990, vol. 2., no. 2, p. 31.
24. Kim, *The New Urban Immigrants*, p. 314.
25. M. C. Madhavan, "Indian Emigrants: Numbers, Characteristics and Economic Impact," *Population and Development Review*, September 1985, pp. 464–65.
26. Edward K. Y. Chen, "The Changing Role of the Asian NICs in the Asia-Pacific Region Towards the Year 2000," in Miyohei Shinohara and Fu-chen Lo, *Global Adjustment and the Future of Asian-Pacific Economy* (Tokyo: Institute of Developing Economies, 1989), p. 220.
27. Tom Rees, "The United Kingdom," in *The Politics of Migration Policies*, Daniel Kubat with Ursula Gehmacher and Ernst Gehmacher, eds. (New York: Center for Migration Studies, 1979), p. 68.
28. Interview with author.
29. Madhavan, "Indian Emigrants," p. 460.
30. "Emigration and Return: Ramifications for India," in *Population Review*, S. Shandrasekhar and Arthur Helweg, eds., vol. 28, nos. 1 and 2, 1984, p. 47.
31. Interview with author.
32. "Britain's Browns," *The Economist*, pp. 21–23.
33. Steven Jones, "Hong Kong to Lose a Growing Share of Its Best, Brightest to Emigration," *The Wall Street Journal*, September 18, 1990.
34. Sam Jameson, "Aussies Say G'Day to Asians," *Los Angeles Times*, November 17, 1989.
35. "Hard-working, Hopeful—and Solvent," *International Herald Tribune*, December 3, 1990.
36. "New Faces in the Crowd," *Canada Year Book 1990* (Ottawa: Economic Council of Canada, 1991), pp. 2–41.
37. Julian Simon, *The Economic Consequences of Immigration* (draft copy) (New York: Basil Blackwell, 1989), p. 44.
38. Ibid., p. 80.
39. David Reimers, *Still the Golden Door* (New York: Columbia University Press, 1985), p. 98.
40. James T. Fawcett and Benjamin V. Carino, "International Migra-

tion and Pacific Basin Development," in *Pacific Bridges: The New Immigration from Asia and the Pacific Islands,* James T. Fawcett and Benjamin V. Carino, eds. (Staten Island, N.Y.: Center for Migration Studies, 1987), p. 9.

41. Interview with author.

42. Jonathan Moore, "Taiwan's New Breed," *Far East Economic Review,* July 21, 1988, p. 56.

43. Fred Arnold, Urmil Minocha, and James T. Fawcett, "The Changing Face of Asian Immigration to the United States," in *Pacific Bridges,* Fawcett and Carino, eds., p. 111; "The New Americans: Yes, They'll Fit In Too," *The Economist,* May 11, 1991, p. 17; William Dunn, "Asians Build New Lives as Immigrants," *USA Today,* November 26, 1990.

44. Julian Simon, "Bring on the Wretched Refuse," *The Wall Street Journal,* January 26, 1990.

45. Richard C. Atkinson, "Supply and Demand of Scientists and Engineers: A Crisis in the Making," *Association Affairs,* April 27, 1990, p. 429; Robert Pool, "Who Will Do Science in the 1990s?," *Science,* April 1990, p. 434.

46. Atkinson, "Supply and Demand of Scientists and Engineers," p. 429; Pool, "Who Will Do Science in the 1990s?," p. 434; "Selected Data on Science and Engineering Awards: 1990," *National Science Foundation,* April 1991.

47. Dan Fost, "California's Asians," *American Demographics,* October 1990, p. 34.

48. Joel Kotkin, "The Spacemen Have Landed," *California,* March 1991, p. 20. CSU fall 1989 enrollment provided courtesy of California State University system.

49. "Foreign Engineering Students at UC Berkeley," Fall 1990, courtesy of the University of California.

50. Carl T. Hall, "Immigrants Mold U.S. Economy," and Don Clark, "Newcomers Put Stamp on Silicon Valley," *San Francisco Chronicle,* July 8, 1991.

51. Stephen Kreider Yoder, "Reverse 'Brain Drain' Helps Asia but Robs U.S. of Scarce Talent," *The Wall Street Journal,* April 18, 1989; Susan Lee, "Train 'Em Here, Keep 'Em Here," *Forbes,* May 27, 1991, p. 112.

52. Like the Jews they have also shown a remarkable propensity to make a long-term commitment to the United States, acquiring citizenship at twice the rate of other groups—J.K.

SOURCE: Elliot R. Barkan, "California at the Forefront: Pacific Rim Migration and Naturalization Patterns in the 1970s and 1980s," *ISSR Working Papers in the Social Sciences*, Institute for Social Science Research, UCLA, 1989–1990, vol. 5, no. 15, p. 55.

53. Selma Cantor Berrol, "Strangers in the City: Migration and Ethnicity," in *The New Ethnics: Asian Indians in the United States*, Parmata Saran and Edwin Eames, eds. (New York: Praeger, 1980), p. 91.

54. Kristin Butcher and David Card, "Immigration and Wages: Evidence from the 1980s," *American Economic Review*, May 1991, pp. 292–96.

55. Richard Levine, "Young Immigrant Wave Lifts New York Economy," *New York Times*, July 30, 1990.

56. "New York City: Looking to the 21st Century," special advertising supplement to *Forbes*, April 15, 1992, p. 98.

57. Benjamin Wong, *Patronage, Brokerage, Entrepreneurship, and the Chinese Community of New York* (New York: AMS Press, 1988), pp. 173–75.

58. "Why Made-in-America Is Back in Style," *Business Week*, November 7, 1988, p. 116; Sandra Bucovaz, "Will America Become Asia's Offshore Garment Maker?," *Am Cham Magazine*, December 1988, pp. 14–15.

59. "Chinatropolis," *The Village Voice*, October 31, 1989, p. 27.

60. Michael A. Goldberg, *The Chinese Connection: Getting Plugged into Pacific Rim Real Estate, Trade, and Capital Markets* (Vancouver: University of British Columbia Press, 1985), p. 117.

61. Michael Specter, "In New York, 'Phenomenal' Boom for Chinatown," *International Herald Tribune*, December 15, 1990.

62. Yuen Ying Chan, "Riding the Dragon," *The Village Voice*, October 31, 1981, p. 34.

63. Interview with author.

64. Smith, *The Patterns of Imperialism*, p. 21.

65. Interview with author.

66. Weber, *The Protestant Ethic*, pp. 51–52.

67. Weiner, *English Culture*, p. 14.

68. Ibid., p. 43.

69. P. L. Payne, "Family Business in Britain," in Akio Okochi and Shigeaki Yasuoka, eds., *Family Business in the Era of Industrial Growth: Its Ownership and Management* (Tokyo: University of Tokyo Press, 1984), p. 189.

70. Weber, *The Protestant Ethic*, pp. 181–82.

71. Weiner, *English Culture*, pp. 101–19.

72. David Cannadine, *The Decline and Fall of the British Aristocracy* (New Haven: Yale University Press, 1990), pp. 262–65.

73. Weiner, *English Culture*, p. 157.

74. Sidney Pollard, *The Wasting of the British Economy: British Economic Policy from 1945 to the Present* (New York: St. Martin's Press, 1982), pp. 41, 79.

75. Weiner, *English Culture*, pp. 125–35.

76. Cannadine, *The Decline and Fall of the British Aristocracy*, p. 407.

77. Leslie Hannah, *The Rise of Corporate Economy* (London: Methuen, 1976), p. 68.

78. Interview with author.

79. *World Competitiveness Report, 1990* (Geneva: Imede, June 1990), p. 153; "German Measles," *The Economist*, August 17, 1991, p. 60.

80. James Risen, "Why Can't America Catch Up?," *Los Angeles Times*, January 14, 1990.

81. *The Economist*, "Survey: Capitalism," May 5, 1990, p. 6.

82. Bradley A. Stertz, "Big Three Boost Car Quality but Still Lag," *The Wall Street Journal*, March 27, 1990; James Risen, "Japan's Edge in Auto Quality," *Los Angeles Times*, January 14, 1990.

83. Pitirim Sorokin, *The Crisis of Our Age: The Social and Cultural Outlook* (New York: E. P. Dutton, 1941), p. 185.

84. Ibid., p. 164.

85. James Risen, "Why Can't America Catch Up?"

86. Barry Wood, "America's Prophet Remains Unimpressed with His Country," *Financial Times*, January 25, 1989.

87. "Management Brief: When GM's Robots Ran Amok," *The Economist*, August 10, 1991, pp. 64–65.

88. "Deming's Demons," *The Wall Street Journal*, June 4, 1990.

89. "Surveying the CEOs," *The Wall Street Journal Europe*, September 29–30, 1989, p. 13.

90. Alan Murray and Urban C. Lehner, "What U.S. Scientists Discover, the Japanese Convert—Into Profit," *The Wall Street Journal*, June 25, 1990.

91. Thomas A. Stewart, "The New American Century," *Fortune*, Spring/Summer 1991 special issue, pp. 12–23.

92. Steve Kelman, "The 'Japanization' of America," *The Public Interest*, Winter 1990, pp. 70–83.

93. Urban C. Lehner and Alan Murray, "Selling of America Touches Some Very Raw Nerves," *The Wall Street Journal*, June 19, 1990.

94. "US-Japan Relations: Fifty Years Beyond Pearl Harbor," *Yomiuri Shimbun*, September 12, 1991.

95. Pat Choate, "Political Advantage: Japan's Campaign for America," *Harvard Business Review*, September–October 1990, pp. 87–103.

96. TRB, "The Nefarious East," *The New Republic*, pp. 6–7.

97. Ian MacGee and Jack Lowenstein, "City of the Future on Starting Blocks," *Asian Business*, July 1990.

98. Lorie Teeter, "French Sound Alarm on Japan High Tech," *Electronic News*, March 5, 1990, p. 22.

99. Interview with author.

100. Joachim Fest, *Hitler* (New York: Vintage Books, 1975), p. 619.

101. Sheridan Tatsuno, *Created in Japan: From Imitators to World Class Innovators* (New York: Harper & Row, 1990), p. 9.

102. T. Iyenaga Sato and Kenoske Sato, *Japan and the California Problem* (New York: G. P. Putnam's Sons, 1921), p. 27.

103. "Survey: International Finance," *The Economist*, April 27, 1991; Michael Smith, "More Work, Less Time," *Financial Times*, May 8, 1990.

104. "Official Reserves," *The Economist*, March 30, 1991, p. 93.

105. Yasusuke Murakami and Yataka Kosai, eds., *Japan in the Global Community* (Tokyo: University of Tokyo Press, 1986), p. 37.

106. Shigekazu Matsumoto, "Asian Pacific Economies in a Changing World: Recent Developments and New Trends in the 1990s," paper presented to the International Symposium on the Economic Cooperation in the Asian-Pacific Region in the 1990s, Shanghai, China, October 15–17, 1990.

107. Interview with author.

108. "The Japanese Are Coming—and Thatcher Is All Smiles," *Business Week*, February 20, 1989.

109. E. S. Browning, "Peugeot Chairman Calvert Continues to Restrict Japanese Imports," *The Wall Street Journal*, March 18, 1991.

110. "World Beaters at the Wheel," *Financial Times*, September 20, 1991.

111. Robert Simison, "Nissan U.K. Plant Teaches E.C. a Lesson," *The Wall Street Journal*, July 23, 1991.

112. *Real Estate Perspectives*, Sumichrest and Associates, February 15, 1991, p. 8.

113. John C. Campbell, *The United States in World Affairs* (New York: Council of Foreign Relations, 1949), p. 290.

114. Jim Mann, "Eisenhower Weighed Asia Pullout in '50's, Files Show," *Los Angeles Times*, September 23, 1991.

115. Paul Ingrassia, "Auto Industry Is Sliding Relentlessly into Japanese Hands," *The Wall Street Journal*, February 16, 1990.

116. Jesus Sanchez, "Cooperation Forges a Success Story," *Los Angeles Times*, April 26, 1991.

117. Bob Baker, "Bringing Teamwork to America," *Los Angeles Times*, June 16, 1990; Joseph B. White, "Japanese Automakers Help U.S. Supplier Become More Efficient," *The Wall Street Journal*, September 9, 1991.

118. Sanchez, "Cooperation Forges a Success Story."

119. "The Best Companies: Scrambling to the Top," *The Economist*, September 7, 1991, pp. 21–24.

120. Michael Schrage, "Applying *Zaibatsu* Principles in the U.S.," *Los Angeles Times*, March 8, 1990.

121. Interview with author.

CHAPTER 5:
DIASPORA BY DESIGN

1. Estimate from Consulate Policy Department, Ministry of Foreign Affairs, Tokyo. Research conducted by Mari Arizumi, 1991.

2. Phaedon Nicolaides, "International Perspective: The Globalization of Japanese Corporations: Investment in Europe," *Business Economics*, July 1991, vol. 26, no. 3, pp. 38–41; "Those Perfidious Japanese," *The Economist*, April 20, 1991, p. 65.

3. Interview with author.

4. W. R. Crocker, *The Japanese Population Problem* (New York: Macmillan, 1931), p. 172.

5. Ibid., p. 173.

6. Ibid., p. 31.

7. Ibid., pp. 202–3.

8. Ibid., p. 174.

9. Ibid., p. 189; Yamato Ichihashi, "International Migrations of the Japanese," in *International Migrations*, Walter Wilcox, ed. (New York: Gordon and Breach, 1931), p. 623.

10. Bouscaren, *International Migrations Since 1945*, p. 122.

11. "Net Foreign Investment Income," *The Economist*, August 30, 1991, p. 90.

12. *World Development Report, 1990* (Washington, D.C.: published for the World Bank by Oxford University Press, 1990), p. 213; *World Competitiveness Report, 1991*, p. 240.

13. Estimate from Consulate Policy Department, Ministry of Foreign Affairs, Tokyo. Research conducted by Mari Arizumi, 1991.

14. 1989 Estimate from Consulate Policy Department, Ministry of Foreign Affairs, Tokyo; 1970 estimate from report of Ministry of Foreign Affairs (Tokyo: 1980), "Survey of Overseas Japanese," p. 9. Research conducted by Mari Arizumi.

15. Fred Hiatt, "It's a Cold, Cruel World Out There," *Washington Post National Weekly*, May 22–28, 1989, p. 17.

16. Kenichi Ohmae, *The Borderless World* (New York: Harper Books, 1991), p. 19.

17. Isaacs, *Idols of the Tribe*, p. 185.

18. Information provided by Returned Educational Promotion Foundation. Research by Mari Arizumi.

19. *Japanese Companies: Consolidated Data 1987–1988* (Tokyo: Nihon Keizai Shimbun, 1989), p. 171.

20. James Davenport Whelpley, *The Trade of the World* (New York: The Century Co., 1913), pp. 247–48.

21. Snyder, *Macronationalisms*, p. 203.

22. Dower, *War Without Mercy*, p. 270.

23. Park, *Race and Culture*, p. 25.

24. William B. Hauser, *Economic and Institutional Change in Tokugawa Japan: Osaka and the Kinai Cotton Trade* (Cambridge, Eng.: Cambridge University Press, 1974), pp. 11, 188–90; Moulder, *Japan, China and the Modern World Economy*, p. 31.

25. Shigeo Shingo, *Non-Stock Production and the Shingo System for Continuous Improvement* (Cambridge, Mass.: Productivity Press, 1988), pp. 19, 416.

26. Edwin Mansfield, "Industrial Innovation in Japan and the United States," *Science*, September 30, 1988, p. 1771. For example, fully one third of Japanese research and development projects are based on suggestions from either production personnel or customers, twice the percentage for American firms.

27. Joel Kotkin, "Secrets of the Orient," *Family Business*, March/April 1991, p. 31.

28. Matao Miyamoto, "The Position and Role of Family Business in

the Development of the Japanese Company System," in *Family Business in the Era of Industrial Growth*, Akio Okuchi and Shigeaki Yasuoka, eds. (Tokyo: University of Tokyo Press, 1984), p. 44.

29. Hiroshi Komai, *Japanese Management Overseas: Experiences in the United States and Thailand* (Tokyo: Asian Productivity Center, 1989), p. 19.

30. Information provided by Jiro Tokuyana, retired dean, Nomura School of Advanced Management.

31. S. N. Eisenstadt, "The Protestant Ethic Thesis: An Analysis," in *The Protestant Ethic and Modernization*, S. N. Eisenstadt, ed. (New York: Basic Books, 1968), pp. 30–31.
    Eisenstadt notes: "Some of the specific structural characteristics of Japanese modernization can be related to specific points of flexibility in the Tokugawa period." He relates specifically to the "social mobility" and opportunities for education there, in comparison with the family-based Chinese system and the domination of intellectual activity by the mandarinate.—J.K.

32. Sol Sanders, *Honda: A Man and His Machines* (Boston: Little Brown, 1975), p. xv.

33. Adrian Furnham and Michele Reilly, "A Cross-Cultural Comparison of British and Japanese Protestant Work Ethic and Just World Beliefs," *Psychologia: A Journal of Psychology in the Orient*, vol. 34, no. 1, March 1991, p. 3; Hidetoshi Kato, "Japanese Social Structure; Achievement and Modernization," private paper, 1990.

34. John G. Roberts, *Mitsui: Three Centuries of Japanese Business* (New York: Weatherhill, 1973), pp. 10–12.

35. Soji Mizuno, *Early Foundations for Japan's 20th Century Emergence* (New York: Vantage Press, 1981), pp. 66–67.

36. "Survey: Business in Europe," *The Economist*, July 8, 1991, p. 6.

37. Park, *Race and Culture*, p. 26.

38. B. Hauser, *Economic Institutional Change in Tokugawa Japan*, p. 190.

39. George Akita and Donald L. Robinson, "Japanese and U.S. Constitutions Celebrate Anniversaries," *Japan Times*, November 28, 1990. In the Charter Oath of the Five Articles, one of the founding documents of the 1868 Restoration, the Emperor Meiji vowed that "wisdom and knowledge shall be sought to strengthen the nation's foundation and well-being."

40. G. C. Allen, *A Short Economic History of Japan* (London: George Allen and Unwin, 1972), p. 167.

41. Ibid.
42. Moulder, *Japan, China and the Modern World Economy*, pp. 184–85.
43. Kunio Yoshihara, *The Rise of Ersatz Capitalism in Southeast Asia* (New York: Oxford University Press, 1988), pp. 41–45.
44. Barbara Molony, *Technology and Investment in the Prewar Japanese Chemical Industry* (Cambridge, Mass.: Council of East Asian Studies, 1990), pp. 39–40.
45. Armytage, *A Social History of Engineering*, pp. 233–34.
46. Molony, *Technology and Investment*, pp. 6–7, 10.
47. Yamato Ichihashi, "International Migration of the Japanese," in *International Migrations*, ed. Wilcox, p. 623. Anti-Japanese agitation began in California as early as 1887, when there were no more than 400 Japanese residents in the state.
48. Howard Hiroshi Sugimoto, *Japanese Immigration, The Vancouver Riots and Canadian Diplomacy* (New York: Arno Press, 1978), p. 29.
49. Roberts, *Mitsui*, p. 263.
50. Ibid., pp. 96–97.
51. Ibid., pp. 108–11.
52. Ibid., p. 112.
53. Ibid., p. 5.
54. Takashi Matsuda, *Japan: Its Commercial Development and Prospects* (London: Sisley's Ltd., 1908), p. 38.
55. Ichihashi, "International Migration of the Japanese," pp. 617–36.
56. Ken-ichi Imai, "Evolution of Japan's Corporate and Industrial Networks," in *Industrial Dynamics*, Bo Carlsson, ed. (Boston: Kluwer Academic Publishers, 1989), pp. 123–55.
57. W. R. Crocker, *The Japanese Population Problem: The Coming Crisis* (New York: Macmillan, 1931), pp. 171, 175.
58. G. C. Allen, *Appointment in Japan* (London: Athlone Press, 1983), pp. 78–79.
59. Allen, *A Short Economic History of Japan*, pp. 64–77.
60. Crocker, *The Japanese Population Problem*, p. 212.
61. Ibid., p. 211.
62. Allen, *Appointment in Japan*, pp. 35–36.
63. Roberts, *Mitsui*, pp. 259–60.
64. Ibid., p. 262.
65. Alvin Yiu-cheong So, "Development Inside the Capitalist World-System: A Study of the Chinese and Japanese Silk Industry," *Journal of Asian Culture*, vol. V, 1981, pp. 33–50.
66. Roberts, *Mitsui*, p. 263.

67. Ibid., pp. 147–48.
68. Ibid., pp. 156–57.
69. Richard Deacon, *Kempei Tai: A History of the Japanese Secret Service* (New York: Beaufort Books, 1983), p. 45.
70. Roberts, *Mitsui*, p. 167.
71. Murphey, *The Outsiders*, p. 203.
72. Roberts, *Mitsui*, pp. 166–67.
73. Crocker, *The Japanese Population Problem*, p. 143.
74. Molony, *Technology and Investment*, pp. 15, 236–37.
75. Robert J. C. Butow, *Tojo and the Coming of the War* (Stanford, Calif.: Stanford University Press, 1961), p. 17.
76. Alfred E. Eckes, *The United States and the Global Struggle for Minerals* (Austin: University of Texas Press, 1979), p. 84.
77. Snyder, *Macronationalism*, p. 221.
78. Deacon, *Kempei Tai*, pp. 84–85.
79. A. Whitney Griswold, *The Far Eastern Policy of the United States* (New York: Harcourt Brace, 1938), p. 377.
80. V. S. Maniam, "Subhas Bose's Odyssey," *India Perspectives*, April 1990, p. 9.
81. Robert Elegant, *Pacific Destiny* (uncorrected proof) (New York: Crown, 1990), p. 9.
82. Interview with author.
83. Dower, *War Without Mercy*, pp. 262–69.
84. M. J. Gayn, *The Fight for the Pacific* (Kingsport, Tenn.: Kingsport Press, 1941), p. 152.
85. Dower, *War Without Mercy*, p. 275.
86. Ibid., pp. 282–84.
87. Ibid., p. 275.
88. David Joel Steinberg, ed., *In Search of Southeast Asia* (New York: Praeger, 1971), pp. 338–39.
89. Dower, *War Without Mercy*, pp. 6–7.
90. Butow, *Tojo and the Coming of the War*, p. 419.
91. Ibid., p. 131.
92. Yoshihara, *The Rise of Ersatz Capitalism*, p. 20.
93. Masasuke Ide, "Corporate Financial Policy and International Competition—A Financial Analyst's View," paper submitted to the Kagami Memorial Foundation of Tokio Marine and Fire Insurance Co., Ltd., September 1991, p. 34.
94. Ibid., p. 13.
95. Ibid., p. 3.

96. Paz Estrella E. Tolentino, "Overall Trends of Foreign Direct Investment," *The CTC Reporter*, no. 29, Spring 1990, p. 29.

97. John Pelzel, "The Small Industrialist in Japan," *Explorations in Entrepreneurial History*, vol. 7–8, 1956, p. 85.

98. Imai, "Evolution of Japan's Corporate and Industrial Networks," in *Industrial Dynamics*, Carlsson, ed., pp. 123–55.

99. Bouscaren, *International Migrations Since 1945*, p. 122.

100. Imai, "Evolution of Japan's Corporate and Industrial Networks."

101. Karel van Wolferen, *The Enigma of Japanese Power* (New York: Knopf, 1989), pp. 47, 396.

102. Hiroyuki Odagiri, "An *Economic* Theory of Japanese Management," London Business School Paper, April 1990.

103. Pelzel, "The Small Industrialist in Japan," p. 81.

104. Sanders, *Honda*, p. 119.

105. Interview with author.

106. Pelzel, "The Small Industrialist in Japan," p. 87.

107. David Friedman, *The Misunderstood Miracle* (Ithaca, N.Y.: Cornell University Press, 1988), pp. 6–11; interview with author.

108. Ibid., pp. 11–13.

109. James Risen, "Tight Network of Suppliers Provides Key Support for Japan's Auto Makers," *Los Angeles Times*, January 17, 1990.

110. Kuniyasu Sakai, "The Feudal World of Japanese Manufacturing," *Harvard Business Review*, November–December 1990, p. 39.

111. Banri Asunama, "Manufacturer-Supplier Relationships in Japan and the Concept of Relation-Specific Skill," *Journal of Japanese and International Economies*, vol. 3, pp. 9–13, 23.

112. Ikuo Umebayashi and JCER Forecasting Associates, "Challenge to Small and Medium Sized Companies Approaching the 21st Century," *Japan Center for Economic Research*, July 1990, p. 35.

113. Tadao Kiyonari, "Competition Strategy of Japan's Small and Medium-Sized Firms vis-à-vis the World," appendix to paper, July 7, 1989. Based on government surveys, Kiyonari reports that the number of smaller industrial firms in Japan that have decided to concentrate on "high technology" increased from 54 percent in 1983 to roughly 84 percent in 1988.

114. Interview with author.

115. Wan Hee Kim, "Korea: A Land of Opportunity, or a Profitless Battleground," *Electronic Business*, March 1, 1987, p. 46.

116. *Industrial Groupings in Japan*, 7th ed. (Tokyo: Dodwell Consulting, 1986), pp. 67–69.

117. *The Case of the Walkman*, Sony Innovation in Management Series, June 1988, p. 4.
118. Interview with author.
119. Interview with author.
120. Dower, *War Without Mercy*, pp. 234–40.
121. Sugimoto, *Japanese Immigration*, p. 6.
122. Dower, *War Without Mercy*, pp. 234–40.
123. Ibid., pp. 248–60.
124. Christopher Chipello and Urban C. Lehner, "Miyazawa Calls U.S. Work Ethic Lacking," *The Wall Street Journal*, February 4, 1992.
125. Dower, *War Without Mercy*, p. 315.
126. Karl Schoenberger, "Issue of Japanese Racism Grows with Immigration," *Los Angeles Times*, January 1, 1990.
127. Hiroshi Komai, *Japanese Management Overseas: Experiences in the United States and Thailand* (Tokyo: Asian Productivity Organization, 1989), p. 28.
128. Mordechai E. Kreinin, "How Closed Is Japan's Market? Additional Evidence," *The World Economy: A Quarterly Journal of International Economic Affairs*, December 1988, pp. 529–41.
129. Alan Murray, "Managed Trade May Serve a Purpose," *The Wall Street Journal*, January 20, 1992.
130. Christopher Bartlett, "Japan's Achilles Heel," *Los Angeles Times*, November 12, 1989.
131. James Risen, "Americans at Japanese Firms Lacking Power," *Los Angeles Times*, October 19, 1989.
132. James Risen, "Some Japanese Firms Moving to Segregate Staffs," *Los Angeles Times*, May 23, 1990. This referred to the operations of Nissan Corp. in Los Angeles.
133. Interview with author.
134. "Osaka Lifts Korean Sports Ban," *Japan Times*, November 26, 1990; "No Way to Treat a Guest," *The Economist*, June 2, 1990, p. 66.
135. Karl Schoenberger, "The Axis: Odd Twins on Ascent," *Los Angeles Times*, August 13, 1990.
136. "When Training Becomes a Rip-off," *Bangkok Post*, March 24, 1991.
137. Elisabeth Rubinfein, "Boat People Arouse Japan's Xenophobia," *The Wall Street Journal*, October 11, 1989.

138. Yamamoto quoted in Kaori Shoji, "The Changing Face of Japanese Labor," *Business Tokyo*, January 1991, p. 22.

139. *Japan 2000*, draft of treatise from discussion at Rochester Institute of Technology, published by Rochester Institute, February 11, 1991, p. 133.

140. Bernard Wysocki, "In Asia, the Japanese Hope to Coordinate What Nations Produce," *The Wall Street Journal*, August 20, 1990.

141. Wysocki, "In Asia, the Japanese Hope to Coordinate What Nations Produce."

142. "Malaysia Envisions a Joining of East Asia's Economic Forces," *International Herald Tribune*, February 23–24, 1991.

143. Raees Mohammed, *Gaijin kacho ga mita Nippon kabushikigaisha (Nippon Inc. in the Eyes of a Foreigner)* (Tokyo: PHP Books, 1989), pp. 75, 83, 85.

144. Interview with Hal Plotkin.

145. Komai, *Japanese Management Overseas*, pp. 69–74, 109.

146. Ibid., pp. 75–80; Dennis S. Tachiki, *Going Transnational: Japanese Subsidiaries in the Asia-Pacific Region* (Tokyo: Center for Pacific Business Studies, Mitsui Research Institute, 1990), p. 17.

147. "Japanese Investment in Thailand: Too Good to Be True," *The Economist*, June 2, 1990, p. 89.

148. Komai, *Japanese Management Overseas*, p. 80.

149. Ibid., pp. 36–38.

150. Steven E. Levingston, "Asian Industry Reaches a New Phase," *The Wall Street Journal*, June 14, 1991. The surveys included such diverse countries as Korea and Malaysia.

151. Dennis Tachiki, *Going Transnational: Japanese Subsidiaries in the Asia Pacific Region* (Tokyo: Mitsui Research Institute, November 1990), pp. 24–25.

152. Kou Hoshino, *"Kokusaika"* ("Internationalization"), in *Nihon Sangyo Ni-ju Issei ki eno torendo o yomu (Industrial Trends in the 21st Century)*, Hiroshi Takeuchi, chief ed. (Tokyo: Yuikaku, 1990), p. 55.

153. *Nippon 1991: Jetro Business Facts and Figures* (Tokyo: 1991), pp. 56–57.

154. Mead Ventures, Inc., *Taiwan Semiconductor Report, 1990* (Phoenix, Ariz.). The survey found Taiwanese firms preferred to work with American firms by a two-to-one margin largely due to their greater openness.

155. Interview with author.

156. Komai, *Japanese Management Overseas*, p. 106. Even in relatively pro-Japanese Thailand a recent poll found most workers expecting anti-Japanese sentiment to grow in coming years.

157. "Asia's Emerging Economies," *The Economist*, March 23, 1991, pp. 3–18.

158. Andrew K. P. Leung, "Japanese Investment and Hong Kong Industries—the Case of a Successful Partnership," paper submitted to symposium on Japan's role in the Asia-Pacific Region, November 7–9, 1989, pp. 2–3.

159. "Postscript," *The Wall Street Journal*, August 7, 1990.

160. *Japan 2000*, p. 14.

161. Ibid., pp. 113–22.

162. Akio Morita, "Japan Must Play According to the Rules of Its Competitors," *Los Angeles Times*, February 9, 1992.

163. Kazuo Nukazawa, "Japan and the USA: Wrangling Toward Reciprocity," *Harvard Business Review*, May–June 1988, p. 4. A Keidanren report predicts Japanese firms will be forced to increase their overseas presence from 4 percent of sales in the mid-1980s to nearly 20 percent by the turn of the century.

164. "Japan's Less-than-invincible Computer Makers," *The Economist*, January 11, 1992, p. 59.

165. Sender, "Inside the Overseas Chinese Network," pp. 29–43; Shigeaki Fujisaki, Nobuaki Hamaguchi, and Tatsufumi Yamagata, "Three Decades of Development in the Pacific Basin: An Overview," in *Perspectives on the Pacific Basin Economy: A Comparison of Asia and Latin America*, Takao Fukuchi and Mitsuhiro Kagami, eds. (Tokyo: The Institute of Developing Economies, 1990), p. 32; "Hong Kong: Asia Its Oyster," *The Economist*, December 8, 1990, p. 30; "Foreign Investment in Indonesia," *The Wall Street Journal*, February 13, 1992.

166. Daniel Burstein, *Yen!: Japan's New Financial Empire and Its Threat to America* (New York: Simon and Schuster, 1988), p. 35.

167. "Interview with Shintaro Ishihara," *Venture Japan*, vol. 2, no. 2, p. 39. In 1990 Ishihara said: "Because of Japan's great financial power, it will be leader of the world."

168. "Foreign Investment in Indonesia," *The Wall Street Journal*, February 13, 1992; Julia Leung, "Asian Borrowers Find Money Scarce Due to Retreat by Japanese Banks," *The Wall Street Journal*, February 7, 1992.

169. "Japanese Capital Flows: Inward Bound," *The Economist*, February 8, 1992, p. 82.

170. "Thumbs Down in Tokyo," *The Economist*, April 11, 1992, pp. 77–78; "Japanese Property: Stuck," *The Economist*, April 11, 1992, pp. 78–79.

171. Robert Metzger and Ari Ginsberg, "The Failure of Japanese Banks in America," research paper, University of Southern California, April 1988. In 1990, for example, a survey by the Sheshenoff Information Service found Japanese return on equity in California was roughly half that of their domestic rivals.—J.K.

172. "Propping Up Detroit," *The Economist*, February 15, 1992, p. 75.

173. *Japan 2000*, p. 16.

174. Leslie Helm, "The Rule of Work in Japan," *Los Angeles Times*, May 17, 1991.

175. "Japanese Less Patriotic Than People in Other Countries," *Mainichi Shimbun*, July 13, 1991.

176. Takeshi Umehara, "The Civilization of the Forest," *New Perspectives Quarterly*, Summer 1990, p. 23.

177. Akiko Kusaoi, "SDF Struggles to Meet Recruiting Quotas," *Japan Times*, December 1, 1990.

178. Karl Schoenberger, "Military in Japan Gets No Respect," *Los Angeles Times*, September 10, 1990.

179. Dentsu Institute for Human Studies, "A New Partnership: New Values and Attitudes of the New Middle Generation in Japan and the USA," pp. 4, 13–15.

180. Interview with author.

181. "Office Workers See Decline in Life at Work," *Los Angeles Times*, October 10, 1991.

182. Interview with author.

183. "Survey of Consciousness of Youngsters Working for Organizations," conducted by Prime Minister's Office, Tokyo, 1979.

184. Dentsu Institute, "A New Partnership" pp. 9, 13.

185. "Land of the Waning Sun," *The Wall Street Journal*, May 20, 1991. By the eve of the twenty-first century Japan's new entrants to the work force are expected to drop by 12 percent, forcing some universities to cut back faculty or even close.

186. "Labor Letter," *The Wall Street Journal*, March 14, 1989: "College Graduate Job Offers Surpass 1 Million Milestone," *Japan Times*, August 21, 1990; "Developing Human Resources to Cope with Restructuring," *KKC Brief*, October 1989, p. 2.

187. Hiroshi Kato, *Jinzai Shin Jidai (New Era for Personnel Utilization)* (Tokyo: President Sha, 1988), p. 75.

188. *Small Business in Japan: 1989* (Tokyo: Small and Medium Enterprise Agency, Ministry of International Trade and Industry, 1989), p. 168.

189. Interview with staff of UPU, Ltd., Tokyo, 1990.

190. Mitsuko Shimomura, "Too Much Mommy-san," *New Perspectives Quarterly*, Winter 1990, pp. 24–27.

191. Interview with author.

CHAPTER 6:
THE SPACEMEN HAVE LANDED

1. Interview with author.

2. Robert W. Gibson, "Networks of Chinese Rim Pacific," *Los Angeles Times*, July 22, 1990.

3. Teresa Watanabe, "Science Park Key to Taiwan's Growth," *Los Angeles Times*, December 29, 1989.

4. Derrik Koo, "Mitac Aims to Be Tops in Quality," *New Straits Times*, September 20, 1990.

5. "Official Reserves," *The Economist*, March 30, 1991, p. 93; *World Competitiveness Report, 1990*, p. 96.

6. James Sterngold, "Japan's Cash Fountain Has All But Dried Up," *New York Times*, December 6, 1991; "Japanese Banks: Deep in Bad Debt," *The Economist*, November 2, 1991, p. 70.

7. Sender, "Inside the Overseas Chinese Network," pp. 29–43; Fujisaki, Hamaguchi, and Yamagata, "Three Decades of Development in the Pacific Basin: An Overview," p.32; "Hong Kong: Asia Its Oyster," *The Economist*, p. 30; "Foreign Investment in Indonesia," *The Wall Street Journal*; Yozo Tanaka, Minako Mori and Yoko Mori, "Overseas Chinese Business Community in Asia: Present Conditions and Future Prospects," *RIM*, Pacific Business and Industries, vol. II, no. 16, 1992, p. 18.

8. John Pomfret, "Taiwan Breaks Out as Global Investor," *Los Angeles Times*, February 10, 1992.

9. Fred S. Worthy, "A New Mass Market Emerges," *Fortune*, Pacific Rim 1990 issue, p. 51.

10. Julia Leung, "Foreign Investment in China Dwindles," *The Wall Street Journal*, August 17, 1990; Yozo Tanaka, Minako Mori and

Yoko Mori, "Overseas Chinese Business Community in Asia: Present Conditions and Future Prospects," p. 19.

11. Joel Millman, "Bienvenidos, Tigers!" *Forbes,* May 27, 1991, pp. 190–91; "Panama and China: Bridging the Pacific," *The Economist,* June 15, 1991, p. 44.

12. Interview with Governor Ernesto Ruffo Appel.

13. Kevin Rafferty, "China's Grasp and Hong Kong's Golden Eggs," *Harvard Business Review,* May–June 1991, p. 55.

14. Sender, "Inside the Overseas Chinese Network," pp. 29–43.

15. Frank Viviano, "Pacific Giants: The Overseas Chinese," *San Francisco Chronicle,* May 27, 1987.

16. Robert Bellinger, "Chinese Engineers: You Have to Prove Yourself," *Electronic Engineering Times,* August 15, 1988.

17. National Science Foundation, "Selected Data on Science and Engineering Doctorate Awards: 1990," Division of Science Resource Studies, April 1991, p. 27.

18. Numbers provided by the University of California system to Hal Plotkin, 1991.

19. Andrew Tanzer, "Bobo Wang's Midlife Crisis," *Forbes,* June 24, 1991, pp. 110–12.

20. Pan, *Sons of the Yellow Emperor,* p. 129.

21. Douglas C. Chen, "Social and Economic Relations of the Overseas Chinese Business," Ph.D. dissertation, Department of Anthropology of the Graduate School of the University of Oregon, June 1976, p. 33.

22. William H. McNeil, *Plagues and Peoples* (New York: Doubleday, 1976), pp. 109–11; Colin MacKerras, *Western Images of China* (Oxford: Oxford University Press, 1989), p. 15.

23. Yuan Li Wu and Chun-Lsi Wu, *Economic Development in Southeast Asia: The Chinese Dimension* (Stanford, Calif.: Hoover Institution, 1980), pp. 122–25.

24. Wu and Wu, *Economic Development in Southeast Asia,* p. 127.

25. Curtin, *Cross-Cultural Trade,* pp. 170–71; Victor Purcell, *The Chinese in Southeast Asia* (London: Oxford University Press, 1965), pp. 7–9.

26. Purcell, *The Chinese in Southeast Asia,* p. 91.

27. Interview with Hal Plotkin.

28. Thomas Sowell, *The Economics and Politics of Race: An International Perspective* (New York: Quill, 1983), p. 34.

29. Pan, *Sons of the Yellow Emperor,* p. 128.

30. Wu and Wu, *Economic Development in Southeast Asia*, p. 48.

31. James V. Jesudason, *Ethnicity and the Economy: The State, Chinese Business, and Multinationals in Malaysia* (Oxford: Oxford University Press, 1989), pp. 38–39.

32. Pan, *Sons of the Yellow Emperor*, p. 152.

33. Garth Alexander, *Silent Invasion: The Chinese in Southeast Asia* (London: MacDonald, 1973), pp. 45–47.

34. Ibid., p. 45.

35. Victor Purcell, "The Position of the Chinese in Southeast Asia," paper presented at the Institute of Pacific Relations, Lucknow, India, October 3–15, 1950, p. 2.

36. David Y. H. Wu, *The Chinese in Papua New Guinea, 1880–1980*, (Hong Kong: The Chinese University Press, 1982), p. 28.

37. Eitzen, "Two Minorities," p. 129.

38. Maurice Freedman, *The Study of Chinese Society: Essays by Maurice Freedman* (Stanford, Calif.: Stanford University Press, 1979). In "The Chinese in Southeast Asia: The Epicycle of Cathay," pp. 56–57, Freedman argues that the Jewish-Chinese analogy breaks down by pointing out that the Chinese diaspora is largely "an illusion" that will disappear over time. They are, he points out, not a "chosen people" like the Jews; he seems to neglect that global tribes can have many other expressions of diaspora besides that which has been experienced by the Jews. In the end, however, only a person in the future can tell whether any of these dispersions will last beyond the next century.—J.K.

39. N. Balakrishnan, "Forked Tongues," *Far East Economic Review*, January 1991, p. 19.

40. Dick Wilson, "Southeast Asia's Chineseness Comes out of the Cultural Closet," *Japan Times*, December 1, 1990.

41. Purcell, "The Position of the Chinese in Southeast Asia," pp. 1–2.

42. Pan, *Sons of the Yellow Emperor*, pp. 10–11; Xing-hu Kuo, *Free China*, trans. Barrows Mussey (Stuttgart: Seewald Publishers, 1984), p. 15.

43. Freedman, *The Study of Chinese Society*, p. 53.

44. Robert Temple, *The Genius of China* (New York: Simon and Schuster, 1987), pp. 9–12; Armitage, *A Social History of Engineering*, p. 38.

45. MacKerras, *Western Images of China*, p. 19.

46. Isaacs, *Idols of the Tribe*, pp. 140–41.

47. Curtin, *Cross-Cultural Trade*, p. 125.

48. Nicholas Roosevelt, *Restless Pacific* (New York: Scribners, 1928), p. 63. As late as the late eighteenth century the Peking mandarins maintained: "Our Celestial Empire possesses all things in prolific abundance and lacks no product within its borders."

49. Wu and Wu, *Economic Development in Southeast Asia*, pp. 126–27.

50. Purcell, *The Chinese in Southeast Asia*, p. 26.

51. Murphey, *The Outsiders*, p. 13.

52. Chen, "Social and Economic Relations of the Overseas Chinese Businesses," pp. 33–34.

53. Shuhua Chang, "Communications and China's National Integration: An Analysis of *People's Daily* and *Central Daily News* on the China Reunification Issue," *Occasional Papers/Reprints Series in Contemporary Asian Studies*, no. 5, 1986, School of Law, University of Maryland, pp. 8–9.

54. Cal Clark, *Taiwan's Development: Implications for Contending Political Economy Paradigms* (Westport, Conn.: Greenwood Press, 1989), pp. 52–53.

55. Clark, *Taiwan's Development*, pp. 55–56.

56. Anthony B. Chan, *Gold Mountain: The Chinese in the New World*, (Vancouver: New Star Books, 1983), p. 37.

57. Yoshihara, *The Rise of Ersatz Capitalism in Southeast Asia*, p. 39.

58. Frank Viviano, "The New Immigrants," *Mother Jones*, January 1983, p. 44.

59. Murphey, *The Outsiders*, p. 105.

60. Michael R. Godley, *The Mandarin-capitalists from Nanyang: Overseas Chinese in the Modernization of China, 1893–1911* (Cambridge, Eng.: Cambridge University Press, 1981), pp. 11–19.

61. Freedman, *The Study of Chinese Society*, pp. 25–26.

62. Ambrose Y. C. King, "The Transformation of Confucianism in the Post-Confucian Era: The Emergence of Rationalistic Confucianism in Hong Kong," unpublished paper, 1987, p. 16.

63. Murphey, *The Outsiders*, p. 24.

64. Yoshihara, *The Rise of Ersatz Capitalism*, p. 43.

65. Tu-wei Ming, *Confucian Thought: Selfhood as Creative Transformation* (Albany: State University of New York Press, 1985), p. 21.

66. Ibid., p. 135.

67. King, "The Transformation of Confucianism in the Post-Confucian Era," p. 12.

68. T. H. Silcock, "Migration Problems of the Far East," in Brinley

Thomas, *Economics of International Migration* (London: Macmillan, 1958), p. 261.

69. T. J. Newbold, *British Settlements in the Straits of Malacca* (Kuala Lumpur: Oxford University Press, 1971), p. 283.
70. Godley, *The Mandarin-capitalists from Nanyang*, pp. 25–33.
71. Ibid., p. 57.
72. T. J. S. George, *Lee Kuan Yew's Singapore* (Singapore: Eastern Universities Press, 1973) p. 17.
73. Ibid., pp. 23–25.
74. Jim Mann, "China's Lost Generation," *Los Angeles Times Magazine*, March 25, 1990, pp. 12–14.
75. "Asia's Emerging Economies," *The Economist*, November 16, 1991, p. 13.
76. Yoshihara, *The Rise of Ersatz Capitalism*, p. 46.
77. Eitzen, "Two Minorities."
78. Davie, *World Immigration*, p. 308.
79. Wu, *The Chinese in Papua New Guinea*, pp. 28–29.
80. Alexander, *Silent Invasion*, p. 52; Thomas Sowell, "Affirmative Action: Lessons from Asia," *The Wall Street Journal*, March 7, 1990.
81. Sender, "Inside the Overseas Chinese Network," p. 32.
82. "Unequal Gains," *The Economist*, August 10, 1991.
83. *Forbes*, July 22, 1991, pp. 160, 164, 166.
84. Tai Yoke Lin, "Ethnic Restructuring in Malaysia," in *From Independence to Statehood: Managing Ethnic Conflict in Five African and Asian States*, Robert B. Goldmann and A. Jeyaratnam Wilson, eds. (New York: St. Martin's Press, 1984), p. 55.
85. Sowell, *The Economics and Politics of Race*, p. 139.
86. Jesudason, *Ethnicity and the Economy*, p. 149.
87. Sowell, *The Economics and Politics of Race*, pp. 33–37; Yoshihara, *The Rise of Ersatz Capitalism*, p. 51.
88. Sowell, *Preferential Policies*, p. 46.
89. Michael Goldberg, "Hedging Your Great-Grandchildren's Bets: The Case of Overseas Chinese Investment in Real Estate Around the Cities of the Pacific Rim," *Journal of Business Administration*, University of British Columbia, vol. 16, nos. 1 and 2, 1986, p. 162.
90. Dower, *War Without Mercy*, pp. 43–45; James M. Chin, *The Sarawak Chinese* (Kuala Lumpur: Oxford University Press, 1981), p. 99.
91. Wu, *The Chinese in Papua New Guinea*, p. 40.

92. Dower, *War Without Mercy,* p. 288.

93. Alexander, *Silent Invasion,* pp. 55–57.

94. Stephen Fitzgerald, *China and the Overseas Chinese: A Study of Peking's Changing Policy, 1949–1970* (Cambridge, Eng.: Cambridge University Press, 1972), p. 69.

95. Charles P. Wallace, "Feeling the Drain in Singapore," *Los Angeles Times,* January 3, 1990.

96. Sender, "Inside the Overseas Chinese Network," pp. 29–43.

97. Jesudason, *Ethnicity and the Economy,* p. 154.

98. Sender, "Inside the Overseas Chinese Network," pp. 29–43; Anthony Rowley, "Imperial Designs of the Overseas Chinese," *Far Eastern Economic Review,* April 14, 1983, p. 75.

99. Sowell, *Preferential Policies,* p. 50; Cait Murphy, "The Grandest Affirmative Action of Them All," *The Wall Street Journal,* December 27, 1990.

100. Interview with Hal Plotkin.

101. Few stories from Taiwan received more one-sided coverage than this alleged return. Among the more recent are: Yoder, "Reverse 'Brain Drain' Helps Asia but Robs U.S. of Scarce Talent," *The Wall Street Journal,* April 18, 1989; Teresa Watanabe, "Taiwanese 'Brains' Leave U.S.," *Los Angeles Times,* December 29, 1989; "Asia's Emerging Economies," *The Economist,* November 16, 1991.

102. Lin Ching-wen, "Overcrowding Creates Taiwan Middle Class Exodus," *Free China Journal,* October 5, 1990.

103. *Commercial Times* quoted in Ching-wen, "Overcrowding Creates Taiwan Middle Class Exodus"; *China Post,* "Emigration: The Third Choice Besides KMT and DPP," January 9, 1990; *China Post,* "Emigrants Say Crime Main Reason for Leaving," January 3, 1990; *The Economist,* "Taiwan: Crime-cracker," June 9, 1990, p. 40.

104. Interview with author.

105. John Pomfret, "Chinese Move Funds Abroad," *San Francisco Chronicle,* December 16, 1991.

106. Sender, "Inside the Overseas Chinese Network," pp. 29-43; David Holley, "Drawn to a Dream," *Los Angeles Times,* October 23, 1990; Sarah Helm, "Fear and Loathing on the Streets of Hong Kong," *San Francisco Examiner,* July 31, 1990; Robert W. Gibson, "Networks of the Overseas Chinese," *Los Angeles Times,* July 22, 1990; Steven Jones, "Hong Kong to Lose a Growing Share of Its

Best, Brightest to Emigration," *The Wall Street Journal*, September 18, 1990. Although capital flows are more diverse, more than 90 percent of all Hong Kong emigrants have gone to three countries —the United States, Canada and Australia.

107. "Leaving Hong Kong," *The Wall Street Journal*, December 19, 1989; Nina McPherson, "Hong Kong's Choice: English or Chinese."

108. Carol J. Williams, "Hungary Offering Passports to Woo Hong Kong Investors," *Los Angeles Times*, November 16, 1990.

109. Bob Drogin, "Passports Hot Item in Hong Kong," *Los Angeles Times*, July 26, 1990.

110. Nicholas D. Kristof, "A Pregnant Pause in Hong Kong as Mothers-to-Be," *International Herald Tribune*, May 17, 1990.

111. Ai Leng Choo, "When Many Are Fleeing Hong Kong, Others Find It's Profitable to Go Back," *The Wall Street Journal*, January 24, 1992.

112. Interview with Hong Kong government officials.

113. Anthony T. Bouscaren, *International Migrations Since 1945*, pp. 112–13.

114. Ibid., p. 113.

115. Interview with author.

116. Interview with author.

117. *Taiwan Republic of China Economic Development* (Ministry of Economic Affairs, April 1987); *Federal Reserve Bank of San Francisco Weekly Letter*, "Taiwan's Trade Surpluses," February 1, 1991.

118. Wong, *Patronage, Brokerage, Entrepreneurship*, p. 55.

119. Catherine Jones, "Hong Kong, Singapore, South Korea and Taiwan: Oikonomic Welfare States," *Government and Opposition*, vol. 25, no. 4, Autumn 1990, p. 462.

120. Interview with author.

121. Purcell, "The Position of the Chinese in Southeast Asia," p. 3; Eitzen, "Two Minorities," p. 129; Wong, *Patronage, Brokerage, Entrepreneurship*, pp. 170–73.

122. Gwen Kinkead, "A Reporter at Large: Chinatown I," *The New Yorker*, June 10, 1991, p. 81.

123. Shih-shan Henry Tsai, *China and the Overseas Chinese in the United States, 1868–1911* (Fayetteville: University of Arkansas Press, 1983), pp. 32–33.

124. Wu and Wu, *Economic Development in Southeast Asia*, p. 49.

125. Yoshihara, *The Rise of Ersatz Capitalism*, p. 53–54; Jesudason, *Ethnicity and the Economy*, p. 31.

126. Siu-kau Lau, "Utilitarian Familism: The Basis of Political Stability," in *Social Life and Development in Hong Kong*, Ambrose Y. C. King and Rance P. L. Lee (Hong Kong: Chinese University Press, 1981), pp. 195–207.

127. King, "The Transformation of Confucianism in the Post-Confucian Era," p. 16.

128. Ibid., p. 7.

129. Jan Woronoff, *Hong Kong: Capitalist Paradise* (Hong Kong: Heinemann Asia, 1980), pp. 115–16.

130. James P. Schriffman and Maria Shao, "South Korea and Taiwan: Two Strategies," *The Wall Street Journal*, May 1, 1986.

131. "Pacific Rim 150," *Fortune*, Pacific Rim 1990 issue, pp. 102–4.

132. Alvin Yiu-cheong So, "Development Inside the Capitalist World System: A Study of the Chinese and Japanese Silk Industry," *Journal of Asian Culture*, vol. V, 1981, pp. 37–50.

133. Rafferty, "China's Grasp and Hong Kong's Golden Eggs," p. 56.

134. Interview with author.

135. "Textiles: Slaves of Fashion," *The Economist*, December 7, 1991, p. 86.

136. Alice Rawsthorn, "A New Set of Challenges," and William Durforce, "So Near, and Yet So Far," *Financial Times*, October 3, 1990, from L. N. Jhunjhunwala, "Export to Save the Country or Perish," reproduced from the *Financial Express* (India), December 9, 1990.

137. "Textiles: Slaves of Fashion," *The Economist*, p. 87.

138. Ibid.

139. Maria Shao and James R. Schiffman, "Taiwan, Korea Battle for Textile Markets by Stressing High Fashion and Flexibility," *The Asian Wall Street Journal Weekly*, April 28, 1986.

140. Edna Bonacich, "Asian and Latino Immigrants in the Los Angeles Garment Industry: An Exploration of the Relationship Between Capitalism and Racial Oppression," *ISSR Working Paper in the Social Sciences*, 1989–1990, vol. 5, no. 13, p. 15.

141. "California: State of the State," *The Bobbin*, April 1991.

142. Interview by author with Mary Stephens, chair of the Fashion Department, Fashion Institute of Design and Merchandising, Los Angeles.

143. Tim W. Ferguson, "Casual-Wear Chief Opposes Hemming in China Trade," *The Wall Street Journal*, May 28, 1991.
144. Interview with author.
145. Godley, *The Mandarin-capitalists*, p. 60.
146. Purcell, *The Chinese in Southeast Asia*, p. 30.
147. Interview with author.
148. Godley, *The Mandarin-capitalists*, pp. 65–73.
149. Tsai, *China and the Overseas Chinese in the United States*, pp. 68–75.
150. Godley, *The Mandarin-capitalists*, pp. 75–82.
151. Ibid., p. 106.
152. Lyon Sharman, *Sun Yat-sen: His Life and Meaning* (New York: John Day, 1934), pp. 35–36, 75–77.
153. Ibid., p. 112.
154. Alfred Crofts and Percy Buchanan, *A History of the Far East* (New York: Longmans, Green, 1958), pp. 312, 323, 326.
155. Joel Kotkin and Vincent Diau, "Red Star over Silicon Valley," *California*, September 1990, p. 24.
156. Interview with author.
157. Fitzgerald, *China and the Overseas Chinese*, p. 193.
158. Anna Wang, "Whither the Work Ethic?," *Free China Review*, September 1989, pp. 35–36.
159. Interview with author.
160. Interview with author.
161. George White, "Laboring over Workers," *Los Angeles Times*, June 24, 1991.
162. Interview with author.
163. Robert W. Gibson, "China, Taiwan Groping Toward Independence," *Los Angeles Times*, April 8, 1991.
164. Leung, "Foreign Investment in China Dwindles," Peter Wickenden, "Taiwan in Two Minds on Trade with China," *Financial Times*, June 6, 1990.
165. "Taiwan: China's Snare," *The Economist*, January 4, 1992, pp. 31–32.
166. Interview with author.
167. David Holley, "Chinese Province Meets the 20th Century," *Los Angeles Times*, September 6, 1987 (stated that 75 percent of all investment in Guandong came from Hong Kong and Macao); Leung, "Foreign Investment in China Dwindles" (stated that 60 percent of all foreign investment throughout China came from Hong Kong alone); Tanaka, Mori, and Mori, "Overseas Chinese

Business Community in Asia: Present Conditions and Future Prospects," p. 19.

168. Andrew Tanzer, "The Mountains Are High, the Emperor Is Far Away," *Forbes*, August 5, 1991, p. 70.

169. David Holley and Sam Jameson, "Province of Wealth and Power," *Los Angeles Times*, November 11, 1991.

170. Leung, "Foreign Investment in China Dwindles"; Wickenden, "Taiwan in Two Minds on Trade with China."

171. "Official Reserves," *The Economist*, March 14, 1992, p. 124. Statement of Hamish Macleod, "Financial Secretary Statement on Exchange Fund," July 15, 1992, faxed to author by Hong Kong Economic and Trade Office, San Francisco. The total numbers from these sources show Taiwan with over $82 billion for foreign reserves, Singapore with nearly $30 billion and Hong Kong with $29 billion. Taken together, these three outposts of the Chinese diaspora boast roughly $142 billion in reserves compared to slightly over $70 billion for Japan.

172. James McGregor, "China's Entrepreneurs Are Thriving in Spite of Political Crackdown," *The Wall Street Journal*, June 4, 1991.

173. David Holley, "China's Coast Luring Visitors from Taiwan," *Los Angeles Times*, January 1, 1989.

174. Interview with author.

175. Interview with author.

176. Leo O. Orleans, *Chinese Students in America: Policies, Issues and Numbers* (Washington, D.C.: National Academy Press, 1988), p. 37.

177. William B. Johnson, "Global Workforce 2000: The New World Labor Market," *Harvard Business Review*, March–April 1991, p. 124.

178. Mann, "China's Lost Generation," pp. 12–14.

179. Nicholas D. Kristof, "Chinese Jam Exits to U.S., the 'Beautiful Country,'" *International Herald Tribune*, September 14, 1990.

180. David Shambaugh and Gregory Wajnowski, "China Is Volcano of Discontent," *The Wall Street Journal*, February 12, 1990.

181. Orleans, *Chinese Students in America*, p. 36.

182. Interview with author.

CHAPTER 7:
THE GREATER INDIA

1. Interview with author.
2. Amit Roy, "The Quiet Millionaires," *Telegraph Weekly Magazine,* August 25, 1990, p. 14.
3. Bouscaren, *International Migrations Since 1945,* p. 101.
4. "Britain's Browns," *The Economist,* October 28, 1989, pp. 21–24; Dr. G. Shantakumar, "The Position of the Indian Community in Singapore: An Economic Profile," *Singapore Indian Chamber of Commerce Bulletin,* pp. 1–4; "Ethnic Origins and the Labor Market," *Employment Gazette,* March 1990, p. 130; "Asians in the US," *Far Eastern Economic Review,* November 22, 1990, p. 32.
5. Oma O. Eleazu, "Interethnic Restructuring in Malaysia," in Robert Goldmann and A. Jeyartnam Wilson, *From Independence to Statehood* (New York: St. Martin's Press, 1984), p. 55.
6. "Britain's Browns," p. 22.
7. Cited in Jay Malhotra, "Economic Status of Foreign Born and US-Born Indian-Americans," a paper based on a report for the U.S. Civil Rights Commission, June 1988; Susumu Awanohara, "In the Melting Pot," *Far East Economic Review,* April 26, 1990, p. 32.
8. Pranay Gupte, "The World Is Their Bazaar," *Forbes,* December 28, 1987, pp. 85–92.
9. Aileen D. Ross, *The Hindu Family in Its Urban Setting* (Toronto: University of Toronto Press, 1961), p. 22.
10. "Thousands of Jainist Followers to Gather at University," *Peninsula Times Tribune,* July 1, 1992.
11. Pranay Gupte, "The Big Money in Cheap Rock," *Forbes,* August 10, 1987.
12. Interview with author.
13. Hugh Tinker, "Indians Abroad: Emigration, Restriction and Rejection," in *Expulsion of a Minority: Essays on Ugandan Asians,* Michael Twaddle, ed. (London: The Athbone Press, University of London, 1975), p. 15.
14. "Britain's Browns," pp. 21–24.
15. M. A. Tribe, "Economic Aspects of the Expulsion of Asians from Uganda," in *Expulsion of a Minority,* Twaddle, ed., pp. 140–57.
16. "Uganda: The Exiles Return," *The Economist,* August 10, 1991, pp. 35–36.
17. Gardner Thompson, "The Ismailis in Uganda," in *Expulsion of a Minority,* Twaddle, ed., pp. 30–38.

18. Interview with author.
19. "Punjabi Orchard Farmers: An Immigrant Enclave in Rural California," *International Migration Review*, vol. 22, issue 1, 1988, pp. 28–47.
20. Interview with Hal Plotkin.
21. Tinker, "Indians Abroad," p. 15.
22. Malhotra, "Economic Status of Foreign Born and US-Born Indian-Americans," pp. 1–30; Awanohara, "In the Melting Pot," p. 32.
23. Monua Janah, "Indian Immigrants Find Room to Grow Beyond Motels," *The Wall Street Journal*, August 25, 1989.
24. Usha R. Jain, *The Gujeratis of San Francisco* (New York: AMS Press, 1989), pp. 128–29.
25. Interview with author; "Jogani's Pooja Owns and Manages Mega Properties and Millions," *L.A. India*, May 25, 1990, p. 23.
26. Prakash Shah, "Indians Abroad in Business and the Professions,"in the report of *The First Global Convention of People of Indian Origin*, September 3, 1989.
27. Roy, "The Quiet Millionaires," p. 19.
28. Gupte, "The World Is Their Bazaar," pp. 85–92.
29. Amit Roy, "The Asian Millionaire," *India Today*, September 15, 1990, pp. 121–22.
30. Kim Foltz, "The RCA Dog Will Have Its Day," *International Herald Tribune*, September 15–16, 1990; Edwin McDowell, "Foreign Flavor for Publishing Leadership," *New York Times*, November 5, 1990; Richard A. Serrano, "LA Record Executive May Be Tapped," *Los Angeles Times*, August 11, 1990.
31. Martha Sherrill, "The Writer from Suburbia," *Washington Post*, July 20, 1990.
32. Kathleen Hendrix, "Vision of a Brave New World," *Los Angeles Times*, November 12, 1987.
33. Roy, "The Quiet Millionaires," p. 19.
34. Interview with author.
35. Arendt, *Imperialism*, p. 92.
36. Tapan Raychaudhuri and Irfan Habib, *The Cambridge Economic History of India, Volume One: 1200–1750* (New Delhi: Cambridge University Press, 1982), pp. 277–78.
37. Armitage, *The Social History of Engineering*, p. 38.
38. Milton Singer, *When a Great Tradition Modernizes* (New York: Praeger, 1972), p. 275.

39. P. N. Agarwala, *A History of Indian Business: A Complete Account of Trade Exchanges from 3000 B.C. to the Present Day* (New Delhi: Vikas Publishing, 1985), pp. 2–3.
40. Raychaudhuri and Habib, *The Cambridge Economic History of India*, pp. 127–31.
41. Mumford, *Technics and Civilization* p. 144.
42. Raychaudhuri and Habib, *The Cambridge Economic History of India*, pp. 77–81.
43. Ibid.
44. Curtin, *Cross-Cultural Trade*, pp. 122–24, 145–48.
45. Ibid.
46. Romila Thapar, *A History of India, Volume One* (London: Penguin Books, 1966), p. 279.
47. Raychaudhuri and Habib, *The Cambridge Economic History of India*, pp. 268–76.
48. Ibid., pp. 300–3.
49. Noburu Tabe, *Indian Entrepreneurs at the Crossroads* (Tokyo: Institute of Developing Economics, 1970), p. 7.
50. Raychaudhuri and Habib, *The Cambridge Economic History of India*, pp. 406–8.
51. Spear, *India*, pp. 229–30.
52. Tabe, *Indian Entrepreneurs at the Crossroads*, p. 13.
53. Curtin, *Cross-Cultural Trade*, pp. 143–45.
54. Immanuel Wallerstein, *The Modern World System I: Capitalist Agriculture and the Origins of the European World-Economy in the Sixteenth Century* (New York: Academic Press, 1974), pp. 50–51.
55. Raychaudhuri and Habib, *The Cambridge Economic History of India*, pp. 406–8; Curtin, *Cross-Cultural Trade*, p. 141.
56. Temple, *The Genius of China*, pp. 9–11; Murphey, *The Outsiders*, p. 13.
57. Kumar, *The Cambridge Economic History of India*, pp. 22–23, 27.
58. Dwijendra Tripathi, "Indian Entrepreneurship in Historical Perspective: A Re-Interpretation," *Economic and Political Weekly*, vol. VI, no. 22, May 29, 1971, p. M-59.
59. Marx, *Capital*, vol. 1, p. 558.
60. Kumar, *The Cambridge Economic History of India*, p. 277.
61. Murphey, *The Outsiders*, p. 21.
62. Curtin, *Cross-Cultural Trade*, pp. 241–42.
63. Kumar, *The Cambridge Economic History of India*, pp. 289–95.
64. Tabe, *Indian Entrepreneurs at the Crossroads*, p. 22.

65. Arthur W. Helweg, "Emigration and Return: Ramifications for India," *Population Review*, vol. 28, nos. 1 and 2, January–December 1984, p. 46.

66. Kumar, *The Cambridge Economic History of India*, p. 359; Strange, *States and Markets*, p. 99.

67. Gita Piramel and Margaret Herdeck, *India's Industrialists, Volume One* (Washington, D.C.: Three Continents Press, 1986), pp. 6–7.

68. Ross, *The Hindu Family in Its Urban Setting*, pp. 8–11.

69. Singer, *When a Great Tradition Modernizes*, p. 366.

70. Piramel and Herdeck, *India's Industrialists*, pp. 6–7.

71. Ibid., pp. 335–40.

72. Shoji Ito, "Ownership and Management of Indian Zaibatsu," in *Family Business in the Era of Industrial Growth*, Okuchi and Yasuoka, eds., pp. 149–59.

73. Robert F. Kennedy, Jr., "The Protestant Ethic and the Parsis," *American Journal of Sociology*, vol. LXVII, July 1962–May 1963, pp. 15–16.

74. Kumar, *The Cambridge Economic History of India*, pp. 342–43, 348–51.

75. Kennedy, Jr., "The Protestant Ethic and the Parsis," p. 17.

76. Ibid., p. 19.

77. Edna Bonacich, "A Theory of Middleman Minorities," *American Sociological Review*, vol. 38, October 1973, p. 583.

78. Amelendu Guha, "Parsi Seths as Entrepreneurs: 1750–1950," *Economic and Political Weekly*, August 1970, p. M-107.

79. Philip Lopate, "Zoroaster in the New World," *New York Times*, October 19, 1986, p. 85.

80. Gita Piramel, "The Rise of the Marwari," *Bombay*, August 22, 1990, p. 44.

81. Isher Judge Ahluwalia, *Industrial Growth in India: Stagnation Since the Mid-Sixties* (New Delhi: Oxford University Press, 1985), pp. 176–77, 187; Kumar, *The Cambridge Economic History of India*, pp. 351, 588.

82. K. N. Vaid, *The Overseas Indian Community in Hong Kong* (Hong Kong: University of Hong Kong, 1972), pp. 54–59, 80.

83. David Joel Steinberg et al., *In Search of Southeast Asia* (New York: Praeger, 1971), p. 217.

84. Bouscaren, *International Migrations Since 1945*, p. 29.

85. Interview with author.

86. Purcell, *The Chinese in Southeast Asia*, p. 71.

87. G. Findlay Shirras, "Indian Migration," in *International Migrations*, Wilcox, ed., p. 592; Jesudason, *Ethnicity and the Economy*, p. 33.

88. Thomas Timberg, *The Marwaris: From Traders to Industrialists* (New Delhi: Vikas Publishing, 1978), pp. 62–63.

89. Interview with author.

90. Vaid, *The Overseas Indian Community in Hong Kong*, pp. 1–15. Estimates by K. Sital, president of the Hong Kong Association of Indian Associations.

91. Ibid., pp. 64–74.

92. "The Harilelas: Leaders of the Indian Community Abroad," *Asia Magazine*, May 19, 1985, pp. 15–18.

93. Frederick Kogos, "This Is Apparel Hong Kong Today!," *Apparel Manufacturer*, July 1961.

94. Vaid, *Indian Community in Hong Kong*, pp. 64–74.

95. Interview with author.

96. Interview with author.

97. Tribe, "Economic Aspects of the Expulsion of Asians from Uganda," in *Expulsion of a Minority*, Twaddle, ed., p. 140.

98. Edna Bonacich, "A Theory of Middleman Minorities," p. 591.

99. "Indians Fear the Future Will Amount to Zero," *Hong Kong Standard*, April 19, 1989.

100. Helweg, "Emigration and Return," pp. 46–47.

101. James Chad, "Paradise Abroad," *Far East Economic Review*, April 26, 1990, p. 26.

102. Interview with author.

103. Spear, *India*, pp. 433–35.

104. Daniel Houston Buchanan, *The Development of Capitalistic Enterprise in India* (New York: A. M. Kelley, 1934), pp. 466–71.

105. Poem quoted in Thomas Timberg, "Industrial Entrepreneurship Among the Trading Communities of India," Harvard University Center for International Affairs, Economic Development Report No. 136, July 1969, p. 41.

106. Piramel and Herdeck, *India's Industrialists*, pp. 68–72.

107. Timberg, "Industrial Entrepreneurship Among the Trading Communities of India," pp. 24–26; Piramel and Herdeck, *India's Industrialists*, pp. 61–70.

108. Timberg, *The Marwaris*, pp. 10–11.

109. Piramel, "The Rise of the Marwari," p. 44.

110. "The Politician Who Knows His Place a Little Too Well," *The Economist*, June 23, 1990, p. 27.

111. Ahluwalia, *Industrial Growth in India*, pp. 2–3.

112. "Survey: India," *The Economist*, May 4, 1991, p. 7.

113. *Handbook of International Trade and Development Statistics, 1989* (New York: United Nations, 1989), pp. 315–16; figures on India are provided courtesy of Price Waterhouse, Madras; Anthony Spaeth, "Firms Find India Welcome Mat Frayed," *The Wall Street Journal*, April 10, 1990.

114. V. G. Bhatia and L. N. Jhunjhunwala, "Export to Save the Country or Perish," *Financial Express*, December 9, 1990, pp. 1–10; "Caught in a Gulf," *Financial Express*, January 4, 1991.

115. "Survey: India," p. 8.

116. Ibid., p. 5.

117. Steve Coll, "Burgeoning Population Threatens India's Future," *Washington Post*, January 21, 1990.

118. Interview with author.

119. Bradford Spangenberg, *British Bureaucracy in India: Status, Policy and the I.C.S. in the Late 19th Century* (Columbia, Mo.: South Asia Books, 1976), p. 351.

120. "The Third World: Survey," *The Economist*, September 29, 1989, p. 9.

121. Ahluwalia, *Industrial Growth in India*, pp. 158–62.

122. "Survey: India," p. 7.

123. Piramel, "The Rise of the Marwari," p. 48. Between 1965 and 1988 the Ambani's Reliance group rose to third among India's top business houses, according to a report by the Lok Sabha Trade Practices Commission, behind only the Birlas and the Tatas; they were not even *listed* in 1965.—J.K.

124. Hardev Sanotra, "Ambani and the System," *Business World*, April 25–May 8, 1990, p. 37.

125. Government of India, Ministry of Finance, "Destination of Indian Exports," *Economic Survey, 1989–1990*. In 1988–1989, for example, the Soviet Union, Eastern Europe and non-OPEC Third World countries accounted for over one third of India's export market. —J.K.

126. Interview with author.

127. Sowell, *Preferential Policies*, pp. 52–53.

128. Murphey, *The Outsiders*, p. 107.

129. Ibid., pp. 107–8.

130. M. J. Akbar, *India: The Siege Within: Challenges to the Nation's Unity* (London: Penguin Books, 1985), pp. 21–22.

131. Ralph Buultjens, "India: Religion, Political Legitimacy and the Secular State," *Annals of the American Academy*, no. 483, January 1986, pp. 101–2.

132. Mark Fineman, "The Killing Ground of Asia," *Los Angeles Times*, May 8, 1990; "Alas, Poor Punjab," *The Economist*, September 22, 1990, p. 40.

133. Mark Fineman, "Lynchings Over Caste Stir India," *Los Angeles Times*, April 12, 1991.

134. Park, *Race and Culture*, p. 351.

135. Interview with author.

136. Interview with Hal Plotkin.

137. Interview by Hal Plotkin with George Abraham, executive director of the Singapore Indian Chamber of Commerce.

138. Interview with author.

139. Kumar, *The Cambridge Economic History of India*, p. 565.

140. Leslie Tilley, "A Passage to India," *Financial Times*, May 17, 1990.

141. Shah, "Indians Abroad in Business and the Professions," p. 53; Robert Bellinger, "Indian EEs: 20,000 Engineers Change Face of U.S. Engineering," *Electrical Engineering Times*, August 1, 1988, p. 40.

142. Arvind Singhal and Everett Rodgers, *India's Information Revolution* (New Delhi: Sage Publications, 1989), pp. 42–43.

143. Ibid.

144. Marianthi Zikopoloulos, ed., "Open Doors: 1989–1990: Report on International Educational Exchange" (Washington, D.C.: Institute of International Education), p. 21.

145. Bellinger, "Indian EEs."

146. Singhal and Rodgers, *India's Information Revolution*, pp. 147–48; Prakash Chandra, "Indians Bring Together Homeland, New Home," *San Jose Mercury News*, October 29, 1989.

147. T. T. Nhu, "Inter-Indian Tensions Fade After Immigration," *San Jose Mercury News*, June 7, 1991.

148. Dr. R. Nagarajan, "The Indian American Family," paper presented at Fifth Annual Convention of Asian Indians in North America, July 1–4, 1988, Cleveland, Ohio.

149. Interview with author.

150. Interview with author.

CHAPTER 8:
FUTURE TRIBES

1. Marshall McLuhan, *The Global Village* (New York: Oxford University Press, 1989), pp. 84–85.
2. John Eckhouse, "Migrant Workers' Economic Impact," *San Francisco Chronicle*, July 1, 1991.
3. "Emigration to Go Up," *Business India*, February 4–17, 1991.
4. George White, "Cheap—and Smart—Labor," *Los Angeles Times*, June 3, 1991.
5. R. Bayley Winder, "The Lebanese in West Africa," *Comparative Studies in Society and History*, vol. 4, 1961–1962, pp. 295–97.
6. Ibid., pp. 320–23.
7. Jennifer Toth, "Study Will Spotlight Record of Success by Arab-Americans," *Los Angeles Times*, January 10, 1991.
8. Peter Fuhrman, "An Oasis of Sanity," *Forbes*, October 2, 1989, pp. 100–1; Michael Cieply, "Something Under the Mattress," *Forbes*, December 6, 1982, pp. 41–42.
9. Geraldine Brooks, "In Humiliating Defeat Can the Palestinians Finally Find Peace," *The Wall Street Journal*, March 6, 1991.
10. Ibid.
11. Interview with author.
12. John P. Tarpey, Kevin Kelly, et al., "The Palestinians Are Lining Up Some Big Backers," *Business Week*, February 22, 1988, pp. 46–47.
13. Interview with author.
14. Friedrich Engels, *The Origin of the Family, Private Property and the State* (New York: International Publishers, 1942), p. 51.
15. Braudel, *The Perspective of the World*, p. 628.
16. Dan Fisher, "Young Emigrés Return to Work for Homeland," *Los Angeles Times*, February 26, 1990; Jeffrey A. Tannenbaum, "East European Descendants Have Edge in Deals There," *The Wall Street Journal*, December 1, 1989.
17. H. Kent Greiger, *The Family in Soviet Russia* (Cambridge, Mass.: Harvard University Press, 1968), pp. 90–94.
18. Adrian Karatnycky, "It's Not Islam That's Uniting Soviet Central Asia," *The Wall Street Journal*, July 28, 1989; Graham E. Fuller, "Azerbaijan: Soon to Be a Household Word," *Los Angeles Times*, January 9, 1990; "The Battle for Uzbekistan," *The Economist*, April 4, 1992, pp. 48–49.

19. Carey Goldberg, "Tidal Wave of Emigration Carries off Soviet 'Brains,' " *Los Angeles Times,* October 8, 1990.

20. "While the Going Is Good," *The Economist,* March 10, 1990, p. 55.

21. David Marshall Lang, *Armenia: Cradle of Civilization* (London: George Allen and Unwin, 1970), pp. 290–91.

22. Lang, *Armenia: Cradle of Civilization,* pp. 86–95.

23. Ibid., pp. 120–35.

24. Phillips, *Symbol, Myth and Rhetoric,* pp. 35–45.

25. Ibid., pp. 60–64.

26. Ibid., pp. 46–48.

27. Lang, *Armenia: Cradle of Civilization,* pp. 285–90.

28. Gary A. Kulhanjian, *A Guide to Armenian Immigrants, Studies and Institutions* (San Francisco: self-published, 1977), p. 2.

29. "Armenians in California: One Day, You Too Could Be Governor," *The Economist,* January 19, 1991, p. 28; Seth Mydans, "Armenians in U.S. Say the People of the Homeland Are in Danger, But What Could Be Done?" *New York Times,* January 23, 1990.

30. Esther Schrader, "L.A.'s Armenia Quake Relief Stuck in Pipeline," *Los Angeles Times,* July 23, 1989.

31. Elizabeth Shogren, "Armenian Nationalist a Hero on Return Home," *Los Angeles Times,* November 13, 1990; Elizabeth Shogren, "Armenian-Americans Drawn to Roots to Assist 'Brothers' in Soviet Union," *Los Angeles Times,* June 30, 1990; Elizabeth Shogren, "Armenia's Leader Seeks Support on U.S. Visit," *Los Angeles Times,* September 30, 1990.

32. Interview with author.

33. Phillips, *Symbol, Myth and Rhetoric,* p. 113.

34. Edward Minasian, "Armenian Immigrant Tide," in *Recent Studies in Armenian History* (Cambridge, Mass.: National Association for Armenian Studies and Research, 1972), pp. 107–11.

35. Jack Danielian, "Armenian Cultural History: Problems of Western Definition," in *Recent Studies in Armenian History,* p. 127.

36. "Armenians in California: One Day, You Too Could Be Governor," *The Economist,* January 19, 1991, p. 28; Jacques Derogy, "*La nostalgie de L'Armenie perdue,*" *L'evénement du Jeudi,* June 6, 1989, p. 61.

37. Joe Queenan, "Will Wonders Ever Cease?" *Forbes,* February 4, 1989, pp. 72–76. The Ghermezian brothers, Armenians from Canada via Iran, have been behind some of the biggest mall develop-

ments in the world, including a massive Edmonton project and the even larger Mall of America in Bloomington, Minnesota.

38. "Armenians in California: One Day, You Too Could Be Governor," *The Economist*, January 19, 1991, p. 28.

39. Interview with author.

40. Burnham P. Beckwith, *Ideas About the Future: A History of Futurism* (Palo Alto: Burnham Beckwith, 1984), pp. 16–25.

41. Ibid., pp. 34, 53, 90–93.

42. James T. Duke and Barry L. Johnson, "Stages of Religious Transformation: A Study of 200 Nations," *Review of Religious Research*, vol. 30, no. 3, March 1989, p. 210.

43. Edward Cornish, *The Study of the Future* (Washington, D.C.: World Future Society, 1977), pp. 162–63.

44. Francis Fukuyama, *The End of History and the Last Man* (New York: The Free Press, 1992), pp. 77, 79, 89, 201.

45. Roderick Seidenberg, *Post-Historic Man: An Inquiry* (Chapel Hill: University of North Carolina Press, 1950), p. 179.

46. Duke and Johnson, "Stages of Religious Transformation," p. 213.

47. Mircea Eliade, *The Myth of the Eternal Return* (Princeton, N.J.: Princeton University Press, 1954), pp. 11, 15, 18, 74.

48. Ibid., pp. 144–46.

49. Walter Zuckerman, "Soviet Russia Solves the Jewish Problem," *The Contemporary Review*, July–December 1931, pp. 741–48.

50. Geraldine Brooks, "The Immigrant Flood of Soviet Jews to Israel Could Beget Big Changes in Nation," *The Wall Street Journal*, April 8, 1990.

51. Christine Demkowych, "Some Jews Forgo Israel's Promise and Elect to Stay in Ukraine," *Los Angeles Times*, March 5, 1991.

52. Interview with author.

53. Kathy Wilhelm, "Monks Join Democracy Movement," *San Francisco Chronicle*, March 28, 1990.

54. Girlal Jain, "End of the Arab Century," *World Press Review*, September 1983, p. 37. This article, "Cross-Cultural Trade," originally appeared in *The Times of India*.

55. Curtin, p. 107.

56. Armytage, *A Social History of Engineering*, pp. 39–40.

57. Said Amir Arjomand, "Social Change in Contemporary Islam," in *New Religious Movements and Rapid Social Change* James A. Beckford, ed. (London: Sage/UNESCO, 1986), p. 101; Kim Murphy, "Islamic Militants Build Power Base in Sudan," *Los Angeles*

Times, April 6, 1992. The Islamic leader of Sudan, Hassan Abdullah-Tarabi, is a Sorbonne-educated academic fluent in English, French and German.

58. Michael Schrage, "Islam Embraces Science on Its Own Terms," *Los Angeles Times,* December 27, 1990.

59. Johnson, "Global Workforce 2000," p. 124.

60. Robert Wuthnow, "Religious Movements in North America," in *New Religious Movements and Rapid Social Change,* Beckford, ed. p. 16.

61. Desda Moss, "Practicing or Not Many Identify with Religion," *USA Today,* April 11, 1991.

62. Wuthnow, "Religious Movements in North America," pp. 16–17, 23–24.

63. Stan Albrecht and Tim Heaton, "Secularization, Higher Education, and Religiosity," *Review of Religious Research,* vol. 26, no. 1, September 1984, pp. 50–51.

64. Ibid.

65. Waxman, *America's Jews in Transition,* pp. 213–14.

66. Roland Enroth, "The Empire Strikes Gold," *Christianity Today,* September 5, 1985, p. 29.

67. Joseph Carey, "A Time of Turmoil for Mormons," *U.S. News & World Report,* April 28, 1986, p. 100.

68. Dennis M. Clark, "Harold Bloom Lauds the Audacity of Joseph Smith," *Sunstone,* April 1991, p. 59.

69. Willa Appel, *Cults in America: Programmed for Paradise* (New York: Holt, Rinehart and Winston, 1983), pp. 3–5.

70. Joan Johnson, *The Cult Movement* (New York: Franklin Watts, 1984), pp. 74–87.

71. Mark P. Leone, "The Economic Basis for the Evolution of Mormon Religion," in *Religious Movements in Contemporary America,* ed. Irving I. Zaretsky and Mark D. Leone (Princeton, N.J.: Princeton University Press, 1974), pp. 729, 739. As Brigham Young, church president and leader of the trek to Utah, once stated: "That religion which cannot save a man temporarily cannot save him physically."

72. Jim Coates, *In Mormon Circles: Gentiles, Jack Mormons and Latter-day Saints* (Reading, Mass.: Addison-Wesley, 1991), pp. 48, 77.

73. Agnes M. Smith, "The First Mormon Mission to Britain," *History Today,* July 1987, p. 31.

74. O. Kendall White, "Mormon Resistance and Accommodation:

From Communitarian Socialism to Corporate Capitalism," in *Self-Help in Urban America: Patterns of Minority Business Enterprise*, Scott Cummings, ed. (Port Washington, N.Y.: Kennikat Press, 1980), p. 90.

75. Dr. E. L. Thorndike, "The Origin of Superior Men," *Scientific Monthly*, May 1943, pp. 425–26.

76. Taken from "Utah: America's Choice," published by the Utah Department of Community and Economic Development in 1991.

77. Maureen Dowd, "Bush's Adviser on Domestic Policy: The Perfect Man to Process Details," *New York Times*, March 29, 1990; *Los Angeles Times*, David Lauter, "'The Man Behind the President," October 14, 1990.

78. Albrecht and Heaton, "Secularization, Higher Education, and Religiosity," pp. 50–51. Mormons attend weekly church services twice as often as their Episcopalian counterparts and three times more often than Catholics.

79. Coates, *In Mormon Circles*, p. 139; Sally B. Donnelly, "The State of Many Tongues," *Time*, April 13, 1992, p. 51.

80. Interview with David Pierson, manager of international sales, Wordperfect Corporation.

81. Interview with author.

82. Sonia Nazario, "Mormon Rules Aid Long Life, Study Discloses," *The Wall Street Journal*, December 6, 1989. According to recent medical surveys religious Mormons tend to live on average eleven years longer than other whites.

83. Rodney Stark, "The Rise of a New World Faith," *Review of Religious Research*, vol. 26, no. 1, September 1984, pp. 18–25.

84. Interview with author.

85. Interviews and charts provided by Donald Snow of the Department of Mathematics, Brigham Young University; Joel Kotkin, "Mission from Utah," *California*, July 1991, pp. 22–23.

86. Stark, "The Rise of a New World Faith." Stark projects that by 2080 the church could boast a membership of between 63 and 245 million members, with the bulk of new converts coming from such newly industrializing countries as Mexico, Brazil and Korea.

87. Interview with author.

88. Charles Hirschman, "America's Melting Pot Revisited," *Annual Review of Sociology*, 1983, p. 397.

89. Thomas Sowell, *The Economics and Politics of Race*, pp. 183–84.

90. Hirschman, *"America's Melting Pot Revisited,"* p. 398.

91. Tony Martin, *Race First: The Ideological and Organizational Struggles of Marcus Garvey and the Universal Negro Improvement Association* (Westport, Conn.: Greenwood Press, 1976), p. 3.

92. Robert Hill, ed., *The Marcus Garvey and Universal Negro Improvement Association Papers* (Berkeley: University of California Press, 1987), p. 5.

93. Theodore G. Vincent, *Black Power and the Garvey Movement* (Berkeley: The Ramparts Press, 1971), p. 13.

94. M. F. Katzin, "Partners: An Informal Savings Institution in Jamaica," *Social and Economic Studies*, VIII, December 1969, pp. 436–40.

95. Martin, *Race First*, pp. 12–13, 19.

96. Ibid., p. 33.

97. Vincent, *Black Power and the Garvey Movement*, p. 169; "Without Commerce and Industry, the People Perish," *Issues and Views*, Spring 1991, pp. 5–6.

98. Martha F. Lee, *The Nation of Islam: An American Millennarian Movement* (Lampeter, Dyfed, Wales: The Edward Mellen Press, 1988), pp. 36–41.

99. Andrea Ford and Russell Chandler, "A Growing Force and Presence," *Los Angeles Times*, January 25, 1990; "America's Blacks: A World Apart," *The Economist*, March 30, 1991, p. 17; Sam Fulwood III, "Gap Grows Between Black Middle Class and Those Mired in Poverty," *Los Angeles Times*, August 9, 1991; Timothy Noah, "Urban League, in Bleak Report, Finds Black Americans' Income Fell in the 1980s," *The Wall Street Journal*, January 9, 1991; Ronald J. Ostrow, "U.S. Imprisons Black Men at Four Times S. Africa's Rate," *Los Angeles Times*, January 5, 1991.

100. Charisse Jones, "The Rebirth of Malcolm X," *Los Angeles Times Magazine*, February 4, 1990, pp. 29–38.

101. Elizabeth Wright, "The True Legacy of Malcolm X: Responsibility Was the Core of His Message to Blacks," *Issues and Views*, Winter 1989, p. 5.

102. Interview with author.

103. Perry Weed, *The White Ethnic Movement and Ethnic Politics* (New York: Praeger, 1973), pp. 43–49.

104. Jill Stewart, "Tribes Aim at Quiet Revolution," *Los Angeles Times*, June 26, 1990.

105. "Cree de coeur," *The Economist*, June 23, 1990, p. 27; Mary Wil-

liams Walsh, "Separatist Fires Burn Again in Quebec," *Los Angeles Times*, May 29, 1990.

106. Judith Waldrop, "Wasp Children Are Waning," *American Demographics*, May 1991, pp. 21–22.

107. "Tomorrow," *U.S. News & World Report*, February 13, 1989, p. 31.

108. Kristin Butcher and David Card, "Immigration and Wages: Evidence from the 1980s," *American Economic Review*, vol. 81, no. 2, May 1991, p. 293.

109. Interview with author.

110. Luis J. Botifol, "How Miami's New Image Was Created," *Occasional Paper Number 1985-1*, Institute of Interamerican Studies, University of Miami, pp. 10–14.

111. Peter McKillop with Cheryl Harrison Miller, "Florida Waits for Fidel to Fall," *Newsweek*, March 26, 1990.

112. William B. Barrett, "Monterey's Revenge," *Forbes*, June 11, 1990, p. 104.

113. Blayne Cutler, "Borderlands," *American Demographics*, February 1991, pp. 45–46.

114. Kwang Chung Kim and Won Moo Hurh, "Ethnic Resources Utilization of Korean Immigrant Entrepreneurs in the Chicago Minority Area," *International Migration Review*, vol. 6, no. 1, p. 109; Mong Hap Ming, "Problems of Korean Immigrant Entrepreneurs," *International Migration Review*, vol. 24, no. 3, p. 441.

115. Isaacs, *Idols of the Tribe*, p. 219.

116. Peter Francese, "Aging America Needs Foreign Blood," *The Wall Street Journal*, March 27, 1990.

EPILOGUE:
THE ROAD TO COSMOPOLIS

1. Toennies, *On Sociology*, pp. 267–68.

2. Fried, *The Notion of Tribe*, p. 110.

3. Andreski, *Military Organization and Society*, pp. 75–78.

4. Snyder, *Macronationalisms*, pp. 71–73.

5. Richard John Neuhaus, "Ortega y Gasset Revisited," *Commentary*, July 1986, p. 56.

6. "North African Unity: One Club to Beat the Other," *The Economist*, May 19, 1990, p. 91.

7. Snyder, *Macronationalisms*, pp. 147–51.

8. Ibid., pp. 204–21.

9. Stanley Meisler, "Despite Ups and Downs, Catalan Language Is Alive, Well," *Los Angeles Times*, January 1, 1991.

10. Kenichi Ohmae, "Toward a Global Regionalism," *Los Angeles Times*, April 27, 1990.

11. Grant, *From Alexander to Cleopatra*, p. xiv.

12. "Et in Cascadia, Ego," *The Economist*, February 29, 1992, pp. 28–29.

13. Ohmae, "Toward a Global Regionalism."

14. *The Politics of Migration Policies*, Kubat, Gehmacher, and Gehmacher, pp. xxii–xxiv.

15. Jim Hoagland, "The Politics of Exclusion: A Witch's Brew Is Bubbling in Europe," *International Herald Tribune*, May 8, 1990.

16. George Melloan, "Can Europe Keep Them Down on the Maghreb?" *The Wall Street Journal*, November 5, 1990.

17. "In Bad Odour," *The Economist*, June 29, 1991, p. 44; Melloan, "Can Europe Keep Them Down on the Maghreb?"

18. "Racism Revived," *The Economist*, May 19, 1990, p. 14; Valéry Giscard d'Estaing, *"La France ne doit plus etre un pays d'immigration,"* *Le Figaro*, May 26, 1990, p. 80.

19. "Berlin: Metropolis Is on the Move," *Das Zeitbild*, January 1991.

20. Interview with author.

21. "The Other Fortress Europe," *The Economist*, June 1, 1991, p. 45.

22. "Turks in Berlin—Mexicans in Los Angeles: What Can We Learn from Each Other?" *Sozialpadagogisches Institut Berlin*, 1986, p. 33; John Bunzel, "Alienation and the Black College Dropout," *The Wall Street Journal*, April 3, 1991.

23. "Scorned Today, Hailed Tomorrow?," *U.S. News & World Report*, January 30, 1989.

24. "Europe's Population Bomb," *Newsweek*, December 15, 1986; "World Population, by Region," *The Economist*, April 11, 1992, p. 107.

25. Statistics from the *Budenstat für Arbeit*, February 1991; estimates by Dr. Frederick Buttler. By the end of the 1990s Germany's shortage of workers should double to nearly one million and by the year 2010 the country will be short at least a half million college graduates.

26. Robert O'Connor, "Who'll Make Up the Slack in Education and Training," *International Herald Tribune*, April 15, 1991; Johnson, "Global Workforce 2000," p. 124; *World Competitiveness Report, 1991* (Lausanne: IMEDE, 1992), p. 323.

27. Interview with author.
28. Elliott, *Imperial Spain*, pp. 376–77.
29. Shigeaki Yasuoka, "Capital Ownership in Family Companies," in *Family Business in the Era of Industrial Growth*, Okochi and Yasuoka, eds., p. 9.
30. Michael Grant, *From Alexander to Cleopatra*, p. 38.
31. Yves Lequin, *La Mosaique France*, pp. 104–9.
32. Yann Moulier and Georges Tapinos, "France," in *The Politics of Migration Policies*, Kubat, Gehmacher, and Gehmacher, eds. pp. 128–33; Peter O'Brien, "Continuity and Change in Germany's Treatment of Non-Germans," *International Migration Review*, vol. 22, no. 3, pp. 111–12; Sarah Gordon, *Hitler, Germans and the "Jewish Question"* (Princeton, N.J.: Princeton University Press, 1984). Even as late as 1933 some Jews saw Berlin as a sort of "haven" from the rabid anti-Semitic wave sweeping the rest of Germany.
33. Armytage, *A Social History of Engineering*, p. 63.
34. Henri Pirenne, "The Stages in the Social History of Capitalism," *American Historical Review*, vol. 19, October 1913–July 1914, pp. 494–515.
35. Braudel, *The Perspective of the World*, pp. 103–4.
36. Gibson-Jarvie, *City of London*, p. 24
37. Braudel, *The Perspective of the World*, pp. 260–62.
38. Ibid., p. 262.
39. Tuchman, *Bible and Sword*, p. 140.
40. Aris, *But There Are No Jews in England*, p. 62.
41. McRae and Cairncross, *Capital City*, p. 9. Of the seventeen merchant banks to survive into the twentieth century, fifteen traced their origins to this varying assortment of immigrants.
42. Lewis Mumford, *The City in History: Its Origins, Its Transformations, and Its Prospects* (New York: Harcourt, Brace and World, 1961), p. 561.

INDEX

About the Author

JOEL KOTKIN is the coauthor of *The Third Century: America's Resurgence in the Asian Era* and *California, Inc.* As a journalist in California for the past two decades, he has worked as a correspondent or editor for *The Washington Post,* the *Los Angeles Times, California Magazine* and *Esquire.* For five years he served as West Coast editor of *Inc.* magazine. He has also written for numerous publications in Japan.

Kotkin currently serves as an international fellow at the Pepperdine University School of Business and Management and a senior fellow at the Center for the New West, which is based in Denver, Colorado. He lives in Los Angeles.

About the Type

The text of this book was set in Palatino, designed by the German typographer Hermann Zapf. It was named after the Renaissance calligrapher Giovanbattista Palatino. Zapf designed it between 1948 and 1952, and it was his first typeface to be introduced in America. It is a face of unusual elegance.